INTERNATIONAL LAW-MAKING BY THE INTERNATIONAL COURT OF JUSTICE AND INTERNATIONAL LAW COMMISSION

This book provides an unparalleled account of the links that draw together the International Court of Justice and the International Law Commission, exposing the depth of the relationship between these central organs of the international legal system and its profound, unintended impact. By drawing upon historical records, as well as interviews with members of both organs, the book reveals that the original vision for interaction between the Court and the Commission has been lost in time. It inquires not only into the cross-fertilization that may be traced in the output of each body, but also into the more subtle ties that they nurture; it also shows how even the rare occasions of disagreement attest to the strength of the inter-institutional relationship rather than undermine it. All this throws light on the largely intangible process of international law-making and challenges the notion that international legislation is the sole preserve of States.

OMRI SENDER is a practitioner and scholar in public international law. He acts as counsel and advisor to States, international organizations, and multinational corporations, including in international dispute settlement proceedings. His writings on public international law, like his practice, cover the full range of the discipline.

CAMBRIDGE STUDIES IN INTERNATIONAL AND COMPARATIVE LAW: 187

Established in 1946, this series produces high quality, reflective and innovative scholarship in the field of public international law. It publishes works on international law that are of a theoretical, historical, cross-disciplinary or doctrinal nature. The series also welcomes books providing insights from private international law, comparative law and transnational studies which inform international legal thought and practice more generally.

The series seeks to publish views from diverse legal traditions and perspectives, and of any geographical origin. In this respect it invites studies offering regional perspectives on core *problématiques* of international law, and in the same vein, it appreciates contrasts and debates between diverging approaches. Accordingly, books offering new or less orthodox perspectives are very much welcome. Works of a generalist character are greatly valued and the series is also open to studies on specific areas, institutions or problems. Translations of the most outstanding works published in other languages are also considered.

After seventy years, Cambridge Studies in International and Comparative Law sets the standard for international legal scholarship and will continue to define the discipline as it evolves in the years to come.

A list of books in the series can be found at the end of this volume.

INTERNATIONAL LAW-MAKING BY THE INTERNATIONAL COURT OF JUSTICE AND INTERNATIONAL LAW COMMISSION

Partnership for Purpose in a Decentralized Legal Order

OMRI SENDER

Partner and Chair of the Public International Law Practice Group, S. Horowitz & Co.

CAMBRIDGE
UNIVERSITY PRESS

CAMBRIDGE
UNIVERSITY PRESS

Shaftesbury Road, Cambridge CB2 8EA, United Kingdom

One Liberty Plaza, 20th Floor, New York, NY 10006, USA

477 Williamstown Road, Port Melbourne, VIC 3207, Australia

314–321, 3rd Floor, Plot 3, Splendor Forum, Jasola District Centre, New Delhi – 110025, India

103 Penang Road, #05-06/07, Visioncrest Commercial, Singapore 238467

Cambridge University Press is part of Cambridge University Press & Assessment, a department of the University of Cambridge.

We share the University's mission to contribute to society through the pursuit of education, learning and research at the highest international levels of excellence.

www.cambridge.org
Information on this title: www.cambridge.org/9781009354325

DOI: 10.1017/9781009354332

First published 2024

A catalogue record for this publication is available from the British Library

A Cataloging-in-Publication data record for this book is available from the Library of Congress

ISBN 978-1-009-35432-5 Hardback

In loving memory of my father, Yoram Sender (1952–2018)

. . . if we can bring ourselves to cease following the mirage of international statute law, we may find that there is developing under our eyes the very machinery of international law-making that we have been looking for all these years.

R.Y. Jennings, 'Recent Developments in the International Law Commission: Its Relation to the Sources of International Law', 13 ICLQ (1964) 385 at 397

CONTENTS

FOREWORD

The United Nations was established, as the Preamble of its Charter proclaims, out of a determination to establish, among other things, conditions under which justice and respect for the obligations arising out of treaties and other sources of international law could be maintained.

For that purpose, the Charter established the International Court of Justice as the principal judicial organ of the United Nations and one of its six main organs. The role assigned to the Court is to decide in accordance with international law such disputes as are submitted to it. In addition, the Court may give advisory opinions on any legal question at the request of whichever body is authorized by or in accordance with the United Nations Charter to make such a request.

The Court succeeded the Permanent Court of International Justice, active in the period 1922 to early 1940, which laid a solid basis for the judicial settlement of disputes between States and rendered twenty-seven advisory opinions.

The new court, the International Court of Justice, was thus able to build on the experience and jurisprudence of its predecessor by further developing the practice of judicial settlement of disputes, and, through its judgments and advisory opinions, make a great contribution to the development of international law.

According to the Charter of the United Nations, it is the General Assembly which shall initiate studies and make recommendations for the purpose of encouraging the progressive development of international law and its codification.

To assist it in the discharge of this task, the General Assembly decided in 1947 to establish the International Law Commission. Over the last seventy-four years, the Commission's activities have substantially changed the landscape of international law. While custom was a predominant form of international law at the moment of the creation of the United Nations, since then, multilateral conventions have come to the foreground. The contribution of the International Law Commission to this phenomenon is unique. This distinguishes the period of the United Nations from the time of the League of Nations. Although, upon the request of the Assembly, the Council of the League convened the Committee of Experts for the Progressive Codification of International Law (active between 1925 and 1928), the results were rather modest. The codification conference organized by the League of Nations in The Hague in 1930 can hardly be considered a milestone in the efforts to codify and develop international law.

While the International Court of Justice is officially the principal judicial organ of the United Nations, the International Law Commission, although formally a subsidiary organ of the General Assembly, deserves to be considered the main legal organ of the United Nations due to its most valuable contribution to the progressive development of international law and its codification.

Although there is no formal link between these two United Nations organs, the work of each has an influence and sometimes strong impact on the work of the other.

This monograph by Dr. Omri Sender engages in a detailed study of how the Court's judgments and advisory opinions have influenced the work of special rapporteurs on various topics with which the International Law Commission has dealt. It considers the extent to which Members of the Commission referred in their discussions to the Court's jurisprudence, and the various ways in which this jurisprudence has found its way into the drafts and reports presented by the Commission to the Member States of the United Nations.

This influence, as the monograph demonstrates, has not been one way. While in the early stage of their work, the Commission benefited perhaps more from the Court's jurisprudence than the Court from the work of the Commission, later on, once the latter elaborated various important codification drafts, which were subsequently adopted as international conventions, the Court started to pay much closer attention to the Commission's work. It regularly turned to the Commission's commentaries when it was required to interpret either the conventions adopted on the basis of the Commission's drafts, or even to draft articles which had not been transformed into conventional instruments. One may thus say that there has been a reciprocal influence between these two important organs of the United Nations. This has had a positive impact on the development and strengthening of the international legal order.

There have been occasional disagreements on substantive issues between the Court and the Commission. They do not escape the attention of Dr. Sender.

He also details the personal connections between the Members of the Court and Members of the Commission, which should not be overlooked. Sometimes the Commission is considered an *antichambre* of the Court; more than one-third of the Members of the Court in its history served on the Commission prior to their election to the principal judicial organ of the United Nations. Significantly, the book also unearths the original vision for the possible interaction between the Court and the Commission, explores the complementarity of their functions, and evaluates the impact of their close relationship on the international legal system.

The book is the result of a meticulous study of a wide array of documents. It is also based on interviews with a number of Members of the Court and Members of the Commission. It is a very solid piece of scholarly research. It represents an important contribution to the literature on these two major legal organs of the United Nations. I have no doubt that it will be of particular interest to all those who follow the activities of the Court and the Commission, their interaction, and their contributions to international law in their respective fields of responsibility.

Peter Tomka
Peace Palace, The Hague

ACKNOWLEDGMENTS

This book is a revised and updated version of a doctoral dissertation I submitted in May 2020 to the George Washington University Law School. While working both on that dissertation and on this book, I have incurred debts which it is a pleasure here to record.

I would first like to register my deep thanks to the supervisor of my dissertation project, Professor Sean D. Murphy. Despite his Olympian schedule, he remained a consistent source of guidance and inspiration, generous with his time and unfailingly kind. His advice, encouragement, and friendship are all greatly appreciated. I am also indebted to the other distinguished members of the dissertation committee: the late Professor Thomas Buergenthal, Professor Martha Finnemore, Dean Susan Karamanian, and Professor Michael Matheson.

In the same breath, a special word of gratitude is due to Sir Michael Wood KC, who opened the doors for me to both the International Law Commission and the International Court of Justice (as well as to international legal practice more broadly). My debt to Sir Michael, for his mentorship, invaluable insights, and support, has been accumulating and continues to grow.

I am privileged also to have benefited from the knowledge and advice of other exceptional public international lawyers, including Michael Becker, Eyal Benvenisti, Eirik Bjorge, Gleider Hernández, Robert Kolb, David Malone, David Nanopoulos, Federica Paddeu, Arnold Pronto, and the late Hugh Thirlway. Several past and present members of the International Court of Justice and the International Law Commission have very generously made themselves available to be interviewed for this study, and I am deeply grateful to them for their time and for their trust.

A warm word of thanks is also owed to the late Irina Gerassimova, Rachel Forman, Amanda Howland, and all the other staff at the Library of the United Nations Office at Geneva for their friendly and efficient assistance in obtaining various research materials.

I also thank His Excellency Judge Peter Tomka, *genius loci* of the two institutions to the study of which this work is dedicated, both for his encouragement to complete the dissertation and for very kindly agreeing to write the Foreword to this book.

Others, too, have been kind enough to contribute much along the way, not least my family, including my mother and, above all, my beloved wife, Nira. I am very grateful to them.

Finally, I would like to thank Marianne Nield and her team at Cambridge University Press for all their support in making this book see the light of day. The decisions of the International Court of Justice and output of the International Law Commission referred to are up to date as of September 2023 unless otherwise indicated.

ABBREVIATIONS

AFDI	*Annuaire français de droit international*
APDI	*Anuário português de direito internacional*
AJIL	*American Journal of International Law*
BYIL	*British Yearbook of International Law*
CJICL	*Cambridge Journal of International and Comparative Law*
CJIL	*Chinese Journal of International Law*
CUP	Cambridge University Press
CYIL	*Canadian Yearbook of International Law*
EJIL	*European Journal of International Law*
FYIL	*Finnish Yearbook of International Law*
GJIL	*Georgetown Journal of International Law*
GYIL	*German Yearbook of International Law*
HICLR	*Hastings International and Comparative Law Review*
HILJ	*Harvard International Law Journal*
HLR	*Harvard Law Review*
ICJ	International Court of Justice
ICLQ	*International and Comparative Law Quarterly*
IJIL	*Indian Journal of International Law*
ILC	International Law Commission
IOLR	*International Organizations Law Review*
JIDS	*Journal of International Dispute Settlement*
LAPE	*Law and Practice of International Courts and Tribunals*
LJIL	*Leiden Journal of International Law*
MPEPIL	*Max Planck Encyclopedia of Public International Law*
MPYUNL	*Max Planck Yearbook of United Nations Law*
MUP	Manchester University Press
NILR	*Netherlands International Law Review*
NYIL	*Netherlands Yearbook of International Law*
OUP	Oxford University Press
PASIL	*Proceedings of the Annual Meeting (American Society of International Law)*
PCIJ	Permanent Court of International Justice

RdC	*Recueil des Cours de l'Académie de La Haye* (The Hague Academy Collected Courses)
SAYIL	*South African Yearbook of International Law*
UNCLOS	United Nations Convention on the Law of the Sea
YBICJ	*Yearbook of the International Court of Justice*
YBILC	*Yearbook of the International Law Commission*
YLJ	*Yale Law Journal*

1

Introduction

The International Court of Justice and the International Law Commission were both set up in the aftermath of the Second World War as part of a wider United Nations system dedicated to creating an international community that is respectful of, and bound by, international law. The Court, as the principal judicial organ of the United Nations,[1] would adjudicate specific disputes between States (and provide advisory opinions), with its decisions having no binding force except between the parties.[2] The Commission, as a subsidiary organ of the United Nations General Assembly, would promote the progressive development and codification of international law, with its products submitted to the Member States of the organization as proposals on which they may then choose to act.[3] By careful design, both organs were configured so as to guarantee that, in fulfilling their mandates, neither would be able to impose its will on States. Indeed, their sovereign masters sought jealously to retain the prerogative of international law-making and would continue to insist that it lie with them alone.

That the Court and the Commission have since then established significant links between themselves is not unknown to international lawyers. Those who follow the work of the two institutions have long observed not only that many members of the Commission have gone on to become members of the Court, but also the exceptional frequency with which each body has relied on the output of the other. Watts, for instance, observed that while the Court "is reluctant to cite as authority the work of individual writers of authority in international law, [it] has

[1] Charter of the United Nations (1945), articles 7, 92.

[2] Statute of the International Court of Justice (1945), article 59; excerpts from the Court's Statute, which is annexed to the UN Charter and forms an integral part thereof, may be found in Annex 1.

[3] Statute of the International Law Commission (1947), as amended, article 1(1); excerpts from the Statute may be found in Annex 2.

been much readier to invoke with approval the work of the International Law Commission"; he further remarked that "[i]t is not just a matter of the International Court relying on the work of the Commission, but of reciprocal action by the Commission building on and developing principles adopted by the Court in its judgments."[4] Others, including members of the Court and the Commission themselves, have similarly noted that the two organs not infrequently "borrow norms from each other"[5] and depicted this interplay as "symbiotic."[6]

When I attended several sessions of the Commission as an assistant to one of its members, I could not help but wonder whether mutual influence was all there is to it. Listening to the Commission's debates, I noticed readily the reverence – if not deference – with which the Court's pronouncements were received, and a more general sentiment that the Court's authority must not be undermined. There was also a sense that endorsement by the Court of the Commission's propositions was the ultimate prize at least some members sought for their labor. Moreover, I was intrigued to hear the President of the Court, during his address before the Commission, refer to the Court and the Commission as "the principal judicial and legal organs of the United Nations, respectively,"[7] notwithstanding the Commission's formal position as only a subsidiary organ of the General Assembly. Having earlier read that the Court and the Commission "rival" each other in their importance for international law,[8] I thought the primary mode was rather one of cooperation. I began asking myself whether consideration was ever given by the founders of the two institutions to how they were to interact, and

[4] A. Watts, *The International Law Commission 1949–1998*, Vol. I (OUP 1999) 12, 13.

[5] W.T. Worster, 'The Transformation of Quantity into Quality: Critical Mass in the Formation of Customary International Law', 31 *Boston University International Law Journal* (2013) 1 at 49–50.

[6] S.M. Schwebel, 'The Influence of the International Court of Justice on the Work of the International Law Commission and the Influence of the Commission on the Court', in *Making Better International Law: The International Law Commission at 50* (United Nations 1998) 161; S.M. Schwebel, 'The Inter-active Influence of the International Court of Justice and the International Law Commission', in C.A. Armas Barea et al (eds.), *Liber Amicorum 'In Memoriam' of Judge José María Ruda* (Kluwer Law International 2000) 479 at 480; A. Pronto and M. Wood, *The International Law Commission 1999–2009*, Vol. IV (OUP 2010) 4.

[7] YBILC 2012, Vol. I, p. 146, para. 92 (Judge Tomka).

[8] R.Y. Jennings, 'Recent Developments in the International Law Commission: Its Relation to the Sources of International Law', 13 ICLQ (1964) 385; Schwebel, 'The Influence of the International Court of Justice on the Work of the International Law Commission and the Influence of the Commission on the Court', *supra* note 6.

whether the current reality accords with any such vision. Bearing in mind the provisions of their constituent instruments, it increasingly appeared to me that a scholarly investigation into the extent and significance of the relationship between the Court and the Commission could usefully shed some light on the largely intangible process of international law-making.

A. Scope and Purpose of the Present Study

This book is about the relationship between the Court and the Commission as it has been shaped through decades of coexistence. As such, it is neither about the Court nor about the Commission per se. While the following chapters deal to a great extent with the mandates, composition, working methods, and output of the two bodies, they do so for the purpose of examining the dynamics of their interaction and the significance of that interaction for the international legal system more broadly.

Previous academic comment on the interplay between the Court and the Commission has been brief and/or noncomprehensive. For the most part, such accounts are found in works that are devoted primarily to one institution or the other,[9] or that zoom in on their impact on a specific field of law.[10] In common with Schwebel's more focused writing on the

[9] General works on the International Court of Justice say very little, if anything, about the Court's relationship with the Commission, but some articles do examine it from that angle: see, for example, S. Villalpando, 'On the International Court of Justice and the Determination of Rules of Law', 26 LJIL (2013) 243–251; P. Tomka, 'Customary International Law in the Jurisprudence of the World Court: The Increasing Relevance of Codification', in L. Lijnzaad and Council of Europe (eds.), *The Judge and International Custom* (Brill Nijhoff 2016) 1–24; and M. Đorđeska, 'The Process of International Law-Making: The Relationship between the International Court of Justice and the International Law Commission', 15 *International and Comparative Law Review* (2015) 7–57. For a view from the side of the Commission, see, for example, B.G. Ramcharan, *The International Law Commission: Its Approach to the Codification and Progressive Development of International Law* (Brill Nijhoff 1977) 15–17; I. Sinclair, *The International Law Commission* (Grotius Publications 1987) 127–136; Watts, *supra* note 4, at 12–14; and R. Higgins et al, *Oppenheim's United Nations*, Vol. II (OUP 2017) 944–945, MN 25.48–25.49.

[10] See, for example, S. Villalpando, 'Le codificateur et le juge face à la responsabilité internationale de l'État: interaction entre la CDI et la CIJ dans la détermination des règles secondaires', 55 AFDI (2009) 39–61; C.J. Tams, 'Law-Making in Complex Processes: The World Court and the Modern Law of State Responsibility', in C. Chinkin and F. Baetens (eds.), *Sovereignty, Statehood and State Responsibility: Essays in Honour of James Crawford* (CUP 2015) 287–306; J. d'Aspremont, 'Canonical Cross-referencing in the Making of the Law of International Responsibility', in S. Forlati, M.M.

topic (now over twenty years old),[11] none is intended to be exhaustive. Moreover, no author seems to have situated the relationship between the Court and the Commission in the broader historical experience of international law, or to go much further than discussing the citations by one organ to the work of the other (and possibly the frequent migration of Commission members to the Court).

This study aims to offer more than a tour d'horizon of the cross-fertilization between the Court and the Commission and to delve deeper than pointing to those tangible instances of explicit reliance by one organ on the work of the other. In putting the relationship between the two institutions under the microscope, it seeks to provide a comprehensive account of all the links that draw them together and to examine them from the point of view of both organs. By uncovering and evaluating the way – indeed ways – in which the Court and the Commission interact, this study hopes to demonstrate that, over time, such interplay has had a profound impact not only on the work and standing of the two bodies but also on the wider phenomenon of international law-making. It will be argued, more specifically, that the relationship between the Court and the Commission runs deeper than what was envisaged when they were founded and what is appreciated still today: that, in effect, it enables them to "legislate" for the world.

While this book is centered on the Court and the Commission, they are by no means the only bodies implicated in international law-making. Indeed, several important developments in the law of nations have occurred without their participation and large swaths of the law so far have remained outside of their reach. Yet the Court and the Commission do occupy a unique position in the international legal system, not least for having mandates that are potentially wide enough to encompass the entire fabric of the law. Their output often constitutes the first port of call for those seeking to learn what the law is and their authority in expounding that law is generally unrivaled.

The picture emerging from this study may be of particular interest to scholars, practitioners, and students of international law. It is hoped, however, that it will capture the attention of larger circles too. While the idea that international legislation is the sole preserve of States continues to hold a deep paradigmatic grip on the imagination of many, it may be

Mbengue and B. McGarry (eds.), *The Gabčíkovo-Nagymaros Judgment and Its Contribution to the Development of International Law* (Brill 2020) 22–40.

[11] See *supra* note 6.

time to acknowledge that both the Court and the Commission often do more than assist in this activity.

B. A Note on Methodology

The research conducted for the present study entailed the examination of a large and varied body of information. Primary materials included some three hundred and thirty judgments, orders, and advisory opinions handed down by the Court since its establishment, as well as many of the individual opinions appended by its judges and some of the pleadings of States appearing before it. The Commission's annual reports to the General Assembly over the past seventy-four years have been combed through as well, along with the thousands of pages recording the Commission's plenary discussions throughout that period and the reports of its special rapporteurs. Other United Nations documents examined include the records of the San Francisco Conference of 1945 (and some of its preparatory papers) as well as the summary records of the meetings held in 1947 by the Committee on the Progressive Development of International Law and Its Codification, which prepared a draft of the Commission's Statute. Archival materials dating from the League of Nations era, including the *procès-verbaux* of the proceedings of the Advisory Committee of Jurists that prepared a draft of the Statute of the Permanent Court of International Justice, were also studied. All these were supplemented by numerous independent observations, made in person, of the Commission and the Court in session.

As indicated by the Bibliography attached to this study, a large volume of academic literature has proven highly useful, too. Writings by former and contemporary members of the Court and the Commission were often of particular interest, as were those examining in detail some of the work products of the two organs. Much of the earlier scholarship was instrumental in making it clear that a number of the pressing questions of the present are, in fact, age-old – and must be approached with that in mind.

Personal interviews were held with some twenty former and present members of the Court and the Commission in order to complement other data by receiving an unmediated insider's perspective on the inter-institutional relationship.[12] These interviews, which indeed have proved

[12] See also S. Brinkmann and S. Kvale, *InterViews: Learning the Craft of Qualitative Research Interviewing*, 3rd ed. (Sage 2015) 3: "qualitative interview research approaches

invaluable, were conducted mostly at The Hague and in Geneva on a not-for-attribution basis, to allow interviewees (whose names are listed in Annex 3) to speak freely.

While the Court and the Commission are, of course, institutions composed of changing casts of individuals, in the present study they are conceived of in a corporate form rather than as collectivities of their members. Observing them as unitary actors is justified given that their powers are assigned to them as such; their work is of a collective nature; and a consistent framework of institutional rules and traditions has guided them over the decades. At the same time, the role of individuals in shaping the relationship between the two organs is duly acknowledged and not infrequently highlighted.

In seeking to provide a detailed exposition of the history and extent of the interplay between the Court and the Commission, the following chapters are perforce descriptive in places. The information presented, however, has been distilled and synthesized, and is considered essential to the offering of abstractions that are embedded in facts.

A final caveat concerns the fact that international lawyers – and the author of this book among them – are for the most part only "amateur social theorists."[13] Our knowledge of political science is often equally limited at best. Immersing myself in some of the leading works on international relations, including those dealing with international organization and international norm dynamics, has greatly enriched my appreciation of the interplay between the Court and the Commission; it has also allowed me to endeavor to apply to this study some of the insights of those neighboring disciplines. The result, however, can only be a modest one in an inquiry so deeply planted in the international legal field.

people not as objects, mechanically controlled by causal laws, but rather as persons, i.e., as subjects who act and are actively engaged in meaning making."

13 M. Koskenniemi, 'The Normative Force of Habit: International Custom and Social Theory', 1 FYIL (1990) 77 (explaining that "[i]n seeking to understand what goes on in the international society [international lawyers] necessarily do this from the vantage point of a theory. For the meaning [of] human behaviour – social actions and events – does not come before the observer's eyes 'an sich'. It appears through multilayered, even chaotic complexes of facts, ideas and texts. Reaching an understanding involves establishing meaningful relationships between these disparate facts, ideas and texts. This again requires that we are in the possession of a code for making distinctions – separating the essential from the non-essential, the cause from the effect, the rule from the regularity, and so on. This code is our more or less explicit social theory. Only by possessing such a code we can understand human behaviour and, by extension, events or actions concerning groups or nations").

Further such attempts may no doubt be worthwhile, especially if one bears in mind that all law-making – including on the international plane – is quintessentially political.

C. Structure of this Book

The book proceeds as follows. Following this brief introduction, Chapter 2 sets the scene for an appreciation of the contemporary relationship between the Court and the Commission by tracing its roots in the broader ideal of the pacific settlement of disputes and the rule of law in international affairs. Taking stock of developments dating back to the nineteenth century, it illustrates that the long-standing movements for an international court and for an international code were not unrelated, and that a certain vision did exist for the way in which their present institutional manifestations were to interact. That original vision, which was lost in time, has thus far attracted less attention from commentators than its importance requires.

Chapter 3 provides a detailed account of the impact that the Commission's work has had in shaping the Court's case-law. In addition to surveying and classifying all those instances in which the Court has to date been ready to refer expressly to the Commission's output, it demonstrates that reliance on the Commission's work has often been more implicit. The question is then posed as to the basis for such recourse and the advantage afforded by it.

Chapter 4 examines the unparalleled influence that the Court's decisions have had on the Commission's codification and progressive development of areas of the law under its consideration. It illustrates not only the great extent to which many of the Commission's propositions have borrowed their authority from the pronouncements of the Court, but also the significant impact of the latter on the Commission's choices concerning terminology and program of work. The chapter further demonstrates the Commission's conscious efforts to support the Court's cause more broadly, including by encouraging the expansion of the Court's jurisdiction and by promoting the doctrine of the sources of international law enshrined in its Statute.

Chapter 5 addresses the relationship between the Court and the Commission beyond the printed page. By focusing attention on the movement of members from one institution to the other, and on the customary exchanges in Geneva between the members of both, it reveals the extent and contribution of the more subtle ties that bind the Court and the Commission.

Chapter 6 addresses in detail those rare occasions in which the Court and the Commission have adopted differing positions on the legal questions before them. In exploring both the potential for such disagreements and how they have been handled, the chapter shows that these instances attest to the strength of the inter-institutional relationship rather than undermine it. It also points out, however, that harmony comes at a cost.

Finally, Chapter 7 seeks to provide an overall assessment of what draws the Court and the Commission together and of the impact that their "special relationship" has produced. By pulling the threads together, it explains that the interaction between the two organs has turned out differently to that which was originally envisaged and that the great weight accorded by each of them to the work of the other has challenged the exclusive basis of State consent for international law's validity. In a legal system that remains heavily dependent on unwritten rules of customary international law that require authoritative determination, the ultimate result has been that the Court and the Commission together assume a public order role not foreseen for either of them by their founders.

2

The International Court of Justice and the International Law Commission: Joined at the Hip

> There can be no real court without law to control its judges, and there can be no effective law without institutions for its application to concrete cases.
>
> (Elihu Root addressing the American Society of International Law, 1921)

> There was naturally a close relationship between the Court as the adjudicator and the Commission as the codifier of international law. Without precise and unambiguous law the adjudicator would be very handicapped, but codification of international law without the existence of an adjudicatory body would be tantamount to law-making in a vacuum. Justice needed both the judge and the legislator.
>
> (Nagendra Singh, Vice-President of the International Court of Justice [and former member of the International Law Commission] addressing the International Law Commission, 1978)

Neither the International Court of Justice, established in 1945, nor the International Law Commission, established two years later, came into being as original, spontaneous creations. Both are reincarnations of older institutions, revived embodiments of ideas the roots of which were planted long before. While the Court is the current working manifestation of the long-standing effort to settle international disputes through judicial means, the Commission is the present pinnacle of the persistent endeavor to reduce the law of nations to a comprehensible set of rules and to secure general agreement upon them. These two movements – one for a world court, the other for a world code – were not unrelated. Those advocating for (or resisting) international adjudication were conscious from the outset that achieving greater clarity with regard to the rules to be applied was of the essence. Codification of international law, for its part, was expected to bring more matters under the sway of an international court, which would, in turn, assist in making more certain the rules in force among the nations (and in further developing or refining them). The historical backdrop to the establishment of both the Court and the Commission is, therefore, not only fascinating in itself, but it is also of vital importance to any attempt at fully comprehending the relationship between the two organs today.

A. The First International Tribunals: "Courts without Law"

The first so-called permanent international court, the Permanent Court of Arbitration, was never intended to be a court. The twenty-six States that established it at The Hague in 1899 had opted instead for a standing International Bureau – one that would do no more than maintain a roster of potential arbitrators from which an ad hoc tribunal might be formed in the event that States sought to settle their dispute in this way. But the States parties to The Hague Convention on the Pacific Settlement of International Disputes did seem to mean it when they chose for their new entity the descriptor 'Arbitration' over 'Justice,' having envisaged the settlement of disputes through this vehicle not in accordance with law, but only "on the basis of respect for law."[1] While there was "no inherent quality of lawlessness in arbitration,"[2] it was regarded as a species of diplomatic process given that "[t]here was at times a tendency for the arbitrators to consider themselves as mediators rather than as faithful interpreters of Law, as diplomats rather than as judges, as conciliators called upon to decide between States in the way least painful to each of them, rather than as judges, whose duty it is to administer impartial justice."[3] The reluctance of States to submit themselves to a system in

[1] 1899 Convention on the Pacific Settlement of International Disputes, article 15. This text was left unchanged in article 37 of the 1907 Convention on the Pacific Settlement of International Disputes.

[2] M.O. Hudson, 'The Permanent Court of International Justice', 35 HLR (1922) 245 at 254.

[3] Final Report of the Advisory Committee of Jurists, in *Advisory Committee of Jurists, Procès-Verbaux of the Proceedings of the Committee, June 16th–July 24th 1920, with Annexes* (Van Langenhuysen Brothers 1920) (hereinafter: *Procès-Verbaux*), p. 694; see also at p. 695 ("It is to be feared that the judges of the Court of Arbitration, being inclined to regard the case from a political standpoint, may not give sufficient weight to the rules of Law") and p. 696 ("Arbitration can take account of a thousand elements of fact and a thousand contingencies and, often, of certain necessities of a political kind. The decrees of justice take account only of a rule defined and fixed by law"). Mr. Léon Bourgeois, speaking to the members of the Advisory Committee on behalf of the Council of the League of Nations, had said that "[t]here is between the sentence in an arbitration and the judgment of a tribunal an essential difference, a difference as profound as that which exists between equity and justice. Arbitration can take account of a thousand elements of fact and a thousand contingencies, and often of certain necessities of a political

which their disputes would be adjudicated in accordance with strict law may well be attributed, in large measure, to the simple fact that the rules of international law, then mostly unwritten and based on international custom, were far from definite.[4] Oppenheim would soon suggest that

> the first and chief task is the exposition of the existing recognized rules of international law... at least partial codification will at some future time become an absolute necessity. The practice and the views of the different states differ so much with regard to many important matters that it is only codification which can create agreement and unanimity, and thereby universally recognized rules of law.[5]

That the absence of a clear and authoritative statement of the law put a heavy strain on the judicial settlement of international disputes was soon brought to light when the States at the Second Hague Conference agreed in 1907 to establish, by international treaty, a permanent International Prize Court.[6] The projected Court, which would sit at The Hague and comprise fifteen judges appointed by the contracting States, was to have a compulsory jurisdiction over appeals against judgments of national prize courts affecting neutral property. Article 7 of the convention establishing the Court stipulated that, where a question of law was to be decided, the Court would apply a treaty in force between the parties, or, in the absence of such a treaty, "the rules of international law"; if no generally recognized rule existed, the Court was to "give judgment in accordance with the general principles of justice and equity."[7] Signatures (and ratifications

kind. The decrees of justice take account only of a rule defined and fixed by law": *ibid*, at p. 8.

4 Another prominent reason was the inability to decide on a method for the appointment of judges.

5 L. Oppenheim, 'The Science of International Law: Its Task and Method', 2 AJIL (1908) 313 at 314 and 320.

6 The Conference also recommended to the Powers a draft convention (which was not eventually adopted) for the creation of a permanent Court of Arbitral Justice, to exist alongside the Permanent Court of Arbitration as a tribunal for adjudication in accordance with law by permanent judges, which, it was expected, "would gradually create a definite system of international law, which would have to be considered by the nations as a rule of conduct": J.B. Scott, 'The Proposed Court of Arbitral Justice', 2 AJIL (1908) 772 at 775 (citing a speaker in the First Subcommittee of the Conference). A Central American Court of Justice (*Corte de Justicia Centroamericana*) was established in 1908, to maintain peace and resolve disagreements among Central American states, "[b]ut the work of this court may be regarded as an experience in federalism, in view of the history of the efforts to unite the Central American peoples into a single state": Hudson, *supra* note 2, at 246.

7 Convention (XII) relative to the Creation of an International Prize Court: The Hague, 18 October 1907.

by the signatory Powers) were withheld, however, mostly because no general agreement could be reached as to what the rules of international law actually were in relation to the questions most likely to come before the Court.[8] The Prize Court was, then, "a court without law":[9] As one contemporaneous commentator observed,

> wide discretion is left to the judges. They are, in fact, in a position to make law by giving their own interpretations and opinions in a case of doubt. Now, what are the rules of International Law referred to? What are the general principles of justice and equity which may be applied where no generally recognized rule of law exists? These are apparently simple questions, but underlying them are historic conceptions and definitions of a diverse character, the application of some of which might infringe seriously upon a nation's sovereignty or cause its citizens to lose millions of dollars' worth of property.[10]

Codification of the relevant rules of international maritime warfare law was one way to address this difficulty, and an international conference was soon held in London (in 1908–1909) with the task "not ... to deliberate *de lege ferenda*" but to adopt a Declaration that would place on record "that those Powers which are best qualified and most directly interested, recognize ... that there exists in fact a common law of nations of which it is the purport of the Declaration, in the common interest, to set out the principles."[11] Such a "Declaration concerning the Laws of

[8] Japan and Russia reportedly abstained from voting at the Conference on the ground that a codification of maritime law ought to precede the institution of such a court: see C.N. Gregory, 'The Proposed International Prize Court and Some of Its Difficulties', 2 AJIL (1908) 458 at 459; A.S. Hershey, 'An International Prize Court', *Articles by Maurer Faculty*, Paper 1960 (1907) 652 at 653. See also J.B. Scott, 'Advancement of International Law Essential to an International Court of Justice', 15 PASIL (1921) 21 at 24 ("Great Britain very properly refused to go into a court of that kind without an understanding upon the law to be observed, because so to do would be in effect, if not in form, to invest the judges of the proposed court with legislative as well as judicial powers").

[9] A. Eyffinger, *The 1899 Hague Peace Conference: The Parliament of Man, the Federation of the World* (Martinus Nijhoff 1999) 456. See also J. Westlake, 'The Hague Conferences', in L. Oppenheim (ed.), *The Collected Papers of John Westlake on Public International Law* (CUP 1914) 531 at 551 ("The greatest difficulty arises from the very fact which is the greatest source of the necessity, namely, the divergent views of prize law entertained in different countries. What is the law which the International Court shall administer?").

[10] J.L. Tryon, 'The International Prize Court and Code', 20 YLJ (1911) 604 at 612.

[11] 'Memorandum communicated by Lord Acton to M. van Swinderen dated 12 November 1908', in G.P. Gooch and H. Temperley (eds.), *British Documents on the Origins of the War 1898–1914*, Vol. VIII (H.M. Stationery Office 1932) 342.

Naval War" was indeed successfully adopted at the Conference,[12] but it failed to secure ratifications by the signatory States and never entered into force as certain matters of law were still considered insufficiently clear.[13] This proved fatal to the International Prize Court as well, which thus never came into being. The experience demonstrated, as Pellet and Müller have observed, "the reluctance of States to be bound by compulsory jurisdiction without a precise framework of legal norms to be applied by such an international tribunal."[14]

B. The Permanent Court of International Justice: A Court in Need of Law

The Great War of 1914–1918 profoundly shook the structure of international law, and when the time had come to consider "not merely what there is left of certain specific rules, but also the fundamental basis of obligation upon which all rules depend,"[15] general agreement was reached that a place should be made for a world court in the system of international organization that was to emerge. This sentiment was enshrined in article 14 of the Covenant of the League of Nations, which directed the League's Council to "formulate and submit to the Members of the League for adoption plans for the establishment of a Permanent Court of International Justice."[16] The text further provided that the envisaged Court "shall be competent to hear and determine any dispute of an international character which the parties thereto submit to it ... [and] may also give an advisory opinion upon any dispute or question referred to it by the Council or by the [League's] Assembly."[17] The need to codify and develop international law was hardly forgotten, but it was recognized that "the process of codifying, clarifying, and improving

[12] In the Preamble, the Contracting Parties refer to "the terms in which the British Government invited various Powers to meet in conference in order to arrive at an agreement as to what are the generally recognized rules of international law within the meaning of article 7 of the Convention of 18 October 1907, relative to the establishment of an International Prize Court": Declaration Concerning the Laws of Naval War, 26 February 1909.

[13] See D. Fleck, 'London Naval Conference (1908–1909)', in MPEPIL (2015), para. 4. For a somewhat different view, see *Procès-Verbaux*, p. 287 (De Lapradelle).

[14] A. Pellet and D. Müller, 'Article 38', in A. Zimmerman et al (eds.), *The Statute of the International Court of Justice: A Commentary*, 3rd ed. (OUP 2019) 819 at 826, MN 14.

[15] E. Root, 'The Outlook for International Law', 10 AJIL (1916) 1 at 3.

[16] Covenant of the League of Nations, 1919 (entered into force on 10 January 1920).

[17] *Ibid.*

international law is necessarily a slow one, and if we wait for a satisfactory body of law before we have a permanent court a generation will pass before it is established."[18] "Meanwhile," it was suggested, "let us supply appropriate means for the application of the law we have. The two projects are not inconsistent; the one can exist along with the other."[19]

At its second meeting, in February 1920, the Council of the League decided to entrust the task of devising a plan for the Permanent Court of International Justice to a designated Committee of Jurists. This Advisory Committee met in The Hague from June 16 to July 24 of that year, being well aware that at stake was "one of the most important of the tasks which [the League] was invited to perform."[20] Over the course of thirty-five meetings, its ten eminent members, presided over by Baron Descamps (Belgium), debated in private the organization, competence, and procedure most appropriate for a permanent international court that was to adjudicate among States.[21] While agreement on certain matters was reached readily, the question of whether the Court's jurisdiction was to be compulsory (to which the Committee eventually replied in the affirmative) was the subject of much debate. It was in this context that Mr. Root (United States of America), one of the leading figures of the Committee, suggested that any such disposition aiming to induce States to agree to obligatory judicial settlement of disputes "should be accompanied by a recommendation to the Council and to the Assembly to the effect that . . . [a] new Conference on international law should be called together as soon as possible; it would have the task of examining what actually are the rules of international law."[22] For Root, this was the clear lesson that had emerged from the abortive attempt to establish the International Prize Court: "The States would not accept a Court which had the right to settle disputes in accordance with rules established by the

[18] C.E. Hughes, 'Address by the Secretary of State of the United States before the American Society of International Law, at Washington, D.C., April 27, 1923', 9 *International Conciliation* (1923) 319 at 344.

[19] *Ibid.*

[20] Words of Sir Eric Drummond, Secretary-General of the League of Nations, as reported by L. Bourgeois in his report of 27 October 1920 to the Council of the League on the matter of the Permanent Court of International Justice: *League of Nations Official Journal*, Issue 8, November–December 1920, 12–13.

[21] See *Procès-Verbaux*. For an interesting insight into the Committee's deliberations, see O. Spiermann, '"Who Attempts Too Much Does Nothing Well": The 1920 Advisory Committee of Jurists and the Statute of the Permanent Court of International Justice', 73 BYIL (2002) 187–260.

[22] *Procès-Verbaux*, at p. 230 (adding that "[t]he Conference should meet periodically").

Court itself, and by the interpretation of more or less vague principles."[23] His warning was taken seriously: A draft report on the work of the Committee recorded that "[t]he danger of conferring on a Court entrusted with the right of compulsory jurisdiction the right to deduce itself the rules according to which the sentences are to be given was put forward with much force; a provision to that effect would make the whole plan unacceptable."[24] Anzilotti, who served at the time as Under-Secretary-General of the League (and later as Judge and President of the Permanent Court of International Justice) soon reported from The Hague to Secretary-General Drummond that codification of international law was "regarded as the necessary consequence of the creation of an International Court of Justice. The law to be applied by the said Court must be determined if States must apply to the Court with confidence."[25]

The need to define the jurisdictional limits of the proposed Court, and to avoid giving it any legislative power in light of the insufficient development of positive international law, resurfaced in the Committee's subsequent discussion on the question of "[w]hat law shall the judge apply in delivering his sentence."[26] The members readily accepted that the sources of law that the Court ought to apply should include any treaties concluded between the parties to the relevant dispute as well as customary international law (Baron Descamps recalled that "a large part of international law, except a few points which are regulated by

[23] *Ibid*, at p. 286. Root had previously made his opinion known that "[w]hen we come to consider the working of an international court … we are forced to realize that the law itself is in many respects imperfect and uncertain. There is no legislature to make law for nations. There is no body of judicial decisions having the effect of precedent to declare what international laws are … any attempt to maintain a court of international justice must fail unless there are laws for the court to administer. Without them the so-called court would be merely a group of men seeking to impose their personal opinions upon the states coming before them. The lack of an adequate system of law to be applied has been the chief obstacle to the development of a system of judicial settlement of international disputes": Root, *supra* note 15, at pp. 5–6.

[24] '*Plan for the Establishment of a Permanent Court of International Justice – Draft Report (historical point of view) – dated 30th July 1920 – by M. Hammarskjöld*, League of Nations Archives 21-6030-859, p. 12.

[25] Report, Anzilotti to Drummond, 27 July 1920, League of Nations Archives 21-5979-4959, p. 5.

[26] *Procès-Verbaux*, at pp. 293–338. This was the last of five questions listed in a questionnaire on the competence of the future Court put together by Baron Descamps and distributed to members of the Committee as a program for discussion: *ibid*, at p. 218.

conventional stipulations, [was] the outcome of custom"[27]). But the other two sources proposed by Descamps as a basis for discussion – "the rules of international law as recognized by the legal conscience of civilized nations" and "international jurisprudence as a means for the application and development of law" – provoked a great deal of debate.[28] Root considered such terms to be too vague and thus to "[constitute] an enlargement of the jurisdiction of the Court which threatened to destroy it."[29] Lord Phillimore (United Kingdom) agreed, suggesting that the two clauses "in fact, gave the Court a legislative power, but legislation in matters of international law could only be carried out by the universal agreement of all States."[30] Mr. Loder (The Netherlands, another future judge and President of the Court), however, considered that "it was precisely the Court's duty to develop law, to 'ripen' customs and principles universally recognized, and to crystallize them into positive rules; in a word, to establish an international jurisprudence."[31] Mr. Hagerup (Norway), in turn, stressed the importance of having a fallback position, in the event that no rule deriving from treaty or international custom was applicable, "to avoid the possibility of the Court declaring itself incompetent (*non liquet*)"; it was this position that most members of the Committee seemed to accept.[32]

When the debate continued, Baron Descamps stressed that any "impression [that] appeared to exist that the rules drawn up by [him] gave to the judges a new power which had never been admitted by the assembly of States" was plainly wrong, as the application in practice of the rules he suggested was "constant in international jurisdictions" and, "far from giving too much liberty to the judges' decision, his proposal would limit it."[33] Mr. Ricci-Busatti (Italy), for his part, agreed with the

[27] *Ibid*, at p. 335; Lord Phillimore, too, expressed the view that "[i]nternational custom, that is, a general practice accepted as law by nations, constitutes in the main international law" (at p. 295).

[28] See also Spiermann, *supra* note 21, at pp. 214–218.

[29] *Procès-Verbaux*, at p. 294 (suggesting also that they amounted to "saying to the States: 'You surrender your rights to say what justice should be'"). Root added that he did not think that the world was disposed to accept "the compulsory jurisdiction of a Court which would apply principles, differently understood in different countries . . . . . . It is inconceivable that a Government would agree to allow itself to be arraigned before a Court which bases its sentences on its subjective conceptions of the principles of justice. The Court must not have the power to legislate": *ibid*, at pp. 308–309.

[30] *Ibid*, at p. 295.

[31] *Ibid*, at p. 294.

[32] *Ibid*, at pp. 296, 307–308, 313, 317–318.

[33] *Ibid*, at pp. 310, 311.

"impossibility of the Court acting as a legislator," but asserted that even where a rule of international law applicable to a case could not be found to exist, "nevertheless a legal situation is established: that which is not forbidden is allowed."[34] After further discussion, a compromise was finally reached on the basis of a draft submitted by Root and Phillimore: The Court would be authorized to apply, in addition to any relevant treaties and customary international law, "the general principles of law recognized by civilized nations" as well as "judicial decisions and the teachings of the most highly qualified publicists of the various nations, as being subsidiary means for the definition of rules of law."[35] Baron Descamps felt it necessary to explain, as regards the latter category, that

> [t]his element could only be of a subsidiary nature; the judge should only use it in a supplementary way to clarify the rules of international law. Doctrine and jurisprudence no doubt do not create law; but they assist in determining rules which exist. A judge should make use of both jurisprudence and doctrine, but they should serve only as elucidation.[36]

It was against this background that Descamps and Root jointly placed before the Committee, some ten days later, a draft resolution concerning the calling of an international conference "for the advancement of international law," which they proposed would be adopted as a recommendation to the Council of the League.[37] Remarkably, despite recognizing that the matter was not squarely within their mandate,[38] the Committee members "very willingly accepted" this proposal,[39] the Committee

[34] *Ibid*, at p. 314.

[35] *Ibid*, at pp. 335–342; see also article 35 of the Committee's draft scheme at pp. 729–730.

[36] *Ibid*, at pp. 336, 337 (adding that "[t]he judge's right to make use of the elements mentioned in this paragraph is not a dangerous one as it would only be for elucidating and supplementary purposes"). Lord Phillimore sought later to emphasize that "judicial decisions state, but do not create, law": *ibid*, at p. 584.

[37] *Ibid*, at pp. 497, 519–520.

[38] *Ibid*, at p. 504 (Loder); see also M.O. Hudson, *The Permanent Court of Justice: A Treatise* (Macmillan 1934) 109, fn. 21 (suggesting that the resolution "went somewhat beyond [the Committee's] mandate"). But see C. Hurst, 'A Plea for the Codification of International Law on New Lines', 32 *Transactions of the Grotius Society* (1946) 135 at 141 ("It must be remembered that in 1914 when war broke out arrangements were in hand for the meeting of a Third Peace Conference at The Hague on the lines of those of 1899 and 1907 – and it was not unnatural that the Jurists Committee should try to ensure the continuance of the successful work of the first two Conferences").

[39] Report dated July 27, 1920, *supra* note 25; see also *Procès-Verbaux*, at pp. 497, 671, 691. The lack of any opposition to the proposal stands out especially when compared with the reaction to another proposal submitted at that same time and signed by Baron Descamps, with respect to the creation of a High Court of International Justice to "try crimes against

stipulating in its final report to the Council that it considered the resolution to be "closely associated with the object of its labors."[40] At a time when the only guides as to what the corpus of international law comprised "were a fairly thin layer of treaties and diplomatic *savoir-faire* in a handful of Chancelleries; and, beyond that, the only systematic treatment was the accumulated knowledge of the great scholars and writers,"[41] the Committee "assumed that the absence of clear and agreed rules of law and the corresponding latitude or discretion of international tribunals are not likely to assist in inducing governments to undertake the commitments of obligatory judicial settlement."[42] The resolution thus suggested that an inter-State conference, "to carry on the work of the two first Conferences at The Hague," should reestablish in the postwar world "the existing rules of the Law of Nations" and formulate and approve "the modifications and additions rendered necessary or advisable by the War, and by the changes in the conditions of international life following upon this great struggle."[43] It was further advised that the conference would be followed periodically by similar conferences, "at intervals sufficiently short to enable the work undertaken to be continued, in so

international public order and the universal law of Nations"; one of the objections raised was that since these categories of crime are vague, the tribunal would effectively be given power to try cases in which there was no law on which to base its judgments: *Procès-Verbaux*, at p. 504 (Loder). A third proposed resolution, on The Hague Academy of International Law, was eventually adopted as well: *Procès-Verbaux*, at p. 749.

40 *Ibid*, at p. 747.

41 F. Berman, 'The International Court of Justice as an "Agent" of Legal Development?', in C.J. Tams and J. Sloan (eds.), *The Development of International Law by the International Court of Justice* (OUP 2013) 7 at 21. Mr. Léon Bourgeois, speaking before the Advisory Committee on behalf of the Council of the League of Nations, had asserted that States "have up to now one towards another uncertain modes of contact, the nature of which is badly defined, the laws of which are still at the mercy of endless differences of opinion, or of arbitrary chance, just as it was between the citizens of each country in the first ages of civilization": *Procès-Verbaux*, at p. 8.

42 H. Lauterpacht, 'Codification and Development of International Law', 49 AJIL (1955) 16 at 20. See also S. Rosenne, 'Codification Revisited After 50 Years', 2 MPYUNL (1998) 1 at 2, fn. 2. Cf. G.W. Wickersham, 'The Codification of International Law', 4 *Foreign Affairs* (1925–1926) 237 at 245 (suggesting that it was "the disregard of the international laws of war, in the great contest of 1914–1918, that led the jurists who framed the Protocol and Statute of the Permanent Court of International Justice" to make this recommendation).

43 *Procès-Verbaux*, at p. 747; other enumerated purposes were "[r]econciling divergent opinions, and bringing about a general understanding concerning the rules which have been the subject of controversy … [and g]iving special consideration to those points, which are not at the present time adequately provided for, and of which a definite settlement by general agreement is required in the interests of international justice."

far as it may be incomplete, with every prospect of success."[44] The result, Root envisioned, would be "continually to extend the domain of international law and thus continually to enlarge the obligatory jurisdiction of the Court without losing the definite limits necessary to guard against the arbitrary exercise of power."[45] Anzilotti wrote to Secretary-General Drummond, in the same spirit, that "[t]he next conference of international law will be in regard to the Permanent Court of International Justice, what the naval conference of London (1909) had to be in regard of the International Prize Court."[46]

C. The Committee of Experts for the Progressive Codification of International Law (1925–1928): Working "for the Assistance of the Permanent Court of International Justice"?

The Advisory Committee's recommendation did not go unnoticed by the Council of the League, which at its session held in Brussels in October 1920 approved and transmitted the recommendation to the Assembly for further action.[47] There, however, the idea of codification of international law at first encountered significant hesitation: being warned by one delegate that codification is "a very dangerous project at this stage in the world's history ... [in which] we have [not] arrived at sufficient calmness of the public mind to undertake that without very serious results to the future of international law," the Assembly voted against further action.[48] The Assembly also rejected a proposal by the Argentine delegation to authorize the PCIJ to apply, in addition to the sources of

[44] *Ibid*, at p. 748.

[45] Final clause of Root's proposal to the Committee, as quoted in Scott, *supra* note 8, at 26.

[46] Report dated 27 July 1920, *supra* note 25.

[47] See *League of Nations Official Journal*, Issue 8, November–December 1920, p. 20.

[48] See Records of the First Assembly, Plenary Meetings: Minutes of the 31st session (1920) 744–747 (Lord Cecil of South Africa). See also UN Doc. A/AC.10/5: 'Historical Survey of Development of International Law and Its Codification by International Conferences' (29 April 1947), pp. 66–67. According to Rosenne, "[i]t is evident from the internal records that considerable skepticism reigned [also] in the highest circles of the [League's] Secretariat, headed by the Secretary-General, Sir Eric Drummond himself, as to the possibility and desirability of the League giving any encouragement to the codification of international law... Nevertheless, this attitude was not unanimously held in the Secretariat": S. Rosenne (ed.), *League of Nations Committee of Experts for the Progressive Codification of International Law (1925–1928)* (Oceana Publications 1972) xxxi. This impasse led Manley O. Hudson to suggest that "[s]ince the judges of the new court are to write reasoned opinions, the decisions themselves should furnish in time a body of international law which the court may apply": Hudson, *supra* note 2, at 256.

law suggested by the Advisory Committee, "[t]he rules drawn up by the Assembly of the League of Nations in the performance of its duty of codifying international law"[49] (the subcommittee designated to review such proposed amendments to the Court's draft Statute having considered that "the stage of development where [giving the Assembly the power to codify international law] would be possible had . . . not yet been reached"[50]). The League's members had also refused the idea of compulsory jurisdiction, which they found to be incompatible with the League's Covenant; and they made sure to insert into the Court's Statute, which entered into force in September 1921, a provision stipulating that "[t]he decision of the Court has no binding force except between the parties and in respect of that particular case."[51]

If members of the League had initially thought that the new Court did not need to operate in tandem with codification efforts, codification was by 1924 back on their agenda. As the Rapporteur of the Assembly's competent subcommittee then put it before them, "everybody was agreed in wishing to see existing international law, which is theoretical and uncertain, converted gradually into precise written law, such conversion having become still more necessary since the creation of the Permanent Court of International Justice."[52] By its resolution dated September 22 of that year, the Assembly, "considering . . . the legislative needs of international relations" and "desirous of increasing the contribution of the League of Nations to the progressive codification of International Law," requested the Council to convene, for this purpose, "a Committee of Experts, not merely possessing individually the required qualifications but also as a body representing the main forms of civilization and the principal legal systems of the world."[53] This standing organ was to draw

[49] League of Nations, Records of the First Assembly, Meetings of the Committees, Vol. I, Geneva, 1920, p. 519.

[50] *Ibid*, at p. 386.

[51] Statute of the Permanent Court of International Justice, article 59.

[52] As reported by the Chairman of the League of Nations Committee of Experts for the Progressive Codification of International Law in describing the lead up to the establishment of the Committee: see Rosenne, *supra* note 48, at p. 5. Manley Hudson, on temporary assignment as an adviser with the League's Legal Section, wrote in a memorandum of August 17, 1927 that "the Assembly resolution of 1924 was almost chiefly due to a desire to meet popular demand": *ibid*, at p. lxxxiii.

[53] *League of Nations Official Journal, Special Supplement*, No. 21, 1924, p. 10. This language drew upon article 9 of the Statute of the Permanent Court of International Justice (1920), which read: "At every election, the electors shall bear in mind that not only should all the persons appointed as members of the Court possess the qualifications required, but the

up, on the basis of consultations with governments, a list of subjects of international law "sufficiently ripe" for regulation by international treaty, and to report to the Council both on these questions and on the procedure that might be followed "with a view to preparing eventually for conferences for their solution."[54]

The Council acted quickly to give effect to the Assembly's resolution by inviting, on December 12, 1924, seventeen persons "to form part of the Committee for the Progressive Codification of International Law."[55] Among these eminent men were two sitting members of the World Court, which decided in principle that it was not incompatible for judges to take part in international conferences concerned with the development of the law:[56] Judge Loder, who had served on the Advisory Committee of Jurists and was now President of the Court, and Mr. Chung Hui Wang (China), a Deputy Judge.[57] Other members of the Committee of Experts, namely Mr. Fromageot (France), Mr. Guerrero (El Salvador), Mr. Schücking (Germany), and Mr. de Visscher (Belgium), were later to become judges of the PCIJ as well. Another prominent member, Mr. Brierly (United Kingdom), would one day be elected a member of the International Law Commission, and his fellow countryman alternate, Mr. McNair, would later serve, like Guerrero, as judge and as president of the International Court of Justice.

Gathered for the first time at the beginning of April 1925 in the Palais Wilson in Geneva, the members of the Committee of Experts were greeted by the Chairman, Mr. Hammarskjöld (Sweden), who stated that "codification is plainly of the greatest value for assuring certainty and clearness in the law."[58] "These advantages," he continued, "are especially

whole body also should represent the main forms of civilization and the principal legal systems of the world."

54 *League of Nations Official Journal, Special Supplement*, No. 21, 1924, p. 10. The Assembly thus "contemplated only a tentative approach to the great problem of codification," as it did not call for the codification of all international law: Wickersham, *supra* note 42, at p. 243.

55 *League of Nations Official Journal*, February 1925, p. 274.

56 *Rapport annuel de la Cour permanente de justice internationale (1 janvier 1922–15 juin 1925)*, P.C.I.J Ser. E, No. 1, p. 239.

57 The Statute of the Permanent Court of International Justice originally provided that if not all of the judges could be present, deputy-judges could be summoned to sit. A revision to the Statute (in 1929) abolished the position of deputy-judges (while increasing the number of judges from eleven to fifteen).

58 Rosenne, *supra* note 48, at p. 3. The Secretary-General of the League spoke briefly before Hammarskjöld, conveying the Council's gratitude for the willingness of members of the

valuable in the case of international law: there legal practice does not possess the same facilities for law-making as it possesses in the field of national legislation for filling gaps and even correcting defects."[59] Referring to article 14 of the Covenant of the League of Nations, "which gave the Council the duty of submitting to the States a plan for a Court of International Justice," Hammarskjöld added that "[w]e know that this duty has been carried out with the greatest success, without it having been thought necessary to postpone establishing the jurisdiction until the law to be applied was fixed. The scruples which prevented the putting into force of the 1907 Convention concerning the Prize Court did not this time prevail."[60]

Following Hammarskjöld's opening remarks, a discussion ensued on the general import of "codification" of international law,[61] a matter to which the Committee was to devote its first four meetings. The discussion afforded members an opportunity to express their views not only on the theoretical distinction between the task of registering the existing unwritten rules and that of progressive development of the law, but also on the Committee's own role and duties. Mr. Wickersham (United States of America), speaking first, had no hesitation in suggesting that much like with restatements "of various topics upon the customary or unwritten law" carried out in the United States, which were prepared not for the purpose of submitting them to the legislatures of States to be enacted into statute law but, rather, for aiding courts in ascertainment of the existing law, the Committee, too, could prepare statements "possibly not for international agreement, but for common acceptance by scholars and for the assistance of the Permanent Court of International Justice or any other tribunals which might deal with questions of International Law."[62]

Committee to serve, and expressing "confident hope that [the Committee's] labours would prove of lasting benefit to the whole world": *ibid.*

59 *Ibid.*

60 *Ibid*, at pp. 3–4.

61 In a working paper circulated by the Chairman to members of the Committee ahead of the Committee's first meeting, it was pointed out that "we shall have to adopt a consistent attitude as regards the nature of the 'codification' which we are instructed to prepare. Are we simply asked to give methodical form and arrangement to rules which already exist, at the most, to reduce to writing ideas on which there is universal agreement? Or are we to go further, and to consider how far innovations are desirable or possible and how far solutions may be found for questions which are still subject of controversy? Though this question may be easy to answer in general terms, it involves many subsidiary problems and considerations which call for examination": [C.P.D.I./2], March 6, 1925.

62 'See Rosenne, *supra* note 48, at p. 6.

This method, he explained with much foresight, "might be a less difficult method than one which sought the assent of Governments to formal agreements of International Law to be embodied in treaties."[63] Other members of the Committee advocated for a less radical but still expansive interpretation of their mandate, according to which their work should not be "confined to codifying points on which the States seemed to be in agreement. The Committee had also an active mission in the sense of drawing attention to general principles and seeking general conclusions, and of settling questions in regard to which the modern international community of interests made it necessary to secure legal uniformity."[64] According to this view, the political interests of governments should be left "quite aside," as "legal experts ought to be above such considerations."[65]

Still others, however, emphasized that the Committee should keep in mind that "[t]he success of its work depended on the attitude adopted by Governments towards the proposals which it would make."[66] Among them was Judge Loder, who, while agreeing that the Committee should not limit itself merely to restating the existing rules of international law but should also engage in the development of the law, made it clear that he considered that "satisfactory results" of the Committee's work would only be achieved "by proceeding by means of conventions and treaties."[67] In his opinion, "the Committee [was to] leave as wide a latitude as possible to the various States, and confine itself to indicating the necessary reforms in general terms."[68] When referring to the subjects to be taken up by the Committee, Loder sought to explain what would be "of

[63] *Ibid.* Wickersham later explained that "[t]he mere preparation of a list [of subjects of international law sufficiently ripe to be regulated by treaty] and its submission to the Governments would not take the Committee very far. He feared that the replies from the Governments would not be of any very considerable value. The foreign offices of the world were at present extremely busy, and were mostly occupied in dealing with pressing questions as they arose from day to day. A list of subjects such as the Committee proposed to draw up would be likely to receive a very superficial consideration. It would be more practicable in present circumstances to propose something definite, and to put forward subjects which, in the opinion of the Committee, were ripe for solution": *ibid*, at p. 22.

[64] *Ibid*, at p. 6 (Suarez (Argentina)); see also at p. 7 (Diena (Italy)), and p. 10 (Schücking), and the statements of Rundstein (Poland) and Mastný (Czechoslovakia), as well as that of de Magalhaes (Portugal), at pp. 12–15 and 18–20, respectively.

[65] See the statements by Suarez and Guerrero, *ibid*, at pp. 21 and 15 respectively.

[66] *Ibid*, at p. 15 (Brierly); see also *ibid*, at pp. 9 and 24 (de Visscher), and p. 16 (Fromageot).

[67] *Ibid*, at p. 8.

[68] *Ibid*, at p. 22.

first importance" for the Court;[69] in this connection, he was speaking "partly from the vantage point of his status as a member of the Permanent Court of International Justice."[70] As regards public (as opposed to private) international law, he noted that there was, "for example, the question of sovereignty. It was only necessary to consult the Statute of the Court in order to realize that the scope of the questions with which it might have to deal with in this field was very extensive."[71] It seems to have been this vantage point that likewise led Loder to suggest that it "would certainly be well for the Committee to put aside the subject of the international law of war" and concentrate on other subjects.[72]

The other member of the PCIJ on the Committee, Deputy Judge Wang (who would also serve on the subcommittee entrusted with collating the various suggestions for subjects that might advantageously be included in the Committee's list), agreed that "it would be convenient to postpone any consideration of the laws of war until a more opportune moment."[73] As to the task of the Committee more generally, he expressed the view that "[c]odification in the narrow sense . . . a reduction to writing of what was already accepted and acted upon in practice . . . would be very useful, as it would give certainty and precision to a good deal that was at present uncertain and vague."[74] But Wang did not consider the need for this work to be urgent; "more apparent and more imperative" was the need for "[c]odification in the broader sense [that] involved proposals for the alteration of existing rules, either by modifications or additions."[75]

The Committee's Chairman, for his part, found it necessary to assert that "it was obvious that no member of the Committee desired to trespass on the competence of the legislature. The part to be played by the Committee was much more modest: it consisted in making proposals to the competent legislative authorities," that is, to States.[76] "Nevertheless," he added, "[w]ere the solution of a question to be found to be unquestionably desirable, and, at the same time, to be realizable, the Committee had the power and the duty to raise the question, it being understood that governments could select or reject any of the proposals

[69] *Ibid*, at p. 8.
[70] *Ibid*, at p. xliii (Rosenne).
[71] *Ibid*, at p. 8.
[72] *Ibid*.
[73] *Ibid*, at p. 21. A majority of the Committee's members supported this position as well.
[74] *Ibid*.
[75] *Ibid*.
[76] *Ibid*, at p. 17.

submitted to them."[77] In summing up the general discussion, he suggested that it was thus neither necessary nor useful for the Committee to determine in the abstract what belonged under the domain of strict codification as opposed to the domain of legislation; going further than merely registering the existing rules of international law was in any case "subject to the caution imposed by the express terms of the [Assembly's] resolution, according to which account must be taken of the fact that the proposed solution must be not only desirable but also realizable."[78] The Committee agreed.

The Committee's second session, held in Geneva from January 12 to 29, 1926, was devoted mostly to examining reports (submitted to it by its subcommittees) on certain subjects of international law that were identified as possibly relevant to its task and finalizing them for submission to the League. It was while considering the report on the topic of nationality, which contained a proposal to confer, in a future convention on the topic, jurisdiction on the PCIJ, that Judge Loder made the suggestion that the Committee should in a general way draw the attention of governments to the advisability of inserting into future conventions clauses providing for compulsory recourse to the Court.[79] But the draft resolution he presented to this effect quickly gave rise to a heated controversy among members of the Committee. Wickersham, for his part, suggested that this would be the surest way to guarantee that the United States would reject all of the Committee's recommendations and explained that the issue at all events fell outside of the Committee's mandate.[80] Brierly adopted a similar line, stressing that this was an essentially political, not legal, question, and reminding members that the United Kingdom's policy was not to accept obligations of this kind.[81] While some members agreed that the matter should be set aside, others favored Loder's suggestion, among them the Chairman, who considered it "essential not to give to the public the impression that the Committee rejected the notion of recourse to the Court."[82] His compromise proposal, that the Committee's general report to the League on the work of its second session would

77 *Ibid.*
78 *Ibid*, at pp. 24, 25.
79 *Ibid*, at pp. 165, 179–180.
80 *Ibid*, at pp. 180, 181.
81 *Ibid*, at pp. 180, 182.
82 *Ibid*, at p. 182 (translation from French).

mention the issue simply by stating that it may always be examined as and when it arises, ultimately won the support of most members.[83]

Despite deep skepticism among the Secretariat of the League with respect to the value of the Committee's work, and broader criticism of the Committee for not sticking closely to its task (of suggesting topics as opposed to attempting their actual codification),[84] in 1927 the League decided, on the basis of the Committee's preparatory reports, to convene at The Hague a conference called the First Codification Conference.[85] The conference was to consider, on account of 'bases of discussion' to be drawn up by a Preparatory Committee, three of the seven topics deemed by the Committee in its third session to be "sufficiently ripe" for codification.[86] The political necessity of carrying on with codification was clear to the decision-makers, not least because across the Atlantic, U.S. politicians continued to warn that "until international law is reduced to the confines of a written code the United States cannot safely give

[83] *Ibid.* For the text of the "general observation" by the Committee, see C.96.M.47.1926.V [C.P.D.I./63], February 9, 1926 ("In some of the conclusions proposed to the Committee in reports of its Sub-Committees, submission of disputes to the jurisdiction of the Permanent Court of International Justice was suggested. It is, of course, to be understood that in any case such suggestions would have constituted merely questions submitted by the Committee for examination by Governments and, eventually, by such conferences as may be called. Even in this form the Committee has not felt that it should deal with the general question whether a clause providing for the obligatory submission of disputes to the Permanent Court of International Justice, of which examples are to be found in various treaties, would or would not be desirable in the instruments which will fall to be drawn up by the contemplated conferences. That course, moreover, would not prejudice the possibility of obtaining advisory opinions from the Court at the request of the League of Nations. The Committee has felt that the above question may always be examined as and when it arises, without being particularly mentioned in the questionnaires [on each subject that may be considered sufficiently ripe for codification, to be sent on the Committee's behalf to Governments]").

[84] See Rosenne, *supra* note 48, at pp. lxxii–lxxxvii; M.O. Hudson, 'The First Conference for the Codification of International Law', 24 AJIL (1930) 447 at 464.

[85] *League of Nations Official Journal, Special Supplement*, No. 53, p. 9. The Assembly recommended the Council to indicate in the invitations to the conference the general rules which should govern the discussions, including as regards "[t]he spirit of codification, which should not confine itself to the mere registration of the existing rules, but should aim at adapting them as far as possible to contemporary conditions of international life": *ibid*, at pp. 9–10.

[86] The Committee of Experts had expressed its preference for a single international conference to consider several subjects together, despite the warning voiced early on by Loder, according to which "[i]n establishing treaties, care must above all be taken to avoid dealing at the same conference with different subjects": see Rosenne, *supra* note 48, at pp. 8 and lxxi respectively.

adhesion to the Permanent Court of International Justice."[87] Root himself persisted in advocating that "[c]odification, so-called, of international law, has a special importance at this time, because it is necessary in order to enlarge the service rendered by the [Court]."[88] This view was publicly endorsed by the League in 1928, when its Ninth Assembly expressed the hope that "the efforts now being made through progressive codification to diminish the uncertainties, and supply the deficiencies, of international law will greatly facilitate the acceptance of the Optional Clause [conferring jurisdiction on the Court]".[89] Meanwhile, it was considered, the Court, "by its decisions, will be helping to make the law more certain and through judicial expression more appropriate for inclusion in convention."[90]

The first international conference specifically called for the purpose of codification convened finally at The Hague in March 1930, comprising delegates of forty-eight States. But its results were very modest, owing, inter alia, to poor preparation, a program too ambitious to attempt at once, inadequate time, and the fact that delegations seemed to have differing views as to the very meaning to be given to the term "codification."[91] A general sense of disillusionment with the idea of

[87] As reported in Wickersham, *supra* note 42, at p. 237; see also Scott, *supra* note 8, at pp. 21–27. Additional arguments put forward at the time against compulsory jurisdiction were the so-called political nature of some disputes, the existence of some disputes in which the subject matter is not a legal right but a so-called conflict of interests, and the fact that there is no international legislature capable of modifying and supplementing existing law: see H. Lauterpacht, 'The Absence of an International Legislature and the Compulsory Jurisdiction of International Tribunals', 11 BYIL (1930) 134.

[88] E. Root, 'The Codification of International Law', 19 AJIL (1925) 675. A memorandum to the League's Secretary-General by Manley O. Hudson (then on temporary assignment as an adviser with the League's Legal Section) had indicated that "demand [for codification] continues and . . . comes from such highly respectable circles," mentioning Root as one of those "eminent men . . . [that] are associating themselves with the inspiration of these expectations": see Rosenne, *supra* note 48, at p. lxxxiii. On this view being held by British statesmen as well, see H. Lauterpacht, *The Function of Law in the International Community* (1933, reprinted OUP 2011) 62–63.

[89] *League of Nations Official Journal, Special Supplement*, No. 64, p. 183.

[90] Wickersham, *supra* note 42, at p. 247.

[91] See A. Alvarez, 'Impressions Left by the First Hague Conference for the Codification of International Law', 16 *Transactions of the Grotius Society* (1931) 119–129; H. Miller, 'The Hague Codification Conference', 24 AJIL (1930) 674–693. See also Hudson, *supra* note 84, at pp. 447–466 (reporting, at p. 449, that "[s]entiment grew quite rapidly against any attempt to state what was the existing law as distinguished from new legislation, and after two weeks it became clear that even the use of the term declaration was stoutly opposed. The discussion in the lobbies of the difference between conventions and declarations was quite interesting").

codification of international law was to follow,[92] so much so that even Brierly, then still a member of the Committee of Experts (which was never again to convene[93]), now lent his support to those calling to abandon entirely the concentrated effort of making the law of nations more definite.[94] Instead, it was suggested, members of the League would resort to international conventions only in special cases where it was of "immediate practical importance" to regulate by general agreement "particular relations" among States; and customary international law, as before, would be left to develop "from the practice of States and the development of international jurisprudence," in particular that of the PCIJ.[95] While decisions of the Court were to have no binding force except between the parties and in respect of the particular case under review, it was indeed well understood – including by those opposing any compulsory jurisdiction – that "the general acceptance of the court's decisions will be continually building up a body of agreement which narrows the field of controversy between nations and prevents future controversies."[96] But it was also noted that in the absence of means for international legislation, international law would be lacking the safeguard

[92] Some did argue at the time, however, that the 1930 Conference "must be viewed as part of a larger picture . . . [that] portrays an effort which ought to be continued": Hudson, *supra* note 84, at p. 465. See also the individual impression of the Rapporteur of the League Assembly's First Committee: *League of Nations Official Journal, Special Supplement*, No. 84, p. 212.

[93] The Committee of Experts' fourth session (held in Geneva from June 22–28, 1928), after which it suspended further work pending fresh instructions from the League, turned out to be its last. On the fascinating exchange that took place within the League on whether the Committee of Experts should be abolished or continue to "go on hunting for new subjects for conferences" for the years to come, and on whether it should at all employ the term "codification," see Rosenne, *supra* note 48, at pp. lxxxv–xciii, xcviii.

[94] J.L. Brierly, 'The Future of Codification', 12 BYIL (1931) 1–12.

[95] See the proposal jointly submitted to the First Committee of the League's Assembly following the Hague Conference by the British, French, German, Greek and Italian delegations: Minutes of the First Committee, Annex 11, Eleventh Ordinary Session of the Assembly of the League of Nations. This proposal served as a basis for the resolution eventually adopted by the League's Assembly on September 25, 1931: *League of Nations Official Journal, Special Supplement*, No. 92, p. 9.

[96] Root, *supra* note 88, at pp. 678. See also Lord Balfour's prediction that a "decision of the Permanent Court cannot but have the effect of gradually moulding and modifying international law," even if that was not contemplated by the Covenant: *P.C.I.J., Documents concerning the Action Taken by the Council of the League of Nations under Article 14 of the Covenant*, p. 38. For the view voiced at that time, that "the supposed non-existence of legal rules applicable to disputes" ought not to limit the international judicial function, see Lauterpacht, *supra* note 88, at pp. 59–143.

(possessed by municipal law) of "correcting" judicial decisions in instances where the existing law ought to be adapted and supplemented in order to be brought into harmony with justice and progress.[97] As Lauterpacht recalled, when the question arose whether to accept obligatory judicial settlement, "international lawyers of repute uttered warnings against pushing too far ahead on one line of international progress so long as the other – institutions of peaceful change – remained stationary."[98]

D. Reincarnations: International Adjudication and Codification of International Law in the United Nations System

The brutal global conflict of 1939–1945 resulted in a more intense exercise of international organization that culminated in the establishment, in October 1945, of the United Nations (UN). A more central place was to be given to the rule of law in international affairs,[99] and the notions of judicial settlement of international disputes as well as progressive development and codification of international law formally found their place within the new UN Charter regime. The San Francisco Conference recognized the persistent need for improving and systematizing international law as a means for securing international peace and security, and the conviction that the substantive insufficiency of international law was intimately tied to the exercise of international judicial powers had not lost its hold. Thus the "conditions under which justice and respect for the obligations arising from treaties and other sources of international law can be maintained," in the words of the Charter,[100]

[97] For more on this argument (and the responses to it), see Lauterpacht, *supra* note 87, at pp. 134–157. See also H. Kelsen, 'Compulsory Adjudication of International Disputes', 37 AJIL (1943) 397 at 400–401. Brierly, too, had earlier contrasted international law with municipal law for lacking the safeguard possessed by the latter, namely that decisions of courts "may be corrected and the law brought into harmony with public opinion by the legislature": J.L. Brierly, *The Law of Nations* (OUP 1928) 189.

[98] H. Lauterpacht, 'The Legal Aspect', in C.A.W. Manning (ed.), *Peaceful Change: An International Problem* (Macmillan 1937) 135 at 138 (referring to the discussion in Great Britain as to its possible acceptance of the obligations of the Optional Clause).

[99] Although not without initial reservations: see H. Lauterpacht, 'The Grotian Tradition in International Law', 23 BYIL (1946) 1 at fn. 2 ("It was with some difficulty that the authors of the Charter of the United Nations were persuaded to assign to international law a place within the scheme of the United Nations. The view is widely held that, conceived in the spirit of realism, the Charter in many respects preferred order to law").

[100] Charter of the United Nations, preambular para. 1.

were to be established by setting up an international court to which States could refer their legal disputes, as well as by charging the General Assembly with a wide-ranging program of codification.[101] International law-making, however, was firmly reserved to States: the United Nations was not conceived of as a legislative body and, in setting it up, its members sought jealously to guard their sovereign prerogative of creating new law or repealing the old.[102]

1. *The International Court of Justice (Re)Born*

Even as the Second World War was still raging, the assumption of those contemplating the postwar international order was that "an International Court in some form will be required in future."[103] The drafters of the UN Charter already had the PCIJ on hand for their rebuilding and it was, in 1945, reinvented as the International Court of Justice when the San Francisco Conference decided to take it over as a principal organ of the United Nations. Despite the insistence of a significant number of States that jurisdiction of the new Court should be compulsory, the extant Optional Clause regime of the PCIJ was preserved to leave States the freedom to accept or reject the Court's compulsory jurisdiction. For States such as the United States – as John Foster Dulles, then an adviser to the State Department, had put it – international law had not yet "developed the scope and definiteness necessary to permit international disputes generally to be resolved by judicial rather than political tests."[104] Nor was any departure made from the old Statute with respect to the law to be applied by the Court: article 38 of the new Statute retained the reference to treaties, customary international law, the general principles

[101] See also I. Sinclair, 'International Law: The Court, Commission and Judges', in E. Jensen and T. Fisher (eds.), *The United Kingdom – The United Nations* (Macmillan 1990) 120.

[102] See also O. Schachter, 'The UN Legal Order: An Overview', in C.C. Joyner (ed.), *The United Nations and International Law* (CUP 1997) 3.

[103] This was the assumption of the informal inter-Allied expert committee set up in 1943 to consider the question of the Permanent Court of International Justice: see M.O. Hudson, 'The Twenty-Third Year of the Permanent Court of International Justice and Its Future', 39 AJIL (1945) 1–7.

[104] As quoted in H.N. Meyer, *The World Court in Action: Judging among the Nations* (Rowman & Littlefield 2002) 97. The United States did finally accept the compulsory jurisdiction of the Court in 1946 (ultimately for only a couple of decades), despite some concern in the Senate that "[w]e should not commit the destiny of this country to a game in which the rules are made by the referee as he goes along": F.O. Wilcox, 'The United States Accepts Compulsory Jurisdiction', 40 AJIL (1946) 699 at 717 (quoting Senator Millikin).

of law, and, as "subsidiary means for the determination of rules of law," to both "judicial decisions and the teachings of the most highly qualified publicists of the various nations." By virtue of article 59 of the Statute, any decision of the Court was still to bind only the States parties to the relevant contentious proceedings and in respect of that particular case alone, and no binding force existed in the case of advisory proceedings.

The Court held its inaugural meeting on April 18, 1946, on the premises of its predecessor at the Peace Palace in The Hague. The Dutch Minister for Foreign Affairs, Jan Herman van Roijen, suggested to the dignitaries assembled on the occasion that the notion of *trias politica* adopted by Montesquieu was perhaps too rigid, and that leaving to judges the role of "mouthpiece[s] which [recite] the law . . . [but] cannot moderate either its force or its vigour" was "still less applicable in international law, in which a written, established rule seldom exists."[105] "Here," he continued,

> the judge finds himself only too often, and whether he wills it or not, obliged to assume the role of the law-maker. The increasing difficulties which, in recent times, have hampered the codification of international law have shown the importance of this aspect of a judge's work. The part played by case-law in the formation of law becomes ever more vital; the world seems disposed to accept and to generalize a ruling given by a Court of high repute; whereas international conferences, after endless discussion, succeed neither in reconciling divergent standpoints nor in framing uniform rules of law.[106]

Remarkably, the very same sentiment was echoed a few months later by the President of the new Court (and former President of the PCIJ), Judge Guerrero, who observed, with reference to the possibility that the new world organization would again seek to codify international law by means of international multilateral conventions, that "[t]he experience already acquired in pursuance of this method has been very far from encouraging . . . and it has to be feared that a second attempt along the same lines will also result in failure."[107] Instead, he observed, "one is justified in wondering whether it would not be preferable to await the gradual development of the jurisprudence of the International Court" alone.[108]

105 YBICJ 1946, p. 33.

106 *Ibid.*

107 J.G. Guerrero, 'The International Court of Justice', 1 *United Nations World* (February 1947) 54 at 55.

108 *Ibid* (adding that "[i]n addition to its judicial and advisory functions, the International Court of Justice is also called upon to continue the work of the old court in connection with the development of international law and thus to open the way to its future

2. *The International Law Commission: International Legislation at Quickened Pace*

For the drafters of the UN Charter, however, past failures did not denote the unwisdom of initial efforts. New life was breathed into the codification and progressive development of international law by article 13 of the Charter, which brought these tasks within the mainstream of the General Assembly's functions.[109] While proposals to vest the General Assembly with legislative authority to enact rules of international law were decisively defeated at the Conference,[110] States did support a more limited mandate of study and recommendation for the purpose of "encouraging the progressive development of international law and its codification."[111] Proposals for the establishment of an "International Legislative Drafting Bureau" of some kind had already been floated,[112] and it was widely felt that "the codification of the law of nations would

codification . . . it is certain that its decisions will possess the great merit of clarifying those rules of law which are the subject of divergent views, and of affirming others which are uniformly recognized by international doctrine and practice. It may be truly said, therefore, that the Court will make a generous contribution to the progress and codification of international law").

109 Article 13(1) reads: "The General Assembly shall initiate studies and make recommendations for the purpose of: (a) promoting international co-operation in the political field and encouraging the progressive development of international law and its codification. . .." For the suggestion that the competence conferred upon the General Assembly by article 13 is covered anyhow by the more general article 10 of the Charter, see H. Kelsen, *The Law of the United Nations: A Critical Analysis of Its Fundamental Problems* (second reprinting, The Lawbook Exchange 2000) 215. On the drafting history of article 13, see C.-A. Fleischhauer and B. Simma, 'Article 13', in B. Simma et al (eds.), *The Charter of the United Nations: A Commentary*, Vol. I, 3rd ed. (OUP 2012) 525 at 528–529.

110 See H.W. Briggs, *The International Law Commission* (Cornell University Press 1965) 6–9; J. Sette-Camara, 'The International Law Commission: Discourse and Method', in *International Law at the Time of Its Codification: Essays in Honour of Roberto Ago* (Dott. A. Giuffrè Editore 1987) 467 at 475–476.

111 See also Y.-L. Liang, 'The Progressive Development of International Law and Its Codification under the United Nations', 41 PASIL (1947) 24 at 28–31. The UN Legal Counsel, Dr. Ivan Kerno, soon explained that the formulation 'progressive development and codification' was "designed to strike a balance between the need for change and the need for stability": 'The International Law Commission', 35 *American Bar Association Journal* (1949) 487.

112 C.W. Jenks, 'The Need for an International Legislative Drafting Bureau', 39 AJIL (1945) 163–179. A similar suggestion was made by the Secretariat of the United Nations in a prior memorandum submitted for the consideration of the 1947 Committee on Development and Codification of International Law: UN Doc. A/AC.10/7.

materially help in re-establishing its prestige."[113] Lending their weight to this cause were former judges of the PCIJ, such as Sir Cecil Hurst (United Kingdom), who publicly voiced his "plea for the codification of international law on new lines" and argued that "a well developed body of law" was an essential component of a sound international legal system.[114] Another former judge of that Court (and future Chairman of the International Law Commission at its first session), Manley O. Hudson (United States of America), had suggested that the Charter offered "an opportunity for a revitalization of international law" and that "[i]nternational legislation . . . must now proceed at quickened pace."[115] Judge Alejandro Alvarez (Chile) of the newly established International Court of Justice expressed support for such efforts as well.[116] The General Assembly unanimously recognized, in its first session in 1946, the obligation laid upon it by article 13 of the Charter and resolved to establish yet another committee of seventeen members to study "[t]he methods by which the General Assembly should encourage the progressive development of international law and its eventual codification."[117]

The Committee on the Progressive Development of International Law and Its Codification, commonly referred to as the "Committee of Seventeen" (of which several members would later go on to serve on the Commission or on the Court, or indeed on both), held thirty meetings at Lake Success, New York, from May 12 to June 17, 1947. When laying down the specific plan for the future International Law Commission, it had before it several valuable studies prepared by the UN Secretariat's Division for the Development and Codification of International Law, a memorandum prepared by its Rapporteur, James Brierly, and a joint proposal of the United States and Chinese delegations.[118] Yet the Committee very much had the Court and its Statute in

113 A. Alvarez, 'The Reconstruction and Codification of International Law', 1 *International Law Quarterly* (1947) 469 at 470 (describing what was felt "on many sides").

114 Hurst, *supra* note 38, at p. 137.

115 M.O. Hudson, 'The New World Court', *Foreign Affairs* (October 1945) 75 at 84.

116 Alvarez, *supra* note 113, at pp. 469–481 (advocating for codification for purposes of progressive development).

117 UNGA resolution 94(I) of 11 December 1946. The Committee was to report back to the General Assembly at its next regular session.

118 See the Supplement to 41 AJIL (1947) 27–147; UN Doc. A/AC.10/26: 'Methods for Encouraging the Progressive Development of International Law and Its Eventual Codification – Memorandum Prepared by the Rapporteur at the Request of the Committee' (16 May 1947); and UN Doc. A/AC.10/33: 'Proposal Regarding the Organization and

mind as well. Its recommendation that the future Commission should comprise fifteen members, for example, was inspired by the size of the Court's bench: several members of the Committee agreed that the number "seemed appropriate in view of the fact that the International Court of Justice also consisted of fifteen Judges," and given that the need to have the different legal systems of the world represented applied equally to the Commission.[119] Similarly, the initial qualification of members of the future Commission as "experts" was soon replaced with the words "persons of recognized competence in international law," also borrowed from the Statute of the Court.[120] The Committee moreover considered the employment terms of the judges of the Court in deciding

Procedures of the Commission of Experts on International Law (CEIL), Proposed Jointly by the Delegations of the United States and China' (23 May 1947).

119 UN Doc. A/AC.10/SR.11: 'Summary Record of the Eleventh Meeting of the Committee on the Progressive Development and Its Codification' (26 May 1947), pp. 3–4 (Bartos (Yugoslavia) and Donnedieu de Vabres (France)); UN Doc. A/AC.10/SR.23: 'Summary Record of the Twenty-Third Meeting of the Committee on the Progressive Development and Its Codification' (10 June 1947), pp. 10–14 (Rudzinski (Poland), Donnedieu de Vabres, Yepes (Colombia), and Koretsky (USSR)). Jessup (United States of America) favored a small group of nine members working together with outside help from experts in various fields, observing that the Permanent Court of International Justice originally had eleven Judges and four alternates, and the increase to fifteen judges had been made not because it was required in order that the Court reflect all the legal systems, but because it had sometimes been difficult to get a quorum; he added that neither in the Committee of Jurists that drafted the new statute of the International Court of Justice nor in the Fourth Committee at the San Francisco Conference had it been said that the number fifteen was required for a proper representation of the various legal systems: *ibid*, at pp. 12–13. The Committee had originally voted in its eleventh meeting for nine members (rejecting the alternatives of eleven, thirteen, and fifteen), but later amended this decision by another vote with nine in favor, five against, and three abstentions. It stuck to fifteen even as doubts were raised whether the number would suffice given the expected workload of the Commission: UN Doc. A/AC.10/SR.24: 'Summary Record of the Twenty-Fourth Meeting of the Committee on the Progressive Development and Its Codification' (11 June 1947), pp. 8–11. Later at the Sixth Committee of the General Assembly, "[some] delegations thought that fifteen members, a number also adopted in the Statute of the International Court of Justice (Article 3), should be considered as a minimum, if it was desired to ensure that the main forms of civilization and the principal legal systems of the world should be represented in the Commission. The Sub-Committee supported a membership of fifteen by thirteen votes to two": UN Doc. A/C.6/193 (18 November 1947), p. 2, para. 4. The Commission's membership was enlarged in 1956 to twenty-one, and in 1961 to twenty-five; since 1981, the Commission has had thirty-four members.

120 A/AC.10/SR.23, *supra* note 119, at p. 5 (another reason for replacing the term 'experts' was "the disparaging sense in which this term sometimes was taken").

to suggest that members of the future Commission should serve full- rather than part-time.[121]

The Committee of Seventeen also proposed that the members of the Commission were to be elected through a procedure identical to that provided for the election of the judges of the Court, that is, by the United Nations General Assembly and the Security Council voting simultaneously but separately on a list of names submitted by the Secretary-General.[122] One remarkable alternative, put forward by Brierly on behalf of the Government of the United Kingdom, was that "[i]n order to eliminate the risk of political appointments ... the members of the International Court of Justice might be invited to nominate the members of this Commission."[123] Brierly explained that "[i]t would, of course, be for the members of the Court to say whether or not they would accept such an invitation, but it does not seem that by doing so they would be in any way departing from the restrictions imposed upon them by the judicial character of the Court."[124] When it was put to a vote, the proposal was defeated by nine against, three in favor, and two abstentions.[125]

121 *Ibid*, at pp. 17–18 (Donnedieu de Vabres); A/AC.10/SR.24, *supra* note 119, at pp. 2–3.

122 UN Doc. A/AC.10/SR.12: 'Summary Record of the Twelfth Meeting of the Committee on the Progressive Development and Its Codification' (27 May 1947), p. 5 (endorsing by majority a United States-Chinese proposal).

123 UN Doc. A/AC.10/16: 'Methods for Encouraging the Progressive Development of International Law and Its Eventual Codification – Memorandum Submitted by the United Kingdom Representative' (12 May 1947), pp. 3–4 (adding that "[i]n many cases international instruments provided for requests to be made to the Permanent Court of International Justice to assume functions such as the appointment of umpires or arbitrators or members of conciliation commissions, and the Permanent Court complied with such requests"). Sjoboeg (Sweden) opined that "it would be simpler to have the members of the Commission appointed by the President of the International Court of Justice," and Rudzinski put forward a scheme which divided the task between the President of the Court, Governments, and the General Assembly: A/AC.10/SR.11, *supra* note 119, at p. 5.

124 A/AC.10/16, *supra* note 123, at p. 3; see also A/AC.10/SR.12, *supra* note 122, at pp. 3, 4 (adding that such a procedure would also assure the equitable representation of the various legal systems of the world; and that he did not think the International Court of Justice would refuse that task).

125 A/AC.10/SR.12, *ibid*, at p. 4. Koretsky, among those opposed, had earlier wondered "whether ... the International Court of Justice would be able to make a better choice than the governments": see UN Doc. A/AC.10/SR.4: 'Summary Record of the Fourth Meeting of the Committee on the Progressive Development and Its Codification' (15 May 1947), p. 6. Interestingly, the idea of appointment of Commission members by the Court resurfaced when the Commission itself, in its third session, reviewed its Statute with the object of recommending revision thereof to the General Assembly. Then Hudson, a former Judge of the Permanent Court of International Justice, suggested that

A suggestion that casual vacancies would be filled by the Court was also rejected.[126]

The question of the position of the future Commission vis-à-vis the Court came more to the fore when the Committee's discussion turned to the issue of possible cooperation between the Commission and other organs of the United Nations. A Sub-Committee that had contemplated this question suggested, among other things, that "[t]he ILC should be authorized to consult with any of the organs of the United Nations on any draft or project, the subject matter of which is relevant to the functions of the particular organ"; it also recommended that "[a]ll ILC documents which are circulated to Governments should be equally circulated to the organs of the United Nations for their information. Such organs should be free to supply any data or make any suggestions."[127] But the Sub-Committee recognized expressly that, "[i]n view of the special position and status of the ICJ," the Committee should carefully consider "whether the foregoing [suggestions] should apply to the Court."[128] It was explained that the Court "was a judicial and not a legislative body. There was some doubt as to whether [it] would have the right to comment on drafts of the International Law Commission in view

"[t]he Commission might look around for some other method of appointment, e.g. the list of candidates might be drawn up by the President of the International Court of Justice following consultation with the judges of the Court, and others. The choice would be governed by concern to put forward candidates likely to make a real contribution to the Commission's work. The list could be either a list of candidates to be voted on by the General Assembly, or, if the General Assembly consented, a list of appointments": YBILC 1951, Vol. I, pp. 122–123, para. 118, and p. 126, para. 6. Although the idea won some support, the Commission eventually decided to recommend the retention of the existing system of appointment. Several years later, Hersch Lauterpacht suggested, when serving as a member of the Commission, that appointment to the Commission by separate or joint action, possibly with or without association with organs of the United Nations such as the International Court of Justice, could better secure the requisite expert element in the composition of the Commission than the method stipulated in the Commission's Statute: Lauterpacht, *supra* note 42, at p. 43.

126 This option was similarly rejected by the Sixth Committee's Sub-Committee 2 that later drafted that Statute of the Commission: UN Doc. A/C.6/193, para. 8 (for reason that the task of progressive development of international law and its codification was entrusted to the General Assembly).

127 Report of the Sub-Committee of 2 June 1947, on Item 3(b) of the agenda: see UN Doc. A/AC.10/SR.17: 'Summary Record of the Seventeenth Meeting of the Committee on the Progressive Development and Its Codification' (3 June 1947), pp. 1–2.

128 *Ibid*, at p. 2.

of the fact that it might have to apply and interpret the same texts later."[129]

In the ensuing debate on the matter, Dr. Kerno, the UN Assistant Secretary-General, informed members of the Committee that the Court "received the most important of the United Nations documents, but the fact of these documents being transmitted did not mean that the Court was asked for comment."[130] He emphasized, however, that "the Court was a United Nations organ and would automatically be included in any decision taken with regard to [cooperation with other UN organs] if it were not expressly excluded."[131] It soon became clear that it was not the receipt by the Court of the Commission's documents that posed a difficulty for members of the Committee, but indeed the possible inference that the Court might or should make any comments on them. In the mind of Mr. Jessup (United States of America), it was certain that "the Committee should avoid placing the International Court of Justice in an embarrassing position by any of its suggestions," and he suggested that its report would clearly indicate that "[i]n view of the special position and status of the International Court of Justice," only the recommendation on the distribution of documents would be relevant to it in this context of cooperation with other UN bodies.[132] Mr. Koretsky (USSR), however, was of the opinion that "[i]t was a matter of course that the Court would abstain from giving any comments or opinions [on the Commission's drafts], but it was not for the Committee to order the Court to do so and it might even be considered a lack of courtesy towards the Court, which would certainly have the same opinion on this subject."[133] He recalled in this context that Judge McNair "had already abstained from signing a text drawn up at an international conference on account of his special position as Judge in the International Court."[134] This opinion was shared by the Secretary of the Committee, Dr. Liang, for whom "it was certain

[129] UN Doc. A/AC.10/SR.16: 'Summary Record of the Sixteenth Meeting of the Committee on the Progressive Development and Its Codification' (2 June 1947), pp. 1–2. The idea that the Permanent Court should "no doubt" be asked "to give its opinion, based on experience" on draft codification conventions had been raised back in 1920 in the Assembly of the League of Nations' Third Committee by Mr. Politis of Greece: League of Nations, Records of the First Assembly: Meetings of the Committees, Vol. II, p. 327.

[130] A/AC.10/SR.16, *supra* note 129, at p. 2.

[131] *Ibid.*

[132] A/AC.10/SR.17, *supra* note 127, at pp. 3, 4.

[133] *Ibid*, at p. 4.

[134] *Ibid.*

that not only would the members of the Court refrain from giving any opinions on drafts of the ILC, but also that the ILC itself would not approach the Court for this purpose."[135]

In reply, Jessup observed that "the matter came down to a difference of opinion as to what could be regarded as courtesy with respect to the Court."[136] He suggested that "[i]n view of the doubts raised by the previous speakers . . . it would be sufficient if mention was made in the report that the Committee had considered the special position of the Court and did not want either to give any foundation for the interpretation that it gave instructions to the Court, or that it had passed over consideration of its particular position."[137] When Brierly voiced his support for Koretsky's preference, however, Jessup withdrew his proposal.[138] No explicit mention of the Court was thus made eventually in the Committee's final recommendations on securing the cooperation of other organs of the United Nations in the Commission's task.[139] The Commission's Statute would remain equally silent on the issue, giving no hint of the underlying understanding of those who envisaged it.[140]

The question of the relationship between the Court and the future Commission again came up when the Committee turned to discuss "methods for encouraging the development of international law through the judicial process." While the debate was cut short after Brierly asserted that "it was not for this Committee to encourage the International Court of Justice in doing what was already its duty to perform,"[141] the Committee did eventually see fit to recommend, in connection with this

[135] *Ibid.*

[136] *Ibid*, at pp. 4–5.

[137] *Ibid.*

[138] *Ibid*, at p. 5.

[139] See UN Doc. A/331: 'Progressive Development of International Law and Its Codification – Note by the Secretary General' (18 July 1947), pp. 11–12, para. 19 (quoting the Committee's Report; original footnote omitted).

[140] Article 25 of the Statute, placed in the chapter entitled "Cooperation with Other Bodies," reads:

> 1. The Commission may consult, if it considers it necessary, with any of the organs of the United Nations on any subject which is within the competence of that organ.
> 2. All documents of the Commission which are circulated to Governments by the Secretary-General shall also be circulated to such organs of the United Nations as are concerned. Such organs may furnish any information or make any suggestions to the Commission.

[141] UN Doc. A/AC.10/SR.9: 'Summary Record of the Ninth Meeting of the Committee on the Progressive Development and Its Codification' (22 May 1947), p. 12 (recording also

item (as well as the question of the development of customary international law), that the future Commission would consider "ways and means for making the evidence of customary international law more readily available."[142] The Committee did not, however, heed the suggestion by Mr. Body (Australia) that, with reference to the question of "methods of securing the co-operation of the several organs of the United Nations in the task of the progressive development of international law and its eventual codification," it should recommend to the General Assembly to adopt a resolution calling on other organs of the United Nations to request the Court's advisory opinion whenever a legal question of special importance arose.[143]

All at once mirroring the debates of the past and prefiguring those of the future, the Committee of Seventeen also deliberated whether a distinction could in practice be drawn between the development of international law and its codification. Differing opinions were voiced over the course of several meetings, with some members emphasizing the necessity of keeping the two tasks generally distinct while others insisted they were not and could not be separated. For members such as Brierly, codification "was a scientific and not a political task," and the method of drawing up international conventions, by contrast, "was appropriate for international legislation but not for codification."[144] Yet for other members, such as Mr. Amado (Brazil), codification was by necessity to "reflect the equilibrium between the static and dynamic aspects of international law";[145] Mr. Hsu (China) similarly considered codification "to be part of the development of international law, the two [being] closely related and influenc[ing] one another."[146] But it also seemed that, at least

that the Chairman, Sir Dalip Singh (India), responded that "the Committee of course agreed on this" and proposed that it move to discuss another topic).

142 A/331, *supra* note 139, at para. 18.

143 UN Doc. A/AC.10/SR.28: 'Summary Record of the Twenty-Eighth Meeting of the Committee on the Progressive Development and Its Codification' (13 June 1947), pp. 3–4.

144 UN Doc. A/AC.10/SR.2: 'Summary Record of the Second Meeting of the Committee on the Progressive Development and Its Codification' (13 May 1947), p. 5; see also, for example, UN Doc. A/AC.10/SR.3: 'Summary Record of the Third Meeting of the Committee on the Progressive Development and Its Codification' (14 May 1947), p. 4 (Vieyra (Argentina)). For Brierly's more nuanced position, with which Jessup expressed his complete agreement, see UN Doc. A/AC.10/SR.6: Summary record of the sixth meeting of the Committee on the progressive development and its codification (20 May 1947), pp. 4–5.

145 A/AC.10/SR.2, *supra* note 144, p. 6.

146 A/AC.10/SR.3, *supra* note 144, at p. 5. See also, for example, A/AC.10/SR.4, *supra* note 125, at p. 8 (Donnedieu de Vabres agreeing that "the two parts of the dual task in the

for some, the question had more to do with concerns over the influence that the future Commission may be able to exert. Koretsky, for example, opined that "codification was not only registering what [law] exists but more," and for that reason favored only the method of elaboration of draft international conventions, explaining that "[n]o agency should be allowed to impose its will on States."[147] Mr. Sjoboeg (Sweden) similarly explained his preference for a single procedure of codification through conventions by arguing not only that the distinction between codification and progressive development (even if possible in theory) could not be maintained in practice, but also that codification by so-called scientific restatements "calls forth very serious objections," including that it was for the International Court of Justice, and not for the Commission, "to state – in the forms provided by the Charter of the United Nations – which is the content of existing international law."[148]

Eventually, a compromise was reached. The Committee elaborated two distinct sets of procedures for the Commission, one for progressive development (by multilateral treaty) and one for codification (by a restatement not embodied in treaty form), explaining, however, that the two terms were "not mutually exclusive" and that "no clear-cut distinction between the formulation of the law as it is and the law as it ought to be could be rigidly maintained in practice."[149] It was also

sphere of international law should not be disconnected"); UN Doc. A/AC.10/SR.5: 'Summary Record of the Fifth Meeting of the Committee on the Progressive Development and Its Codification' (19 May 1947), pp. 6–8 (Bartos and de Beus (Netherlands)); A/AC.10/SR.6, *supra* note 144, at p. 5 (Rocha (Colombia)).

147 See respectively A/AC.10/SR.4, *supra* note 125, at p. 5 (having pointed out earlier that "Article 13(a) of the Charter puts both terms next to one another and . . . it was not necessary to make such a marked distinction between them") and A/AC.10/SR.9, *supra* note 141, at pp. 13–14. See also UN Doc. A/AC.10/SR.13: 'Summary Record of the Thirteenth Meeting of the Committee on the Progressive Development and Its Codification (28 May 1947), pp. 14–15. For the argument that codification of international law is a term susceptible to several meanings and the suggestion that the debate was often "really a political debate couched, however, in terms acceptable to the legal discipline and the standards of parliamentary diplomacy of the time," see Rosenne, *supra* note 48, at p. cii.

148 A/AC.10/SR.24, *supra* note 119, at pp. 14–15 (adding that "[a]ll interference by the General Assembly in the field thus reserved for the competence of the Court would seriously endanger the letter's authority and consequently have extremely regrettable results").

149 A/331, *supra* note 139, at paras. 7, 10. See also A/AC.10/SR.5, *supra* note 146, at p. 9 (Dr. Liang, the Secretary of the Commission, expressing his hope "that the Committee would bear in mind that it would be unnecessary to decide upon an academic distinction between development and codification; if a distinction is to be decided upon, the

accepted, including by members such as Brierly, that even restatements produced by the Commission would not be "binding either on governments or on the International Court, and that [their] authority was merely 'persuasive', that is to say, that [their] influence on governments or courts was dependent upon its scientific merits only."[150] Any output of the Commission was to be only *ad referendum*, with the ultimate decision as to whether to affix to it any binding force (by being ratified as conventional rules or through practice coupled with acceptance as law) lying solely in the hands of States.

The Committee's final report[151] was taken up in September 1947 by the Sixth Committee of the General Assembly, which established a subcommittee "to draft a resolution and report back to the Committee."[152] After fifteen meetings, the Sub-Committee presented to the Sixth Committee a detailed report and a draft resolution to which a draft Statute of the International Law Commission was attached. In these, the Sub-Committee rejected the suggestion that members of the Commission would be elected by both the General Assembly and the Security Council, having considered that "the International Court of Justice was a special case which should not serve as a precedent for the appointment of the ILC," and because "there was no reason to associate the Security Council with the work of codifying international law which ... was entrusted [under the UN Charter] to the General Assembly."[153] The Sub-Committee proposed, instead, election (for a three-year term) by the General Assembly alone and suggested that the Commission would function on a part-time basis only (primarily for budgetary reasons).[154] It moreover decided it was inadvisable "to reopen the inconclusive discussion" on the distinction between the methods of codification and progressive development, and voted by overwhelming majority to retain both, while recognizing (like the Committee of

distinction between the task of development of international law and the task of its codification should be in terms of methods").

150 A/AC.10/16, *supra* note 123, at p. 4, para. 9 (adding that "[b]ut it may be expected that the persuasive authority of a restatement made under the procedure here outlined, though lacking imperative-force, would be considerable"); see also A/AC.10/SR.2, *supra* note 144, at p. 5.

151 UN Doc. A/AC.10/51 (17 June 1947), reissued as A/331, *supra* note 139.

152 UN Doc. A/C.6/SR.38, p. 15. The sub-committee's Rapporteur, Mr. J.P.A. Francois (The Netherlands) would soon serve as a member of the Commission.

153 UN Doc. A/C.6/193, para. 7.

154 *Ibid*, at para. 4. Members now serve five-year terms.

Seventeen before it) that "the terms employed were not mutually exclusive."[155] One stated reason for maintaining the method of scientific restatement was "the mediocre results" that codification by international conventions had achieved in the past.[156] Still, the importance of close consultation with States, as a lesson learned from past attempts at the codification of international law, was a cornerstone in the proposal put forward by the Sub-Committee. Combining the requirements of scientific expertise with the realities of political life was deemed essential: law-making was not to be entrusted only to lawyers.

On November 20, 1947 the Sixth Committee approved the proposed Statute,[157] and the next day the General Assembly adopted it by resolution 174(II), thereby establishing the International Law Commission as a subsidiary organ with a general mandate to consider any topic of international law. The first elections to the Commission took place in the following year, and on April 12, 1949, the Commission opened the first of its annual sessions under the chairmanship of Hudson, the former American judge of the PCIJ. A 'Survey of International Law in Relation to the Work of Codification of the International Law Commission',[158] prepared by the UN Secretariat with the assistance of Professor Hersch Lauterpacht (later a member of the Commission and then judge of the Court), served as a basis for the initial program of work. As was perhaps to be expected, it did not take long before the question of the distinction between the methods of codification and progressive development was

[155] *Ibid*, at para. 15. In his opening remarks during the Commission's first session, Mr. Kerno, the UN Assistant Secretary-General in charge of Legal Affairs, stated that the Statute "offered compromise between the codification of international law through official conventions, as had been tried under the auspices of the League of Nations, and codification through the unofficial scientific restatement of positive law": YBILC 1949, p. 9, para. 3.

[156] A/C.6/193, para. 15 (put forward, *inter alia*, by the representatives of the United States and the United Kingdom).

[157] See UN Doc. A/504.

[158] UN Doc. A/CN.4/1 (5 November 1948), reissued as Rev.1 in February 1949 (noting, at para. 12, that "What is required – for the sake of the authority of international law, the alleviation of the task of international tribunals, and the removal of one of the traditional causes of the unwillingness of States to submit disputes to the compulsory jurisdiction of international tribunals – is the introduction of certainty, precision and uniformity in matters of detail. That task is in fact comprised within the terms of reference of the International Law Commission"). The Survey has been supplemented by later reviews of the general scope of the Commission's future program of work.

raised within the Commission.[159] Yet no decision was taken as to more precise definitions of the terms, and the understanding was that "the approach to [the Commission's] work [was to remain] open and flexible."[160] At that first session, the Commission also interpreted its own Statute to decide that it was not obliged to seek the General Assembly's permission in selecting topics for codification.[161] No member challenged the conception put forward in the course of the plenary debate on this matter by Mr. Scelle (France), who asserted that "[i]t was clear from the preparatory work which had preceded the establishment of the Commission that the latter was a body with complete freedom, the equal of the International Court of Justice. In matters of codification it had the same free authority that the Court had with regard to disputes."[162]

E. Conclusion

A common thread unites the events and achievements of the long-standing movements for judicial settlement of international disputes and for codification (and development) of international law: the idea that a world court and a world code would ideally go hand in hand, one being necessary for the optimal advance of the other. The existence of an international court has indeed made increasingly apparent the need for a clear and more authoritative statement of international law (while operating, to a limited extent, to satisfy it).[163] Codification, for its part, intensified the demand for international adjudication, so that uniform

[159] See YBILC 1949, pp. 14–22. In opening the general debate on the organization of the Commission's work, the Chairman commented, with regard to the distinction made by the Commission's Statute between the progressive development and codification of international law (and the procedures to be followed for each), that "[e]xamination of those articles led to the conclusion that, by drafting rules of so elastic a nature, the authors of the Statute had wished to grant the Commission a great deal of freedom in choosing the method for studying a definite question" (*ibid*, at p. 14, para. 4).

[160] C. Eagleton, 'First Session of the International Law Commission', 43 AJIL (1949) 758 at 760.

[161] YBILC 1949, pp. 14–32; for the vote (10 in favor, 3 against), see p. 32, para. 15.

[162] *Ibid*, at p. 19, para. 45.

[163] See also H.W.A. Thirlway, *International Customary Law and Codification* (A.W. Sijthoff 1972) 34; and the Annual Report of the United Nations Secretary-General on the Work of the Organization (1 July 1954–15 June 1955), U.N. General Assembly Official Records: 10th Sess., Supp. No. 1 (A/2911), p. xiii (observing that "the reluctance of Governments to submit their controversies to judicial settlement stems in part from the fragmentary and uncertain character of much of international law as it now exists").

interpretation and application of the law might be achieved.[164] This general notion was carried over in 1945 to the United Nations system, in which the International Court of Justice and the International Law Commission were to proceed from where their predecessors had left off and perform their respective tasks in the service of their sovereign masters.

As the historical records further illustrate, an interaction between the Court and the Commission was indeed anticipated from the outset. The texts that would emanate from the Commission were presumed to be of much interest to (and likely to come before) the Court, while the decisions of the Court were to be studied carefully by the Commission in formulating and proposing the rules of international law. It was moreover understood that, to a certain extent, the two organs shared the task of codification and progressive development of the law: within their distinct institutional constraints, each of them was to say what the law is and contribute to its evolution. But it was also thought that, in view of their separate yet complementary mandates, some distance between the Court and the Commission was appropriate, and that their partner in making international law more definite would be States; by careful original design, it was undoubtedly the latter that were to have the last word. Thus the Court's decisions could develop the law only if supported by general State practice, and were anyhow to bind only those States that had willingly put themselves under the authority of the Court in a particular case. The Commission's output, be it restatements of the law or draft multilateral conventions, was likewise to have no binding force without the seal of approval of States (through their practice or otherwise). The diffused process of law-making on the international plane, in which it was not always clear where codification ended and progressive development began, was to combine the requirements of scientific expertise with the harsh realities of political life, by no means being left to the lawyers alone.

It is this rich context in which the relationship between the Court and the Commission, as it has evolved, must be placed and examined. Having learned how the two organs were configured and mandated for interaction, we may now explore just how that original vision played out in practice.

[164] See also M.O. Hudson, *International Tribunals: Past and Future* (Carnegie Endowment for International Peace and Brookings Institution 1944) 109–110 (referring to treaty-making in particular).

3

"An Invaluable Guide": The Commission's Contribution to the Court's Work

As was anticipated by those who drafted the Commission's Statute, the texts emanating from the Commission did prove to be of interest to the Court and did in time come before it for interpretation and application. Judge Koretsky could thus say by 1968 that the Court, "for its part, did not merely study the Commission's work. Norms drafted by the Commission had crossed and continued to cross the threshold of the Peace Palace, where the Court sat, and were increasingly interpreted and applied by the Court in its examination of the cases referred to it."[1]

The progress achieved by the Commission in codifying and progressively developing international law was not only highly relevant to the Court's work: it was also of great benefit to it. In addition to generating a need for uniform interpretation and application of the law, and in this way encouraging more applications to the Court,[2] the Commission's work has been relied on by the Court in determining the applicable law in a notable number of cases whose subject matter coincided with an issue already considered by the Commission. President Abraham had no hesitation, therefore, in telling Commission members in 2016 that the Court "always examined the Commission's work with the greatest interest and it never decided a point of law without giving due consideration

[1] YBILC 1968, Vol. I, p. 161, para. 3. The Court's awareness of the work accomplished by the Commission was perhaps all the more notable in those early days, as judges were then not assisted by law clerks and were required to do their own legal research. Judges of the Court are nowadays unlikely to miss any output of the Commission that may be relevant to a case, in particular as the parties to the case may refer to it; the Court's Registry, which prepares a formal bibliography on matters pending before the Court, may bring it to the judges' attention; and members of the Court who are former members the Commission may share their personal knowledge of such work.

[2] General Assembly resolution 3232(XXIX) of November 12, 1974, titled 'Review of the Role of the International Court of Justice', recalled "the increasing development and codification of international law in Conventions open for universal participation and the consequent need for their uniform interpretation and application" (preambular para. 7). See also Chapter 4, Section B.3.

to the Commission's opinion on the matter."[3] His successor, President Yusuf, remarked in the same spirit that to him, "[a]s a judge of the International Court, but also first and foremost as an international lawyer, the work of the ILC has played, and continues to play, a crucial role in my daily work."[4]

For a judicial institution that relies mostly on its own authority (and that of its predecessor) in order to sustain its findings in law,[5] the Court's recourse to the Commission's work has indeed been remarkable. Even if the Court has on occasion referred to other sources for such purposes, it "uniquely privileges some of the drafts, reports, and other work product of the Commission through citations in its decisions."[6] Inquiry into the ways in which the Court has made use of the Commission's output – and even works-in-progress – reveals the significant extent of its reliance on the latter's work, including the fact that there is more beneath the surface. It also raises the question of the basis for such reliance.

The present chapter proceeds by considering, in Part A, the occasions on which the Court has made express reference to the work product of the Commission. These occasions may be divided into three categories.

[3] YBILC 2016, Vol. I, p. 232, p .19. President Owada had earlier stated in Geneva that "the Commission's work was extremely useful to the Court in its judicial activities": YBILC 2009, Vol. I, p. 125, para. 47.

[4] Address of President Yusuf before the International Law Commission on the Occasion of Its Seventieth Anniversary (5 July 2018), available at <http://legal.un.org/docs/?path=../ilc/sessions/70/pdfs/english/key_note_address_5july2018.pdf&lang=E>.

[5] See also W. Alschner and D. Charlotin, 'The Growing Complexity of the International Court of Justice's Self-Citation Network', 29 EJIL (2018) 83–112.

[6] D.J. Bederman, 'Counterintuiting Countermeasures', 96 AJIL (2002) 817 at 819. See also, for example, M. Peil, 'Scholarly Writings as a Source of Law: A Survey of the Use of Doctrine by the International Court of Justice', 1 CJICL (2012) 136 at 152 (concluding, on the basis of empirical research, that "[t]he International Law Commission is far and away the most common source relied upon by the judges … This is as large as the next four sources combined"); F. Berman, 'Authority in International Law', KFG Working Paper Series, No. 22, Berlin Potsdam Research Group (2018) 16 (referring to the "favoured treatment" of ILC work in the Court's jurisprudence); C.J. Tams, 'The ICJ as a "Law-Formative Agency": Summary and Synthesis', in C.J. Tams and J. Sloan (eds.), *The Development of International Law by the International Court of Justice* (OUP 2013) 377 at 386 ("In a surprisingly large number of areas, ICJ decisions have drawn on, and confirmed, views of the ILC"); A. Watts, *The International Law Commission 1949–1998*, Vol. I (OUP 1999) 12–13; S.M. Schwebel, 'The Influence of the International Court of Justice on the Work of the International Law Commission and the Influence of the Commission on the Court', in *Making Better International Law: The International Law Commission at 50* (United Nations 1998) 161 at 163 (referring to the "unusual degree of endorsement given by the Court itself to the Commission's statements").

First (in Part A(1)), the focus is on reference by the Court to the Commission's work as a supplementary means for treaty interpretation; second (in Part A(2)), the analysis turns to reference to the Commission's work in the context of the Court's pronouncements on customary international law; and, third (in Part A(3)), the focus of analysis turns to reference to the Commission's work as part of the Court's own reasoning. In Part B, the argument is made that there is much more than meets the eye, given indirect reliance by the Court on the work product of the Commission (Part B(1)) as well as implicit reliance (Part B(2)). Part C looks to instances of reference to the work product of the Commission in individual opinions of the judges of the Court, and Part D considers the justification for the Court's reliance on the output of the Commission. A conclusion draws the present chapter to a close in Part E.

A. Explicit References

If the judicial decision is "the pulse of legal life, and it is here that the analysis of the legal forces comes into play,"[7] then the Commission's work has very much been injected into the bloodstream of international law through repeated references to it in the Court's decisions. In over thirty cases, which address a wide range of legal issues, the Court has invoked not only draft articles adopted by the Commission, but also the commentaries thereto as well as reports and summary records of the Commission (and even a report of a Special Rapporteur). While in some cases the Court has mentioned only the position adopted by the Commission, in others, references were more extensive, even running to a detailed account of the Commission's debates and quotations from relevant passages.

Nor is it the case, as Judge Schwebel observed some twenty years ago, that the Court has always referred to the Commission for the same reasons.[8] The Commission's work has in his account been resorted to by the Court for three different purposes: first, to interpret conventions that are based on draft articles elaborated by the Commission; second, to support the Court's determinations as to the existence or otherwise of rules of customary international law; and, finally, to supplement and

[7] A. Ross, *A Textbook of International Law* (Longmans, Green & Co. 1947) 80.

[8] S.M. Schwebel, 'The Inter-active Influence of the International Court of Justice and the International Law Commission', in C.A. Armas Barea et al (eds.), *Liber Amicorum 'In Memoriam' of Judge José María Ruda* (Kluwer Law International 2000) 479 at 484.

reinforce the Court's legal reasoning more broadly.[9] The present section will apply this typology (despite the risk that its categories may overlap as, for example, when the Court resorts to preparatory work in examining whether a certain treaty provision reflects customary international law) in offering a comprehensive account of all those instances to date where the Court has referred to the Commission's work.

1. *Reference to the Commission's Work as a Supplementary Means for Treaty Interpretation*

Perhaps the most natural occasion for the Court to refer to the Commission's work has been in those cases where the Court was called upon to interpret a treaty that was concluded on the basis of draft articles prepared by the Commission. In such instances, the Commission's output has mostly been resorted to as preparatory work (*travaux préparatoires*) offering an authoritative explanation of what the treaty provision in question was originally intended to mean. This was the case in *Continental Shelf (Tunisia/Libyan Arab Jamahiriya)* (1982), in which the Court referred to "the records of the International Law Commission and other *travaux préparatoires* of the 1958 Geneva Convention on the Continental Shelf" in its interpretation of the term "continental shelf."[10] By the same token, the Commission's commentaries on its draft articles on the law of treaties were quoted in the judgment on preliminary objections in the case concerning *Land and Maritime Boundary between Cameroon and Nigeria* (1998) when the Court sought to explain the scope of certain provisions of the 1969 Vienna Convention on the Law of Treaties.[11] These commentaries were again referred to by the Court in its judgment on the merits of that case (2002), when clarifying the scope of article 7(2) of the same Convention;[12] in the *Kasikili/Sedudu Island* judgment (1999), when the Court sought to clarify the concepts of

[9] *Ibid*, at 484–485.

[10] *Continental Shelf (Tunisia/Libyan Arab Jamahiriya), Judgment, I.C.J. Reports 1982*, p. 45, para. 41.

[11] *Land and Maritime Boundary between Cameroon and Nigeria, Preliminary Objections, Judgment, I.C.J. Reports 1998*, pp. 293–294, para. 31 (referring to article 78 of the Convention together with articles 16 and 24). The Commission's own position in 1966 relied on the Court's holding in the *Right of Passage* case: YBILC 1966, Vol. II, p. 201, para. 3.

[12] *Land and Maritime Boundary between Cameroon and Nigeria (Cameroon* v. *Nigeria: Equatorial Guinea intervening), Judgment, I.C.J. Reports 2002*, p. 430, para. 265.

"subsequent agreement" and "subsequent practice" as employed in article 31(3) of the Convention (which it found to reflect customary international law);[13] and in the *Pulp Mills* judgment (2010), when the Court determined the scope of article 57 of the Convention.[14]

Other output of the Commission was similarly referred to as a supplementary means for treaty interpretation. Thus, in the *Avena* case (2004), the Commission's discussion of the text that later became article 36 of the Vienna Convention on Consular Relations was referred to by the Court in interpreting the words "without delay" as used in subparagraph (b)(1).[15] That same discussion was again referred to in the *Jadhav* case (2019) to establish that article 36 applied also to persons suspected of espionage; the original text of article 36, as prepared by the Commission, was also used in interpreting the meaning of the words "if he so requests."[16] In the same vein, the Court had recourse to the Commission's deliberations from the early 1950s in its judgment concerning the *Territorial and Maritime Dispute between Nicaragua and Honduras in the Caribbean Sea* (2007), when interpreting article 15 of the United Nations Convention on the Law of the Sea (UNCLOS) (which it found to be "virtually identical" to article 12 of the 1958 Convention on the Territorial Sea and the Contiguous Zone, drawn up on the basis of the Commission's draft articles on the topic).[17] The Court again relied on the Commission's deliberations in the case concerning the *Maritime Delimitation in the Black Sea* (2009) when interpreting article 12 of UNCLOS (some elements of which had been discussed by the Commission in connection with what later became article 8 of the 1958 Convention on the Territorial Sea and the Contiguous Zone).[18] In *Jurisdictional Immunities of the State* (2012), the Court referred to the Commission's commentary on the text of what became article 12 of the United Nations Convention on Jurisdictional Immunities of States and

[13] *Kasikili/Sedudu Island (Botswana/Namibia), Judgment, I.C.J. Reports 1999*, pp. 1075–1076, paras. 48–49.

[14] *Pulp Mills on the River Uruguay (Argentina* v. *Uruguay), Judgment, I.C.J. Reports 2010*, p. 66, para. 141.

[15] *Avena and Other Mexican Nationals (Mexico* v. *United States of America), Judgment, I.C.J. Reports 2004*, pp. 48–49, para. 86.

[16] *Jadhav (India* v. *Pakistan), Judgment, I.C.J. Reports 2019*, pp. 439–441, paras. 77–83 and p. 447, para. 108.

[17] *Territorial and Maritime Dispute between Nicaragua and Honduras in the Caribbean Sea (Nicaragua* v. *Honduras), Judgment, I.C.J. Reports 2007*, p. 744, para. 280.

[18] *Maritime Delimitation in the Black Sea (Romania* v. *Ukraine), Judgment, I.C.J. Reports 2009*, pp. 106–107, para. 134.

Their Property, when holding that the provision was not intended to be restricted to *acta jure gestionis* and did not apply to situations involving armed conflict.[19] Some ten years later, in *Alleged Violations of Sovereign Rights and Maritime Spaces in the Caribbean Sea* (2022), the commentary to the Commission's articles concerning the law of the sea was pointed to by the Court yet again in determining the scope of articles 33 and 303 of UNCLOS.[20]

While recourse to the Commission's work as *travaux préparatoires* in such circumstances hardly seems objectionable, it is nonetheless remarkable that, when interpreting a convention based on draft articles proposed by the Commission, the Court has tended to rely far more on the Commission's deliberations than on the records of the diplomatic conferences or other meetings convened by States to negotiate and conclude the convention in question. This has not been lost on the Commission.[21]

It also bears mention that it is in fact the Commission itself that has bolstered such use of its work by suggesting, when laying the foundation to article 32 of the Vienna Convention on the Law of Treaties, that recourse may be had to the preparatory work of a treaty as a

[19] *Jurisdictional Immunities of the State (Germany* v. *Italy: Greece intervening), Judgment, I.C.J. Reports 2012*, p. 127, para. 57 and pp. 129–130, para. 69; see also p. 127, para. 64. For the subtle criticism that the Court "has not hinted at the possible discrepancy between an article and its commentary and at the resulting problem of interpretation," see G. Gaja, 'Interpreting Articles Adopted by the International Law Commission', 85 BYIL (2015) 10 at 17.

[20] *Alleged Violations of Sovereign Rights and Maritime Spaces in the Caribbean Sea (Nicaragua* v. *Colombia), Judgment, I.C.J. Reports 2022*, pp. 327-328, paras. 151–152 and pp. 337-338, para. 184.

[21] See YBILC 1977, Vol. II, Part Two, p. 132, para. 125 (the Commission explaining to the General Assembly that its commentaries "are an essential element of the codification process, facilitating . . . the understanding and interpretation of the rules embodied in the codification conventions. They are an important part of the *travaux préparatoires* of those conventions, being frequently referred to or quoted in the diplomatic correspondence of States as well as by the International Court of Justice"); YBILC 1986, Vol. II, Part Two, p. 65, para. 253 (the Commission explaining to the General Assembly the "fundamental importance" of continuing the system of summary records by noting that these "also have their utility for international adjudications and settlements. The ICJ has, in fact, referred to them on a number of occasions in applying and interpreting international conventions concluded on the basis of draft articles prepared by the Commission"); YBILC 1989, Vol. I, p. 2, para. 7 (the Commission's outgoing Chairman, Díaz González, saying, in response to criticism emanating from the Sixth Committee that the Commission's reports were too voluminous, that "[i]t should not be forgotten in that connection that the Commission's report was also a working tool much appreciated by specialists in international law and that it had at times even been cited in judgments of the ICJ").

supplementary means of its interpretation.[22] Even if the Commission did not necessarily have its own work in mind when making that suggestion, it was certainly well served by deciding back then that "[nothing] would be gained by trying to define *travaux préparatoires*."[23]

2. *Reference to the Commission's Work in the Context of Pronouncements on Customary International Law*

Reference by the Court to the Commission's work has also been made in those cases where the other primary source of international law, custom, was at issue. It is here that the Court, which "relies on customary international law constantly and as a matter of course,"[24] has probably found the Commission's output the most useful, and where the latter's influence on the Court's determinations has been the most visible.

One way in which the Court has relied on the Commission's work when it has been called upon to determine and apply customary international law is by referring to it as evidence supporting the Court's own analysis as to the state of such law. This was the way in which the Commission's work made its debut in the jurisprudence of the Court, when the latter observed, in the *North Sea Continental Shelf* cases

[22] Article 32 (on 'Supplementary means of interpretation') reads:

> Recourse may be had to supplementary means of interpretation, including the preparatory work of the treaty and the circumstances of its conclusion, in order to confirm the meaning resulting from the application of article 31, or to determine the meaning when the interpretation according to article 31: (a) leaves the meaning ambiguous or obscure; or (b) leads to a result which is manifestly absurd or unreasonable.

It may be recalled that "[t]he first two of the Commission's Special Rapporteurs on the law of treaties in their private writings ... expressed doubts as to the existence in international law of any technical rules for the interpretation of treaties": YBILC 1964, Vol. II, p. 199, para. (1) to the commentary to draft articles 69–71.

[23] YBILC 1966, Vol. II, p. 223, para. (20) to the commentary to draft articles 27–28 (adding that "to do so might only lead to the possible exclusion of relevant evidence"). That the Commission probably did not fully have in mind that its own work would fall within the term *travaux préparatoires* may perhaps be gleaned from the fact that it debated whether, with regard to multilateral treaties, the article should authorize the use of *travaux préparatoires* only as between States which took part in the negotiations (*ibid*). By 2018, the Commission "reiterated its firm view that the summary records of the Commission, constitute[ed] crucial *travaux préparatoires* in the progressive development and codification of international law": YBILC 2018, Vol. II, Part Two, p. 207, para. 384.

[24] H. Lauterpacht, *The Development of International Law by the International Court* (Stevens & Sons 1958, reprinted by Grotius Publications 1982) 392–393.

(1969),[25] that the question whether the equidistance principle laid down in article 6 of the 1958 Convention on the Continental Shelf originally figured therein as a customary rule "depend[ed] mainly on the processes that led the Commission to propose it."[26] Having recognized that the work of the Commission, being based to a large extent on State practice and input, may well embody or indeed crystallize a rule of customary international law,[27] the Court drew primarily on the Commission's extensive debates in deciding that the rule in question was not to be regarded as declaratory of a preexisting or emergent rule of customary international law.[28] Such recourse to the Commission, here and elsewhere in this judgment (as described below), expressed a clear vote of confidence by the Court in the working procedures of the Commission and in the quality of its output.[29] Judge Waldock later recalled that "it was in the *North Sea Continental Shelf* Cases . . . that the Commission's work had for the first time been a central feature of the proceedings [before the Court] and had helped to guide the Court to its conclusions."[30]

Reference to the Commission's work in support of the Court's assessment as to the state of customary international law was also made in

[25] The Court had mentioned the Commission once before, in its advisory opinion on *Reservations to the Convention on Genocide*, but only to note that the General Assembly had invited the Commission to study the general question of reservations to multilateral conventions both from the point of view of codification and from that of the progressive development of international law: *Reservations to the Convention on Genocide, Advisory Opinion: I.C.J. Reports 1951*, p. 20.

[26] *North Sea Continental Shelf, Judgment, I.C.J. Reports 1969*, p. 38, para. 62. The Court's President at that time, Judge Bustamante y Rivero, had said just a few months earlier that the Commission's codifications, in which it stated legal principles formulated and refined by it on the basis of careful sifting of theory of the law, the doctrine of writers, and court decisions, "later served – until multilateral treaties were concluded by States – as a guide to judges adjudicating in specific cases": YBILC 1969, Vol. I, p. 70, para. 5.

[27] See also the Court's description of Denmark and the Netherland's general argument in this regard, which was not rejected: *North Sea Continental Shelf, Judgment, I.C.J. Reports 1969*, p. 28, para. 37.

[28] *Ibid*, at p. 39, para. 64 (the Court "having regard also to the attitude of the International Law Commission to this provision").

[29] See also *ibid*, at p. 51, para. 95 (the Court recognizing "the care which, at the beginning of its investigation, the International Law Commission took to acquire exact information" as to the characteristics of the continental shelf, and referring to the Commission's 1956 Yearbook); and p. 222 (Judge Lachs writing in his Dissenting Opinion that "[i]t is all to the credit of the International Law Commission that it discussed the issues involved in Article 6 at such length before adopting its final text").

[30] YBILC 1974, Vol. I, p. 70, para. 29.

Military and Paramilitary Activities in and against Nicaragua (1986), where the Court relied on the Commission's commentary to article 50 of its draft articles on the law of treaties as "a further confirmation" of the customary status of the principle of the prohibition of the use of force expressed in article 2(4) of the UN Charter.[31] In *Jurisdictional Immunities of the State* (2012), the Court's inquiry into the existence of a customary rule conferring immunity on States in foreign courts began with the pronouncement that in 1980 the Commission concluded, "upon an extensive survey of State practice," that the rule did exist; the Court then observed that the conclusion was confirmed by the record of a wide array of practice.[32] Moreover, the Commission's decision not to include a provision limiting State immunity in cases of violations of peremptory norms in its draft articles on jurisdictional immunities of States and their property was relied on by the Court in that case as one indication that no such rule of customary international law had existed at that time;[33] and the Court also made it explicit that statements made by States in connection with the Commission's work may well give rise to or evince the existence of customary international law.[34] In the case concerning the *Maritime Dispute* between Peru and Chile (2014), the Court again referred to the Commission's work on the law of the sea from the 1950s (in addition to the practice of States) as the basis for its conclusion that "the evidence at its disposal does not allow it to conclude that the agreed maritime boundary along the parallel extended beyond 80 nautical

[31] *Military and Paramilitary Activities in and against Nicaragua (Nicaragua* v. *United States of America), Merits, Judgment, I.C.J. Reports 1986*, p. 100, para. 190. In his Separate Opinion appended to the advisory opinion in the *Chagos* case, Judge Robinson suggested that here "the Court apparently [also] cit[ed] with approval the observation of the International Law Commission that the prohibition of the use of force is a norm of *jus cogens*": *Legal Consequences of the Separation of the Chagos Archipelago from Mauritius in 1965, Advisory Opinion, I.C.J. Reports 2019*, p. 312, para. 59.

[32] *Jurisdictional Immunities of the State (Germany* v. *Italy: Greece intervening), Judgment, I.C.J. Reports 2012*, p. 123, para. 56 (having noted, in the previous paragraph, "the extensive study of the subject" by the Commission). President Tomka later said to the Commission that "[t]he Court had relied on conclusions drawn by the Commission more than 30 years previously in order to point to the prevalence of the relevant rule of customary international law": YBILC 2012, Vol. I, p. 144, para. 78.

[33] *Jurisdictional Immunities of the State (Germany* v. *Italy: Greece intervening), Judgment, I.C.J. Reports 2012*, pp. 138–139, para. 89 (referring to a report by a Working Group of the Commission).

[34] *Ibid*, at p. 123, para. 55 and p. 135, para. 77.

miles from its starting-point."[35] The Court's observation, in *Dispute over the Status and Use of the Waters of the Silala* (2022), that the Commission "did not appear to consider that Article 11 of . . . [its] Draft Articles [on the law of the non-navigational uses of international watercourses] reflected an obligation under customary international law" was likewise made in support of the conclusion that article 11 of the 1997 Convention on the Law of the Non-Navigational Uses of International Watercourses did not reflect customary international law.[36] The Court further stated that the formulations used in article 12 of the Convention and the ILC commentary regarding the threshold for the application of the customary obligation to notify and consult, and the duty to conduct a prior environmental impact assessment, had essentially the same meaning as the formulation used in the Court's subsequent case-law.[37]

But the Court has also cited the Commission's pronouncements – at times independently from any convention or resolution and often with little or no further comment – as precise restatements of customary international law, such references being "as brief and categorical as its own autonomous determinations of the rules of law."[38] In these cases the Court has indeed avoided detailing (if not conducting altogether) an inquiry of its own as to the existence of a certain general practice accepted as law, conveniently treating statements adopted by the Commission as authoritative articulations of the international law in

[35] *Maritime Dispute (Peru* v. *Chile), Judgment, I.C.J. Reports 2014*, p. 47, para. 117 (having earlier defined, at para. 112, the relevant "context" for examining the rules of general international law at issue to be one "provided by the State practice and related studies in, and proposals coming from, the International Law Commission and reactions by States or groups of States to those proposals concerning the establishment of maritime zones beyond the territorial sea and the delimitation of those zones").

[36] *Dispute over the Status and Use of the Waters of the Silala (Chile* v. *Bolivia), Judgment, I.C.J. Reports 2022*, pp. 650–651, para. 111).

[37] *Ibid*, at p. 652, paras. 115–117.

[38] S. Villalpando, 'On the International Court of Justice and the Determination of Rules of Law', 26 LJIL (2013) 243 at 247 (adding that this "apparently indicates an increasing trust placed by the Court on the Commission"). See also P. Tomka, 'Customary International Law in the Jurisprudence of the World Court: The Increasing Relevance of Codification', in L. Lijnzaad and Council of Europe (eds.), *The Judge and International Custom* (Brill Nijhoff 2016) 1 at 5 (explaining that in some cases the Court has indeed found it "sufficient to look to the considered views expressed by States and bodies like the International Law Commission (ILC) as to whether a rule of customary law exists and what its content is"); G. Hernández, *The International Court of Justice and the Judicial Function* (OUP 2014) 159.

force. This "favorite shortcut" of the Court, as it has been termed,[39] was first taken in the *North Sea Continental Shelf* cases, when the Court indicated, almost by a side-wind, that articles 1–3 of the 1958 Convention on the Continental Shelf, which were based on the Commission's draft articles on the law of the sea, reflected or crystallized "received or at least emergent rules of customary international law relative to the continental shelf."[40] In its advisory opinion on the *Interpretation of the Agreement of 25 March 1951 between the WHO and Egypt* (1980), the Court similarly invoked the Commission's draft articles on treaties between States and international organizations or between international organizations – then not yet put to the Commission's second and final reading – in suggesting that draft article 56 (on the denunciation of or withdrawal from a treaty containing no provision on the matter) specified some of the applicable legal principles and rules.[41]

It is the 1997 judgment in the *Gabčíkovo-Nagymaros Project* case, however, which was "[t]he watershed precedent" in the Court's reliance on the Commission's work to support its findings in law.[42] Here the

[39] S. Talmon, 'Determining Customary International Law: The ICJ's Methodology between Induction, Deduction and Assertion', 26 EJIL (2015) 417 at 437 (suggesting that this "simply may be an example of the Court outsourcing the inductive process to the Commission" and adding that "[i]n none of the cases where the Court has found a (draft) article of the ILC to reflect customary international law did it enquire whether the Commission was actually codifying international law or whether it was not perhaps progressively developing international law. In all cases, the ILC has served as a kind of pseudo-witness for a rule having acquired the status of customary international law").

[40] *North Sea Continental Shelf, Judgment, I.C.J. Reports 1969*, p. 39, para. 63.

[41] *Interpretation of the Agreement of 25 March 1951 between the WHO and Egypt, Advisory Opinion, I.C.J. Reports 1980*, pp. 94–95, para. 47 and p. 96, para. 49 (referring to draft article 56 as the corresponding provision to article 56 of the Vienna Convention on the Law of Treaties, itself a convention adopted on the basis of draft articles produced by the Commission). See also YBILC 1981, Vol. I, p. 208, para. 5 (Judge El-Erian telling members of the Commission that "[t]he Commission's work was indeed useful to the Court even before it became an international convention. Article 56 of the Commission's draft articles on treaties concluded between States and international organizations or between international organizations had been relied upon by the Court as illustrative of customary law and a guiding indication of a residual rule"). The Commission was aware of this use of its work: see YBILC 1982, Vol. II, Part Two, p. 57, commentary to draft article 56.

[42] Villalpando, *supra* note 38, at p. 245. See also S.M. Schwebel, 'Speech by Judge Stephen M. Schwebel on the Report of the International Court of Justice', 92 AJIL (1998) 612 at 613 (referring to the judgment as "notable ... because of the breadth and depth of the importance given in it to the work product of the International Law Commission ... it illustrates the fact that, just as the judgments and opinions of the Court have influenced

Court did not just quote from the Commission's commentary to its draft articles on succession of States in respect of treaties in order to assert that article 12 of the 1978 Vienna Convention bearing that same name (and providing that "treaties of a territorial character" are unaffected by a succession of States) was expressive of customary international law;[43] it also referred to several of the Commission's draft articles on State responsibility – then only provisionally adopted by the Commission on first reading – as authoritative restatements of customary international law. Draft article 17, on "Irrelevance of the origin of the international obligation breached," was invoked (alongside the Court's previous case-law) in support of the Court's view that it was "well established that, when a State has committed an internationally wrongful act, its international responsibility is likely to be involved whatever the nature of the obligation it has failed to respect."[44] The conditions set forth in draft article 33, which dealt with the state of necessity as a ground for precluding wrongfulness of State action, and was at that time still very much debated within the Commission, were likewise held to "reflect customary international law."[45] Choosing not to limit itself to stating that it was the parties who were in agreement that the draft article on necessity represented international law, the Court thus affixed to the article its own seal of approval by accepting it without further analysis as an authoritative statement of positive international law.[46] Draft articles 47–50 were

the work of the International Law Commission, so the work of the Commission may influence that of the Court"); I. Sinclair, 'The International Lawyer and the Codification of International Law', in C. Wickremasinghe (ed.), *The International Lawyer as Practitioner* (BIICL 2000) 41 at 49 (referring to "a significant departure by the Court from its hitherto cautious treatment of the extent to which it can properly invoke, as a firm statement of the law, draft articles drawn up by the Commission on a particular topic when those draft articles, even though adopted by the Commission on first reading, have not yet been subjected either to a second reading in the light of comments by Governments or to the critical scrutiny which they should receive at a codification conference").

[43] *Gabčíkovo-Nagymaros Project (Hungary/Slovakia), Judgment, I.C.J. Reports 1997*, p. 72, para. 123.

[44] *Ibid*, at p. 38, para. 47.

[45] *Ibid*, at pp. 40–41, paras. 51–52. The Court's analysis of Hungary's conduct followed the expressions adopted by the Commission in its draft article and the meaning ascribed to them by it in the commentary: *ibid*, at p. 41, para. 53 and p. 46, para. 58.

[46] President Shi later told the members of the Commission that the Court "in its turn, reinforced the value of the draft articles by declaring some of the principles contained therein as being of a customary nature; and it had done so some four years before the adoption of the draft on second reading or before the General Assembly took note of the draft articles": YBILC 2003, Vol. I, p. 164, para. 7.

similarly mentioned (together with the Court's case-law and an arbitral award) in support of the Court's assertion that countermeasures must meet certain conditions in order to be justifiable under international law.[47]

These references, once again to an incomplete and provisional text still under consideration by the Commission, were a far cry from the expectation of the members of the Committee of Seventeen in 1947, that the Court would most certainly abstain from expressing any opinion on the Commission's working drafts.[48] The Court's endorsement of draft article 33, which some members of the Commission had considered to be too permissive and looked forward to reconsidering at the second reading stage, indeed limited, if not foreclosed, any possibility of the Commission making such changes.[49]

The judgment in the *Gabčíkovo-Nagymaros Project* case was the first in a long line of decisions in which the Court has pronounced on, agreed with, and found useful the Commission's draft articles on State responsibility (whether in provisional or final form), relying on their substance as

[47] *Gabčíkovo-Nagymaros Project (Hungary/Slovakia), Judgment, I.C.J. Reports 1997*, p. 55, para. 83.

[48] See Chapter 2, Section D.2. President Schwebel later suggested that "[d]raft articles were, of course, only drafts and therefore could not be accorded the same weight [as that of conventions elaborated by the Commission], but in cases where the parties to a dispute agreed that certain draft articles were an authoritative statement of the law on a particular point, the Court naturally gave relevant weight to them": YBILC 1998, Vol. I, p. 145, para. 73. President Abraham has similarly said that "the Court was generally reluctant to refer to articles that were only provisional, but it still took such work into account in determining applicable law": UN Doc. A/C.6/70/SR.21: 'Summary Record of the General Assembly's Sixth Committee Meeting of 6 November 2015', p. 6, para. 25.

[49] Simma later recognized that "[t]he Commission would create a problem for itself, were it to decide to eliminate provisions on which some international judgement or arbitral award had already been based": YBILC 1998, Vol. I, pp. 91–92, para. 38; see also p. 95, para. 69 and p. 228, para. 1 (Crawford). For the explicit explanation that article 33 no doubt "survived the debate [in the Commission's Drafting Committee] materially unscathed . . . because ICJ had approved it almost word for word in its judgment in the *Gabčíkovo-Nagymaros Project* case," see YBILC 1999, Vol. I, p. 180, para. 45 (Crawford); see also p. 72, para. 50 (Gaja sounding "a note of caution about altering some provisions that had become an authoritative restatement of the law") and pp. 140–141, paras. 26, 29 (Crawford). The Commission had already in 1994 decided to delay the adoption of a certain draft article on the topic 'State responsibility' after the Special Rapporteur, who had found the provision unsatisfactory, warned that "[o]nce adopted on first reading, draft articles served as one basis for developing international law": YBILC 1994, Vol. I, pp. 266, 270 (in reference to draft article 12 (on "Conditions relating to resort to countermeasures")).

well as "generally follow[ing] the terminology used in [them]."[50] This very much fulfilled the prophecy of Judge Waldock, who suggested already in 1974 that an output of the Commission on the topic was destined to play an increasingly frequent role in the proceedings and decisions of the Court: "Few contentious cases came before the Court which did not, to a greater or lesser degree, raise some aspect of State responsibility," he explained, adding that "he was convinced that the Commission's work on that topic would . . . have a large and continuing interest for the Court."[51]

Two years after the *Gabčíkovo-Nagymaros Project* judgment, the Court endorsed yet another proposition contained in the Commission's provisional draft articles on State responsibility by holding, in its advisory opinion on *Difference relating to Immunity from Legal Process of a Special Rapporteur* (1999), that draft article 6 thereof reflected the well-established customary rule that the conduct of any organ of a State must be regarded as an act of that State.[52] The draft articles on State responsibility, by then adopted by the Commission on second and final reading, were also referred to in the *Wall* advisory opinion (2004), in which the Court again chose to articulate one of the conditions under which the state of necessity might be invoked by quoting the terms used by the Commission.[53] In *Armed Activities on the Territory of the Congo* (2005), the Court's statement of the law relied on articles 4, 5, and 8 of the Commission's draft articles on State responsibility;[54] the Court also quoted the Commission's commentary to article 45 in support of its observation that waivers or renunciations of claims or rights must either

[50] YBILC 1998, Vol. I, p. 193, para. 23 (Crawford). See also C.J. Tams, 'Law-making in Complex Processes: The World Court and the Modern Law of State Responsibility', in C. Chinkin and F. Baetens (eds.), *Sovereignty, Statehood and State Responsibility: Essays in Honour of James Crawford* (CUP 2015) 287–306 (suggesting that the Court has operated within the Commission's "master plan" for the law on State responsibility, and that the two bodies (through "normative ping-pong") have been partners in law-making in this field).

[51] YBILC 1974, Vol. I, p. 70, para. 30.

[52] *Difference relating to Immunity from Legal Process of a Special Rapporteur of the Commission on Human Rights, Advisory Opinion, I.C.J. Reports 1999*, p. 87, para. 62.

[53] *Legal Consequences of the Construction of a Wall in the Occupied Palestinian Territory, Advisory Opinion, I.C.J. Reports 2004*, p. 195, para. 140.

[54] *Armed Activities on the Territory of the Congo (Democratic Republic of the Congo v. Uganda), Judgment, I.C.J. Reports 2005*, p. 226, para. 160. President Higgins later recalled that the court "rel[ied] in its reasoning on the Commission's draft articles": YBILC 2006, Vol. I, p. 213, para. 20.

be express or unequivocally implied from the conduct of the State alleged to have waived or renounced its right.[55]

The Commission's draft articles on State responsibility were once again "central to the Court's reasoning"[56] in the *Genocide case (Bosnia and Herzegovina* v. *Serbia and Montenegro)* (2007), where the Court found several of them to reflect customary international law without referring to any further evidence of State practice or *opinio juris.* More specifically, the Court noted that article 4 reflected the customary rule that the conduct of any State organ is to be considered an act of the State under international law and may therefore give rise to the responsibility of that State,[57] and then applied the rule, as captured in that article and its commentary, in analyzing whether the acts of genocide committed in Srebrenica were perpetrated by persons or entities having the status of organs of the Federal Republic of Yugoslavia.[58] The Court also held that article 8 (on conduct directed or controlled by a State) laid down a rule of a customary character,[59] and added that this rule (itself based on the Court's 1986 judgment in *Military and Paramilitary Activities in and against Nicaragua*) "must be understood in the light of the Court's jurisprudence."[60] In addition, the Court asserted that article 16 (on aid

[55] *Armed Activities on the Territory of the Congo (Democratic Republic of the Congo* v. *Uganda), Judgment, I.C.J. Reports 2005*, p. 266, para. 293 (the Court stating that the Commission referred to this issue "similarly" to the way the Court has).

[56] YBILC 2007, Vol. I, p. 122, para. 15 (President Higgins addressing the Commission).

[57] *Application of the Convention on the Prevention and Punishment of the Crime of Genocide (Bosnia and Herzegovina* v. *Serbia and Montenegro), Judgment, I.C.J. Reports 2007*, pp. 202–203, paras. 385, 388.

[58] *Ibid*, at p. 203, para. 388.

[59] *Ibid*, at pp. 207–208, para. 398 and pp. 210–211, para. 407. In his Dissenting Opinion, Judge Al-Khasawneh stated that "[i]n applying the effective control test, the Court followed Article 8 of the International Law Commission Articles on State Responsibility": *ibid*, at p. 255, para. 36.

[60] *Ibid*, at p. 208, para. 399; having explained the criterion of 'effective control' endorsed by it, the Court again stressed that "[t]his is the state of customary international law, as reflected in the ILC Articles on State Responsibility" (at p. 209, para. 401). Cassese has observed that "[t]he Court's basic assumption, that Article 8 of the ILC Articles reflects customary law, is undemonstrated, being simply predicated on the authority of the Court itself (the *Nicaragua* precedent), as well as the authority of the ILC. The logical sequences of propositions in which the Court's holding is grounded could perhaps be set out as follows: (1) The Court in *Nicaragua* enunciated the test [as an apodictic truth in the Kantian sense, namely as enouncing an absolute and necessary truth] (2) the ILC upheld the same test (based only on *Nicaragua*); (3) hence the test is valid and reflects customary international law": A. Cassese, 'The *Nicaragua* and *Tadić* Tests Revisited in Light of the ICJ Judgment on Genocide in Bosnia', 18 EJIL (2007) 649 at 651.

or assistance in the commission of an internationally wrongful act) – which was initially considered even within the Commission to be of the nature of progressive development of the law[61] – reflected a customary rule.[62] The judgment also made it clear that there was no criminal responsibility of States in international law, "thereby endorsing the basic strategy of the second reading of the [Commission's] Articles."[63] Higgins, who was President of the Court at the time of the judgment, would later say in reference to the articles on State responsibility that "the quality of an ILC report may be such that governments and indeed courts will refer to large parts of it as an authoritative statement of international law – and even turn to the text concerned to guide them in relation to particular legal problems."[64] Another commentator put it more bluntly in suggesting that the Court "treated the ILC Articles on State Responsibility as holy scripture."[65]

[61] See J. Crawford, 'The Progressive Development of International Law: History, Theory and Practice', in D. Alland et al (eds.), *Unity and Diversity of International Law: Essays in Honour of Professor Pierre-Marie Dupuy* (Martinus Nijhoff 2014) 3 at 20; H. Thirlway, *The Sources of International Law*, 2nd ed. (OUP 2019) 23.

[62] *Application of the Convention on the Prevention and Punishment of the Crime of Genocide (Bosnia and Herzegovina* v. *Serbia and Montenegro), Judgment, I.C.J. Reports 2007*, p. 217, para. 420. For the suggestion that this assertion was not actually required, see A. Gattini, 'Breach of the Obligation to Prevent and Reparation Thereof in the ICJ's Genocide Judgment', 18 EJIL (2007) 695 at 696–697, fn. 7.

[63] J. Crawford, 'The International Court of Justice and the Law of State Responsibility', in C.J. Tams and J. Sloan (eds.), *The Development of International Law by the International Court of Justice* (OUP 2013) 71 at 85 (citing to paras. 167–170 of the 2007 judgment).

[64] R. Higgins, 'The United Nations at 70 Years: The Impact Upon International Law', 65 ICLQ (2016) 1 at 2 (adding that "[t]hat has been true of the ILC Articles on State Responsibility"). The Court's reference to several of the Commission's articles in this *Genocide* case owed also to the fact that it "took the opportunity to pronounce on virtually every matter that could arise under the Genocide Convention, in the belief that substantive claims relating to genocide would be very, very rare, and that this pedagogical opportunity should be taken": *ibid*, at p. 17. See also YBILC 2007, Vol. I, p. 125, para. 33 (President Higgins telling the Commission that "[w]hat the Court had sought to do in its Judgment in the *Bosnia and Herzegovina* v. *Serbia and Montenegro* case had not only been to answer the claims before it, but also systematically to elaborate and explain each and every element in the Genocide Convention, believing, exceptionally, that the latter task was also a necessary contribution to clarity and understanding. The Court regarded as extremely important, for the future, its views on the bases of State responsibility for genocide and the precise circumstances in which the duty of a State to prevent genocide in another State's territory might arise as well as the scope of that duty").

[65] M. Milanović, 'State Responsibility for Genocide: A Follow-Up', 18 EJIL (2007) 669 at 693.

The articles on State responsibility were again drawn upon by the Court in the *Pulp Mills* judgment (2010), in which the Court referred (together with some of its own case-law) to articles 34–37 as reflecting customary international law on the issue of reparation.[66] The judgment in the following year in *Application of the Interim Accord of 13 September 1995* applied the notion enshrined in article 22, when rejecting Greece's claim that its conduct could be justified as a countermeasure precluding the wrongfulness of its conduct.[67] In 2012, in the *Diallo* judgment on the compensation owed by the Democratic Republic of the Congo to the Republic of Guinea, the Court similarly invoked, inter alia, the commentary to article 36 of the articles on State responsibility in support of its view that a claim concerning compensation relating to loss of future earnings cannot be purely speculative.[68] That year the Court also asserted, in *Jurisdictional Immunities of the State*, that general international law was "expressed" in article 30(a) (on cessation of a wrongful act) and "reflected" in article 35 (on restitution).[69]

The articles on State responsibility were further endorsed in the *Genocide case (Croatia* v. *Serbia)* (2015), where the Court asserted that article 3 (on characterization of an act of a State as internationally wrongful) reflected a rule of customary international law;[70] and in the compensation phase of the case concerning *Certain Activities Carried Out by Nicaragua in the Border Area* (2018), where the Court referred to the Commission's commentary to article 38 in support of its assertion that under international law, interest is neither an autonomous form of reparation nor a necessary part of compensation in every case.[71] In the

[66] *Pulp Mills on the River Uruguay (Argentina* v. *Uruguay), Judgment, I.C.J. Reports 2010*, p. 104, para. 273.

[67] *Application of the Interim Accord of 13 September 1995 (the former Yugoslav Republic of Macedonia* v. *Greece), Judgment of 5 December 2011, I.C.J. Reports 2011*, pp. 691–692, para. 164.

[68] *Ahmadou Sadio Diallo (Republic of Guinea* v. *Democratic Republic of the Congo), Compensation, Judgment, I.C.J. Reports 2012*, p. 342, para. 49.

[69] *Jurisdictional Immunities of the State (Germany* v. *Italy: Greece intervening), Judgment, I.C.J. Reports 2012*, p. 153, para. 137. The Court did not cite this case, but only the Commission's work, when holding again in *Certain Iranian Assets* that article 30(a) reflects customary international law: *Certain Iranian Assets (Islamic Republic of Iran* v. *United States of America)*, judgment of 30 March 2023, paras. 226–227 (also referring to the commentary).

[70] *Application of the Convention on the Prevention and Punishment of the Crime of Genocide (Croatia* v. *Serbia), Judgment, I.C.J. Reports 2015*, p. 61, para. 128.

[71] *Certain Activities Carried Out by Nicaragua in the Border Area (Costa Rica* v. *Nicaragua), Compensation, Judgment, I.C.J. Reports 2018*, p. 58, para. 151.

reparation phase of *Armed Activities on the Territory of the Congo* (2022), article 31 was said – again, without more – to reflect customary international law, and the commentary to articles 31 and 47 was referred to in support of the Court's statements concerning the law on allocation of responsibility for reparation and the necessary causality.[72] The Court similarly endorsed article 34 as a restatement of the customary international law in force,[73] as it did provisions of article 37 (on satisfaction) and the commentary thereto.[74] Soon thereafter, in *Alleged Violations of Sovereign Rights and Maritime Spaces in the Caribbean Sea* (2022), the Court quoted the Commission's commentary to article 12 of the articles on State responsibility, according to which there is no general rule applicable to the question whether a State engages its international responsibility by the enactment of national legislation; it then applied it as the applicable rule.[75] One of the Commission's former special rapporteurs on State responsibility (and future judge of the Court), commenting on the multiple references made over the years by the Court to the articles on State responsibility, acknowledged that in some cases the articles endorsed did, in fact, represent progressive development rather than codification of international law.[76] The application of such articles by the Court, he suggested, amounted to "[c]ustomary international law by stealth, perhaps."[77]

Similar treatment was accorded by the Court to provisions put forward by the Commission in its work on other topics as well. In the *Diallo* judgment on preliminary objections (2007), it was the definition of diplomatic protection provided by article 1 of the Commission's draft articles on that topic that was held to be reflective of customary international law,[78] even though the Commission had adopted that text only

[72] *Armed Activities on the Territory of the Congo (Democratic Republic of the Congo* v. *Uganda), Judgment, I.C.J. Reports 2022*, p. 43, paras. 70, pp. 49-50, para. 98, p. 64, para. 148 and p. 130, para. 382.

[73] *Ibid*, at p. 50, para. 101.

[74] *Ibid*, at p. 132, paras. 388–389.

[75] *Alleged Violations of Sovereign Rights and Maritime Spaces in the Caribbean Sea (Nicaragua* v. *Colombia), Judgment, I.C.J. Reports 2022*, p. 339, paras. 191–192.

[76] J. Crawford, 'Chance, Order, Change: The Course of International Law', 365 RdC (2013) 108.

[77] *Ibid.*

[78] *Ahmadou Sadio Diallo (Republic of Guinea* v. *Democratic Republic of the Congo), Preliminary Objections, Judgment, I.C.J. Reports 2007*, p. 599, para. 39; see also at p. 606, para. 64. The Commission did not miss an opportunity to note this in the commentary to its draft articles on the responsibility of international organizations:

months earlier as a compromise, marking a retreat from the approach taken in the *Mavrommatis Palestine Concessions* case and, moreover, actually noted in the commentary that the article "makes no attempt to provide a complete and comprehensive definition of diplomatic protection."[79] This once again led a former member of the Commission (who, too, was soon to be elected a judge of the Court) to wonder whether one could "take this as an example of instant customary law."[80] The Court further added that "[o]wing to the substantive development of international law over recent decades in respect of the rights it accords to individuals, the scope *ratione materiae* of diplomatic protection . . . has subsequently widened to include, *inter alia*, internationally guaranteed human rights,"[81] a remark that very much accorded with the Commission's chosen approach to the topic and has indeed been viewed as "just one example of the many ways in which the Court in this judgment has shown its appreciation for the work of the ILC on diplomatic protection."[82] In the judgment on preliminary objections in the *Application of the ICSFT and CERD* case (2019), the Court cited the Commission's draft articles on diplomatic protection and on State responsibility, together with its own case-law, in support of the statement that local remedies must be previously exhausted as a matter of customary international law in cases in which a State brings a claim on behalf of one or more of its nationals.[83] The draft articles on diplomatic protection were again cited with approval by the Court in *Certain Iranian Assets* (2023), where the Court treated article 14(3) and article 15(a) of the draft

YBILC 2011, Vol. II, Part Two, p. 86, fn. 300. The Court again held that article 1 reflects customary international law in its judgment of 30 March 2023 in *Certain Iranian Assets (Islamic Republic of Iran* v. *United States of America)*, para. 61.

79 YBILC 2006, Vol. II, Part Two, p. 26, paragraph (1) of the commentary to draft article 1; paragraph (7) of the commentary similarly states that the definition does not cover exceptions (at p. 27). See also A. Vermeer-Künzli, '*Diallo* and the Draft Articles: The Application of the Draft Articles on Diplomatic Protection in the *Ahmadou Sadio Diallo* Case', 20 LJIL (2007) 941 at 943–944.

80 G. Gaja, 'The Protection of General Interests of in the International Community', 364 RdC (2012) 39.

81 *Ahmadou Sadio Diallo (Republic of Guinea* v. *Democratic Republic of the Congo), Preliminary Objections, Judgment, I.C.J. Reports 2007*, p. 599, para. 39.

82 Vermeer-Künzli, *supra* note 77, at p. 942.

83 *Application of the International Convention for the Suppression of the Financing of Terrorism and of the International Convention on the Elimination of All Forms of Racial Discrimination (Ukraine* v. *Russian Federation), Preliminary Objections, Judgment, I.C.J. Reports 2019*, p. 605, para. 129.

articles, along with their commentary, as restating customary rules.[84] The Court's frequent reference to the Commission's texts in ascertaining rules of customary international law has indeed been so extensive that a judge of the Court (himself a former member of the Commission) saw it necessary to consider, in broad terms, what the appropriate methodology for interpreting articles adopted by the Commission should be.[85]

All this is not to say that the Court has unquestioningly accepted all of the Commission's propositions as restatements of positive law, or that it has treated all of the Commission's work products as being of equal authority: it has not. In each case, the Court seems to have either "carefully decided if the ILC work referred to, while an important *œuvre*, does or does not yet represent the law on a certain matter,"[86] or – perhaps more accurately – at the very least considered whether that work has attracted sufficient support from States so as to merit being endorsed as such. Bearing in mind the Commission's dual function, judges of the Court have indeed been at pains to note that the Court must "apply existing law and therefore needed to distinguish in the texts adopted by the Commission between matters relating to the codification of customary law and issues of progressive development."[87] They have also been conscious that, in President Higgins's words, "[d]ifficulties might arise when the Court came to deal with a provision that might be regarded by scholars as a development of international law rather than a restatement of it."[88] The Court has on a limited number of occasions

[84] *Certain Iranian Assets (Islamic Republic of Iran* v. *United States of America)*, judgment of 30 March 2023, paras. 66, 68.

[85] Gaja, *supra* note 19, at pp. 10–20.

[86] R. Higgins et al, *Oppenheim's International Law: United Nations*, Vol. II (OUP 2017) 1182, para. 29.186 and p. 944, para. 25.49 ("The ICJ does not automatically accept ILC draft articles or other work products as statements of customary international law. It assesses their applicability on a case-by-case, article-by-article basis"). See also YBILC 1999, Vol. I, p. 124, para. 19 (President Schwebel saying that "[o]f course, the Court did not adopt that approach lightly, but would consider carefully whether a draft article formulated by the Commission was in fact a reflection of customary international law, or whether it was a development in that law"); A/CN.4/SR.3639: 'Provisional Summary Record of the Commission's 3639th Meeting' (18 July 2023), p. 7 (President Donoghue saying that "[t]he Court made extensive use of the Commission's outputs, including its commentaries, although it did not accept them uncritically").

[87] UN Doc. A/C.6/70/SR.21, *supra* note 48, at p. 6, para. 23 (President Abraham, adding that "[t]hose texts could not always have the value of positive law for the Court, but it nevertheless took them into account in determining the current state of customary international law in any particular area").

[88] YBILC 2007, Vol. I, p. 128, para. 55.

even contradicted the Commission with regard to a certain point of law.[89]

By the same token, the Court has generally been reluctant to endorse the work of the Commission on a given topic as a whole, instead preferring to refer only to specific provisions thereof and to avoid taking a position on provisions that were not directly at issue in a given case.[90] In the *Diallo* judgment on preliminary objections (2007), therefore, the Court expressly left undecided the question as to whether article 11(b) of the Commission's draft articles on diplomatic protection reflected customary international law, holding that the "special case" covered by that article did not arise in the circumstances of the case.[91] Similarly, in its judgment that year in the *Genocide case (Bosnia and Herzegovina* v. *Serbia and Montenegro)*, the Court stated, after holding that articles 4 and 8 of the Commission's draft articles on State responsibility reflected customary international law, that it "does not see itself required to decide at this stage whether the ILC's Articles dealing with attribution, apart from Articles 4 and 8, express present customary international law, it being clear that none of them apply in this case."[92] In the following year, the Court refrained from deciding, in its judgment on the preliminary objections raised by Serbia in the *Genocide case (Croatia* v. *Serbia)*, whether article 10(2) of the draft articles on State responsibility reflected customary international law on the grounds that further elements of fact in any event would be required in order to consider the applicability of that article to the particular case.[93] The same approach was followed in the judgments on jurisdiction and admissibility in *Obligations concerning*

[89] See Chapter 6, Section B.1.

[90] On some exceptions, see Section B.1 below.

[91] *Ahmadou Sadio Diallo (Republic of Guinea* v. *Democratic Republic of the Congo), Preliminary Objections, Judgment, I.C.J. Reports 2007*, pp. 615–616, paras. 91–93. In fact, the Court did not agree with the Commission on the matter: see Chapter 6, Section B.1.

[92] *Application of the Convention on the Prevention and Punishment of the Crime of Genocide (Bosnia and Herzegovina* v. *Serbia and Montenegro), Judgment, I.C.J. Reports 2007*, p. 215, para. 414.

[93] *Application of the Convention on the Prevention and Punishment of the Crime of Genocide (Croatia* v. *Serbia), Preliminary Objections, Judgment, I.C.J. Reports 2008*, p. 459, para. 127. At the merits stage, the Court again found it unnecessary to consider that question, having held that the article did not apply to the facts of the case: *Application of the Convention on the Prevention and Punishment of the Crime of Genocide (Croatia* v. *Serbia), Judgment, I.C.J. Reports 2015*, pp. 52–53, paras. 104–105 (but suggesting again that article 13 of the articles on State responsibility is expressive of customary international law).

Negotiations relating to Cessation of the Nuclear Arms Race and to Nuclear Disarmament (2016), where the Court avoided a decision as to whether article 43 of the draft articles on State responsibility reflected a rule of customary international law by noting that the Commission's commentary itself specifies that the articles are not concerned with jurisdiction of international courts or admissibility of cases before them.[94] In its judgment on reparation in *Armed Activities on the Territory of the Congo* (2022), the Court similarly quoted only two of three paragraphs of article 37 of the articles on State responsibility, leaving no hint that a third paragraph even exists.[95] President Abraham was right to make the general observation that "[a]s to whether the text on State responsibility was part of custom, although the Court had had occasion to speak to that point concerning individual articles, it had not taken a position in general, and had avoided doing so when there was any doubt."[96]

All the same, concerns have been raised as to the Court's "too ready acceptance that the substance of particular proposals adopted by the Commission . . ., with their accompanying commentaries, can without more analysis be regarded as authoritative statements of general international law."[97] As Berman has put it,

[94] *Obligations concerning Negotiations relating to Cessation of the Nuclear Arms Race and to Nuclear Disarmament (Marshall Islands* v. *India), Jurisdiction and Admissibility, Judgment, I.C.J. Reports 2016*, pp. 272–273, para. 42; *Obligations concerning Negotiations relating to Cessation of the Nuclear Arms Race and to Nuclear Disarmament (Marshall Islands* v. *United Kingdom), Preliminary Objections, Judgment, I.C.J. Reports 2016*, p. 852, para. 45.

[95] *Armed Activities on the Territory of the Congo (Democratic Republic of the Congo* v. *Uganda), Judgment, I.C.J. Reports 2022*, p. 132, para. 388.

[96] YBILC 2015, Vol. I, p. 233, para. 28 (having just said that "[i]n general . . . [the Court] avoided taking positions on matters of international law that were not strictly and directly at issue in a given case, tending to defer such pronouncements": see p. 232, para. 24). President Higgins had similarly clarified that "it would not be correct to say that the Court regarded the totality of the draft articles on responsibility of States as customary international law; to date, it had had occasion only to pronounce on, agree with and find useful formulations in certain specific articles, to which it had referred as customary international law": YBILC 2007, Vol. I, p. 128, para. 55.

[97] Sinclair, *supra* note 42 (adding that "the reasoning underpinning the invocation by the Court of the work product of the Commission, at least in some instances, has been foreshortened if not glossed over entirely"). See also, for example, YBILC 2000, Vol. I, p. 276, para. 89 (Pellet saying, in reference to the Court's judgment in the *Gabčíkovo-Nagymaros Project* case, that "ICJ had perhaps accorded much more weight to the Commission's draft articles than was justified by texts adopted on first reading").

> [i]f there has been a problem, it is not [the privileging of the Commission's work], but rather the somewhat indiscriminate approach the Court has taken toward the ILC's working product, without on occasion sufficient attention to whether the particular item cited is the final product, or indeed to whether it should be regarded as the ILC's considered reflection of the *lex lata*, as opposed to a proposal *de lege ferenda*, which marks in turn that boundary between law-making and the determination of established law which underlies the whole structure of Article 38 of the ICJ Statute.[98]

Such concerns are exasperated given the fact that the Commission itself generally has refrained, notwithstanding the explicit instructions of its Statute, from placing its output (or even particular rules set out therein) in one or the other category.[99]

3. *Reference to the Commission's Work as Part of the Court's Own Reasoning*

A third avenue along which the Court has utilized the Commission's output has been to cite the latter's views in setting out its own legal reasoning, in the sense that "arguments of the Court go hand-in-hand with arguments of the Commission."[100] This additional role accorded by the Court to the Commission's work was referred to by Judge Schwebel as "exceptional."[101] Yet, already in the *North Sea Continental Shelf* cases, the Court referred to the ideas propounded within the Commission from 1950 to 1956 on the question of delimitation of the continental shelf between adjacent States to confirm its own conclusion that the rule of equidistance was not to be viewed as an inherent necessity of continental shelf doctrine.[102] In the *Gulf of Maine* judgment (1984), a Chamber of

98 Berman, *supra* note 6, at p. 16.

99 On this, and on the age-old conceptual and practical tension between codification of international law and its progressive development, see, for example, M. Wood, 'The UN International Law Commission and Customary International Law', in E. Cannizzaro et al (eds.), *Discourses on Methods in International Law: An Anthology*, Gaetano Morelli Lectures Series, Vol. 3 (International and European Papers Publishing 2020) 65–102; Crawford, *supra* note 61, at pp. 3–22.

100 Schwebel, *supra* note 8, at p. 485.

101 *Ibid.*

102 *North Sea Continental Shelf, Judgment, I.C.J. Reports 1969*, pp. 33–36, paras. 49–50, 54–56. See also Schwebel, *supra* note 6, at p. 162 ("In a passage which is central to that Judgment, the Court attached decisive weight to the fact that, in the Commission's debates, the equidistance rule 'was never given any special prominence at all, and certainly no priority'").

the Court similarly referred, as part of its reasoning as to which continental shelf delimitation method was to be applied, to the Commission's prior choice as to delimitation methods that merited legal attention;[103] President Nagendra Singh would soon say, with regard to matters pertaining to maritime jurisdiction, that

> the Court's activity has run parallel in this domain with that of the International Law Commission, . . . and of the codification conferences . . . summoned to consolidate and develop the law of the sea. Judges and legislators have thus systematically learned from each other in this field of international law, in what I have ventured to call a symbiotic relationship of case-law and codification.[104]

An additional example may be found in the case concerning *Maritime Delimitation and Territorial Questions between Qatar and Bahrain* (2001), where a 1958 report by the Commission's Special Rapporteur on the topic 'Arbitral procedure' was used to confirm the Court's observation as to the meaning of the term "arbitration" for purposes of public international law.[105]

More remarkable in this context is the *Gabčíkovo-Nagymaros Project* judgment, where the Court's reasoning, "especially in its discussion on the notion of state of necessity, [was] intermingled with citations from the commentaries of the Commission."[106] Thus, in expressing its view that necessity as a ground for precluding wrongfulness can be accepted only on an exceptional basis, the Court added that "[t]he International Law Commission was of the same opinion when it explained that it had opted for a negative form of words in Article 33 of its Draft [articles on State responsibility adopted on first reading]."[107] The Court similarly relied on the Commission, after holding that a state of necessity could not exist without a peril duly established at the relevant point in time, by

[103] *Delimitation of the Maritime Boundary in the Gulf of Maine Area, Judgment, I.C.J. Reports 1984*, pp. 319–320, para. 175. The Chamber also referred to the Commission's work as covered in the Court's earlier *North Sea Continental Shelf* judgment: *I.C.J. Reports 1969*, p. 293, para. 91; p. 297, para. 107; and p. 313, para. 159.

[104] 'Work of the Court in 1985–1986', 40 YBICJ (1985–1986) 127 at 176–177.

[105] *Maritime Delimitation and Territorial Questions between Qatar and Bahrain, Merits, Judgment, I.C.J. Reports 2001*, pp. 76–77, para. 113 (citing first the Hague Conventions of 1899 and 1907 as well an advisory opinion of the PCIJ, then the work of the Commission and then an arbitral award).

[106] Schwebel, *supra* note 8, at p. 485.

[107] *Gabčíkovo-Nagymaros Project (Hungary/Slovakia), Judgment, I.C.J. Reports 1997*, p. 40, para. 51.

adding that "[a]s the International Law Commission emphasized in its commentary, the 'extremely grave and imminent' peril must 'have been a threat to the interest at the actual time.'"[108] The Commission's words again became the Court's when it held (by quoting once more from the Commission's commentary) that the respect by Hungary, in 1989, of its obligations under the terms of the 1977 Treaty, would not have resulted in a situation "characterized so aptly by the maxim *summum jus summa injuria*."[109] Recourse to the Commission's output was also made in this way when the Court, by citing the commentary to (then) article 41 of the Commission's draft articles, distinguished between, on the one hand, actual commission of a wrongful act and, on the other, conduct prior to that act which is of a preparatory character and which "does not qualify as a wrongful act."[110]

In the *Genocide case (Bosnia and Herzegovina* v. *Serbia and Montenegro)* (2007), the Court quoted article 58 of the Commission's articles on State responsibility, and its commentary, in support of its assertion that responsibility for international wrongful acts may lie with individuals as well as States.[111] It also referred to the rule stated by the Commission in article 14(3) of the articles on State responsibility, in support of its assertion that a breach of an obligation to prevent genocide may occur only when the commission of a prohibited act begins;[112] and to articles 31 and 36 thereof (alongside its own case-law), in support of its pronouncements as to the rules of international law governing the determination of reparation for an internationally wrongful act.[113] The Court also used the Commission's words, as borrowed from the interpretation of the crime of genocide offered by it in its commentary to article 17 of the Draft Code of Crimes against the Peace and Security of Mankind, in explaining that the acts comprising genocide include mental elements,[114] and that it is not necessary to intend to achieve the complete annihilation of a group from every corner of the globe for the crime of

[108] *Ibid*, at p. 42, para. 54.
[109] *Ibid*, at p. 45, para. 57.
[110] *Ibid*, at p. 54, para. 79.
[111] *Application of the Convention on the Prevention and Punishment of the Crime of Genocide (Bosnia and Herzegovina* v. *Serbia and Montenegro), Judgment, I.C.J. Reports 2007*, p. 116, para. 173.
[112] *Ibid*, at pp. 221–222, para. 431.
[113] *Ibid*, at pp. 232–233, para. 460.
[114] *Ibid*, at p. 121, para. 186.

genocide to be found to have been committed.[115] That commentary to article 17 was again referred to by the Court (along with rulings of the International Criminal Tribunal for the former Yugoslavia and the International Criminal Tribunal for Rwanda) to support both its own interpretation that the intent, for purposes of the crime of genocide, must be to destroy at least a substantial part of the particular group concerned,[116] and its own view that destruction of historical, cultural, and religious heritage does not fall within the categories of acts of genocide set out in the Convention.[117]

The Commission's legal reasoning was once more adopted in the *Jurisdictional Immunities of the State* case (2012), in which the Court observed that "in accordance with the principle stated in Article 13 of the International Law Commission Articles on Responsibility of States for Internationally Wrongful Acts, the compatibility of an act with international law can be determined only by reference to the law in force at the time when the act occurred."[118] Article 41 (on consequences of a serious breach of an obligation under *jus cogens*) was similarly mentioned by the Court (and thus implicitly endorsed as a statement of positive law) as part of its clarification of the relationship between *jus cogens* and the rules of State immunity.[119] Not long after, in the merits judgment in the *Genocide case (Croatia* v. *Serbia)* (2015), the Commission's views regarding the scope of the Genocide Convention were again invoked by the Court in support of the latter's own interpretation of the meaning and scope of the term "destruction" as found in the Convention,[120] as well as the meaning and scope of certain acts which constitute the *actus*

[115] *Ibid*, at p. 126, para. 199.

[116] *Ibid*, at p. 126, para. 198.

[117] *Ibid*, at p. 186, para. 344.

[118] *Jurisdictional Immunities of the State (Germany* v. *Italy: Greece intervening), Judgment, I.C.J. Reports 2012*, p. 124, para. 58. For Tladi, "[h]ere the Court seems to be applying the Draft Articles [on State responsibility] directly *as law* and not as reflecting law": D. Tladi, 'The Fate of the Draft Articles on State Responsibility: Act Soon or Face the Further Erosion of the Role of States in the International Law-Making Process', APDI 2013 (2015) 87 at 90.

[119] *Jurisdictional Immunities of the State (Germany* v. *Italy: Greece intervening), Judgment, I.C.J. Reports 2012*, p. 140, para. 93.

[120] *Application of the Convention on the Prevention and Punishment of the Crime of Genocide (Croatia* v. *Serbia), Judgment, I.C.J. Reports 2015*, p. 63, para. 136 (citing the commentary to the Commission's Draft Code of Crimes against the Peace and Security of Mankind).

reus of genocide.[121] In *Certain Iranian Assets* (2023), the Court supported its cautious approach to the 'clean hands' doctrine by noting that the Commission declined earlier to include the doctrine among the circumstances precluding wrongfulness in its articles on State responsibility.[122]

B. There Is More Beneath the Surface

Notwithstanding the prevalent references to the Commission's work in the Court's decisions, the full extent of the Court's reliance on such output does not properly come into sight by reading the case-law alone. This is because the Court not infrequently resorts to the Commission's output only indirectly, or without making such recourse explicit. Any comprehensive appreciation of the Commission's impact on the Court's judicial activity ought to take such implicit reliance into account.

1. *Indirect Reliance*

To begin with, the Court frequently relies on the Commission's work indirectly when basing itself on rules clearly set out in conventions that were concluded on the basis of draft articles elaborated by the Commission.[123] In its *Tehran Hostages* judgment (1980), for example, the Court applied several of the provisions of the 1961 Vienna Convention on Diplomatic Relations and the 1963 Vienna Convention on Consular Relations, both of which it regarded in general terms as instruments that "codify the law of diplomatic and consular relations";[124] it also "examined with great care and appreciation" the 1973 Convention on the Prevention and Punishment of Crimes against Internationally Protected Persons, including Diplomatic Agents, which was likewise prepared on the basis of the Commission's draft articles.[125] In the

[121] *Ibid*, at p. 69, para. 157 (citing the commentary to the Commission's Draft Code of Crimes against the Peace and Security of Mankind).

[122] *Certain Iranian Assets (Islamic Republic of Iran* v. *United States of America)*, judgment of 30 March 2023, para. 81.

[123] These conventions often provide for the Court's jurisdiction in the first place: see also Chapter 4, Section B.3.

[124] *United States Diplomatic and Consular Staff in Tehran, Judgment, I.C.J. Reports 1980*, p. 24, para. 45; see also the Court's Order of 15 December 1979 on the request for the indication of Provisional Measures in this case, at p. 16, para. 25.

[125] YBILC 1981, Vol. I, p. 208, para. 4 (Judge El-Erian addressing the Commission).

Gabčíkovo-Nagymaros Project judgment (1997), the Court drew upon the 1969 Vienna Convention on the Law of Treaties, the 1978 Vienna Convention on Succession of States in respect of Treaties, and the 1997 Convention on the Law of the Non-Navigational Uses of International Watercourses, all of which had their origin in the Commission's work.[126] Particularly noteworthy is the Court's general statement in that case, that it

> has no need to dwell upon the question of the applicability in the present case of the Vienna Convention of 1969 on the Law of Treaties. It needs only to be mindful of the fact that it has several times had occasion to hold that some of the rules laid down in that Convention might be considered as a codification of existing customary law. The Court takes the view that in many respects this applies to the provisions of the Vienna Convention concerning the termination and the suspension of the operation of treaties, set forth in Articles 60 to 62.[127]

By endorsing so sweepingly a convention based on the Commission's work as reflecting customary international law, and by habitually treating various provisions set out in such conventions in the same manner (including when the convention in question has not come into force, either generally or as between the parties), the Court has reinforced the value of the Commission's output as authoritative statements of law. As Gaja observed, the Court has "clearly increased the significance of

[126] *Gabčíkovo-Nagymaros Project (Hungary/Slovakia), Judgment, I.C.J. Reports 1997*, p. 7.

[127] *Ibid*, at p. 38, para. 46. In its advisory opinion on the *Legal Consequences for States of the Continued Presence of South Africa in Namibia (South West Africa) notwithstanding Security Council Resolution 276 (1970)*, and in its judgment concerning the jurisdiction of the Court in the *Fisheries Jurisdiction* case, the Court had relied on two of the most important articles in part V of the Vienna Convention: article 60 (on termination or suspension of the operation of a treaty as a consequence of its breach) and article 62 (on fundamental change of circumstances): see, respectively, *Legal Consequences for States of the Continued Presence of South Africa in Namibia (South West Africa) notwithstanding Security Council Resolution 276 (1970), Advisory Opinion, I.C.J. Reports 1971*, p. 47, para. 94, and *Fisheries Jurisdiction (United Kingdom* v. *Iceland), Jurisdiction of the Court, Judgment, I.C.J. Reports 1973*, p. 18, para. 36. The Court has also ruled that articles 31 and 32 of the Convention reflected customary international law: see, for example, *Territorial Dispute (Libyan Arab Jamahiriya/Chad), Judgment, I.C.J. Reports 1994*, p. 21, para. 41; *Kasikili/Sedudu Island (Botswana/Namibia), Judgment, I.C.J. Reports 1999*, p. 1059, para. 18. See also YBILC 1999, Vol. I, p. 125, para. 19 (President Schwebel addressing the Commission and conceding that the view that article 31 did reflect customary international law "would have been widely contested in 1969 but had become less controversial with the passing of time [and the Court's endorsement of it]").

various codification conventions by giving weight to certain articles of these conventions even when they had been ratified by only few States."[128]

2. *Implicit Reliance*

There are, moreover, instances in which the Court has clearly consulted the Commission's work but has chosen not to mention it despite adopting a position very much compatible with that of the Commission. In *Tehran Hostages* (1980), for instance, the Court had before it article 8 (as it then was) of the Commission's first reading draft articles on State responsibility, which dealt with circumstances in which the conduct of a person or group of persons shall also be considered as an act of a State under international law,[129] but it did not refer to that text when accepting that "the militants, authors of the invasion and jailers of the hostages, had now become agents of the Iranian State for whose acts the State itself was internationally responsible."[130] More broadly, the judgment essentially followed both the structure and reasoning of the Commission's draft articles by first examining the question of attribution, then proceeding to inquire whether a breach of an international obligation had occurred and whether any special circumstances may have excused such a breach, and finally indicating the specific obligations resulting from the breach.[131] This was evident to Schwebel, who told his fellow members of the Commission that he "now felt able to tell the most pragmatic of lawyers who queried the practical use of the Commission's work on State responsibility that they should read the judgment of the Court in the [Iran] *hostages* case."[132]

A very similar path was soon followed by the Court in *Military and Paramilitary Activities in and against Nicaragua* (1984), again without

[128] Gaja, *supra* note 80, at p. 38.

[129] See Memorial of the Government of the United States of America, available at <www.icj-cij.org/files/case-related/64/9551.pdf>, p. 157.

[130] *United States Diplomatic and Consular Staff in Tehran, Judgment, I.C.J. Reports 1980*, p. 35, para. 74.

[131] See also B. Graefrath, 'The International Law Commission Tomorrow: Improving Its Organization and Methods of Work', 85 AJIL (1991) 595; S. Villalpando, 'Le codificateur et le juge face à la responsabilité internationale de l'État: interaction entre la CDI et la CIJ dans la détermination des règles secondaires', 55 AFDI (2009) 39 at 50–51; W. Riphagen, 'State Responsibility: New Theories of Obligation in Interstate Relations', in R. MacDonald and O. Johnston (eds.), *The Structure and Process of International Law* (Martinus Nijhoff 1983) 587–588.

[132] YBILC 1980, Vol. I, p. 91, para. 11.

any reference to the Commission's draft text.[133] In *Armed Activities on the Territory of the Congo* (2005), too, the Court found that acts and omissions of the Uganda Peoples' Defence Forces (UPDF) and its soldiers were attributable to Uganda given that UPDF was a part of its armed forces and regardless of whether they acted contrary to the instructions given or exceeded their authority,[134] thereby accepting almost verbatim the rule reflected in article 7 of the Commission's articles on State responsibility (by now finally adopted) but making no express reference to it.[135] Nor did the Court refer to the articles on State responsibility in its judgment in *Dispute regarding Navigational and Related Rights* (2009), despite pronouncing in general terms on the international legal obligation incumbent upon States to cease wrongful conduct.[136] In the *Pulp Mills* judgment of the following year, the Court held that customary international law required States to undertake an environmental impact assessment where there is a risk that the relevant proposed industrial activity may have a significant adverse impact in a transboundary context,[137] apparently relying on – but not citing – article 7 of the Commission's draft articles on the prevention of transboundary harm from hazardous activities, "which would have supported the

[133] See also K. Keith, 'The International Law Commission's Work and the Shaping of International Law', in *Making Better International Law: The International Law Commission at 50* (United Nations 1998) 285 at 314 (observing that "in the case concerning *United States Diplomatic and Consular Staff in Tehran* and the case concerning *Military and Paramilitary Activities in and against Nicaragua (merits)* the Court based itself squarely upon the Commission's [unfinished, draft] conclusions on two basic aspects of the law of State responsibility, using almost identical terms to those employed by the Commission in order to deal with problems of immutability and circumstances precluding wrongfulness"); S. Scott, 'Codification of State Responsibility in International Law: A Review and Assessment', 9 *ASILS International Law Journal* (1985) 1 at 31–35.

[134] *Armed Activities on the Territory of the Congo (Democratic Republic of the Congo* v. *Uganda), Judgment, I.C.J. Reports 2005*, p. 242, paras. 213–214.

[135] See also P. Couvreur, 'The ICJ and the Implementation of the Law on State Responsibility', in *The International Court of Justice and the Effectiveness of International Law* (Brill Nijhoff 2016) 205 at 220.

[136] *Dispute regarding Navigational and Related Rights (Costa Rica* v. *Nicaragua), Judgment, I.C.J. Reports 2009*, p. 267, para. 148. President Tomka later confirmed that the Court did rely on the Commission's articles and added, almost apologetically, that "one explanation [for not citing them] might be the composition of the drafting committee. In any event, that was the only case in which he had not fully participated owing to health problems": YBILC 2012, Vol. I, p. 148, para. 110.

[137] *Pulp Mills on the River Uruguay (Argentina* v. *Uruguay), Judgment, I.C.J. Reports 2010*, p. 83, para. 204.

Court's conclusions"[138] and which was indeed referred to by Uruguay in its pleadings before it.

Several possible reasons exist for such deliberate omissions. First, as noted above, the Court's general tendency is to invoke mainly its own jurisprudence (and that of its predecessor) in support of its statements; this approach serves to explain the relatively rare references by it to other authorities.[139] The Court may also wish, perhaps, that a certain idea be seen to be its own: as one of its presidents once conceded, "judges were men just like others and they might, for example, want to differentiate themselves or to assert themselves as a body."[140] Yet another reason may be that the Court wishes to avoid constraining the Commission if its relevant work product has not yet been finalized. This appears to have been the case in *LaGrand* (2001), where the Court confirmed the possibility that a State might be required to offer assurances and guarantees of non-repetition; while such measures were envisaged in draft article 30 of the Commission's unfinished articles on State responsibility, the Court made no mention of the Commission's work on that subject.[141] President Guillaume later explained that

> [i]t was by no means from lack of respect that the Court had not cited the work of the Commission on non-repetition in its judgment ... The various special rapporteurs had taken different positions on the matter and the Commission itself had not taken a final position, having left the relevant article in abeyance pending the judgment of the Court.[142]

[138] Gaja, *supra* note 80, at pp. 41–42. At least one member of the Commission also found "elements" of the Commission's work "readily recognizable" in a previous Order given by the Court in this case on 13 July 2006: see YBILC 2006, Vol. I, p. 211, para. 2 (Pambou-Tchivounda).

[139] President Guillaume, for one, was "a proponent of autonomy and [of] not citing other bodies": M. Andenas, 'Reassertion and Transformation: From Fragmentation to Convergence in International Law', 46 GJIL (2015) 685 at 729. According to several accounts (on file with the author), President Guillaume was during his term in office thus not in favor of citing the Commission's output even in those instances when the Court agreed with it.

[140] YBILC 2000, Vol. I, p. 360, para. 24 (President Guillaume addressing the Commission and referring to judges generally in the context of discussing the question of cooperation among different international courts). Granted, this may well be the case where a proposition put forward by the Commission is not particularly novel.

[141] *LaGrand (Germany* v. *United States of America), Judgment, I.C.J. Reports 2001*, pp. 508–514, paras. 117–127; see also Couvreur, *supra* note 135, at p. 234.

[142] YBILC 2001, Vol. I, p. 213, para. 32. This was not the approach taken by the Court when citing article 33 of the draft articles on State responsibility in *Gabčíkovo-Nagymaros*: see *supra* note 45 and the accompanying text.

A further reason for not explicitly referring to a proposition adopted by the Commission when the Court has relied on it may be because the proposition is not broadly accepted as settled law. The Court, or at least some of its judges, may have reservations as to the customary status of a certain rule proposed by the Commission and are then unwilling to give it their blessing as a statement of law having a general application, even if they accept in a given case a result that is consistent with that rule. In *Questions relating to the Obligation to Prosecute or Extradite* (2012), for example, the Court referred only to its own jurisprudence in connection with the question of Belgium's ability to invoke the responsibility of another State for an alleged failure to comply with obligations *erga omnes*, without any reference to articles 42 and 48 of the Commission's articles on State responsibility that deal precisely with such a situation.[143] President Tomka later revealed that the reason for this was the desire to achieve consensus in drafting the judgment, as "one judge . . . had argued vehemently that article 48 of the articles on State responsibility did not reflect customary international law."[144]

Relatedly, the Court's reluctance to refer explicitly to the Commission's work may be because the proposition in question has only little support among States (who may consider its customary status debatable). This seems to have been the case when the words of article 41 in the Commission's draft articles on State responsibility,

[143] *Questions relating to the Obligation to Prosecute or Extradite (Belgium* v. *Senegal), Judgment, I.C.J. Reports 2012*, pp. 449–450, paras. 68–69. See also L. Crema, 'The ILC's New Way of Codifying International Law, the Motives Behind It, and the Interpretive Approach Best Suited to It', in P. Merkouris, J. Kammerhofer and N. Arajarvi (eds.), *The Theory, Practice, and Interpretation of Customary International Law* (CUP 2022) 161 at 179-180.

[144] YBILC 2012, Vol. I, p. 148, para. 109 (addressing the Commission and adding that that one judge "was a former member of the Commission" and noting that this is an exception to the fact that "[i]t was generally helpful to have former members of the Commission as members of the Court, since they tended to draw more on the work of the Commission"). President Tomka very likely referred to Judge Xue, who in any event appended a dissenting opinion on the relevant point but appears to have influenced the drafting of the majority's judgment (the desire for a broad consensus again playing its role); if that is indeed the case, it is interesting to think of this as an example of a former member of the Commission holding on, in The Hague, to opinions that he or she had voiced when in Geneva: see also Chapter 5, Section 1.A(i).

a "residue of the old concept of State crimes" that had been so controversial among States, were essentially quoted in the *Wall* advisory opinion but without actually attributing them to the articles.[145] Article 48 of the same articles, which was proposed by the Commission *de lege ferenda* and was similarly not adopted without criticism, was likewise endorsed by the Court only implicitly in the *Genocide case (Bosnia and Herzegovina* v. *Serbia and Montenegro)* (2007).[146] The Court made it clear in the compensation phase of the *Diallo* case (2012) that the sum awarded to Guinea in the exercise of diplomatic protection of Diallo was intended to provide reparation for the latter's injury,[147] but did not cite in support the "recommended practice" (clearly an attempt at progressive development of the law) included in the Commission's draft articles on diplomatic protection.[148] In such cases, the Court's abstention from referring expressly to the Commission, while at the same time essentially endorsing its position, does not cast doubt on the authority of the rule proposed by the Commission:[149] instead it entrenches that rule and confers upon it the status of positive international law. In this way, as one member of the Court has acknowledged, the Court is "part of the process of the norm's consolidation."[150]

145 See also Crawford, *supra* note 63, at p. 82. Bordin has suggested an alternative reason – that the Court was reluctant at that time to refer to the notion of peremptory norms upon which article 41 is based: F.L. Bordin, 'Reflections of Customary International Law: The Authority of Codification Conventions and ILC Draft Articles in International Law', 63 ICLQ (2014) 535 at 545, fn. 59.

146 *Application of the Convention on the Prevention and Punishment of the Crime of Genocide (Bosnia and Herzegovina* v. *Serbia and Montenegro), Judgment, I.C.J. Reports 2007*, p. 43, p. 104, para. 147; see also Crawford, *supra* note 63, at p. 78. President Tomka suggested with respect to the later judgment in the case concerning *Questions relating to the Obligation to Prosecute or Extradite* that "it was not always necessary to refer specifically to the number of the article but rather to its substance. A careful reading of the judgment . . . showed that the Court's views closely reflected the content of article 48 of the articles on State responsibility": YBILC 2012, Vol. I, p. 148, para. 109.

147 *Ahmadou Sadio Diallo (Republic of Guinea* v. *Democratic Republic of the Congo), Compensation, Judgment, I.C.J. Reports 2012*, p. 344, para. 57.

148 See also L. Condorelli, 'Protection diplomatique réussie et réparation due: une glose', in D. Alland et al (eds.), *Unity and Diversity of International Law: Essays in Honour of Professor Pierre-Marie Dupuy* (Brill 2014) 477 at 481. President Tomka has confirmed that the Court, in assessing the compensation claimed, took an approach consistent with that of the Commission: YBILC 2012, Vol. I, p. 143, para. 65.

149 Cf. Bordin, *supra* note 145, at p. 545.

150 Interview with member of the Court in April 2016, on file with the author.

C. Reference in Individual Opinions

If the Commission's work features quite often in the Court's decisions, even more extensive references to it may be found in individual opinions of the Court's judges. The extent to which individual judges refer to the Commission's output is remarkable not only for showing "how keenly Members of the Court follow" the work of the Commission,[151] but also because dissenting and separate opinions, as Crawford has observed more generally, often set out in more detail the workings of the Court and reflect its actual methods.[152] While taking stock of all such references falls outside the scope of the present study, pointing to even some of these opinions readily illustrates both the high regard paid by judges of the Court to the Commission's output and the comfort with which they refer to it.[153]

Individual opinions referred to the Commission's work long before a decision of the Court first did so in 1969. Already in 1950, for example, Judge Alvarez referred, in his dissenting opinion in the *Asylum* case, to a provision included in "the Declaration of the rights and duties of States which was drafted by the Codification Commission of the United

[151] Schwebel, *supra* note 8, at p. 504 (also noting, at p. 485, that "[w]hile the Court is characteristically cautious in making references to the work of the Commission, this certainly does not hold true for the separate and dissenting opinions of individual judges in relation to a particular case before the Court").

[152] J. Crawford, *Brownlie's Principles of Public International Law*, 9th ed. (OUP 2019) 40. As one clear example, in his Dissenting Opinion in *Application of the Convention on the Prevention and Punishment of the Crime of Genocide (Bosnia and Herzegovina* v. *Serbia and Montenegro)*, Judge Al-Khasawneh stated that "[i]n applying the effective control test, the Court followed Article 8 of the International Law Commission Articles on State Responsibility": see *supra* note 59. See also S. Rosenne, 'Codification Revisited after 50 Years', 2 MPYUNL (1998) 1 at 14 ("It is clear, for instance from Judge Schwebel's dissenting opinion in the 1995 judgment concerning *Maritime Delimitation and Territorial Questions between Qatar and Bahrain* (Jurisdiction and admissibility) that in its deliberations where a text originating in the ILC has been relevant, the Court has not passed over the commentaries").

[153] See also I. Sinclair, *The International Law Commission* (Grotius Publications 1987) 131 (suggesting that such frequent reference to the Commission's work in individual opinions "is not very surprising, since the records of the Commission are so extensive and the topics the Commissions has had under consideration are so wide-ranging that it is not difficult to buttress support for particular propositions of international law by reference to the Commission's deliberations"); Schwebel, *supra* note 8, at p. 485 ("Due to the extensive records of the Commission, and the wide range of topics the Commission has had under its consideration, it is not difficult to find support for a particular proposition of international law in the Commission's work").

Nations" just a year earlier during its very first session.[154] The Commission's work was again referred to by Judge Alvarez in his individual opinion in the *Fisheries* case (1951), when discussing the means by which the contemporary international law finds expression;[155] and in the dissenting opinion he appended to the Court's advisory opinion on *Effect of Awards of Compensation Made by the United Nations Administrative Tribunal* (1954), where he mentioned more broadly that the law "on maintenance of peace and the development of confidence and co-operation between States" was applied within the United Nations also "in the work of the Codification Commission in the preparation of regulations governing certain matters."[156] In the preliminary objections phase of the *South West Africa* cases (1962), it was judges Jessup, Spender, and Fitzmaurice who all referred to the still ongoing work of the Commission on the law of treaties (and to views of its special rapporteurs on the topic), albeit in support of different propositions they sought to sustain.[157] At the merits phase of the same cases (1966), Judge Tanaka's dissenting opinion referred both to the Commission's Draft Declaration on Rights and Duties of States (among "evidence" he listed for the interpretation and application of certain UN Charter provisions) and to its consideration of *jus cogens* as a category of international law.[158]

After the exceptional homage paid to the Commission's work in the Court's 1969 judgment in the *North Sea Continental Shelf* cases, dozens of references to the Commission's work would follow in individual opinions, judges citing the Commission's products in support of various arguments and sometimes devoting lengthy passages to describing (and commenting on) its views. Judge Schwebel, for example, referred to the Commission's work no fewer than thirteen times in his dissenting opinions in the two phases of the case concerning *Military and Paramilitary Activities in and against Nicaragua*, with regard to such matters as the law of treaties, the use of force, offenses against the peace and security of

[154] *Colombian-Peruvian Asylum Case, Judgment of November 20th 1950: I.C.J. Reports 1950*, p. 301.

[155] *Fisheries Case, Judgment of December 18th, 1951: I.C.J. Reports 1951*, p. 149.

[156] *Effect of awards of Compensation Made by the U.N. Administrative Tribunal, Advisory Opinion of July 13th, 1954: I.C.J. Reports 1954*, p. 70.

[157] *South West Africa Cases (Ethiopia* v. *South Africa; Liberia* v. *South Africa), Preliminary Objections, Judgment of 21 December 1962: I.C.J. Reports 1962*, pp. 402–404 and 407–410 (Separate Opinion of Judge Jessup); p. 475 (Joint Dissenting Opinion of Judge Spender and Judge Fitzmaurice).

[158] *South West Africa, Second Phase, Judgment, I.C.J. Reports 1966*, pp. 293, 298.

mankind, the rights and duties of States, and the law of State responsibility.[159] One of these references concerned what he termed "elemental aspects of accepted international law . . . illustrated in the draft articles on State Responsibility which my eminent colleague, Judge Ago, prepared and which the International Law Commission has adopted."[160] In another separate opinion that highlighted the personal ties uniting the Court and the Commission, Judge Jiménez de Aréchaga supported his assertion in the *Continental Shelf (Tunisia/Libyan Arab Jamahiriya)* case (1982) that the Court's interpretation of the concept of "natural prolongation" in the *North Sea Continental Shelf* judgment was consistent with the 1958 Convention on the Continental Shelf, by saying, inter alia, that this was "confirmed by the fact that several Members of the Court in 1969 had taken an active part in the work of the International Law Commission and the Geneva Conference, where these questions were discussed."[161] Judges of the Court, in their individual opinions, have also commented sometimes on the Commission more generally, for example by referring to it as being composed of "eminent jurists,"[162] and to its members as being "highly qualified internationally well-known legal scholars representing the main legal systems of the world."[163]

Some judges of the Court have referred in their individual opinions to their own past work as members of the Commission, again drawing attention to the personal links uniting the two organs.[164] To mention

[159] *Military and Paramilitary Activities in and against Nicaragua (Nicaragua* v. *United States of America), Jurisdiction and Admissibility, Judgment, I.C.J. Reports 1984*, p. 607; *Military and Paramilitary Activities in and against Nicaragua (Nicaragua* v. *United States of America), Merits, Judgment. I.C.J. Reports 1986*, p. 259.

[160] *Military and Paramilitary Activities in and against Nicaragua (Nicaragua* v. *United States of America), Jurisdiction and Admissibility, Judgment, I.C.J. Reports 1984*, p. 607, para. 74 (referring to draft article 27 and the commentary thereto in connection with the argument that the conduct of Honduras, Costa Rica, and El Salvador was in the nature of aid or assistance to the United States).

[161] *Continental Shelf (Tunisia/Libyan Arab Jamahiriya), Judgment, I.C.J. Reports 1982*, p. 113, para. 48 (Separate Opinion).

[162] *North Sea Continental Shelf, Judgment, I.C.J. Reports 1969*, p. 108 (Separate Opinion of Judge Ammoun).

[163] *Ibid*, at p. 177 (Dissenting Opinion of Judge Tanaka). Judge Azevedo noted already in 1949, in his individual opinion in *Reparation for Injuries*, that "in the appointment of Members of the International Court of Justice or of the new International Law Commission, much more attention is paid to personal qualities than to nationality": *Reparation for Injuries Suffered in the Service of the United Nations, Advisory Opinion: I.C.J. Reports 1949*, p. 194.

[164] See also Chapter 5, Section A.1(i).

but two examples, Judge Lauterpacht referred in his separate opinion in the case concerning *Certain Norwegian Loans* (1957) to a report on the law of treaties that he himself had submitted to the Commission as a Special Rapporteur in 1953 (if only to depart from the view expressed therein).[165] Judge Crawford, for his part, did not miss the opportunity to give another boost to the Commission's articles on State responsibility, which he as Special Rapporteur had brought to final adoption, in his dissenting opinion in the *Obligations concerning Negotiations relating to Cessation of the Nuclear Arms Race and to Nuclear Disarmament* cases (2016). Being well aware that the Court had hitherto found it difficult to endorse article 48 as reflecting a rule of customary international law,[166] Judge Crawford referred to the "established" rule that States can be parties to disputes about obligations the performance of which they have no specific material interest in, only to cite article 48 as an authority for this general proposition.[167] In addition, although the Court had found article 43 of those articles to be inapplicable to the cases in question, Judge Crawford seized the moment in order to comment on the scope and meaning of that article, including by interpreting the judgment of the Court referred to by the Commission in its commentary to the article.[168]

More recently still, judges Cançado Trindade, Robinson, and Sebutinde each referred to the Commission's work in separate opinions they appended to the Court's advisory opinion on *Legal Consequences of the Separation of the Chagos Archipelago from Mauritius in 1965*. Judge Sebutinde cited not only the view of the Commission, but also of some of its individual members, in support of her contention that the right to self-determination possessed the character of *jus cogens*; and she further

[165] *Case of Certain Norwegian Loans, Judgment of July 6th, 1957: I.C.J. Reports 1957*, p. 52.

[166] See *supra* note 144 and the accompanying text; see also Chapter 6, Section B.1.

[167] *Obligations concerning Negotiations relating to Cessation of the Nuclear Arms Race and to Nuclear Disarmament (Marshall Islands* v. *India), Jurisdiction and Admissibility, Judgment, I.C.J. Reports 2016*, p. 522, para. 21; *Obligations concerning Negotiations relating to Cessation of the Nuclear Arms Race and to Nuclear Disarmament (Marshall Islands* v. *United Kingdom), Preliminary Objections, Judgment, I.C.J. Reports 2016*, p. 1102, para. 22.

[168] *Obligations concerning Negotiations relating to Cessation of the Nuclear Arms Race and to Nuclear Disarmament (Marshall Islands* v. *India), Jurisdiction and Admissibility, Judgment, I.C.J. Reports 2016*, pp. 522–523, paras. 22–23; *Obligations concerning Negotiations relating to Cessation of the Nuclear Arms Race and to Nuclear Disarmament (Marshall Islands* v. *United Kingdom), Preliminary Objections, Judgment, I.C.J. Reports 2016*, pp. 1102–1103, paras. 23–24 (also noting, in a footnote, a view that he proposed to the Commission in this context and was rejected by it).

relied on a report of the Commission's Special Rapporteur on 'Peremptory norms of general international law (*jus cogens*)', published only a few months earlier, to sustain her finding that articles 53 and 64 of the Vienna Convention on the Law of Treaties were part of customary international law.[169] Judge Robinson saw no difficulty in referring to the Commission's still ongoing work on 'Peremptory norms of general international law (*jus cogens*)' either, citing reports of the Special Rapporteur (as well as the Commission's commentaries on the law of treaties and on State responsibility) in support of his own argument that the right to self-determination was a peremptory norm.[170] The views of individual members of the Commission were also cited in the Separate Opinion of Judge Cançado Trindade, again in support of the argument that the right to self-determination possessed the character of *jus cogens*.[171]

The high regard paid by judges of the Court to the Commission's output was again made evident when no less than six individual opinions appended to the Court's judgment in *Question of the Delimitation of the Continental Shelf beyond 200 Nautical Miles* (2023) made reference to the Commission's output on the topic 'Identification of customary international law'.[172] The case turned on the question whether, under customary international law, a State's entitlement to a continental shelf beyond 200 nautical miles from its baselines may extend within 200 nautical miles from the baselines of another State; endorsement of the Commission's guidance as to how such a question ought to be approached can be seen as a clear expression of confidence in the Commission's own ability to say authoritatively what the law is.[173]

[169] See *Legal Consequences of the Separation of the Chagos Archipelago from Mauritius in 1965, Advisory Opinion, I.C.J. Reports 2019*, pp. 284–285, paras. 28 (fn. 22) and 30.

[170] *Ibid*, at pp. 320–321, para. 73(a) and 73(b); he also referred to articles 40 and 41 of the Commission's articles on State responsibility, saying that these "would appear to reflect general international law" (at p. 326, para. 89).

[171] *Ibid*, at pp. 194–195, paras. 123–124.

[172] *Question of the Delimitation of the Continental Shelf between Nicaragua and Colombia beyond 200 nautical miles from the Nicaraguan Coast (Nicaragua* v. *Colombia)*, Judgment of 13 July 2023, Separate Opinion of Judge Xue, paras. 17–18, 47; Separate Opinion of Judge Iwasawa, paras. 11, 14; Dissenting Opinion of Judge Tomka, fn. 70; Dissenting Opinion of Judge Robinson, para. 9; Dissenting Opinion of Judge Charlesworth, para. 26, fns. 15, 39; Dissenting Opinion of Judge ad hoc Skotnikov, para. 16.

[173] The Commission's guidance was itself based largely on the Court's jurisprudence: see Chapter 4, Section A.1.

D. Justification for Reliance?

The Court's readiness to consult and refer to the Commission's output raises the question as to the basis for such reliance, especially when bearing in mind the prescriptions of the Court's Statute as regards its competence in deciding disputes that are brought before it. Article 38.1 (*d*) of the Statute, as already noted,[174] directs the Court to apply, as subsidiary means for determining the law (including customary international law), judicial decisions or "the teachings of the most highly qualified publicists of the various nations." Does the Commission's output fall within the ambit of the latter formulation?

The notion of "subsidiary means" as enshrined in the Court's Statute predates the establishment of the Commission. This is so even if the idea and relevance of codification, as discussed in Chapter 2, were not lost on the members of the Advisory Committee of Jurists who drafted that Statute. At least some members of the Committee of Seventeen that laid out the plan for the Commission, however, did consider that scientific restatements by it might be regarded as "teachings" within the meaning of article 38.1(*d*).[175] This accorded with the contemporaneous view of Jennings, a future judge and President of the Court, who submitted that "[a] carefully compiled restatement of the law by an international body of jurists working under the auspices of the United Nations might well win for itself a special position in the ranks of such evidences of the law."[176] The 1949 'Survey of International Law in Relation to the Work of Codification of the International Law Commission,' published by the UN Secretary-General in advance of the Commission's first session, similarly suggested that texts produced by the Commission but not turned into

[174] See Chapter 2, Section D.1.

[175] See, for example, UN Doc. A/AC.10/SR.10 (23 May 1947), p. 5 (Bartoš). Gilberto Amado (Brazil), who was a member of the Committee of Seventeen and later served on the Commission, suggested in his latter capacity, during the Commission's first session, that the Commission "was in a better position than the codifiers of The Hague or Geneva, since it had more time at its disposal and since there would, as a result, be more continuity in its work. Further, although it also must seek to have its drafts accepted by States, in order to give them the form of international conventions, there were other ways open to it. Its reports could be approved by the General Assembly and would thus not fail to influence States when they came to deal with them. If the Assembly merely took note of them, they would still have a value as subsidiary means for the determination of rules of law, according to sub-paragraph (d) of the first paragraph of Article 38 of the Statute of the International Court of Justice": YBILC 1949, p. 18, para. 30.

[176] R.Y. Jennings, 'The Progressive Development of International Law and Its Codification', 24 BYIL (1947) 301 at 308.

conventions "would be at least in the category of writings of the most qualified publicists, referred to in article 38 of the Statute of the International Court of Justice as a subsidiary source of law to be applied by the Court."[177] Yet the *Survey* went on to say that "[m]ost probably their authority would be considerably higher. For they will be the product not only of scholarly research, individual and collective, aided by the active co-operation of Governments, of national and international scientific bodies, and the resources of the United Nations. They will be the result of the deliberations and of the approval of the International Law Commission."[178]

The Commission itself remained unable, in its work on the topic 'Identification of customary international law', to agree on whether its output might properly be labeled as "teachings": some members (including the Special Rapporteur) supported such a classification, while others considered this position as "reductive" and argued that the Commission's output had a different, "special status," not least because of its contribution to the Court's work.[179] Divergent views have been put forward in the literature as well: while some have argued that "[t]hat the work of the ILC qualifies under the terms of Article 38(1)(d) should be clear,"[180] others have suggested that "there is something inappropriate" about such

[177] UN Doc. A/CN.4/1/Rev.1: 'Survey of International Law in Relation to the Work of Codification of the International Law Commission: Preparatory Work within the Purview of Article 18, Paragraph 1, of the Statute of the International Law Commission (Memorandum submitted by the Secretary-General)' (1949), p. 16.

[178] *Ibid* (adding that "[o]utside the sphere of international judicial settlement they will be of considerable potency in shaping scientific opinion and the practice of Governments"). For some interesting comments made on this matter in the UN General Assembly's Sixth Committee following the Commission's first session in 1949, see Y.-L. Liang, 'The First Session of the International Law Commission: Review of Its Work by the General Assembly', 44 AJIL (1950) 527 at 538–540.

[179] See the Special Rapporteur's summary of the debate on this issue at YBILC 2015, Vol. I, p. 72, para. 55; see also Wood, *supra* note 99, at paras. 97–102. A clearer position may be adopted by the Commission in its work on 'Subsidiary means for the determination of rules of international law': see A/78/10: 'Report of the International Law Commission on the Work of Its Seventy-Fourth Session' (24 April–2 June and 3 July–4 August 2023), p. 83, para. 14 of the commentary to provisionally adopted draft conclusion 2.

[180] Berman, *supra* note 6, at p. 16. See also, for example, B.A. Chigara, 'The Administration of International Law in National Courts and the Legitimacy of International Law', 17 *International Criminal Law Review* (2017) 909 at 913 (describing the Commission as "the institutional embodiment of the publicist under Article 38(1)[(d)] of the Statute of the ICJ"); Peil, *supra* note 6, at pp. 136–161; S. Sivakumaran, 'The Influence of Teachings of Publicists on the Development of International Law', 66 ICLQ (2017) 1 at 5; A. Pellet, 'L'adaptation du droit international aux besoins changeants de la société internationale', 329 RdC (2007) 42.

classification, in part because "the membership of the Commission goes beyond the ranks of such highly qualified publicists, and ... has a collegiate character which confers on its work much greater authority than that which would attach to its members as mere individuals."[181]

The Court, for its part, does not seem to have concerned itself with this formal question when invoking the work of the Commission.[182] Judge Shi was therefore rather ambiguous when telling members of the Commission in 1997 that the Court "viewed the draft articles produced by the Commission and the reports prepared for it as sources *at least as authoritative as* the writings of the most eminent publicists."[183] President Schwebel observed, more specifically, that "[i]t is difficult to confine [the Commission's] relevance to any one of the four sources [which the Court is bound to apply in accordance with article 38], though I have yet to hear anyone suggest that the work of the Commission is a fifth source of its own."[184] Other judges, too, have considered the question to be neither

181 Watts, *supra* note 6, at pp. 14, 15. Bishop has suggested that the work of the Commission is a "separate source of international law" other than those listed in article 38 of the Court's Statute, arguing that "[t]hrough its official and multi-national character, the texts agreed upon by the ILC would seem to merit special mention as a source": W.W. Bishop, 'General Course of Public International Law', 115 RdC (1965) 245 (adding, however, that "[a]t the very least the joint efforts of the members of this Commission should rank on a par with the 'teachings of the publicists of the various nations' [referred to in article 38.1(*d*) of the Statute]"). See also, for example, Bordin, *supra* note 143, at p. 559 ("[c]-odification conventions and ILC draft articles are not, of course, to be assimilated with custom, and their characterization as subsidiary sources remains technically correct. And yet, the tendency to associate these texts with customary international law makes it somewhat simplistic to treat them as mere evidence of State practice or as the work of publicists").

182 See also Watts, *supra* note 6, at p. 14 ("it is by no means that Article 38 attempts to identify the sources of international law (it nowhere uses the term 'sources'); even if it does, it is not certain that the list of categories in Article 38 of the Statute is an exhaustive enumeration of those sources ... It may therefore not matter unduly if the International Law Commission's work does not fit tidily within those categories ... the Court has not hesitated to invoke the work of the International Law Commission where it seemed appropriate to do so, without concerning itself with the formal question of how that work might fall within Article 38 of the Court's Statute").

183 YBILC 1997, Vol. I, p. 214, para. 64 (addressing the Commission; emphasis added). In addressing the Commission again several years later, as President of the Court, Judge Shi was no clearer, saying that "*[i]f* the Commission's work was only a subsidiary means of determining international law, according to Article 38 of the Statute of the International Court of Justice, its very high quality had undoubtedly made it one of the most reliable, and relied upon, of those subsidiary means": YBILC 2003, p. 163, para. 4 (emphasis added).

184 Schwebel, *supra* note 6, at p. 163. Perhaps one such suggestion was made by Judge Alvarez, who submitted in 1951 that among the "new elements on which the new

important nor useful. Several of them have stated that there was simply no need to try to fit the Commission's output within the confines of article 38.1, given that it was a matter of common sense that the Court is free to have recourse to any evidence it may deem useful in determining the law.[185] For them, the Commission's products may well offer quality and clarity of considerable utility, especially when the Commission has had the chance to "subject these same topics [that come before the Court] to minute, critical and objective scrutiny from all relevant angles before making its recommendations ... [and] as part of its standard working method ... factors in the observations of States on its drafts as they evolve."[186] At times, the Commission's output may be "the only game in town" in connection with a certain legal issue, making it both difficult to ignore and potentially highly influential in affecting how judges may conceive of that issue whatever the pedigree that aligns it to the Court's

international law, still in the process of formation, will be founded" beyond conventions and customary international law are "especially the decisions of the International Court of Justice" and "the works of the Codification Commission set up by the United Nations": *Fisheries Case, Judgment of December 18th, 1951: I.C.J. Reports 1951*, p. 149 (Separate Opinion). See also the Dissenting Opinion of Judge *ad hoc* Mahiou in *Ahmadou Sadio Diallo (Republic of Guinea* v. *Democratic Republic of the Congo), Merits, Judgment, I.C.J. Reports 2010*, p. 828 ("This viewpoint, widely accepted within the doctrine, is also taken up in the draft Articles adopted by the International Law Commission in 2006 ...").

185 Interviews with several members of the Court in April 2016, on file with the author. When pressed, the judges did say that, if need be, it would be possible to fit the Commission's output under the heading of "teachings." Some judges do seem to have categorized the Commission's output as such when advancing various arguments in their individual opinions: see, for example, the Declaration of Judge Guillaume in *Dispute regarding Navigational and Related Rights (Costa Rica* v. *Nicaragua), Judgment, I.C.J. Reports 2009*, p. 294, para. 9; and the Declaration of Judge *ad hoc* Van den Wyngaert in *Arrest Warrant of 11 April 2000 (Democratic Republic of the Congo v. Belgium), Provisional Measures, Order of 8 December 2000, I.C.J. Reports 2000*, p. 232, para. 7, fn. 14.

186 Schwebel, *supra* note 6, at p. 163. See also UN Doc. A/CN.4/SR.3548: 'Provisional Summary Record of the Commission's 3548th Meeting' (22 July 2021), p. 10 (President Donoghue explaining that "[a]lthough the Court did not cite scholarship in its judgments, it did cite the Commission's outputs, which, because of how the Commission was comprised, the role that it played in the United Nations system, the diversity of its membership and the deliberative and collaborative methodology that it followed, enjoyed a different status, despite their apparent similarities to other types of analyses"); J. Dugard, 'How Effective Is the International Law Commission in the Development of International Law? A Critique of the International Law Commission on the Occasion of Its Fiftieth Anniversary', 23 SAYIL (1998) 34 at 38 (observing that the Commission's drafts are "thoroughly researched and carefully worded" and that "[t]his explains why the International Court of Justice has had no hesitation in relying upon [it]").

Statute.[187] Such pragmatic views are reminiscent of the approach taken as long ago as in the *Lotus* case, in the course of which the Court's predecessor observed that

> in the fulfilment of its task of itself ascertaining what the international law is, it has not confined itself to a consideration of the arguments put forward, but has included in its researches all precedents, teachings and facts to which it had access and which might possibly have revealed the existence of one of the principles of international law [that might be of relevance].[188]

In identifying rules of customary international law, in particular, the work of the Commission has often been "the best and most expedient evidence available," giving definition to a sometimes amorphous State practice and providing "for a much more comprehensive examination of a rule of customary international law than is possible by the Court in the context of a judicial proceeding."[189] It has, especially when based on copious research and input from States, enabled the Court to avoid carrying out an inductive examination of custom's constituent elements on its own and afforded it a most valuable ability to check the pulse of States – its primary stakeholders – as to their possible acceptance of the

187 Interview with member of the Court in April 2016, on file with the author. Gaja explained the Court's frequent reference to the Commission's articles on State responsibility in very much these terms: *supra* note 19, at p. 11. See also D.D. Caron, 'The ILC Articles on State Responsibility: The Paradoxical Relationship between Form and Authority', 96 AJIL (2002) 857 at 866 ("when there is a 'legal vacuum' of authority relevant on an issue, courts and arbitral panels will turn to whatever is available ... In that situation, a set of articles adopted by the ILC will be quite influential, perhaps even more influential than a treaty").

188 *The Case of the S.S. "Lotus", P.C.I.J., Series A*, No. 10 (1927), p. 31.

189 Tomka, *supra* note 38, at pp. 5, 10–11. See also Schwebel, *supra* note 8, at p. 485 ("the Commission may have more effective means to determine the existence of State practice than the Court"); YBILC 2013, Vol. I, p. 87, para. 19 (President Tomka telling the Commission that "[l]acking the time or resources to carry out inductive studies on State practice in all cases, the Court welcomed the Commission's commentaries, which it found to be an extremely important resource when it was establishing the existence of customary international law"); UN Doc. A/CN.4/SR.3380: 'Provisional Summary Record of the Commission's 3380th Meeting' (25 July 2017), p. 11. (President Abraham addressing the Commission in saying that "[w]hat was important for the Court was the Commission's role in clarifying customary international law and to be able to refer to the Commission's work insofar as it reflected that area of international law"). Another judge has similarly said that the Commission's output offers the "best available and widest evidence of State practice and *opinio juris*": interview with member of the Court in April 2016, on file with the author.

rule in question.[190] As one judge stated, "the Court needs places to go to for propositions on customary international law. The Commission interacts with States, which is very important. It has been reasonably systematic over time in its approach to codification and is a reliable, relatively non-partisan source."[191] The "increasing relevance of codification" for the Court's jurisprudence on customary international law has indeed been attributed chiefly to the Commission's texts.[192]

The Commission's tendency to avoid labeling its pronouncements as either codification or progressive development has proven highly useful to the Court also in those cases where it has sought to push the envelope of positive law, in that citing the Commission's output in support of its positions has enabled the Court to make those positions appear more rooted. At the same time, the argument that recourse to the Commission's output "does not so much owe to any form of reverence . . . by the Court for its 'little sister' as it does to the convenience of hiding behind the Commission's work" so as not to appear as an international legislator (when

[190] For the observation made already in 1930, that the carefully considered opinions of governments received in response to attempts at codification is a result that "[n]o private writer could ever have achieved . . . this collation of various views is obviously the first step towards reaching that measure of agreement upon which any codification must rest," see H.A. Smith, 'Codification of International Law', 12 *Journal of Comparative Legislation and International Law* (1930) 131 at 132.

[191] Interview with member of the Court in April 2016, on file with the author. In the *North Sea Continental Shelf* cases, Judge Ammoun made it a point to note that "all nations are called upon to sit" on the Commission; and Judge Tanaka referred to it as "representing the main legal systems of the world": see, respectively, *North Sea Continental Shelf, Judgment, I.C.J. Reports 1969*, p. 133 and p. 174. Judge Gaja (writing in his private capacity) has said that "draft articles adopted by the Commission may be considered, at least to a certain extent, as a first approximation to the current appraisal by States of the applicable rules": *supra* note 80, at 41. Abi-Saab said in the seminar on the Commission that "My experience on the bench bears out the conclusion that, when judges are faced with the possibility of a legal vacuum, they will go to the greatest lengths to avoid that result. They will search for anything out of which they might construct a conclusion. They will hang on to whatever they can find and will even fabricate title for the propositions that they adopt. If they have in front of them an instrument which has been very carefully negotiated and drafted and which has been widely accepted by States, they will hang on to it like a lifeboat in a storm. Whatever theoretical explanations we may concoct to explain their behaviour and to justify their conclusions, this phenomenon remains a fact of legal life": G. Abi-Saab, in *Making Better International Law: The International Law Commission at 50* (United Nations 1998) 83.

[192] Tomka, *supra* note 38, at pp. 1–24.

it does effectively act as one)[193] is too sweeping. In particular, it fails to appreciate not only those instances where the Court has referred to the Commission in other situations,[194] but also the personal links and shared sense of mission that unite the two organs.[195] Furthermore, as some of its judges have observed, the Court may well be expected to cite the Commission's work when one or both of the parties to a case have referred to it, or simply by virtue of its formal status as an organ of the General Assembly.[196]

E. Conclusion

The growing availability of texts produced by the Commission has had a profound impact on the Court's jurisprudence, in that the rules formulated and refined by the Commission have repeatedly served as "a guide to judges adjudicating in specific cases."[197] As we have seen, the Court has invoked the Commission's work as evidence of the state of international law not only when seeking authoritative explanations of what certain treaties have meant, but also in support of its findings as to

193 A. Pellet and D. Müller, 'Article 38', in A. Zimmerman et al (eds.), *The Statute of the International Court of Justice: A Commentary*, 3rd ed. (OUP 2019) 819 at 915, MN 231 (my translation from French).

194 See also Villalpando, *supra* note 131, at p. 54 ("Pourtant, il ne paraît pas y avoir de critères définis à cet égard: la Cour, par exemple, semble récemment employer le projet d'articles comme un moyen simple et rapide de determination des règles en matière d'attribution, bien que sa jurisprudence puisse tout aussi bien lui permettre d'identifier les mêmes critères; en revanche, elle continue de donner plus d'importance à ses propres précédents qu'au projet au sujet des conséquences du fait illicite. De plus, l'autorité inconditionnelle que certains arrêts semblent attribuer à ce projet dans certaines hypothèses est relativisée par les nombreux cas dans lesquels la Cour semble contourner la codification de la Commission").

195 See Chapters 5 and 7.

196 Interviews with several members of the Court in April 2016, on file with the author. See also YBILC 2006, Vol. I, p. 217, para. 47 (President Higgins telling members of the Commission more generally that "as part of the United Nations systems, the Court started from the assumption that all United Nations materials would be useful. The truth was, however, that some were more useful than others").

197 YBILC 1969, Vol. I, p. 70, para. 5 (President Bustamante y Rivero addressing the Commission); see also YBILC 1979, Vol. I, p. 65, para. 10 (President Waldock addressing the Commission in saying that "the Commission had helped to point the way for the Court on such matters as the continental shelf and certain aspects of the law of treaties"); YBILC 2003, Vol. I, p. 163, para. 7 (President Shi addressing the Commission in saying that "[t]he Commission's codification of the rules of State responsibility had been an invaluable guide to the Court when it had dealt with complex issues"); Higgins, *supra* note 64, at p. 2.

customary international law, including when the Commission's pronouncements, relied upon as codification of established rules, were clearly in the nature of progressive development. The Commission's legal reasoning has also been relied on more broadly, which again affected how the Court has viewed and decided a number of the legal questions put to it. The remarkable extent of this recurrent practice becomes ever clearer when considering all those instances where the Court has consulted the Commission's work but has chosen not to make such recourse explicit.

The great weight attributed to the Commission's texts – whether as "teachings" within the meaning of article 38.1(*d*) or otherwise – transcends any auxiliary role envisaged for materials on which the Court might rely in the determination of rules of international law.[198] This has certainly been the case when the Commission's unfinished drafts, or other of its pronouncements not yet having earned the imprimatur of States, have been invoked as authoritative restatements of customary international law notwithstanding their formal status or uncertain provenance. In such instances (of which the Commission is well aware[199]), the Court has not merely applied the law, but has assisted in its consolidation, the Commission's abandonment of the distinction between codification and progressive development affording it a creative discretion to say what the law is. This synergistic interaction has over time made it increasingly clear that it was no longer accurate to consider that the Commission can only accomplish what States want it to.

[198] See also Schwebel, *supra* note 8, at 504.

[199] See, for example, YBILC 1979, Vol. II, Part One, pp. 126–127, paras. 1–2; YBILC 2001, Vol. II, Part Two, p. 55, para. 4 of the commentary to draft article 12.

4

"An Inexhaustible Treasury of Experience": The Court's Influence on the Commission's Work

The Court's utilization of the work of the Commission is not a one-way affair. Even more visible is the influence of the Court's judgments and opinions on the Commission's work, which has indeed been profound. The output of the Commission, together with the reports by its special rapporteurs and thousands of pages of recorded debates, make clear that in the course of determining and developing the rules of international law, the Commission's first recourse is always to the Court's jurisprudence.[1] This case-law, no matter how advanced in age and whether or not the Court had adjusted or expatiated its underlying reasoning, has been meticulously digested by the Commission, treated as authoritative, and often serves as the basis for the Commission's propositions of law. In Yasseen's memorable words at the Commission, "[t]he cases of the International Court were an inexhaustible treasury of experience [for the Commission,] and were of great value in drawing up rules of international law."[2] The definite impact of that jurisprudence on the formation of legal opinion in the Commission extends, moreover, to the terminology adopted by it and to its program of work more generally; it may also be seen in the exceptional care taken by the Commission to

[1] See also YBILC 1968, Vol. I, p. 162, para. 21 (Sir Humphry Waldock); YBILC 1999, Vol. I, p. 127, para. 38 (Chairman Galicki observing that "[t]he importance of the Court's jurisprudence for the Commission's work could not be overestimated"). For the recognition by a member of the Commission that "[t]he Court's jurisprudence has implications way beyond the binding effects upon the States that appear before it . . . One effect may be seen in the work of the International Law Commission, which pays close attention to the Court's jurisprudence when engaging in the Commission's mandate to codify and progressively develop international law," see S.D. Murphy, 'What a Difference a Year Makes: The International Court of Justice's 2012 Jurisprudence', 4 JIDS (2013) 539 at 548.

[2] YBILC 1968, Vol. I, p. 162, para. 11 (adding that "[t]he International Court of Justice applied the rules of international law and the International Law Commission helped to draw them up, but on several occasions the Commission had found passages in the judgments of the Court which provided excellent formulations for rules of international law").

preserve the Court's authority and to promote its mission. All these elements will now be examined in turn.

A. Endorsing the Court's Pronouncements

The Commission's Statute refers to judicial decisions as "relevant data" for any exercise of codification, and to decisions of international courts more specifically among the "evidence of customary international law."[3] This requires the Commission merely to consult such jurisprudence (along with other evidence, namely, practice, treaties, and doctrine); yet from the outset, it has been clear that the decisions of the Court – more than any other judicial decisions and indeed any other material – carried far greater weight. The tone was set as early as in the Commission's first session, when its Chairman Hudson (formerly a judge of the PCIJ) successfully set aside opposition to a certain draft provision by asserting that it "had been taken from an advisory opinion of the Permanent Court of International Justice, the authority of which could not be challenged."[4] A working paper presented by Hudson in the following year suggested, in defining how a rule of customary international law may be said to have come into existence, that "[o]f course the presence of each of these elements [that constitute customary international law] is to be established (*doit être constaté*) as a fact by a competent international

[3] Statute of the International Law Commission (1947), as amended, article 20(a) and article 24, respectively. See also YBILC 1950, Vol. II, p. 368, para. 30 (the Commission explaining that "including judicial decisions on questions of international law among the evidences of customary international law . . . may be defended logically . . . for such decisions, particularly those by international courts, may formulate and apply principles and rules of customary international law. Moreover, the practice of a State may be indicated by the decisions of its national courts"). The *Handbook on the International Court of Justice* published by the Court itself recalls that "[t]he Court's role is effectively institutionalized in the Statute of the United Nations International Law Commission, which provides for the Commission to submit its draft articles to the Assembly together with a commentary containing an adequate presentation of precedents and other relevant data, including 'judicial decisions'. As can be seen from the Commission's drafts, decisions of the ICJ take pride of place in its presentation of relevant judicial decisions": *Handbook on the International Court of Justice* (2019), available at <www.icj-cij.org/files/publications/handbook-of-the-court-en.pdf>, p. 100.

[4] YBILC 1949, p. 105, para. 7 (referring, in the context of the draft Declaration on Rights and Duties of States, to the rule that a State may not invoke provisions in its constitution or its laws as an excuse for failure to perform this duty to carry out in good faith its international obligations, later incorporated in article 13 of the draft Declaration). At the Commission's third session, Hudson again stated that "the judgments of the Court were accepted as authoritative": YBILC 1951, Vol. I, p. 142, paras. 89–90.

authority."[5] He soon made it clear, at the plenary debate, that "what he had in mind was the International Court of Justice,"[6] and virtually all members of the Commission concurred.[7] When the role of judicial decisions in the determination of rules of customary international law came up for reconsideration some seventy years later (as part of the work on the topic 'Identification of customary international law'), the Commission's conclusion on the matter made express mention of the Court, "in recognition of the significance of its case law and its particular position as the only standing international court of general jurisdiction."[8]

To be sure, the Court's decisions are by no means the only source considered and referred to by the Commission. Relevant practice and doctrine are surveyed for each topic under examination; governmental input is always encouraged; and even scientific expertise has been sought on occasion. The Commission also studies (and often cites) the decisions of other courts and tribunals, as it is indeed required to do, and is well aware that there is no formal hierarchy among international judicial bodies. The fact remains, however, that no "evidence" of the law is ever relied upon with the comfort and reverence reserved for decisions of the Court, which the Commission at one point tellingly depicted as "the supreme world tribunal."[9] While the degree to which the Court has influenced the work of the Commission has naturally turned on whether the subject matter of its case-law has coincided with a topic under the consideration of the Commission,[10] and even though the Commission does derive its propositions also from State practice and from general

5 YBILC 1950, Vol. II, p. 26, para. 11.

6 YBILC 1950, Vol. I, p. 6, para. 39.

7 *Ibid*, at para. 40 (also recording that only Scelle "felt that national courts of justice were equally competent, since any court could establish the existence of custom"). Surprisingly, no member of the Commission suggested that the Commission itself may be that "competent international authority."

8 YBILC 2018, Vol. II, Part Two, p. 109, para. 4 of the commentary to draft conclusion 13. The Special Rapporteur for the topic, Sir Michael Wood, had earlier said that "decisions of international courts . . . were of particular significance, especially those of the International Court of Justice as the principal judicial organ of the United Nations": YBILC 2015, Vol. I, p. 42, para. 36. On the classification of the Court's decisions as "subsidiary means" for the determination of rules of international law, see Section B.1 as well as Chapter 7.

9 YBILC 1980, Vol. II, Part Two, p. 87, para. 9 (commentary to the Commission's draft articles on the law of treaties between States and international organizations or between international organizations, as adopted on first reading).

10 See also S.M. Schwebel, 'The Inter-active Influence of the International Court of Justice and the International Law Commission', in C.A. Armas Barea et al (eds.), *Liber Amicorum 'In Memoriam' of Judge José María Ruda* (Kluwer Law International 2000)

legal ideas, the general sentiment is indeed that, as one member observed, "decisions of the International Court of Justice . . . are probably the most widely used source for [the Commission's] draft texts."[11]

The heavy reliance placed by the Commission on the Court's case-law owes, first and foremost, to the Court's position as the principal judicial organ of the United Nations.[12] That position entails for the Court an undeniable authority to say what the law is, and commands the respect of other United Nations organs, including the Commission, not least for purposes of systemic consistency. In addition, at least for some Commission members, decisions of the Court are themselves evidence of State practice having "particular value as being objective appreciations of the practice of States on the points which they were called upon to deal with."[13] Earthlier considerations bear mention as well: First, it is more convenient for the Commission to be able to rely on a limited number of cases than to undertake a thorough inductive enquiry into the practice

479 at 480. See also Section B.3, which explains that the Court's decisions have also impacted the Commission's work program.

11 Tladi's summary of the Commission's debate on his fourth report on Peremptory norms of international law (*jus cogens*) during the Commission's 3465th meeting on May 16, 2019, a recording of which may be accessed at <https://conf.unog.ch/digitalrecordings/index.html?guid=public/12.0110/AB3C35F1-50A2-4727-A709-96FAF4A3900D_10h07&position=0> (adding, in response to the comments of another member, that "[t]his is my seventh year on the Commission and I have attended all but maybe 7 plenaries and it is the first time that I have heard that there is too much reliance on the ICJ"). See also A/CN.4/SR.3639: 'Provisional Summary Record of the Commission's 3639th Meeting' (18 July 2023), p. 6 (Mr Fife saying that "[a]s a new member of the Commission, he had been struck by the number of references made to decisions of the Court in the Commission's internal discussions"); YBILC 2007, Vol. I, p. 121, para. 1 (Brownlie observing that "the Court's work had special relevance for the work of the Commission"). Bennouna, as a member of the Commission, had noted in the same spirit that when the Court was suffering from difficult working conditions it was also "the Commission [that] suffered the consequences because it referred to the Court's jurisprudence": YBILC 1997, Vol. I, p. 215, para. 74 (responding to Judge Shi's depiction of the financial difficulties encountered by the Court).

12 See also Murphy, *supra* note 1 (suggesting that the Commission's close attention to the Court's jurisprudence may be explained by the fact that "especially given the Court's stature as the judicial organ of the United Nations . . . in a world of limited international jurisprudence it is inevitable that the Court's reasoning will impact in new and different ways the development of international law").

13 YBILC 1964, Vol. I, p. 86, para. 69 (Sir Humphrey Waldock); see YBILC 1968, Vol. I, p. 162, para. 21 (Sir Humphrey Waldock explaining the Commission's primary recourse to the Court's decision in that the Commission's work is "based on the practice of States and that had to be interpreted in the light of the Court's findings"). Simma observed that members of the Commission have sometimes been speaking of State practice when they had "referred really to the practice of ICJ": YBILC 1999, Vol. I, p. 211, para. 34.

and *opinio juris* of almost two hundred States.[14] Second, as one member of the Commission has put it, "[w]e cannot just make it all up, and it really is the best we have got."[15] Finally, the Commission's adherence to the Court's pronouncements also derives from the concern that diverging from a position adopted by the Court would cast a doubt over the Commission's own output. As another member has said, for the Commission "to go beyond the judgment of the Court into the realm of the progressive development of the law ... would give rise to even greater objections than those levelled against any objectionable decision of the Court. It might also invite retaliation by the Court, which could result in instability of the law."[16]

The close attention paid by the Commission to the Court's jurisprudence is evident in all stages of its work, on almost any topic of its choice. Where relevant, decisions of the Court take pride of place in preliminary surveys included in proposals for topics that the Commission may take up, and sometimes (as elaborated below) serve as impetus for such proposals in the first place. The reports of the Commission's special rapporteurs, too, "clearly [show] how much its work had been inspired by the Court's decisions,"[17] as special rapporteurs habitually take account of all relevant pronouncements by the Court and closely model their proposals on the Court's *dicta*.[18] President Tomka has indeed explained that "the work of the Court provided a solid basis for Special Rapporteurs and the International Law Commission to codify customary international law."[19] Ago similarly said – after recognizing more broadly that "the

[14] Interview with member of the Commission in July 2014, on file with the author.

[15] Interview with member of the Commission in May 2015, on file with the author.

[16] YBILC 1955, Vol. I, p. 203, para. 20 (Amado). On disagreements between the Court and the Commission, see Chapter 6.

[17] YBILC 1968, Vol. I, p. 162, para. 21 (Sir Humphrey Waldock). See also YBILC 2012, Vol. I, p. 146, para. 92 (President Tomka addressing the Commission in saying generally that "the Commission had studied carefully the judgments of the Permanent Court of International Justice and the International Court of Justice, with special rapporteurs taking them into account when drafting various proposals").

[18] See, for example, YBILC 1954, Vol. I, p. 158, para. 42 (François, Special Rapporteur on the topic 'Régime of the high seas', clarifying that a paragraph in his proposed article on passage of warships "had been added to take into account the ruling of the International Court of Justice in the *Corfu Channel* case"). Similarly, García Amador, as Special Rapporteur on State responsibility, noted that he added a paragraph to his draft Sixth Report "in order to incorporate the rule laid down by the International Court of Justice in the *Nottebohm* case": YBILC 1961, Vol. II, p. 53.

[19] P. Tomka, 'Remarks', 106 PASIL (2012) 195 (adding that that work also "provided support for the views of the Commission").

work of the International Court of Justice was extremely useful to the International Law Commission" – that "[a]s Special Rapporteur for the draft on State responsibility, he had been able to appreciate the need to refer to the [judgments] and advisory opinions of the International Court of Justice."[20]

In the Commission's debates, recourse to the Court's case-law is a matter of course. The thousands of pages recording these debates are replete with references to the Court's decisions and make readily apparent the exceptional respect held within the Commission for the Court and its pronouncements. As President Schwebel recalled, "[t]he importance accorded to the Court's jurisprudence in the individual reports of rapporteurs is reflected in the discussions among members of the Commission. During meetings of the Commission, members have often cited cases of the Court mentioned in the report under discussion."[21] Indeed, pointing to a judgment of the Court in support of a certain view is considered a sort of a trump card, "proof" of the validity of a legal argument.[22] As a case in point, Verdross defended in plenary the position that responsibility operated as between States, and not as between a State and an individual, by suggesting that this principle "formed part of the general international law as recognized by the highest judicial authority in the world, the International Court of Justice."[23] More recently, Sir Michael Wood shrugged off skepticism about the possible existence of a bilateral rule of customary international law by simply pointing out that such a view had been explicitly rejected in the *Right of Passage* case.[24] Nolte similarly deflected criticism made against proposals he put forward

[20] YBILC 1968, Vol. I, p. 162, para. 17.

[21] Schwebel, *supra* note 10, at p. 481 (adding that "[t]he same is true with respect to the Commission's reports to the General Assembly which are a reflection of those reports and the Commission's discussions and drafts"). One example of the remarkable extent of references to the Court's case-law may be found in a plenary debate on the topic 'Identification of customary international law', during which Huang felt compelled to say that "he was not in favour of extensive quotes from the judgments of the International Court of Justice in statements during plenary debates, as it gave the impression that the Commission relied too heavily on such judgments instead of on the opinions of its members": YBILC 2014, Vol. I, p. 130, para. 6; Saboia "shared the view that the Commission should be careful not to show undue reliance on the judgments of the Court" (at p. 135, para. 74).

[22] See YBILC 1994, Vol. I, p. 106, para. 38 (Pellet); see also YBILC 1995, Vol. I, pp. 163–164, para. 14 (Villagrán Kramer); YBILC 1998, Vol. I, p. 36, para. 32 (Brownlie).

[23] YBILC 1960, Vol. I, p. 276, para. 3.

[24] UN Doc. A/CN.4/717: 'Fifth Report on Identification of Customary International Law by Michael Wood, Special Rapporteur' (2018), para. 115.

as Special Rapporteur on the topic 'Subsequent agreements and subsequent practice in relation to the interpretation of treaties' by saying that "[t]hose concerns were somewhat surprising because he had been careful in trying to adhere strictly to the case law of international courts, in particular that of the International Court of Justice."[25] By the same token, members have sometimes found it difficult to accept a certain statement of the law as *lex lata* if it has not yet been recognized as such by the Court.[26] Any criticism of the Court's case-law during the Commission's debates is rare and usually provokes opposition:[27] the common view is that, in the words of one member, "[t]he Commission must, of course, strive to reflect the Court's rulings closely."[28] This is most visibly seen in the Commission's own texts, which are surveyed in some detail below.

1. *Incorporation of the Court's Determinations into the Commission's Output*

Pronouncements of the Court have provided the basis for a great many of the provisions put forward by the Commission, often being the first point of reference (if not the point of departure) in the Commission's endeavors to codify the law.[29] This has been particularly noticeable in

[25] YBILC 2015, Vol. I, p. 139, para. 28.

[26] See, for example, YBILC 2000, Vol. I, p. 296, para. 43 (Rosenstock objecting to the proposed formulation of article 48 of the draft articles on State responsibility (on 'Conditions relating to resort to countermeasures') in saying that "[i]t reflected no customary law and no statement by ICJ"); YBILC 2013, Vol. I, p. 58, para. 16 (Murase arguing that the precautionary principle did not have the status of an obligation for States by pointing out, inter alia, that the Court "had yet to recognize a precautionary 'principle'"); YBILC 2015, Vol. I, p. 11, para. 4 and p. 12, para. 10 (Murphy); YBILC 2016, Vol. I, p. 96, para. 74 (Murphy). The Commission as a whole argued, in support of its statement that the breach of an international obligation is always a wrongful act that entails international responsibility, that "[t]here is not a single judgment of the Permanent Court of International Justice or of the International Court of Justice, or a single international arbitral award, that recognizes either explicitly or implicitly [otherwise]": YBILC 1976, Vol. II, Part Two, p. 96, para. 4.

[27] See also Chapter 6.

[28] YBILC 2016, Vol. I, p. 232, para. 25 (Kamto).

[29] See also YBILC 1979, Vol. I, p. 65, para. 10 (President Waldock saying that "the pronouncements of the Court had provided the basis for the Commission's codification and development of some important areas of the law"). President Tomka echoed this sentiment some thirty-five years later in saying that "the Court's work has been highly influential in informing the codification projects undertaken by the International Law Commission, with that entity relying heavily on the Court's pronouncements in its efforts to codify international law": Statement by H.E. Judge Peter Tomka, President of the

fields in which the Court's jurisprudence was abundant, such as the law of treaties, the law of the sea, and the law on State responsibility; but the tendency to extract as much as possible from decisions of the Court may be observed in the work on almost any topic examined by the Commission,[30] which has not shied away from interpreting the Court's decisions for this purpose.[31] When invoking a decision of the Court in support of its own propositions, the Commission often indicates that the

International Court of Justice, on Panel titled 'The Hague International City of Peace and Justice' (16 May 2013), available at <www.icj-cij.org/files/press-releases/6/17376.pdf>, p. 2 (adding that the Commission "continue[s] to cite liberally to the Court's precedents in its codification work"). See also S. Villalpando, 'On the International Court of Justice and the Determination of Rules of Law', 26 LJIL (2013) 243 at 247; S. Rosenne, *The Law and Practice of the International Court 1920–2005*, Vol. III (Martinus Nijhoff 2006) 1554 ("Probably the most concentrated application of dicta of the International Court is seen in the ongoing work of the International Law Commission, where the contribution of the Court to the codification and progressive development of international law is most conspicuous").

[30] The Court's case-law features in the vast majority of the Commission's final products; the exceptions are 'Formulation of the Nürnberg principles' (1950); 'Draft Code of Offences against the Peace and Security of Mankind' (1954); 'Draft Articles on Diplomatic Intercourse and Immunities' (1958); 'Draft Articles on Consular Relations' (1961); 'Extended Participation in General Multilateral Treaties Concluded under the Auspices of the League of Nations' (1963); 'Draft Articles on Special Missions' (1967); 'Draft Articles on the Representation of States in Their Relations with International Organizations' (1971); 'Draft Articles on the Prevention and Punishment of Crimes against Diplomatic Agents and Other Internationally Protected Persons' (1972); 'Review of the Multilateral Treaty-Making Process' (1979); 'Draft Articles on the Status of the Diplomatic Courier and the Diplomatic Bag Not Accompanied by Diplomatic Courier and Draft Optional Protocols Thereto' (1989); 'Draft Code of Crimes against the Peace and Security of Mankind', including that Draft Statute for an International Criminal Court (1996 and 1994, respectively); 'Draft Articles on the Law of Transboundary Aquifers' (2008); and 'Guide to Provisional Application of Treaties' (2021). In these cases, no relevant decision of the Court had been identified at the time of the Commission's work.

[31] For the general view that "it was the Commission's job to interpret judicial decisions" on which it seeks to rely, see YBILC 2002, Vol. I, p. 257, para. 13 (Pellet). Ushakov explained in 1969 that "in its work the Commission was called upon to ponder the judgments of the Court and draw the necessary conclusions to assist it in its task of codification and progressive development of international law" (YBILC 1969, Vol. I, p. 69, para. 1); Fomba similarly said in 2002 that "[i]t was for the Commission to 'decode' the Court's 'message' with intelligence, subtlety and practicality" (YBILC 2002, Vol. I, p. 98, para. 3). Examples are indeed numerous: see, for instance, *infra* note 47; YBILC 1954, Vol. II, p. 154, the commentary to draft article 4; YBILC 1966, Vol. II, p. 225, para. 8 of the commentary to draft article 29; YBILC 1974, Vol. II, Part One, p. 197, paras. 3–4 of the commentary to draft article 12; YBILC 1976, Vol. II, Part Two, p. 99, para. 10 (commentary to article 19); YBILC 2014, Vol. II, Part Two, p. 103, para. 46; YBILC 2018, Vol. II, Part Two, p. 55, para. 36 of the commentary to draft conclusion 7; A/74/10: 'Report of the International

rule in question has been "confirmed" by the Court's case-law,[32] or that it is "consistent" with it;[33] at times, however, the transplantation is acknowledged more clearly.[34] Either way, as the following chronological record indicates, such recourse to the Court's case-law may be observed already in the Commission's earliest years. Ever since, and almost without exception, that case-law has been studied (and presented) not only before that of other international courts and tribunals, but also before State practice.

In its early work on *Arbitral procedure*, the Commission very much took cognizance of the Court's *Peace Treaties* advisory opinion,[35] putting forward a set of provisions that proposed the exercise of various functions by the President of the Court, or by the Court itself, in the event that an arbitral procedure is derailed. Soon thereafter, in 1953, it was the

Law Commission on the Work of Its Seventy-First Session' (29 April–7 June and 8 July–9 August 2019), p. 201, para. 3 of the commentary to draft conclusion 21. The Commission's equation of the concept 'intransgressible norms' with *jus cogens* was likewise a matter of interpretation: see also YBILC 2004, Vol. I, p. 158, para. 38 (President Shi saying that "the question as to whether the intransgressible norms of international humanitarian law [referred to in the *Nuclear Weapons* case] could be deemed to be *jus cogens* was one of interpretation. There was certainly no mention of it in the Court's judgment").

32 See, for example, YBILC 1956, Vol. II, p. 273, para. 1 of the commentary to article 16; YBILC 1981, Vol. II, Part Two, p. 34, para. 19 of the commentary to draft article 13; YBILC 2001, Vol. II, Part Two, p. 40, para. 6 of the commentary to article 4; YBILC 2006, Vol. II, Part Two, p. 39, para. 1 of the commentary to draft article 11; YBILC 2011, Vol. II, Part Three, p. 155, para. 5 of the commentary to draft guideline 2.6.3; YBILC 2014, Vol. II, Part Two, p. 28, para. 6 of the commentary to article 4; YBILC 2016, Vol. II, Part Two, p. 35, para. 3 of the commentary to draft article 6 of the Commission's draft articles on the protection of persons in the event of disasters; YBILC 2018, Vol. II, Part Two, p. 75, para. 6 of the commentary to conclusion 12 of the draft conclusions on subsequent agreements and subsequent practice in relation to the interpretation of treaties.

33 See, for example, YBILC 1959, Vol. II, p. 92, para. 2 of the commentary to draft article 1; YBILC 2011, Vol. II, Part Three, p. 74, para. 9 of the commentary to guideline 1.5.3.

34 See, for example, YBILC 1964, Vol. II, p. 206, para. 18 ("The present article thus reflects the position taken by the Court on this point"); YBILC 2015, Vol. II, Part Two, p. 94, para. 14 (the Final Report of the Study Group on the most-favoured-nation clause referring to "the Commission ... giving effect to what had already been decided by the International Court of Justice in the *Anglo-Iranian Oil Co.* case").

35 The Special Rapporteur, Scelle, noted that this "most important" advisory opinion "came at the right moment" and "showed the rightness of the Commission's opinion" that stopping such evasion by recourse to the President of the Court for the appointment of an arbitrator, as a matter of *lege ferenda*, was desirable: YBILC 1950, Vol. I, p. 257, paras. 1, 4. See also T.D. Grant and R. Nicholson, 'The Early *United Nations* Advisory Opinions (1948–62)', in E. Bjorge and C. Miles (eds.), *Landmark Cases in Public International Law* (Hart 2017) 222 at 245 et seq.

Court's advisory opinion in *Reparation for Injuries Suffered in the Service of the United Nations* that served to support the Commission's assertion, in the context of its work on the topic 'Nationality, including statelessness', that "[t]he rule as to nationality of claims is not an absolute rule of international law."[36]

The jurisprudence of the Court next played a role in the Commission's work on the law of the sea, in particular as regards the regime of territorial sea. Draft article 4 on the topic, concerning normal base lines for measuring the breadth of the territorial sea, was said by the Commission to reflect the international law in force because "[t]his [was] the Commission's interpretation of the judgment of the International Court of Justice rendered on 10 December 1951 in the Fisheries Case between the United Kingdom and Norway."[37] The draft article on "Straight base lines" brought into an even sharper focus the significance of the Court's pronouncements to the Commission's work, when the Special Rapporteur for the topic, François, based his proposal for a special regime in the case of special circumstances on the Court's *Fisheries* judgment but sought to supplement the general method applied by the Court with "certain desirable particulars."[38] In response to criticism that this text was incompatible with the judgment of the Court, François maintained that that was not the case: it was simply that "certain more precise formulations were necessary to put those principles [pronounced by the Court] into practice," and "[f]or that reason, a committee of eminently qualified [nautical] experts had been consulted and it was on the basis of their report that the rule set out in paragraph 2 had been adopted."[39] Sir Gerald Fitzmaurice sided with the Special Rapporteur,[40] but the position quickly met with strong opposition among members who favored close adherence to the Court's text.

[36] YBILC 1953, Vol. II, p. 227, fn. 17.

[37] YBILC 1954, Vol. II, p. 154 (commentary to draft article 4).

[38] *Ibid*, at p. 155 (commentary to draft article 5; the Commission made it clear that the additions proposed "represent[ed] a progressive development of international law").

[39] YBILC 1955, Vol. I, p. 196, para. 22 (adding that the criteria proposed "were simply necessary practical criteria for the application of the general principles which the International Court of Justice had laid down in the *Fisheries Case*, and which the Commission had adopted for paragraph 1" (at para. 23)).

[40] *Ibid*, at p. 198, paras. 45–46 (saying that "the considerations laid down in the International Court of Justice's decision in the *Fisheries* Case had been of a rather too general – and in some respects altogether too vague – nature to be suitable for inclusion in the Commission's draft articles," and that "[i]t was essential to give [some of them] a more precise character"); see also p. 199, para. 54 (noting also, in paras. 50 and 52 and

García Amador emphatically asserted that "[t]he International Court of Justice, constituting the greatest authority on international law, had been satisfied with the three criteria [for the special regime]," and that it was thus "incumbent upon the Commission to adhere to those three criteria instead of reproducing them in part only."[41] Krylov (a former judge of the Court) concurred, saying that "the Commission should not go any further than the International Court in the formulation of the basic considerations involved,"[42] and Hsu added that "faced with the choice between a decision of the International Court of Justice and the opinion of the group of nautical experts, he had no hesitation in siding with the former."[43] When some resistance persisted to García Amador's proposal that the Commission's text be amended so as to "reproduce as closely as possible the three criteria laid down by the International Court,"[44] Krylov protested vehemently, saying that he was "astonished by the unexpected attack made on the decision of the International Court of Justice, which in the *Fisheries Case* had made a contribution to case-law."[45] Following a lively debate, Sir Gerald withdrew a proposal for the total deletion of the draft article concerned, but stressed his disagreement with its text and urged the Commission to reconsider it. His plea was rejected by a vote, and the draft, as amended, was adopted by 10 votes to 3.[46] The accompanying commentary explained that the Commission "interpreted the Court's [*Fisheries*] judgment, which was delivered on the point in question by a majority of 10 votes to 2, as expressing the law in force," and "accordingly drafted the article on the basis of this judgment."[47] It was further made clear that "the Commission made a number of changes [to its earlier draft of the article] designed to bring the text even more closely

also later on, other difficulties with the judgment, which he said the UK government had received with a great deal of dismay).

41 *Ibid*, at p. 197, para. 36 (also proposing to incorporate, "in the terms by the International Court of Justice, the third of the three basic considerations which the Court had regarded as inherent in the nature of the territorial sea").

42 *Ibid*, at p. 198, para. 40.

43 *Ibid*, at para. 43.

44 *Ibid*, at p. 202, paras. 3, 5–7.

45 *Ibid*, at para. 9.

46 *Ibid*, at p. 205, paras. 36–37, 41–42.

47 YBILC 1956, Vol. II, p. 267, para. 2 of the commentary to draft article 5. One observer has remarked that the Commission has "extended the doctrine of the Norwegian Fisheries Case almost beyond recognition and applied it in a context completely different from that from which the Court spoke": R.N. Swift (ed.), *Annual Review of United Nations Affairs 1961–1962* (Oceana Publications 1963) 38 (citing McDougal).

into line with the Court's judgement."[48] The Court's jurisprudence, virtually by itself, also inspired draft article 16 (on "Duties of the coastal State"), which was said by the Commission to "confirm the principles which were upheld by the International Court of Justice in its judgement of 9 April 1949 in the *Corfu Channel Case* between the United Kingdom and Albania."[49]

The Commission's Draft articles on the law of treaties likewise drew heavily on the case-law of the Court and its predecessor, including with respect to the rules on treaty interpretation.[50] Notably, the Commission retained its position that preparatory work should be afforded only a subsidiary role in the interpretation of a treaty, despite the strong criticism of some States, by saying that it "accords with the jurisprudence of the International Court of Justice on the matter."[51] As regards the general rule on formulation of reservations to multilateral treaties, which has been considered "[t]he most powerful instance of the influence of the Court on the work of the Commission,"[52] the Commission reversed its original stated position on the matter in order to fall into line with the widely differing view adopted by the Court in the *Reservations to the Genocide Convention* advisory opinion.[53] The Court's decisions have similarly been invoked in the draft articles on the law of treaties in support of the rule that a foreign minister may be considered to represent her State without being asked for evidence of it;[54] the rule that the deposit of an instrument itself establishes the legal nexus at once with other contracting States, unless the treaty otherwise provides;[55] the obligation of a State not to frustrate the object of a treaty prior to its entry into

48 YBILC 1956, Vol. II, p. 268, para. 4.

49 *Ibid*, at p. 273, para. 1 of the commentary to draft article 16.

50 See YBILC 1966, Vol. II, p. 219, para. 6; p. 220, paras. 10 and 11; p. 221, paras. 12 and 14; p. 222, paras. 15, 17, and 18; p. 223, paras. 18, 19, and 20; p. 224, para. 4; p. 225, para. 8 (referring to several decisions).

51 *Ibid*, at p. 220, para. 10.

52 Schwebel, *supra* note 10, at p. 488.

53 YBILC 1966, Vol. II, p. 208, para. 23; see also Chapter 6, Section B.2. The Commission's use of the Court's jurisprudence makes no distinction between legally binding decisions in contentious cases and non-binding advisory opinions, perhaps because technically even binding decisions only bind the two States before the Court.

54 *Ibid*, at p. 193, para. 4 of the commentary to draft article 6 (referring to the PCIJ in the *Legal Status of Eastern Greenland* case).

55 *Ibid*, at p. 201, para. 3 of the commentary to draft article 13 (referring to *Right of Passage over Indian Territory (preliminary objections)*).

force;[56] the rule that consent to a reservation may be implied from absence of objection;[57] the principle of good faith as a legal principle, which forms an integral part of the rule *pacta sunt servanda*;[58] the rule that a treaty is not to be regarded as intended to have retroactive effect unless such an intention is expressed in the treaty or is clearly to be implied from its term;[59] the rule that the starting point of interpretation is the elucidation of the meaning of the text;[60] the general rule regarding third States;[61] the operation of the rule on treaties providing for obligations for third States;[62] the principle that a party is not permitted to benefit from its own inconsistencies;[63] and the rule that a State may invoke an error in a treaty as invalidating its consent to be bound by the treaty.[64] Upon the final adoption of the draft articles in 1966, Tunkin felt compelled to register his regret that "although the commentaries on the draft articles were in general excellent, they did not adequately reflect the practice of States, and placed undue emphasis on pronouncements by the International Court of Justice."[65]

In its work on the Draft articles on most-favoured-nation clauses, the Commission paid particular attention to the three cases dealt with by the Court that were of relevance to the topic, while adopting the Court's general view of the purpose of such clauses as set out in *U.S. Nationals in*

56 *Ibid*, at p. 202, para. 1 of the commentary to draft article 15 (referring to the PCIJ in the *Certain German Interests in Polish Upper Silesia* case).

57 *Ibid*, at p. 208, para. 23 (referring to the *Reservations to the Genocide Convention* advisory opinion).

58 *Ibid*, at p. 211, para. 2 of the commentary to draft article 23 (referring to the *Rights of Nationals of the United States of America in Morocco* case and to judgments of the PCIJ, as well as arbitral decisions).

59 *Ibid*, at p. 211, paras. 1–2 of the commentary to draft article 24 (referring to the *Ambatielos case (Preliminary Objections)* and to the PCIJ in the *Mavrommatis Palestine Concessions* case).

60 *Ibid*, at p. 220, para. 11 (specifying that "the jurisprudence of the International Court contains many pronouncements" to this effect).

61 *Ibid*, at p. 226, para. 2 (referring to the PCIJ in the *Free Zones of Upper Savoy and the District of Gex* case, the *Territorial Jurisdiction of the International Commission of the River Oder* case, and the *Status of Eastern Carelia* case).

62 *Ibid*, at p. 227, para. 2 (referring to the PCIJ in the *Free Zones* case).

63 *Ibid*, at p. 239, para. 1 (referring to *The Arbitral Award made by the King of Spain* case and *The Temple of Preah Vihear* case).

64 *Ibid*, at p. 243, para. 2 (referring to the *Legal Status of Eastern Greenland* case before PCIJ, and to *The Temple of Preah Vihear* case before the Court).

65 YBILC 1966, Vol. I, Part Two, p. 348, para. 188; Bartoš agreed (at para. 189). See also Tunkin's earlier note of caution at YBILC 1964, Vol. I, p. 85, para. 56 and p. 87, para. 72.

Morocco.[66] The Commission also gave effect to what had been decided by the Court in the *Anglo-Iranian Oil Company* case, by stating that the treaty containing the most-favoured-nation clause is the basic treaty in a situation where a third-party treaty exists.[67]

The Court's case-law had also been relied on in the Commission's Draft articles on succession of States in respect of treaties, adopted on second reading in 1974. The second Order of the PCIJ in the *Free Zones of Upper Savoy and the District of Gex* case, for example, was described by the Commission as "perhaps the most weighty endorsement of the existence of a rule requiring a successor State to respect a territorial treaty affecting the territory to which a succession of States relates," which it enshrined in draft article 12.[68] Draft article 18, according to which a newly independent State may establish its consent to be bound by a treaty in virtue of its predecessor's signature of the treaty, relied to a great extent on the Court's decisions in the *North Sea Continental Shelf* cases and in *Reservations to the Convention on the Prevention and Punishment of the Crime of Genocide*.[69]

By the same token, the jurisprudence of the PCIJ dealing with the dissolution of the German and Austro-Hungarian empires was of much use to the Commission in its work on the topic 'Succession of States in respect of matters other than treaties', concluded in 1981. This is made evident, inter alia, by the commentaries on draft article 8 (on "State property") and draft article 13 (on "Transfer of part of the territory of a State").[70] The Commission also "[had] in mind the Court's elaboration of the concept of equity," especially in the *North Sea Continental Shelf* cases, when employing it as a supplementary element and part of the material content of certain draft articles.[71]

[66] YBILC 1978, Vol. II, Part Two, p. 11, para. 49. See also YBILC 1976, Vol. II, Part Two, p. 7, para. 39.

[67] YBILC 1978, Vol. II, Part Two, p. 25, paras. 2–3 of the commentary to draft article 8. See also YBILC 2015, Vol. II, Part Two, p. 94, para. 14.

[68] YBILC 1974, Vol. II, Part One, p. 197, para. 3 of the commentary to draft article 12; see also the references to the cases *Temple of Preah Vihear* and *Right of passage* at pp. 198–199, paras. 6 and 8 of the commentary.

[69] *Ibid*, at p. 221, paras. 4–5 of the commentary to draft article 18 (the Commission first referring to the Court's case-law and only then to corresponding provisions of the Vienna Convention on the Law of Treaties); see also Schwebel, *supra* note 10, at p. 499.

[70] YBILC 1981, Vol. II, Part Two, p. 25, para. 7 of the commentary, and p. 34, para. 19 of the commentary. See also Schwebel, *supra* note 10, at pp. 499–500.

[71] YBILC 1981, Vol. II, Part Two, p. 20, paras. 83–85; see also YBILC 1976, Vol. II, Part Two, p. 133, para. 24.

In the Commission's 1982 Draft articles on treaties concluded *between States and international organizations or between international organizations*, the view that international organizations may have a body of practice that forms an integral part of their rules was derived from the *Namibia* advisory opinion.[72] The Commission also endorsed the Court's reasoning in the advisory opinion on the *Interpretation of the Agreement of 25 March 1951 between the WHO and Egypt* with regard to denunciation of a treaty, noting that the decision had referred to the Commission's own past work on this matter.[73] More generally, the draft articles continued the process of establishing the status of international organizations as subjects of international law, which the Court had begun in the *Reparation for Injuries* case.

The commentary to the Draft articles on jurisdictional immunities *of States and their property*, adopted on second reading in 1991, contains a reference to the judgment of the PCIJ in the *Société Commercial de Belgique* case, as an example confirming that no measures of constraint by way of execution or coercion can be exercised by the authorities of one State against another State and its property, even in international litigation.[74]

The Commission's work on the law of the non-navigational uses of international watercourses, which culminated in 1994 with the adoption of draft articles of the topic, drew upon the Court's jurisprudence as well. The obligation of States to negotiate the apportionment of the waters of an international watercourse, eventually incorporated in draft article 3 (on "Watercourse agreements"), was based by the Commission on the Court's case-law concerning fisheries and maritime delimitation, including the *North Sea Continental Shelf* cases and *Fisheries Jurisdiction* cases.[75] Similarly, the statement that a watercourse State cannot be deemed to have violated its due diligence obligation if it did not know (or did not have to know) that the particular use of an international watercourse would cause significant harm to other watercourse States, was supported in the commentary by reference to the *Corfu Channel* judgment.[76] The obligation that the State whose use causes the harm shall

[72] YBILC 1982, Vol. II, Part Two, p. 21, fn. 53.
[73] *Ibid*, at p. 57.
[74] YBILC 1991, Vol. II, Part Two, p. 56, fn. 170.
[75] See YBILC 1994, Vol. II, Part Two, p. 95, fn. 196; YBILC 1980, Vol. II, Part Two, p. 116, para. 31.
[76] YBILC 1994, Vol. II, Part Two, p. 104, paras. 8–9 of the commentary to draft article 7.

consult with the State suffering such harm, laid down in draft article 7 (on "Obligation not to cause significant harm"), found its inspiration in the *Fisheries Jurisdiction* cases;[77] as did the obligation that consultations and negotiations shall be conducted on the basis that each State must in good faith pay reasonable regard to the rights and legitimate interests of the other State, laid down in draft article 17 (on "Consultations and negotiations concerning planned measures").[78] The *North Sea Continental Shelf* judgment was again invoked in support of the stated principle that the parties to a dispute should conduct their negotiations in good faith and in a meaningful way.[79] Some of these provisions, as incorporated in the Watercourses Convention elaborated by States on the basis of the Commission's draft articles, were referred to in the Commission's Draft articles on the law of transboundary *aquifers* (2008),[80] which thereby relied on the Court's jurisprudence yet again, even if indirectly. Notably, the Commission did not include therein a draft article endorsing the 'precautionary principle', because the Court has been reticent about its status as a binding principle of international law.[81]

The Draft articles on nationality of natural persons in *relation to the succession of States*, finally adopted by the Commission in 1999, refer to the advisory opinion of the PCIJ on *Acquisition of Polish Nationality* in support of draft article 15, which prohibits discrimination.[82] Draft article 19 (on 'Other States') borrows from the *Nottebohm* judgment with regard to the question of the link required between an individual and a third State.[83]

The Commission's output on *State responsibility*, which was forty-five years in the making, has the fingerprints of the Court's jurisprudence all

[77] *Ibid*, at p. 104, para. 13 of the commentary to draft article 7.

[78] *Ibid*, at p. 116, para. 3 of the commentary (also referring to the *North Sea Continental Shelf* cases).

[79] *Ibid*, at p. 134, para. 3 of the commentary to article 33 (on 'Settlement of disputes').

[80] YBILC 2008, Vol. II, Part Two, p. 33, para. 1 of the commentary to draft article 9, and p. 38, para. 1 of the commentary to draft article 15.

[81] Draft article 12 ('Prevention, reduction and control of pollution') employed the "less disputed formulation" 'precautionary approach', which is referred to as necessary not by virtue of a legal obligation but because of "the fragility and scientific uncertainty of aquifers": YBILC 2008, Vol. II, Part Two, pp. 34–35, para. 5 of the commentary (where it is also noted that "[t]he Commission was well aware of the differing views on the concept of 'precautionary approach' as opposed to that of 'precautionary principle'"). See also YBILC 2008, Vol. I, p. 248, para. 108 (Escarameia).

[82] YBILC 1999, Vol. II, Part Two, p. 37, para. 1 of the commentary to draft article 15.

[83] *Ibid*, at pp. 39–40, paras. 3, 5 of the commentary.

over it. As others have already observed, the central issues covered under the draft articles on the topic, including the definition of an international wrongful act, the nature of the conduct constituting a breach of an international obligation, the attribution of conduct to a State, the circumstances precluding wrongfulness, and the consequences of an international wrongful act, all find support – if not their *fons et origo* – in the case-law of the Court or its predecessor.[84] The commentary accompanying the draft articles adopted in 2001 contains no fewer than 222 references to the case-law of the Court, and a further 76 references to the formative judgments of its predecessor, with such references often constituting the first step in the justification supporting the draft article in question.[85] The Commission also followed the Court on the controversial issue of the degree of control required for attribution of conduct to a State, by adopting (in the commentary to draft article 8) the test of effective control employed in *Military and* Paramilitary Activities *in and against Nicaragua.*[86] In the words of one observer, "the PCIJ and ICJ were of crucial importance [to the Commission's work on State responsibility]: their jurisprudence shaped many of the building blocks, and some

84 To name but a few examples, article 1, which states the basic principle underlying the articles as a whole, and article 2, on "Elements of an internationally wrongful act of a State," both reflect a number of decisions of the Court and its predecessor. Article 4 (on "Conduct of organs of a State") likewise enshrines a rule already pronounced by the two courts. Article 26, according to which a State may not take countermeasures which conflict with *jus cogens*, reflects the position adopted by the Court in its Order on the admissibility of counter-claims in the *Genocide case (Bosnia and Herzegovina* v. *Serbia and Montenegro)*, where it was held that "in no case could one breach of the Convention serve as an excuse for another" (*Application of the Convention on the Prevention and Punishment of the Crime of Genocide (Bosnia and Herzegovina* v. *Yugoslavia), Counter-Claims, Order of 17 December 1997, I.C.J. Reports 1997*, p. 258, para. 35). Article 31 incorporated the Permanent Court of International Justice's principle of "integral reparation" for an injury. Article 51, on the requirement of proportionality in countermeasures, echoes the Court's judgment in the *Gabčíkovo-Nagymaros Project* case.

85 See also S. Villalpando, 'Le codificateur et le juge face à la responsabilité internationale de l'État: interaction entre la CDI et la CIJ dans la détermination des règles secondaires', 55 AFDI (2009) 39 at 42–43.

86 YBILC 2001, Vol. II, Part Two, pp. 47–48, paras. 4–5 (indicating subtly that the alternative test adopted by the international criminal tribunal for the former Yugoslavia was not a suitable one). As already noted, the Court endorsed this article in the *Genocide case (Bosnia and Herzegovina* v. *Serbia and Montenegro)*. A more recent example of the Commission following the Court even when its assertion of the legal position has been controversial may be found in the incorporation in 2014 into the Commission's draft article 3 on the immunity of State officials from foreign criminal jurisdiction, of the Court's pronouncement in the *Arrest Warrant* case as to the immunity *ratione personae* of ministers for foreign affairs.

of the cornerstones, of the eventual edifice."[87] For Pellet, the Commission "took largely note of this judge-made law without calling into question its fundamentals, nevertheless filling in some of its gaps and dissipating some of its uncertainties, while adding a prudent and still welcome flavour of progressive development."[88]

The long period in which the Commission was engaged with the topic of State responsibility had indeed afforded an opportunity for an "intellectual interaction" between the Court and the Commission that benefited the work greatly.[89] In the years leading up to the first reading stage, the Court made significant contributions to the law in a series of important cases that the Commission quickly took into account: *Barcelona Traction, United States Diplomatic and Consular Staff in Tehran, Military and Paramilitary Activities in and against Nicaragua*, and the *Gabčíkovo-Nagymaros Project*. In the latter case, in particular, the Court "played an important role in consolidating some of the ideas of the ILC *avant le lettre*," especially those relating to countermeasures and to necessity as a circumstance precluding wrongfulness.[90] The Commission later

[87] C.J. Tams, 'Law-Making in Complex Processes: The World Court and the Modern Law of State Responsibility', in C. Chinkin and F. Baetens (eds.), *Sovereignty, Statehood and State Responsibility: Essays in Honour of James Crawford* (CUP 2015) 287 at 306; see also Villalpando, *supra* note 85, at p. 46. Crawford, the Commission's Special Rapporteur on the topic at the time, remarked in 2001 that "the history of the development of [the Commission's articles on] State responsibility showed how much the Commission owed to the Court for the clarification it had provided in such cases as the *Gabčíkovo Nagymaros Project* and the *Differences relating to Immunity from Legal Process of a Special Rapporteur of the Commission on Human Rights*": YBILC 2001, Vol. I, p. 213, para. 37.

[88] A. Pellet, 'Some Remarks on the Recent Case Law of The International Court of Justice on Responsibility Issues', in P. Kovács (ed.), *International Law – A Quiet Strength* (Pázmány Press 2011) 111 at 113.

[89] See R. Rosenstock and M. Kaplan, 'The Fifty-Third Session of the International Law Commission', 96 AJIL (2002) 412 at 414–415; J. Crawford, 'The International Court of Justice and the Law of State Responsibility', in C.J. Tams and J. Sloan (eds.), *The Development of International Law by the International Court of Justice* (OUP 2013) 71 at 73–75 (referring to a "symbiotic relationship between the ILC and the ICJ in this field" and to "a dialectical relationship" that exists between the two organs).

[90] Crawford, *supra* note 89, at p. 79. While serving as Special Rapporteur on the topic, Crawford said that "[t]he conditions laid down by the Court [in the *Gabčíkovo-Nagymaros Project* case] as justification for countermeasures under general international law would therefore have to be borne in mind when the articles in part two came to be redrafted": YBILC 1999, Vol. I, p. 235, para. 84. He later recalled, however, that "[i]n fact, government comments on the countermeasures articles were of greater significance than the Court's statements, useful as the latter were in providing support and occasional

postponed its adoption of provisions on assurances and guarantees of non-repetition until the Court delivered its judgment in *LaGrand*.[91]

Also of note is that the Court's holding in *Barcelona Traction*, "in the most *obiter* of dicta,"[92] that certain obligations were owed to the international community as a whole, served essentially by itself as the foundation of the pivotal distinction initially drawn by the Commission between an international crime and an international delict.[93] The Commission noted that "however isolated the expression of such an opinion in an international judgment may still appear to be," the apparent support for it in the Court's decision "seem[s] an important argument in support of the theory that there are . . . two different types of internationally wrongful acts of the State."[94] While that controversial distinction was eventually dropped at the second reading stage, draft article 48 (on "Invocation of responsibility by a State other than an injured State") retained the notion that all States can be held to have a legal interest in protection of some obligations, and its commentary states expressly that it "give[s] effect to the statement by ICJ in the *Barcelona Traction* case."[95] This was in keeping with the approach of Crawford, as Special Rapporteur, who said that "the Commission had not invented the concept of 'obligations owed to the international community as a whole': it had been introduced by ICJ. The Commission could only endorse it, the question being to what extent."[96] The Commission's ultimate position, as already noted, was later endorsed by the Court in the *Genocide case (Bosnia and Herzegovina* v. *Serbia and Montenegro)*.[97]

In the *Draft articles on prevention of transboundary harm from hazardous activities*, adopted in 2001 as well, the Commission explained that

language for the text": J. Crawford, 'The ILC's Articles on Responsibility of States for Internationally Wrongful Acts: A Retrospect', 96 AJIL (2002) 874 at 875, fn. 5.

[91] See also Chapter 6, Section B.2.

[92] Crawford, *supra* note 89, at p. 77.

[93] See also R. Rosenstock, 'The Forty-Sixth Session of the International Law Commission', 89 AJIL (1995) 390 at 394.

[94] YBILC 1976, Vol. II, Part Two, pp. 99–100, para. 11.

[95] YBILC 2001, Vol. II, Part Two, p. 127, para. 8 of the commentary. See also M. Lachs, 'Some Reflections on the Contribution of the International Court of Justice to the Development of International Law', 10 *Syracuse Journal of International and Commerce* (1983) 239 at 266 (observing that "the reliance of the International Law Commission on this formulation in its subsequent work on state responsibility is a clear demonstration of the Court's contribution to the development of the law").

[96] YBILC 2000, Vol. I, p. 87, para. 68.

[97] See Chapter 3, Section B.2.

the prevention of transboundary harm arising from hazardous activities is "confirmed by ICJ in its advisory opinion on the *Legality of the Threat or Use of Nuclear Weapons* as now forming part of the corpus of international law."[98] It also explained the function of the concept of "control" in international law by reference to the *Namibia* advisory opinion,[99] and relied on the judgment in the *Nuclear Tests* cases when describing the principle of good faith in international law.[100] The commentary to draft article 6 (on "Authorization") recalled that the "ICJ in the *Corfu Channel* case held that a State has an obligation 'not to allow knowingly its territory to be used for acts contrary to the rights of other States',"[101] and the commentary to draft article 8 (on "Notification and information") referred to that same judgment in saying that "[t]he obligation to notify other States of the risk of significant harm to which they are exposed is reflected in the *Corfu Channel* case."[102] The Court's judgments in the *Fisheries Jurisdiction* and *North Sea Continental Shelf* cases were referred to in support of the statement that the principle of good faith is an integral part of any requirement of consultations and negotiations,[103] and the judgment in the *Gabčíkovo-Nagymaros Project* case was referred to in an attempt to ground the precautionary approach in international law.[104]

The influence of the Court's case-law on the Commission's work is no less sharply demonstrated by the *Draft articles on diplomatic protection*, finalized in 2006.[105] Despite significant pressure to overturn the traditional notion of diplomatic protection enshrined in such cases as *Mavrommatis Palestine Concessions* and *Barcelona Traction*, the Commission's debates were dominated by that jurisprudence and it decided to proceed on such a basis.[106] Accordingly, even if the criterion

98 YBILC 2001, Vol. II, Part Two, p. 148, para. 3 of the general commentary.

99 *Ibid*, at p. 151, para. 12 of the commentary to draft article 1.

100 *Ibid*, at p. 155, para. 2 of the commentary to draft article 4.

101 *Ibid*, at p. 157, para. 3 of the commentary to draft article 6.

102 *Ibid*, at p. 159, para. 3 of the commentary to draft article 8.

103 *Ibid*, at p. 161, para. 4 of the commentary to draft article 9.

104 *Ibid*, at p. 163, para. 7 of the commentary to draft article 10.

105 See also P. Couvreur, 'The ICJ and the Implementation of the Law on State Responsibility', in *The International Court of Justice and the Effectiveness of International Law* (Brill Nijhoff 2016) 205 at 243–258; K. Parlett, 'Diplomatic Protection and the International Court of Justice', in C.J. Tams and J. Sloan (eds.), *The Development of International Law by the International Court of Justice* (OUP 2013) 87 at 93–105.

106 See Chapter 6, Section A. It is also interesting to observe, in this context, that in the early stages of adopting some of the Commission's draft articles on this topic, Escarameia (seeking to extend the scope of the draft articles to cover diplomatic protection of crew

of effective nationality employed in the *Nottebohm* case was subtly set aside by the Commission,[107] the Court's case-law served to uphold several of the central provisions adopted by the Commission. This is the case with article 2, which restates the very right of States to exercise diplomatic protection by reference to *Barcelona Traction*;[108] and with article 9, which "accepts the basic premise of *Barcelona Traction* that it is incorporation that confers nationality on a corporation for the purposes of diplomatic protection."[109] The commentary to article 11 likewise refers to *Barcelona Traction* in support of the general rule that a corporation is to be protected by the State of nationality of the corporation and not by the State or States of nationality of the shareholders,[110] as does the commentary to article 12, according to which shareholders qualify for diplomatic protection when their own rights are affected.[111] Article 14, in codifying the rule requiring the exhaustion of local remedies as a prerequisite for the exercise of diplomatic protection, points to the *Interhandel* and *ELSI* cases;[112] and the Court's jurisprudence is likewise invoked in support of the statement that waiver of local remedies must

members and passengers on ships) pointed to an evolution of the law in the judgment of the International Tribunal for the Law of the Sea in *M/V "Saiga" (No. 2)* and voiced the opinion that "[i]t was not logical that the Commission should rigidly follow ICJ, but not ITLOS. That was all the more important since the Commission was focusing on the fragmentation of international law": YBILC 2002, Vol. I, p.136, para. 71 (adding that "[w]hen there was a clear judicial precedent, the Commission should follow it"). Chairman Rosenstock was quick to respond that the judgment "would be noted in the commentary" (*ibid*, at p. 137, para. 72), but no such reference was eventually added. Instead, the Commission's report that year indicated that during the general debate on the topic, the ITLOS case was referred to in support of the proposal to extend the scope of the draft articles, but also that "caution was advised regarding the M/V 'Saiga' (No. 2) case . . . which had been brought before ITLOS under the special provisions contained in article 292 of the United Nations Convention on the Law of the Sea, and not as a general case of diplomatic protection": YBILC 2002, Vol. II, Part Two, p. 51, para. 127.

107 See Chapter 6, Section B.2. The *Nottebohm* judgment (alongside the Court's advisory opinion in *Reparation for Injuries*) was nevertheless relied on by the Commission's in support of its proposed draft article 7 (on "Multiple nationality and claim against a State of nationality"): YBILC 2006, Vol. II, Part Two, p. 34, para. 3.

108 YBILC 2006, Vol. II, Part Two, p. 28, para. 2; see also p. 54, para. 3 of the commentary to draft conclusion 19.

109 *Ibid*, at p. 38, para. 4 of the commentary (the Commission did, however, provide for an exception dictated by "policy and fairness").

110 *Ibid*, at p. 39, para. 1. At the same time, the exceptions in draft article 11 do not implement fully the *dicta* in *Barcelona Traction*.

111 *Ibid*, at pp. 42–43, paras. 1, 3 (also paying attention to the *ELSI* case at para. 2).

112 *Ibid*, at p. 44, para. 1; pp. 45–46, paras. 6 and 10.

not be readily implied.[113] The Commission's statement that individual rights under international law may also arise outside the framework of human rights, too, is substantiated by reference to the Court's pronouncements (in *LaGrand* and *Avena*),[114] and the general commentary provides, without further explanation, that "[t]he question whether a State may exercise diplomatic protection in respect of a national who is an agent of an international organization was answered by the ICJ in the *Reparation for Injuries* case."[115]

In the *Draft principles on the allocation of loss in the case of transboundary harm arising out of hazardous activities*, finally adopted in 2006 as well, the Commission described its holistic approach to the definition of the term "environment" by adopting as its own the Court's words in the *Gabčíkovo-Nagymaros Project* judgment.[116] That judgment was also referred to by the Commission in support of the principle that the State of origin must continuously monitor hazardous activities;[117] and as "an important recognition under general international law of the duty imposed on States affected by transboundary harm to mitigate the damage to the best extent they can."[118] The *Corfu Channel* judgment was also cited, both in explaining that the duty of the State of origin to consult all States affected or likely to be affected owes to "elementary considerations of humanity,"[119] and in support of the statement that compensation to victims must be prompt and adequate.[120] The commentary further states that the *Chorzów Factory* standard applies in respect of internationally wrongful acts, even though they were not covered by the draft principles, only to appreciate "the limits and the parallels that ought to be drawn in respect of activities covered."[121] Finally, the Court's case-law served more generally to support a list of general principles concerning payment of compensation.[122]

[113] *Ibid*, at p. 50, para. 15 of the commentary to draft article 15 (referring to the *ELSI* judgment).
[114] *Ibid*, at p. 51, para. 4 of the commentary to draft article 16.
[115] *Ibid*, at p. 26, para. 3 of the general commentary.
[116] *Ibid*, at p. 69, para. 21 of the commentary to draft principle 2.
[117] *Ibid*, at p. 84, para. 3 of the commentary to principle 5.
[118] *Ibid*, at p. 85, para. 10 of the commentary to draft principle 5, fn. 460.
[119] *Ibid*, at p. 84, para. 9 of the commentary to draft principle 5.
[120] *Ibid*, at p. 72, para. 3 of the commentary to draft principle 3.
[121] *Ibid*, at p. 75, para. 17 of the commentary to draft principle 3.
[122] *Ibid*, at p. 76, para. 18 of the commentary to draft principle 3, fn. 412.

Extensive references to the Court's case-law may also be found in the Commission's *Guiding principles applicable to unilateral declarations of States capable of creating legal obligations* of 2006, most of which have been inspired by that jurisprudence. The commentaries accompanying the guiding principles are indeed said to be "explanatory notes reviewing the jurisprudence of the ICJ and pertinent State practice" (and that they do, precisely in that order),[123] and the definition of unilateral acts is itself described as "very directly inspired" by the Court's *dicta*.[124] The Court's judgments also form the foundation of the guideline according to which every State possesses capacity to undertake legal obligations through unilateral declarations;[125] the guidelines on how the legal effect of such declarations is to be determined;[126] and the guidelines on who can issue a binding unilateral declaration and in what form.[127] Other guidelines (on a unilateral declaration conflicting with *jus cogens*, on unilateral declarations and third States, and on the revocation of unilateral declarations) are likewise supported by references to the Court's pronouncements.[128]

The Commission's *Draft articles on the effects of armed conflicts on treaties*, adopted in 2011, cite the Court's decisions in support of the statements that customary international law continues to apply independently of treaty obligations;[129] that treaties relating to international humanitarian law continue in operation during armed conflict;[130] that non-derogable provisions of human rights treaties apply during armed conflict;[131] that there is a presumption that environmental treaties apply in case of armed conflict;[132] and that treaties relating to diplomatic and consular relations continue to apply even in armed conflict.[133]

The *Draft articles on the responsibility of international organizations*, also adopted in 2011, further consolidated the status of international

[123] *Ibid*, at p. 161, fn. 873.
[124] *Ibid*, at p. 162, para. 1 of the commentary to guideline 1.
[125] *Ibid*, at para. 1 of the commentary to guideline 2.
[126] *Ibid*, at para. 1 of the commentary to guideline 3, and pp. 164–165, paras. 1–3 of the commentary to guideline 7.
[127] *Ibid*, at pp. 163–164, paras. 1 and 3 of the commentary to guideline 4, and paras. 1 and 3 of the commentary to guideline 5.
[128] *Ibid*, at pp. 165–166, commentary to guideline 8; para. 2 of the commentary to guideline 9; and paras. 1 and 3 of the commentary to guideline 10.
[129] YBILC 2011, Vol. II, Part Two, p. 116, para. 2 of the commentary to draft article 10.
[130] *Ibid*, at pp. 120–121, para. 6.
[131] *Ibid*, at p. 127, para. 49.
[132] *Ibid*, at paras. 54–55.
[133] *Ibid*, at pp. 129–130, paras. 72, 75.

organizations as subjects of international law as pronounced upon by the Court in the *Reparation for Injuries* case.[134] They too contain ample references to the Court's case-law, including in support of some of the basic terms employed by the Commission, such as "international organization," "rules of the organization," and "agent."[135] In this context, the Commission's statement on acquisition of legal personality by an international organization under international law is expressly said to be a generalization of the two advisory opinions pertaining to the World Health Organization alone.[136] Similarly, several of the Court's advisory opinions concerning the United Nations are cited in reference to "conduct of organs or agents of an international organization," with the Commission explaining that "[w]hat was said by the International Court of Justice with regard to the United Nations applies more generally to international organizations."[137] The principle that a wrongful act committed by an international organization entails responsibility is supported, inter alia, by reference to the Court's advisory opinion on *Difference relating to Immunity from Legal Process of a Special Rapporteur of the Commission on Human Rights*;[138] and one of the essential elements of such an international wrongful act is explained by citing the advisory opinion on *Interpretation of the Agreement of 25 March 1951 between the WHO and Egypt*.[139] The Court's decisions are also referred to in defining the parameters of *ultra vires* conduct.[140] Chapter IV of the draft articles, which deals with "responsibility of an international organization in connection with the act of a State or another international organization" and is largely based on articles 16 to 18 of the draft articles on State responsibility, is supported by an indication that the Court had found article 16 to reflect a customary

[134] See also Crawford, *supra* note 89, at p. 73. That international organizations may bear responsibility for the conduct of their organs or agents was mentioned already in the commentary to the draft articles on State responsibility, adopted in 2001, by reference to the Court's jurisprudence: YBILC 2001, Vol. II, Part Two, p. 34, para. 7 of the commentary to draft article 1.

[135] YBILC 2011, Vol. II, Part Two, p. 50, paras. 8–9 and 11 of the commentary to draft article 2; p. 51, para. 18 of the commentary to draft article 2; p. 52, para. 23 of the commentary to draft article 2; p. 63, para. 6 of the commentary to draft article 10.

[136] *Ibid*, at p. 50, para. 8 of the commentary to draft article 2.

[137] *Ibid*, at p. 55, paras. 2–4 of the commentary to draft article 6.

[138] *Ibid*, at p. 53, para. 3 of the commentary to draft article 3.

[139] *Ibid*, at para. 2 of the commentary to draft article 4.

[140] *Ibid*, at p. 60, para. 1 of the commentary to draft article 8, fn. 147; p. 61, paras. 6–7 of the commentary to draft article 8.

rule.[141] Other references to the Court's case-law are made, for example, in reference to the obligation to pay compensation;[142] obligations in respect of a serious breach committed by an international organization;[143] the entitlement of an international organization to invoke international responsibility;[144] the requirement of proportionality of countermeasures;[145] and the interpretation of article 103 of the Charter of the United Nations.[146]

The Commission's elaborate *Guide to practice on reservations to treaties*, finally adopted in 2011 as well, contains over one hundred references to the Court's case-law. It clearly follows the line adopted by the 1951 advisory opinion on *Reservations to treaties*, most notably by adopting the notion of the object and purpose of the treaty as a condition for the permissibility of reservations not prohibited by the treaty,[147] and by seeking to extract from the Court's case-law guidance as to determining the object and purpose of a treaty.[148] The Court's case-law is also invoked to sustain the Commission's pronouncements on such issues as late formulation of reservations;[149] advance objections;[150] specified reservations;[151] validity of the reservations to dispute settlement clauses;[152] and interpretation of reservations.[153] It is further cited in support of the Commission's statements on various other related issues, such as the definition of a treaty;[154] denunciation of a treaty;[155] and the impact of estoppel and the principle of good faith.[156]

In 2014, the Commission sought to soften the reception of its *Draft articles on expulsion of aliens* (a topic for which States had shown little

141 *Ibid*, at p. 65, para. 1 of the general commentary to Part IV.
142 *Ibid*, at p. 80, para. 3 of the commentary to draft article 36.
143 *Ibid*, at p. 83, para. 6 of the commentary to draft article 42.
144 *Ibid*, at p. 84, para. 3 of the commentary to draft article 43; p. 86, para. 5 of the commentary to draft article 45; p. 83, para. 3 of the commentary to draft article 47.
145 *Ibid*, at pp. 94–95, para. 1 of the commentary to draft article 54.
146 *Ibid*, at p. 104, para. 1 of the commentary to draft article 67.
147 YBILC 2011, Vol. II, Part Three, p. 209, para. 3 of the commentary to guideline 3.1.3.
148 *Ibid*, at p. 216, para. 3 of the commentary to guideline 3.1.5.1.
149 *Ibid*, at p. 112, para. 2 of the commentary to guideline 2.3.
150 *Ibid*, at p. 153, para. 34 of the commentary to guideline 2.6.1.
151 *Ibid*, at p. 207, para. 7 of the commentary to guideline 3.1.2.
152 *Ibid*, at p. 231, para. 1 of the commentary to guideline 3.1.5.7.
153 *Ibid*, at p. 276–277, paras. 5, 9 of the commentary to guideline 4.2.6; p. 319, para. 6 of the commentary to guideline 4.7.1.
154 *Ibid*, at p. 147, fn. 1010.
155 *Ibid*, at p. 132, fn. 868.
156 *Ibid*, at p. 324, fns. 2601–2602.

appetite) by suggesting that the basis in international case-law applicable to the topic "has recently been reinforced by a judgment of the International Court of Justice."[157] The commentary then referred to the *Diallo* case as confirming the rules set out in draft article 4 (on "Requirement for conformity with law");[158] draft article 5 (on "Grounds for expulsion");[159] draft article 17 (on "Prohibition of torture or cruel, inhuman or degrading treatment or punishment");[160] draft article 19 (on "Detention of an alien for the purpose of expulsion");[161] draft article 20 (on "Protection of the property of an alien subject to expulsion");[162] draft article 26 (on "Procedural rights of aliens subject to expulsion");[163] draft article 30 (on "Responsibility of States in cases of unlawful expulsion");[164] and draft article 31 (on "Diplomatic protection").[165]

The *Final report on the obligation to extradite or prosecute* (aut dedere aut judicare), also adopted by the Commission in 2014, relied to a great extent on the Court's judgment in *Questions relating to the Obligation to Prosecute or Extradite*, which the Commission expressly waited to consider before finalizing its work (and indeed found "helpful in elucidating some aspects relevant to the implementation of the obligation to extradite or prosecute"[166]). While recognizing that "the Court's reasoning relates to the specific implementation and application of issues

[157] YBILC 2014, Vol. II, Part Two, p. 24, para. 1 of the general commentary (citing *Diallo*). The Special Rapporteur, Kamto, had earlier said that "[w]hat made that judgment so important was that it addressed no fewer than seven legal issues raised by the expulsion of aliens . . . Those points constituted the nub of the topic which the Commission had been examining for more than five years. In his seventh report, the Special Rapporteur reviewed them and, in each case, reproduced the relevant passages from the judgment and showed how the Court's position matched the arguments set out in the reports presented to the Commission on the subject of the expulsion of aliens. Since the Court's judgments were significant points of reference for codification, it seemed as if the Commission was on the right track": YBILC 2011, Vol. I, p. 154, para. 8.

[158] YBILC 2014, Vol. II, Part Two, pp. 28–29, paras. 6, 7 of the commentary to article 4.

[159] *Ibid*, at p. 29, para. 2 of the commentary.

[160] *Ibid*, at p. 39, para. 1 of the commentary.

[161] *Ibid*, at p. 41, para. 2 of the commentary.

[162] *Ibid*, at p. 44, para. 4 of the commentary.

[163] *Ibid*, at p. 54, para. 10 of the commentary (referring also to the *LaGrand* and *Avena* cases).

[164] *Ibid*, at p. 59, para. 6 of the commentary.

[165] *Ibid*, at para. 2 of the commentary.

[166] *Ibid*, at p. 96, para. 3(b)(15) of the report; see also Chapter 6, Section B.2. The Commission also cited the *Genocide case (Bosnia and Herzegovina* v. *Serbia and Montenegro)* in connection with its analysis of the obligations arising under the Genocide Convention: see YBILC 2014, Vol. II, Part Two, p. 96, para. 3(a)(14).

surrounding [the Torture Convention alone]," the Commission drew upon the judgment in order to establish the meaning of the obligation to extradite or prosecute more broadly.[167] It also endorsed (albeit in a footnote) Judge Donoghue's statement in that case, that even if dispositive paragraphs of the judgment bind only the parties to the case, "the Court's interpretation of a multilateral treaty (or of customary international law) can have implications for other States."[168] The judgment was further invoked in support of the notions that the obligation to cooperate in combating impunity is given effect, inter alia, through the obligation to extradite or prosecute;[169] that universal jurisdiction of domestic courts must be established as a necessary condition for enabling a preliminary inquiry and for submitting a case to the competent authorities for the purpose of prosecution;[170] that a case ought to be submitted for the purpose of prosecution, irrespective of the existence of a prior request for the extradition of the suspect;[171] and that a delay in enacting necessary legislation in order to prosecute suspects adversely affects the State party's implementation of its obligations.[172] The judgment was moreover relied upon for purposes of clarifying the elements comprising the obligation to investigate;[173] the elements comprising the obligation to prosecute;[174] the obligation to extradite;[175] the need to take into account the object and purpose of the relevant instrument;[176] the temporal scope of the obligation to extradite or prosecute under a treaty;[177] the consequences of non-compliance with the obligation;[178] and the relationship of the obligation with *erga omnes* obligations or *jus cogens* norms.[179] Remarkably, the Commission explicitly avoided taking a position on whether the obligation to extradite or prosecute belongs to the corpus of customary international law, having noted that the Court had

[167] *Ibid*, at para. 3(b)(15) (referring to "The Hague formula," which has served as a model for most contemporary conventions containing the obligation to extradite or prosecute).
[168] *Ibid*, at p. 97, fn. 441.
[169] *Ibid*, at p. 92, para. 65.1(1), fn. 414.
[170] *Ibid*, at p. 97, para. 65.3(b)(18), fn. 447.
[171] *Ibid*, at p. 102, para. 65.3(d)(41).
[172] *Ibid*, at p. 98, para. 65.3(b)(19).
[173] *Ibid*, at para. 65.3(b)(20).
[174] *Ibid*, at para. 65.3(b)(21).
[175] *Ibid*, at 65.3(b)(22).
[176] *Ibid*, at p. 99, para. 65.3(b)(23).
[177] *Ibid*, at para. 65.3(b)(25).
[178] *Ibid*, at para. 65.3(b)(26).
[179] *Ibid*, at p. 103, para. 65.3(e)(46).

not had an opportunity to do so in that judgment by reason of jurisdictional limits.[180]

Moreover, the Court's case-law was cited in support of several provisions contained in the Commission's *Draft articles on the protection of persons in the event of disasters*, adopted on second reading in 2016, namely those on the relevant humanitarian principles,[181] on the role of the affected State,[182] on the duty of the affected State to seek external assistance,[183] and on the consent of the affected State to external assistance.[184]

The Commission's *Draft conclusions on subsequent agreements and subsequent practice in relation to the interpretation of treaties*, as finally adopted in 2018, give pride of place to the Court's case-law, which is virtually always referred to first when the decisions of international courts and tribunals are referred to in support of a conclusion.[185] That jurisprudence greatly informed the Commission's approach to such matters as the possible effects of subsequent agreements and subsequent practice in interpretation;[186] the notion of evolutionary interpretation of treaty terms;[187] the weight of subsequent agreements and subsequent practice as a means of interpretation;[188] the possibility of expressing agreement regarding interpretation by silence or inaction;[189] and the applicability of

[180] *Ibid*, at pp. 103–104, paras. 65.3(f)(49)–(55).

[181] YBILC 2016, Vol. II, Part Two, p. 35, para. 3 of the commentary to draft article 6 (referring to the *Corfu Channel* case).

[182] *Ibid*, at p. 45, para. 2 of the commentary to draft article 10, fn. 173 (referring to the *Corfu Channel* case, in support of "the core principle of sovereignty").

[183] *Ibid*, at p. 47, para. 4 of the commentary to draft article 11 (referring to the *Corfu Channel* case).

[184] *Ibid*, at p. 52, para. 11 of the commentary to draft article 13 (referring to several decisions of the Court as illustrating the function of good faith as limiting the admissible exercise of rights and discretion).

[185] See, for example, YBILC 2018, Vol. II, Part Two, p. p. 27, para. 4 of the commentary to conclusion 2; pp. 33, 35 and 37, paras. 7, 14 and 26 of the commentary to conclusion 4; pp. 39–40, para. 6 of the commentary to conclusion 5; and pp. 44–45, para. 12 of the commentary to conclusion 6. That approach was also reflected in the Special Rapporteur's reports: see, for example, YBILC 2013, Vo. II, Part One, p. 56, para. 10, pp. 62–66, paras. 42–63, and p. 71, paras. 93–95.

[186] YBILC 2018, Vol. II, Part Two, pp. 48–49; p. 51, para. 16; p. 52, para. 23; pp. 53–54, paras. 27–31 (all in the commentary to conclusion 7).

[187] *Ibid*, at pp. 56–58, paras. 6 and 11–12 of the commentary to conclusion 8.

[188] *Ibid*, at p. 60, para. 3 of the commentary to conclusion 9; see also pp. 61–62, para. 10 of the commentary to that conclusion, which clearly favors the approach of the Court over that of the World Trade Organization Appellate Body (while blurring the differences between them).

[189] *Ibid*, at pp. 65–66, paras. 14, 16–17, and 20 of the commentary to conclusion 10.

articles 31 and 32 of the 1969 Vienna Convention to treaties that are constituent instruments of international organizations.[190]

Much reliance on the Court's case-law was also placed by the Commission in its work on the topic 'Identification of customary international law', which culminated in 2018 with a set of sixteen draft conclusions. While based on a wide array of materials, the conclusions drew primarily on the Court's stated methodology in such cases as *North Sea Continental Shelf* and *Jurisdictional Immunities of the State*,[191] including in defining the key terms "a general practice" and "acceptance as law."[192] The conclusions on how a rule set forth in a treaty may be considered to reflect a rule of customary international law, on the probative value of resolutions of international organizations and conferences, and on particular (as opposed to general) customary international law, were likewise supported (if not shaped) mainly by references to the Court's decisions.[193]

In the *Draft articles on prevention and punishment of crimes against humanity*, adopted on second reading in 2019, the Commission referred to the Court's case-law as confirming the status of the prohibition on crimes against humanity as *jus cogens*;[194] in support of the statement that obligations of a State party under a convention would usually only operate with respect to a situation that existed after the convention enters into force for that State;[195] in explaining the contours of the obligations not to engage in acts constituting crimes against humanity and to prevent and punish crimes against humanity;[196] in support of the directive that preventing crimes against humanity must be done in conformity with international law;[197] in explaining the character of the obligation to

[190] *Ibid*, at pp. 75–80, paras. 6, 8, 10–12, 20–22 and 24–32 of the commentary to conclusion 12.

[191] *Ibid*, at pp. 93–94, paras. 2–3 of the commentary to conclusion 2; pp. 95–96, paras. 3, 5 and 7 of the commentary to conclusion 3.

[192] *Ibid*, at pp. 100–103, paras. 2 and 4–9 of the commentary to conclusion 8 and paras. 2–6 of the commentary to conclusion 9.

[193] *Ibid*, at pp. 105–107, paras. 2 and 5–8 of the commentary to conclusion 11; p. 108, paras. 5–6 of the commentary to conclusion 12; and pp. 112–113, paras. 1, 4 and 6 of the commentary to conclusion 16.

[194] A/74/10, *supra* note 31, at p. 25, para. 5 of the commentary to the preamble.

[195] *Ibid*, at p. 27, para. 3 of the commentary to draft article 1.

[196] *Ibid*, at pp. 48–50, paras. 3–5 and 7–9 of the commentary to draft article 3 (noting, inter alia, that the "Court's approach is consistent with views previously expressed by the Commission").

[197] *Ibid*, at p. 57, para. 5 of the commentary to draft article 4.

establish national jurisdiction, and of the purpose and function of preliminary measures when an alleged offender is present;[198] in describing the obligation of *aut dedere aut judicare*;[199] in support of the notion that an alleged offender must be treated fairly;[200] and in clarifying the essence of negotiation as a dispute settlement means.[201]

The Commission's *Draft guidelines on the protection of the atmosphere* of 2021 contain some two dozen references to the Court, including in support of the guidelines on "Obligation to protect the atmosphere,"[202] "Environmental impact assessment,"[203] "Sustainable utilization of the atmosphere,"[204] and "International cooperation."[205] The role of the Court as a forum for settlement of disputes relating to the protection of the atmosphere is highlighted as well.[206]

The Court's case-law also served to inspire or substantiate several propositions contained in the Commission's *Draft principles on protection of the environment in relation to armed conflicts*, which were adopted on second reading in 2022. That may be said, for example, of the draft principle concerning the obligation to make full reparation for environmental damage caused in relation to an armed conflict;[207] the draft principle incorporating the Martens Clause with respect to the protection of the environment in relation to armed conflicts;[208] the draft principle on application of the law of armed conflict to the environment (with regard to the rule on proportionality);[209] the draft principle on prohibition of pillage;[210] and the draft principle on prevention of transboundary

198 *Ibid*, at p. 85, para. 4 of the commentary to draft article 7, and at p. 91, para. 5 of the commentary to draft article 9, respectively.
199 *Ibid*, at pp. 93–94, paras. 4–5 of the commentary to draft article 10 (extensively quoting from *Questions relating to the Obligation to Prosecute or Extradite (Belgium* v. *Senegal)*).
200 *Ibid*, at p. 101, para. 11 of the commentary to draft article 11.
201 *Ibid*, at p. 130, para. 3 of the commentary to draft article 15.
202 A/76/10: 'Report of the International Law Commission on the Work of Its Seventy-Second Session' (26 April–4 June and 5 July–6 August, 2021), p. 28, para. 9 of the commentary to guideline 3.
203 *Ibid*, at p. 29, para. 2 of the commentary to guideline 4.
204 *Ibid*, at p. 31, para. 5 of the commentary to guideline 5.
205 *Ibid*, at p. 36, para. 3 of the commentary to guideline 8.
206 *Ibid*, at p. 51, para. 3 of the commentary to guideline 12.
207 A/77/10: 'Report of the International Law Commission on the Work of Its Seventy-Third Session' (18 April–3 June and 4 July–5 August, 2022), p. 123, para. 7 of the commentary to principle 9.
208 *Ibid*, at pp. 137 and 139–140, paras. 1–2 and 8–9 of the commentary to principle 12.
209 *Ibid*, at p. 145, paras. 4, 6 of the commentary to principle 14.
210 *Ibid*, at p. 150, para. 3 of the commentary to principle 16.

harm.[211] In offering support for the draft principle on "General environmental obligations of an Occupying Power," the Commission referred to the Court's case-law before drawing upon its own past work bearing on the matter.[212]

The *Draft conclusions on identification and legal consequences of peremptory norms of general international law (jus cogens)*, as finally adopted by the Commission in 2022, contain multifold references to the decisions of the Court, which is recognized for "[leaving] a mark on the development both of the general concept of peremptory norms and of particular peremptory norms, even in cases where such norms were not explicitly invoked."[213] The Court's case-law is cited in support of, among others, the conclusions on "Nature of peremptory norms of general international law";[214] "Bases for peremptory norms of general international law";[215] "International community of States as a whole";[216] "Evidence of acceptance and recognition";[217] and "Rules of customary international law conflicting with a peremptory norm of general international law."[218]

In paying close attention to the Court's decisions, the Commission has not passed over the individual opinions associated with them, including dissenting opinions.[219] These have been referred to – sometimes quite extensively – not only in the reports of special rapporteurs and during

[211] *Ibid*, at pp. 169–170, paras. 1 and 4 of the commentary to principle 21.

[212] *Ibid*, at p. 160, para. 4 of the commentary to principle 19; see also p. 161, para. 5 of the commentary ("The reference to environmental considerations is drawn from and inspired by the Advisory Opinion of the International Court of Justice on *Legality of the Threat or Use of Nuclear Weapons*").

[213] *Ibid*, at p. 45, para. 4 of the commentary to conclusion 9.

[214] *Ibid*, at pp. 18–19 and 23, paras. 3–4 and 11 of the commentary to conclusion 2.

[215] *Ibid*, at pp. 31, 32–33 and 34, paras. 2, 5 and 8 of the commentary to conclusion 5.

[216] *Ibid*, at p. 38, para. 4 of the commentary to conclusion 7.

[217] *Ibid*, at p. 41, para. 2 of the commentary to conclusion 8, as well as p. 42, fns. 119 and 121–122.

[218] *Ibid*, at p. 56, para. 4 of the commentary to conclusion 14.

[219] See also YBILC 2012, Vol. I, p. 117, para. 20 (McRae saying that "[i]t was not the Commission's task first to identify the law and then to apply it, as if it were a court. Hence, as Mr. Tladi had said, separate and dissenting opinions to the decisions of international judicial bodies might well be as important for the Commission as majority opinions. Even if a well-reasoned separate or dissenting opinion did not have the same legal status, it might have more significance for the Commission's work than a poorly reasoned majority opinion that was not supported by practice"), and p. 125, para. 67 (Kamto responding that "he did not go so far as to endorse the position put forward by Mr. McRae when he said that it was sometimes necessary to place the individual or dissenting opinions of some judges of the International Court of Justice at the same level

plenary debates but also in the Commission's final output. Examples are plentiful,[220] but particular mention may be made of the Commission's reliance, in formulating in 1951 the (now outdated) rule of unanimous consent concerning reservations to treaties, on the dissenting opinions of several of the Court's judges in the advisory opinion on *Reservations to the Convention on Genocide*.[221] Attention may also be drawn to the terms of paragraph 1 of the Commission's draft article 56 on the law of treaties (dealing with termination or suspension of the operation of a treaty implied from entering into a subsequent treaty), which were based on the separate opinion of Judge Anzilotti in the *Electricity Company of Sofia and Bulgaria* case, despite the fact that the Court itself did not accept his

as the decisions of the Court, as he considered that to be going too far"); YBILC 2016, Vol. I, p. 232, para. 25 (Kamto).

220 See Special Rapporteur Waldock's explanation that paragraph 3 of draft article 62 that he proposed with regard to treaties providing obligations or rights of third State, "was inspired by the view expressed in the *Free Zones* case by Judges Altamira and Hurst in their dissenting opinion," and that he preferred this view over that proposed by some members of the Commission: YBILC 1964, Vol. I, p. 86, para. 66. See also the references to individual opinions in the commentary to several draft articles on the law of treaties (YBILC 1966, Vol. II, p. 203, para. 3; p. 228, fn. 178; p. 238, para. 1; p. 239, fn. 202; p. 243, para. 2; p. 254, para. 4); the reference, in the commentary to the State responsibility draft article on '*Force majeure* and fortuitous event', to the *Corfu Channel* case and the conflict between the views expressed by the majority of the Court and by Judge Krylov in his dissenting opinion (YBILC 1979, Vol. II, Part 2, p. 130, para. 31); the references in the draft articles on diplomatic protection (YBILC 2006, Vol. II, Part Two, p. 41, para. 10; p. 42, para. 12; p. 43, fn. 162); the reference in the draft articles on the responsibility of international organizations to Judge Fitzmaurice's Separate Opinion in the *Certain Expenses of the United Nations* case (YBILC 2011, Vol. II, Part Two, p. 82, para. 5); the references to individual opinions in the commentary to several guidelines of the Guide to practice on reservations to treaties (YBILC 2011, Vol. II, Part Three, p. 74, fn. 305; p. 86, para. 15; p. 162, fn. 1150; p. 197, fn. 1435; p. 216, fns. 1630, 1633; p. 221, fns. 1675, 1678–1679; p. 221, para. 6 and fns. 1682, 1686; p. 224, fns. 1737–1738; p. 232, fn. 1789; p. 236, fn. 1829; p. 293, para. 6; p. 311, para. 23; p. 324, fn. 2601; p. 335, para. 13); the references in the final report on the obligation to extradite or prosecute (*aut dedere aut judicare*) (YBILC 2014, Vol. II, Part Two, p. 95, para. 11; p. 99, fn. 449; p. 100, para. 28; p. 101, fn. 498; p. 103, fn. 507, p. 104, fns. 513–514); the references in the commentary to the draft conclusions on subsequent agreements and subsequent practice in relation to the interpretation of treaties (YBILC 2018, Vol. II, Part Two, p. 44, para. 7 of the commentary to conclusion 6); the reference in the commentary to the draft articles on prevention and punishment of crimes against humanity (A/74/10, *supra* note 31, at p. 85, para. 5 of the commentary to draft article 7); and the references in the commentary to the draft conclusions on Peremptory norms of general international law (*jus cogens*) (A/77/10, *supra* note 207, at p. 28, fn. 58 and p. 42, fn. 122).

221 See also Chapter 6, Section B.2.

application of these conditions in that case.[222] In a similar vein, one of the exceptions adopted by the Commission (in its work on diplomatic protection) to the rule on exhaustion of local remedies was described by it as having "its origin in a separate opinion of Sir Hersch Lauterpacht in the *Certain Norwegian Loans* case."[223] The term "universal jurisdiction" was likewise defined, in the Commission's final report on the obligation to extradite or prosecute (*aut dedere aut judicare*), by reference to the Joint Separate Opinion of Judges Higgins, Kooijmans, and Buergenthal in the *Arrest Warrant* case.[224] These and other examples show that the Commission has indeed referred to separate and even dissenting opinions of the Court's judges not only where a certain decision of the Court was not determinative of a specific question pending before the Commission, but also where the Court's holding on a certain question was unambiguous.[225] Either way, the Commission has thus allowed for such opinions (that is, for individual judges of the Court in such capacity) a significant role in the codification and development of international law.

2. *Tracking the Court's Language*

The Commission's reliance on the Court's decisions entails a clear preference for following closely the wording employed in them. Tracking the Court's language in the Commission's output is indeed a conscious choice of drafting, and even a slight departure from such phraseology is generally made only for a reason.[226]

Examples of the Commission endorsing the Court's formulations are abundant. In 1978, for instance, in connection with article 24 of the draft articles on succession of States in respect of matters other than treaties,

[222] YBILC 1966, Vol. II, p. 253, para. 2.

[223] YBILC 2006, Vol. II, Part Two, p. 47, para. 3 of the commentary to draft article 15.

[224] YBILC 2014, Vol. II, Part Two, p. 97, para. 3(b)(18), fn. 449.

[225] See also Schwebel, *supra* note 10, at p. 482.

[226] Thus a term may be opposed within the Commission, or avoided by it, on the ground that it has been avoided or not been used by the Court: see, for example, YBILC 1981, Vol. I, p. 11, para. 36 (the Special Rapporteur for the topic 'Law of treaties between States and international organizations or between international organizations', Reuter, suggesting that using the term 'international personality' in connection with the definition of the term 'international organization' would not be wise, primarily because "[i]n its 1949 advisory opinion on *Reparation for Injuries Suffered in the Service of the United Nations*, the International Court of Justice had noted that that was a doctrinal expression which had sometimes given rise to controversy"); YBILC 1955, Vol. I, p. 205, para. 39; YBILC 1999, Vol. I, p. 155, para. 9.

the Commission readily accepted Díaz González's suggestion that "the word 'factors' should be replaced by the word 'circumstances', so as to adhere as closely as possible to the wording used by the International Court of Justice in setting out, in its judgment in the *North Sea Continental Shelf Cases*, the equitable considerations applicable to the delimitation."[227] Similarly, the language employed in article 17 of the Commission's draft articles on the law of non-navigational uses of international watercourses (dealing with how inter-State consultations and negotiations concerning planned measures are to be carried out) was "inspired chiefly by the judgment of the ICJ in the *Fisheries Jurisdiction (United Kingdom* v. *Iceland)* case."[228] The stated intention in qualifying the term "link" by the adjective "effective" in article 19 of the draft articles on nationality of natural persons in relation to the succession of States was likewise "to use the terminology of ICJ in the *Nottebohm* case";[229] and for the wording of article 1 of the draft articles on diplomatic protection, the Commission "had been guided by the language used by ICJ in its judgment in the *Interhandel* case."[230] In working on its draft articles on State responsibility, the Commission "preferred the phrase 'basic human rights', chosen by ICJ in its judgment in the *Barcelona Traction* case, to the phrase 'fundamental human rights' which appears in Article 1, paragraph 3, of the Charter of the United Nations."[231] The term "State which has committed an internationally wrongful act," which was used for years in the Commission's drafts on the topic, was replaced in 1998 with "wrongdoing State" on the advice of the Special Rapporteur, Crawford, who said that the latter term was preferable, inter alia, because the Court had used it in its *Gabčíkovo-Nagymaros Project* judgment.[232] In another article, on the proportionality

[227] YBILC 1978, Vol. I, p. 220, para. 56. Yasseen noted a decade earlier that "on several occasions the Commission had found passages in the judgments of the Court which provided excellent formulations for rules of international law": *supra* note 2.

[228] YBILC 1988, Vol. II, Part Two, p. 52, para. 3.

[229] YBILC 1999, Vol. II, Part Two, p. 40, para. 5. See also YBILC 1997, Vol. II, Part Two, p. 35, para. 5 (commentary to draft article 18(1) concerning "Other States"); YBILC 1997, Vol. I, p. 173, paras. 41–49.

[230] YBILC 2002, Vol. I, p. 129, para. 6 (Yamada, Chair of the Drafting Committee); see also p. 130, para. 9 (referring to draft article 2 in saying that "the Committee had preferred to emphasize that notion, which was also compatible with the wording used in the decision of [PCIJ] in the *Mavrommatis* case").

[231] YBILC 1995, Vol. II, Part Two, p. 74, para. 24; see also YBILC 1993, Vol. I, p. 145, para. 32.

[232] YBILC 1998, Vol. I, p. 193, para. 23 (noting also the reasons that "the new phrase was much more succinct and would save about 100 words overall. Secondly, the use of the past tense implied that the wrongful act had been completed, and was in the past.

of countermeasures, the Commission's Drafting Committee, "[c]onsidering that the words 'proportional' and 'commensurate' were interchangeable . . . had opted for the latter because it was the word ICJ had used."[233] The Commission likewise preferred a wording "more faithful to the language of the *Arrest Warrant* judgment" in describing the acts covered by immunity *ratione personae* in the draft articles provisionally adopted on 'Immunity of State officials from foreign criminal jurisdiction'.[234] The commentary to the Commission's guideline on "sustainable utilization of the atmosphere" makes it plain that "[p]aragraph 2 builds upon the language of the International Court of Justice in its judgment in the *Gabčíkovo-Nagymaros Project* case,"[235] just as the preamble to the Draft principles on protection of the environment in relation to armed conflicts "borrows language from the Advisory Opinion of the International Court of Justice in *Legality of the Threat or Use of Nuclear Weapons*."[236]

The Commission's preference to track the Court's formulations may be evident even in those instances where such language is thought of as being obscure or imprecise, as the view that "[t]he language of judgements, being frequently loose, was generally not appropriate for inclusion

However, the draft clearly also applied to wrongful acts of a continuing character"); see also YBILC 1998, Vol. II, Part One, p. 24, para. 98.

233 YBILC 2001, Vol. I, p. 112, para. 57 (Tomka, Chairman of the Drafting Committee (adding that "... As for the words 'the rights in question' adopted by the Committee at the previous session, they came from the decision of the Court in the *Gabčíkovo-Nagymaros Project* case")). See also Crawford, *supra* note 89, at p. 81 (noting, with reference to the *Gabčíkovo-Nagymaros Project* judgment, that "[t]he Court's language was quoted in the eventual ILC articles on countermeasures. This illustrates how the Court and the ILC can and do mutually endorse aspects of each other's work"); D.J. Bederman, 'Counterintuiting Countermeasures', 96 AJIL (2002) 817 at 822 (referring to draft article 51, which borrows the word "commensurate" from the Court's jurisprudence, as "a provision whose key term is based exclusively on isolated language in a recent World Court decision"). The use of the word "countermeasures" in preference of "reprisals" was similarly made primarily because it was found "in the jurisprudence of ICJ itself": see, for example, YBILC 1992, Vol. I, p. 176, para. 28 (Razafindralambo).

234 YBILC 2013, Vol. I, p. 52, para. 16 (Tladi, Chairman of the Drafting Committee). See also YBILC 2015, Vol. II, Part Two, p. 73, para. 187 ("It was acknowledged that a variety of terms have been used to refer to the concept, but in this case the term 'act performed in an official capacity' was employed to ensure continuity of terminological usage within the Commission, following the terminology used by the International Court of Justice in the *Arrest Warrant of 11 April 2000* case").

235 *Supra* note 204.

236 A/77/10: *supra* note 207, at p. 99, para. 6 of the commentary to the preamble.

in an instrument of a legislative character,"[237] has never won support within the Commission. This was the case when, as already noted, the Commission in 1955 made a number of changes designed to bring its text on straight baselines "even more closely into line with the Court's judgment in the ... *Fisheries* case,"[238] despite the criticism of the Special Rapporteur, François, that some of the Court's expressions were too imprecise.[239] Even a plea made "with all due deference to the International Court of Justice," that "in [a] particular context the Commission could depart somewhat from that wording [used by the Court] in order to reflect faithfully what the Court had [clearly] had in mind,"[240] may be defeated in the interest of retaining the precise wording of the Court.[241] The Commission has also accepted that "[t]he sensitivity of the party that had lost a case should not cause the Commission to refrain from using wording drawn from rulings of the Court."[242]

At the same time, there are exceptions to the Commission's attachment to the Court's formulations, which again reflect the understanding among its members that they complement the work of the Court, or at the very least that they "should not always be bound by the exact language of the ICJ, which after all is not a legislator, and [they] could certainly seek to clarify what the Court was saying."[243] Thus, for example, although the Commission in 1955 "felt bound to retain" the expression "used for navigation between two parts of the high seas" in its draft text on the non-suspension of innocent passage through straits, "particularly in view of its use by the International Court of Justice in the *Corfu Channel* case,"[244] it nevertheless deemed it appropriate to insert the word "normally" before the word "used."[245] The Commission similarly codified the exception to the rule regarding the effect of error in the law of

[237] YBILC 1955, Vol. I, p. 203, para. 19 (Edmonds, adding that "it would be well to bear in mind that there was a great difference between the legislative and the judicial function"). See also YBILC 1964, Vol. I, p. 163, para. 66 (Lachs).

[238] YBILC 1955, Vol. II, p. 36, para. 3 of the commentary to draft article 5.

[239] See YBILC 1955, Vol. I, p. 199, para. 63; p. 204, para. 28; and p. 205, paras. 34–35.

[240] YBILC 1966, Vol. I, Part I, p. 116, para. 29 (Reuter).

[241] *Ibid*, at p. 117.

[242] *Ibid*, at pp. 20–21, para. 38 (Briggs, pointing out that "[w]ith regard to the use of phraseology from International Court of Justice decisions, he must point out that when the Court decided a case there was always one dissatisfied party").

[243] Interview with member of the Commission in July 2016, on file with the author.

[244] YBILC 1955, Vol. II, p. 39.

[245] *Ibid* (stating its opinion that this addition is "in conformity with the Court's decision"). See also YBILC 1956, Vol. II, p. 273, para. 3 of the commentary to article 17.

treaties by drawing upon the terms used in the *Temple of Preah Vihear* case, but "felt . . . that there is substance in the view that the Court's formulation of the exception . . . is so wide as to leave little room for the operation of the rule" and thus, "without questioning the Court's formulation of the exception in the context of the particular case," omitted certain of its words.[246] The Commission also accepted the suggestion by Crawford, as Special Rapporteur on State responsibility, to retain the term "attribution" despite being aware that the Court had continued to use "imputability."[247] Similarly, it preferred to speak of "formation" of customary international law in its draft conclusions on identification of customary international law, even though the Special Rapporteur had pointed out that the Court referred to "creation."[248] The Commission also favored the word "assessed" for the requirement that a State's practice be considered as a whole,[249] even though the Court had previously employed the word "taken" in a case referred to in this context.[250]

3. *The Court's Influence on the Commission's Program of Work*

The Court's decisions have inspired not only individual provisions adopted by the Commission but also the selection of topics that it has taken up. This is not altogether surprising, given that subjects considered ripe for codification are defined in the Commission's Statute as those in

246 YBILC 1966, Vol. II, p. 244, para. 8. For the earlier resistance within the Commission to depart from the Court's wording, see YBILC 1963, Vol. I, p. 39, para. 72 (Rosenne) and p. 41, para. 23 (Jiménez de Aréchaga).

247 YBILC 1998, Vol. I, pp. 228–229, para. 2 (defending this position by explaining that "[t]he Commission's choice was nevertheless right, since 'imputability' introduced an element of fiction where none existed," and noting that the term "imputability" was in fact used at the outset by the former Special Rapporteur, Roberto Ago). At least a couple of members were uncomfortable with disfavoring a term employed by the Court: *ibid.* at p. 239, para. 53 (Kabatsi), and p. 243, para. 17 (Illueca).

248 For the suggestion by the Special Rapporteur on the topic, Sir Michael Wood, to replace "the words 'formation, or expression' with the words 'expressive, or creative', which were employed by the International Court of Justice in the *Continental Shelf (Tunisia/Libyan Arab Jamahiriya)* case," see UN Doc. A/CN.4/717: 'Fifth Report on Identification of Customary International Law by Michael Wood, Special Rapporteur' (2018), para. 46. For Kolodkin's observation that "as currently worded, [the draft conclusion] was not incompatible with the Court's judgment and there was no reason to amend it," see YBILC 2016, Vol. I, p. 104, para. 45.

249 YBILC 2018, Vol. II, Part Two, p. 99 (conclusion 7, paragraph 1).

250 *Ibid*, at p. 100, para. 3 of the commentary (referring to *Jurisdictional Immunities of the State*).

which "there already has been extensive State practice, precedent and doctrine."[251] As early as the Commission's first session, in 1949, when it was engaged in initial planning for the codification of international law, Spiropoulos observed with regard to the law of treaties that "[t]he Permanent Court of International Justice had established a jurisprudence in the matter which far from preventing the work of codification should on the contrary encourage and help it."[252] This approach has guided the Commission ever since (the topics 'State responsibility' and 'Diplomatic protection' come easily to mind), and has meant that the Commission continues to be very attentive to the Court's case-law in considering its own program of work. The Court's influence in this regard is even more significant when considering that the General Assembly, which the Commission's Statute calls upon to specify topics for the Commission to work on, virtually never does so.

A clear example of the Court's influence on the Commission's agenda may be found in the work on 'Unilateral acts of State', a topic to which the Commission turned its attention in 1996. Indeed, one of the primary stated reasons for taking up the topic was that "[i]t has been touched upon by several judgments of ICJ, and especially in the *Nuclear Tests* cases, but the celebrated dicta leave room for uncertainties and questions."[253] Despite a warning that the Commission "should avoid taking the view that the law [on the topic] depended on a small number of maverick decisions of ICJ,"[254] and a concern that the topic was not a unified subject,[255] members of the Commission considered that the Court's case-law provided sufficient material,[256] and the work of the Special Rapporteur was described as intended "to uncover the constituent

[251] Statute of the International Law Commission (1947), article 15.

[252] YBILC 1949, p. 48, para. 17.

[253] YBILC 1996, Vol. II, Part Two, p. 141, para. 3(b). See also YBILC 2002, Vol. I, p. 98, para. 3 (Fomba saying that "ICJ had dispelled such mysteries [relating to the scope of unilateral acts] ... However, in view of the difference in nature and mandate between the Court and the Commission, and without prejudice to the results of the ongoing study of practice, the Commission should be able to proceed further than the Court had done and to propose a genuine legal regime for unilateral acts").

[254] YBILC 1998, Vol. I, p. 49, para. 8 (Brownlie).

[255] *Ibid*, at p. 35, para. 30 (Brownlie); see also p. 39, para. 67 (Ferrari Bravo expressing the concern that the Commission might find itself "sailing on a boundless ocean"). Brownlie later suggested that the study on the topic 'Unilateral acts' should focus on cases heard by the Court: YBILC 2004, Vol. I, p. 180, para. 31.

[256] See, for example, YBILC 1998, Vol. I, p. 41, para. 83 (Economidas stating that the Court had already accepted unilateral acts as a source of international rights and obligations, and that, "[i]n fact, the discussion in the Commission could not take place unless there was some relevant case law, and it had all the material necessary for studying unilateral

elements of what ICJ had described in many of its decisions as a purely unilateral legal act."[257] Of the resulting ten *Guiding principles applicable to unilateral declarations of States capable of creating legal obligations*, adopted by the Commission in 2006, no fewer than nine give expression to the case-law of the Court.[258]

The Commission's work on 'Immunity of State officials from foreign criminal jurisdiction', too, was "triggered in large part" by the Court.[259] If any proof is needed, during the annual exchange between members of the Commission and the President of the Court in 2006, when President Higgins was asked whether there were any topics that "the Commission might take up that would be useful to the Court in its work,"[260] she replied that "[o]ne topic on which she personally would warmly welcome a study by the Commission was the relationship between the global push for measures to combat impunity, on the one hand, and the international law in immunity, on the other."[261] The Commission took up the topic 'Immunity of State officials from foreign criminal jurisdiction' the following year, and members of the Commission later recalled President Higgins's words when highlighting the benefit of having done so.[262]

In a similar vein, the Commission did not take up the topic of *jus cogens* until after several decisions of the Court had considered the scope, content, and impact of the concept (which had first been endorsed by the Commission, in connection with its work on the law of treaties). An initial proposal made in 1993 by Jacovides was rejected by the Commission's Planning Group, which considered that because practice on *jus cogens* "did not yet exist," it would be "premature for [the

acts"), and p. 48, para. 2 (Dugard recognizing that "[t]he doctrine of unilateral acts was based on a handful of judicial decisions, particularly in the *Nuclear Tests* cases in 1974").

257 *Ibid*, at p. 45, para. 27 (Herdocia Sacasa). The Court itself may well have been aware, throughout this time, that the Commission had identified already in 1967 "the basic notion of the concept of 'unilateral acts'" as a subject worthy of study, also by virtue of the decisions of the Court and other tribunals: YBILC 1971, Vol. II, Part Two, pp. 60–61.

258 YBILC 2006, Vol. II, Part Two, p. 164 (Guiding principle 6, which concerns more of a factual point regarding the possible addressees of a unilateral declaration, being the exception); see also the details provided earlier in this chapter.

259 R. O'Keefe, 'Jurisdictional Immunities', in C.J. Tams and J. Sloan (eds.), *The Development of International Law by the International Court of Justice* (OUP 2013) 147.

260 YBILC 2006, Vol. I, p. 218, para. 50 (Escarameia).

261 *Ibid*, at para. 52. Presidents of the Court have advised the Commission as to its program of work on more than one occasion when paying it their annual official visits: see Chapter 5, Section B.

262 See YBILC 2008, Vol. I, p. 204, para. 2 (Jacobsson); p. 217, para. 18 (Vázquez-Bermúdez); and p. 226, para. 91 (Saboia).

Commission] to enter into this kind of study."[263] By 2015, however, after it was pointed out that practice had developed at a rapid pace and attention was drawn primarily to decisions of the Court,[264] the Commission felt comfortable enough to add the topic '*Jus cogens*' to its long-term program of work.[265]

A different, but no less remarkable, example of the influence that the Court may have on the Commission's agenda may be seen in the latter's decision in 2002 to add the topic 'Fragmentation of international law' to its long-term program of work. Members of the Court have since the mid-1990s voiced their apprehension, both before the Commission and elsewhere, about fragmentation as a threat to international law as a system, with particular repercussions for the Court's influence.[266] Members of the Commission paid close attention to such rather alarmist statements, and by the time President Guillaume told them in 2000 that the challenge of fragmentation was "a subject of common interest" to both the Court and the Commission,[267] they were ready to pick up the gauntlet. A proposal that the Commission take up the topic, presented that year by Hafner, gave prominence to the concern earlier expressed by

263 See YBILC 2014, Vol. II, Part Two, pp. 170–171, paras. 3–4. See also 'Presentation by Mr. Vaughan Lowe', in *The International Law Commission Fifty Years After: An Evaluation* (United Nations 2000) 122 at 134.

264 YBILC 2014, Vol. II, Part Two, p. 171, fn. 9; pp. 172–173, paras. 10–12.

265 The topic was later renamed 'Peremptory norms of general international law (*jus cogens*)'; the output was titled 'Draft conclusions on identification and legal consequences of peremptory norms of general international law (*jus cogens*)'.

266 See, for example, S. Oda, 'The International Court of Justice Viewed from the Bench (1976–1993)', 244 RdC (1993) 145; Address to the Plenary Session of the General Assembly of the United Nations by Judge Stephen M. Schwebel, President of the International Court of Justice, (26 October 1999), available at <https://undocs.org/pdf?symbol=en/A/54/PV.39>; Speech by His Excellency Judge Gilbert Guillaume, President of the International Court of Justice, to the Sixth Committee of the General Assembly of the United Nations (27 October 2000), available at <www.icj-cij.org/files/press-releases/1/3001.pdf>; YBILC 2003, Vol. I, p. 166 (President Shi telling members of the Commission that "the members of ICJ were concerned about the fragmentation of international law"). See also M. Koskenniemi and P. Leino, 'Fragmentation of International Law? Postmodern Anxieties', 15 LJIL (2002) 553–556; H. Caminos, 'The Growth of Specialized International Tribunals and the Fears of Fragmentation of International Law', in N. Boschiero et al (eds.), *International Courts and the Development of International Law* (Asser Press 2013) 55–64.

267 YBILC 2000, Vol. I, p. 358, para. 4. An earlier study on the Commission from 1981 by the United Nations Institute for Training and Research (UNITAR) "implie[d] that if the tendency towards legal fragmentation is not arrested, the [UN] system may soon have no further significant use for the ILC, in which case it should be retired": T.M. Franck and M. El Baradei, 'The Codification and Progressive Development of International Law: A UNITAR Study of the Role and Use of the International Law Commission', 76 AJIL (1982) 630 at 639.

President Schwebel before the UN General Assembly, that a multitude of courts, tribunals, and similar instances could eventually create a risk to the homogeneity of international law.[268] It also indicated at that very early stage that one envisaged solution would have to do with endowing the Court with some sort of monitoring authority to ensure consistency and harmony of the international legal order.[269] The Commission's subsequent decision to study the topic, which was far from a natural choice,[270] soon received support from President Shi, who told the Commission in the following year that the judges of the Court remained concerned about the fragmentation of international law, and that "it would be helpful if the General Assembly were to adopt a resolution indicating how to deal with [the matter]."[271] President Higgins, for her part, had no reservations in pointing out to the Commission in 2006 that cases such as *Armed Activities on the Territory of the Congo* and the *Genocide case (Bosnia and Herzegovina* v. *Serbia and Montenegro)* constituted "exemplary material for the topic."[272] While the Commission's work, which was pursued under the title 'Fragmentation of international law: difficulties arising from the diversification and expansion of international law' did not eventually make recommendations such as giving the Court the possibility of being seized by other international courts with preliminary issues,[273] it may well be said that in its aftermath "the polemics have subsided."[274]

268 YBILC 2000, Vol. II, Part Two, p. 148. The name originally proposed for the topic was 'Risks ensuing from fragmentation of international law'.

269 *Ibid*, at p. 149 (relying also on a statement by President Schwebel).

270 See also C. Tomuschat, 'The International Law Commission – An Outdated Institution?', 49 GYIL (2006) 77 at 83 (referring to the topic when suggesting that "[a]nalytical research of that kind is normally carried out by academic lawyers").

271 YBILC 2003, Vol. I, p. 166, paras. 25–26.

272 YBILC 2006, Vol. I, p. 214, para. 25. President Higgins also made it known that she "greatly welcome[d] this study, and the interesting reports produced by Professor Koskenniemi thus far": R. Higgins, 'A Babel of Judicial Voices? Ruminations from the Bench', 55 ICLQ (2006) 791 at 800.

273 A suggestion raised before the Commission by President Guillaume: YBILC 2000, Vol. I, p. 359, para. 14. For possible reasons for the Commission's decision to avoid proposing an institutional hierarchy in the international legal system, see M.J. Matheson, 'The Fifty-Eighth Session of the International Law Commission', 101 AJIL (2007) 407 at 429 ("Commission members . . . were obviously not eager to plunge into such delicate questions as the degree to which international tribunals are bound to defer to pronouncements by the International Court of Justice"); C. Leathley, 'An Institutional Hierarchy to Combat the Fragmentation of International Law: Has the ILC Missed an Opportunity?', 40 *New York University Journal of International Law & Politics* (2007) 259 at 268–270.

274 T. Treves, 'The Expansion of International Law', 398 RdC (2015) 201 (adding that "[t]he undertones of competition between courts and tribunals are gone and the discussions, while continuing, are going in the direction of more detailed scholarly investigations").

B. Supporting the Court

The exceptional position reserved for the Court in the Commission's work finds expression not only in the consistent endorsement and dissemination of the Court's pronouncements; it is also visible in the Commission's conscious approach of seeking to respect and support the Court so as to preserve and promote its authority. That approach may be gleaned from the Commission's output as well, in particular where it reflects the Commission's careful consideration of any reference to the Court's role and its deliberate efforts to expand it.

1. *Respecting the Court and Seeking to Safeguard It from Criticism*

A striking illustration of the Commission's concern with preserving and promoting the Court's authority may be found in the Commission's decision in 1950 not to recommend the establishment of a criminal chamber of the Court for purposes of trying persons charged with international crimes, out of concern that this would be harmful to the Court. Despite the conclusion of the Commission's special rapporteurs on the question of 'International criminal jurisdiction', Alfaro and Sandström, that it would be both possible and preferable to provide for such an option,[275] the Commission eventually decided to state that "it has paid attention to the possibility of establishing a criminal chamber of the International Court of Justice and that, though it is possible to do so by amendment of the Court's Statute, the Commission does not recommend it."[276] This came after Hudson, with much diplomatic skill, threw his full weight behind an effort to prevent such a recommendation, urging his colleagues that the Commission "must avoid any step which might make that great institution [i.e. the Court] a centre of grave controversy."[277] Brierly agreed: "The real reason why it would be unwise

See also Murphy's observation that the Commission's final report may have "place[d] too much emphasis on the need to promote the coherence of the international law system, rather than recognizing and celebrating, for example, the value of competition between international tribunals": S.D. Murphy, 'Deconstructing Fragmentation: Koskenniemi's 2006 ILC Project', 27 *Temple International & Comparative Law Journal* (2013) 293 at 302.

275 See YBILC 1950, Vol. II, p. 17, paras. 130–134 (Report by Ricardo J. Alfaro, Special Rapporteur) and p. 23, para. 40 (Report by Emil Sandström, Special Rapporteur).

276 *Ibid*, at p. 379, para. 145.

277 YBILC 1950, Vol. I, p. 23, para. 60 (earlier saying that "as one who for thirty years had exerted every effort on behalf of the Court at The Hague – one of the essential organs of

to confer criminal jurisdiction on the present International Court had been given by Mr. Hudson… It would be disastrous if such discredit spread to the Court."[278] Being "anxious to safeguard the [International] Court of Justice from criticism,"[279] Hudson and Brierly managed to sway the Commission. A similar position was adopted several decades later, in the early 1990s, when the Commission was asked by the General Assembly to consider "the question of establishing an international criminal court or other international criminal trial mechanism" and recommended the establishment of a separate international criminal court.[280]

As another early example, in 1958, a draft provision of the Commission's model rules on arbitral procedure that would have enabled parties engaged in arbitration, "in exceptional circumstances," to replace by agreement an arbitrator appointed by the President of the International Court of Justice, was dropped due to concerns raised by several members that permitting such conduct would undermine the prestige and authority of the President of the Court.[281]

international life – [he] feared it might mean the utter destruction of the Court's prestige if an international criminal jurisdiction were added to it. The International Court should remain an instrument solely for the settlement of disputes between States, and for giving advisory opinions"); see also p. 25, para. 21 (Hudson saying that "[i]t would be most unfortunate for the authority of the International Court, which was set up to settle disputes between States, if it were to be associated with the idea of a police court. The International Court had a mission to fulfil. To create a criminal chamber of the Court or to confer criminal jurisdiction on the Court would be a fatal blow") and p. 26, para. 34 (Hudson saying that "any international criminal jurisdiction was bound to become deeply embroiled in political controversies. This would mean less frequent recourse to the Hague Court in a sphere in which it had done admirable work, namely, in disputes between States; and even if States still submitted their disputes to the Court, its prestige would nevertheless be lowered"). Hudson made sure to be the one proposing the text of the Commission's conclusion that no criminal chamber should be established: see *ibid*, at p. 27, paras. 46–47 and pp. 316–317.

278 *Ibid*, at p. 25, para. 22. One other reason that was discussed was that a major amendment to the Court's Statute would be required in order to empower it to hear criminal trials.

279 *Ibid*, at p. 26, para. 32 (Chairman Scelle, who earlier indicated that even if the Commission had not explicitly been asked about the desirability of such a criminal chamber of the Court, but only of the possibility of setting it up, in view of the concerns expressed by Hudson it should express a definite opinion about it (at p. 24, paras. 6, 8)).

280 YBILC 1992, Vol. II, p. 16, para. 104 and pp. 58–80. See also YBILC 1992, Vol. I, p. 204, para. 42 (Al-Khasawneh saying that he "did not think that the Commission was in a position to comment on the competence of the members of the ICJ in matters of criminal law").

281 YBILC 1958, Vol. I, pp. 27–30, 39.

The Commission's consciousness of not being discourteous toward the Court may also be seen in its more recent work on the topic 'Identification of customary international law', which sought to provide guidance on how rules of customary international law are to be determined. The Special Rapporteur, Sir Michael Wood, and the Commission following his lead, made it clear early on that such guidance was directed mainly at "judges in domestic courts, and judges and arbitrators in specialized international courts and tribunals."[282] It was also agreed that the primary materials for the Commission's work on the topic would include the practice of international courts and tribunals, "first among them the International Court of Justice,"[283] and, as already noted, the draft conclusions eventually adopted indeed rely heavily on the Court's decisions.[284] The Commission was also at pains, when referring (in line with the Court's Statute) to judicial decisions as "subsidiary means" for the determination of rules of customary international law, not to be seen as downplaying the importance of the Court's decisions:[285] draft

282 YBILC 2013, Vol. II, Part One, p. 120, para. 14. See also YBILC 2014, Vol. II, Part One, p. 170, para. 12 (referring "especially" to "those who are not necessarily specialists in the general field of public international law").

283 *Ibid*, at p. 169, para. 3(b). See also YBILC 2014, Vol. I, p. 122, para. 8 (Vázquez-Bermúdez saying, with reference to the general methodology, that "[t]he Court and the Commission had a significant influence on each other's work. The Court also influenced other international courts, States and domestic courts, which did not replicate the work done by the Court to identify the existence and scope of a customary rule. It would be useful for the Special Rapporteur to refer to the Court's practice and its recognized authority, which the Commission shared, to identify rules of customary international law"). The role given to decisions of the Court was so significant that some members "cautioned against exclusive reliance on the jurisprudence of the International Court of Justice": YBILC 2014, Vol. II, Part Two, p. 149, para. 151; see also YBILC 2014, Vol. I, p. 130, para. 6 (Huang saying that "he was not in favour of extensive quotes from the judgments of the International Court of Justice in statements during plenary debates, as it gave the impression that the Commission relied too heavily on such judgments instead of on the opinions of its members").

284 See also O. Sender and M. Wood, 'The International Court of Justice and Customary International Law: A Reply to Stefan Talmon', *EJIL:Talk!* (30 November 2015), available at <www.ejiltalk.org/the-international-court-of-justice-and-customary-international-law-a-reply-to-stefan-talmon/>. Murase's view that "[t]he International Court of Justice was by no means a central decision-making organ for matters of customary international law, and it would therefore not be appropriate to take the Statute of the International Court of Justice as a basis for preparing a general definition of customary international law for the entire international community" (YBILC 2013, Vol. I, p. 83, para. 15) did not gain any traction within the Commission.

285 See YBILC 2015, Vol. II, Part Two, p. 30, para. 86; see also the Statement of the Chairman of the Drafting Committee at YBILC 2015, Vol. I, p. 282, para. 26.

conclusion 13 (on 'Decisions of courts and tribunals') highlights expressly the decisions of the Court,[286] and its commentary makes it clear that "[t]he use of the term 'subsidiary means' does not, and is not intended to, suggest that such decisions are not important for the identification of customary international law."[287] It further explains that

> [e]xpress mention is made of the International Court of Justice, the principal judicial organ of the United Nations whose Statute is an integral part of the Charter of the United Nations and whose members are elected by the General Assembly and Security Council, in recognition of the significance of its case law and its particular position as the only standing international court of general jurisdiction.[288]

The Commission's draft conclusion 9 on the topic 'Peremptory norms of general international law (*jus cogens*)' similarly highlights the particular importance of the Court's decisions as subsidiary means for the determination of *jus cogens* norms.[289]

In its annual reports to the General Assembly, too, the Commission has been very conscious to exhibit courtesy toward the Court and not to include any text that may be seen as passing judgment on it. Amendments to the Commission's draft annual reports have been made time and again specifically for such a purpose, as was the case in 1952 when Hudson suggested that "it was not for the Commission to declare that some particular provision confirmed the traditional practice of the International Court" and proposed, in connection with a draft commentary that the Commission was considering, "the substitution of the words 'is in accord with' for the word 'confirms'."[290] In 2007, the Commission deemed it appropriate to include in its annual report a

[286] See YBILC 2018, Vol. II, Part Two, p. 109, draft conclusion 13(1): "Decisions of international courts and tribunals, in particular of the International Court of Justice, concerning the existence and content of rules of customary international law are a subsidiary means for the determination of such rules."

[287] *Ibid*, at para. 2 of the commentary.

[288] *Ibid*, at para. 4 (which further indicates, at fn. 743, that "[a]lthough there is no hierarchy of international courts and tribunals, decisions of the International Court of Justice are often regarded as authoritative by other courts and tribunals").

[289] A/77/10, *supra* note 207, at p. 43, para. 1 of conclusion 9; see also the explanation provided at pp. 44–45, para. 4 of the commentary to the conclusion.

[290] YBILC 1952, Vol. I, p. 231, para. 73 (the amendment was accepted). Other examples are abundant: see, for instance, YBILC 1950, Vol. I, p. 303, paras. 101, 104 (acceptance of Hudson's proposal that the passage "a positive principle which could supplement the negative opinion ordered by the Permanent Court of International Justice" be deleted); YBILC 1958, Vol. I, p. 39, paras. 68–69 (rejection of a sentence that would have placed

paragraph "[r]ecalling that the ICJ as the principal judicial organ of the United Nations has played an important role in adjudicating disputes among States in accordance with international law" and requesting the UN Secretariat "to make every effort to continue the publication Summaries of Judgements, Advisory Opinions and Orders of the International Court of Justice, in all the official languages of the United Nations."[291]

2. *Promoting the Doctrine of Sources Enshrined in the Court's Statute*

Another noteworthy contribution by the Commission to the Court's standing has been its consistent treatment of article 38.1 of the Court's Statute – formally an instruction to the Court alone as to the law to be applied by it – as an authoritative enumeration of the sources of international law more generally. Despite various suggestions over the decades that a broader spectrum of international law exists beyond the

co-opted arbitrators on the same footing as arbitrators appointed by the President of the Court); YBILC 1990, Vol. I, pp. 326–327, para. 55 (acceptance of Njenga's proposal that, "[o]ut of respect for the ICJ," the Commission indicates explicitly in its 1990 annual report that the views of the ICJ should be obtained as regards the option of conferring upon it jurisdiction over individuals); YBILC 1997, Vol. I, p. 306, para. 72 (acceptance of Pellet's proposed amendment to the text of the Commission's annual report "in the interest of greater courtesy towards ICJ"); YBILC 2001, Vol. I, p. 274, paras. 62–63 (acceptance of Pellet's suggestion that a formulation that "appeared to award points to the ICJ and should be deleted"); YBILC 2006, Vol. I, p. 274, para. 26 (acceptance of Gaja's remark, made in connection with the adoption of the commentaries on the draft articles on diplomatic protection, that the Commission should not seem "to imply that the ICJ had been confused in its reasoning [in the *Avena* and *LaGrand* cases as regards the difference between diplomatic protection and consular assistance]; that was not a fair comment or something which the Commission should presume to say"); YBILC 2006, Vol. I, p. 309, para. 84 (acceptance of Pellet's observation that "it would be only reasonable to place the ICJ at the top of the list [included in the Commission's annual report] of organizations with which the Commission had continued traditional exchanges of information"); YBILC 2011, Vol. I, p. 352, para. 30 (acceptance of Nolte's suggestion to amend a sentence which stated that the Court paid little attention to the declaration by Romania, as it "sounded derogatory"); YBILC 2014, Vol. I, p. 219, para. 8 (Vázquez-Bermúdez suggesting the deletion of a paragraph in saying that "there was a close, even symbiotic, relationship between the Court and the Commission, as reflected in the work of each. The last sentence of paragraph 17 could send an unfortunate message"). Such an approach of seeking to avoid any appearance of criticism of the Court is moreover often evident in the debates of the Commission's Drafting Committee and working groups, which are not recorded.

291 YBILC 2007, Vol. II, p. 102, para. 394.

contours of that provision,[292] the Commission has persistently continued to consider that codification of the sources of international law "has been successfully accomplished by the definition of the sources of international law as given in article 38 of the Statute of the International Court of Justice."[293] Thus, for example, the Commission adopted *en toto* the text of article 38 in its model rules on arbitral procedure, when laying down the law to be applied by any tribunal in the absence of an agreement between the parties.[294] It similarly referred to "the main sources of international law (treaties, custom and general principles of law as laid out in Article 38 of the Statute of the International Court of Justice)" in its study on 'Fragmentation of international law'.[295] The Commission's work on these sources of international law has very much been grounded in their definition in article 38.1 and their application thereunder;[296] and the foray into the subject of obligations arising for States out of unilateral acts – as we have seen – has been largely defined by the Court's pronouncements on the matter. The more recent topics aiming to clarify the meaning of 'General principles of law' and 'Subsidiary means for determination of rules of international law', in which both terms are used by the Commission expressly within their meaning in article 38.1,[297] further illustrate the point. It might also suggest a certain self-confidence on the part of the Commission that the interpretation of this provision in the Court's Statute is not the sole prerogative of the Court.

Significantly, the Commission has also endorsed article 38.1 as the standard approach to law finding: as McRae has observed, the legal research undertaken by the Commission into a topic under its

[292] See, for example, R.Y. Jennings, 'The Identification of International Law', in B. Cheng (ed.), *International Law: Teaching and Practice* (Stevens & Sons 1982) 3 at 9; D.P. Verma, 'Rethinking about New International Law-Making Process', 29 IJIL (1989) 38–51.

[293] UN Doc. A/CN.4/1/Rev.1: 'Survey of International Law in Relation to the Work of Codification of the International Law Commission: Preparatory Work within the Purview of Article 18, Paragraph 1, of the Statute of the International Law Commission (Memorandum submitted by the Secretary-General)' (1949), p. 22.

[294] YBILC 1958, Vol. II, p. 83, article 10.

[295] YBILC 2006, Vol. II, Part Two, p. 182, conclusion (31).

[296] See Section A.1. See also the commentary to conclusions 5 and 9 of the Commission's Draft conclusions on 'Identification and legal consequences of peremptory norms of general international law (*jus cogens*)', in A/77/10, *supra* note 207, at pp. 33–35, paras. 7–10 and pp. 43 and 45, paras. 2 and 5–6.

[297] See, respectively, YBILC 2017, Vol. II, Part Two, p. 155, para. 4; and A/76/10, *supra* note 202, at pp. 186–187, paras. 1–4.

consideration is "essentially a utilization of the classic sources of international law as set out in Article 38(1) of the Statute of the International Court of Justice."[298] With regard to the identification of customary international law, in particular, the Commission's stated methodology has been closely modeled on that of the Court.[299] In employing the same foundational doctrines and argumentative techniques that are resorted to by the Court, the Commission has thus contributed to their wider appeal and application, and to maintaining the Court at the center (if not the apex) of a unified system of law tailored to its design.

3. *Seeking to Expand the Court's Jurisdiction*

It is commonly thought that the Commission's usual practice is to leave the essentially political question of dispute settlement outside of its work products, for negotiation between States at any conference to which such products are submitted.[300] In fact, however, the Commission has often included dispute settlement clauses in its output, and these have not infrequently reserved for the Court the role of ultimate arbiter.[301] As the following account indicates, such references to the Court may be seen to reflect a general preference of the Commission to broaden the reach of the Court's jurisdiction, motivated not only by a desire to promote the ideal of compulsory judicial settlement of international disputes, but also

[298] D. McRae, 'The Work of the International Law Commission 2007–2011: Progress and Prospects', 106 AJIL (2012) 322 at 331 (suggesting, however, that for some topics, in which the relevant practice is elusive, other methods may and have been resorted to). See also YBILC 1967, Vol. I, p. 88, para. 6 (Judge Sir Gerald Fitzmaurice addressing the Commission in saying that "[t]he Court had to declare the law, not as an arbitrary process but in accordance with the provisions of Article 38, paragraph 1 of its Statute. The Commission's task was less circumscribed, for it was the main international codifying agency, but it still had to take into account the elements laid down in that article"). For the suggestion that the enumeration of the sources of international law in the ICJ Statute (including the distinction between principal and 'subsidiary' means for determining the law) expedited the codification of international law by spelling out the "normative specter" to those categories of law, see F. Villagrán Kramer, 'The First Fifty Years of the U.N. International Law Commission', 16 *Chinese Taiwan Yearbook of International Law and Affairs* (1997) 1 at 19.

[299] See *supra* notes 191–193 and the accompanying text.

[300] See, for example, E. Candioti, 'Comment: International Law of Shared Natural Resources and Peace', in G. Nolte (ed.), *Peace through International Law: The Role of the International Law Commission* (Springer 2009) 151 at 154.

[301] For a general survey of the Commission's practice in relation to settlement of disputes clauses, see UN Doc. A/CN.4/623: 'Settlement of Disputes Clauses – Note by the Secretariat', YBILC 2010, Vol. II, Part One, pp. 427–440.

by the perception that this may be a significant guarantee that codified law would be applied.

Already at the Commission's first session in 1949, its Chairman Hudson drew the attention of his colleagues to the possibility of extending the Court's jurisdiction if the Commission were to include the topic 'Arbitral procedure' in its program of work.[302] The Commission's draft convention on arbitral procedure, adopted in 1953, followed that lead, designating for the Court compulsory jurisdiction over such matters as the arbitrability of a dispute, the disqualification of a sole arbitrator, and the interpretation of an arbitral award as well as its annulment.[303] The view that making provision for interventions by the Court in arbitral proceedings, "as it were by the back door," might be incompatible with the fundamental principle of State sovereignty,[304] ultimately succumbed within the Commission (by a vote) to the sentiment that "the ideal of the international community [included] . . . the obligatory jurisdiction of the International Court of Justice."[305] The

[302] YBILC 1949, p. 50, para. 33.

[303] See YBILC 1953, Vol. II, pp. 208–212. The Commission debated whether it was at all appropriate to impose such roles on the Court in this way, but in the end "felt that, as the International Court of Justice is the principal judicial organ of the United Nations, it is proper, with regard to an instrument brought into existence under the aegis of the United Nations, that certain functions or powers shall be conferred upon the Court and that it was unnecessary that the Court should in each case signify the acceptance of the powers and functions thus conferred upon it. It was also noted that the simple conferment of such powers, without any further formalities, constitutes a frequent feature of instruments of pacific settlement": *ibid*, at p. 206, para. 45). The Commission also felt it necessary to explain that "[w]hile it is to be hoped that the activity and the jurisdiction of the International Court of Justice will substantially increase, it is clear, in the light of experience, that international arbitration will continue to constitute a widely accepted means of pacific settlement through binding decisions based on law": *ibid*, at p. 208, para. 56.

[304] See, for example, YBILC 1953, Vol. I, pp. 43–44, paras. 59, 62, 65 (Kozhevnikov, Žourek) and p. 144, para. 5 (Kozhevnikov); YBILC 1958, Vol. I, p. 233, para. 62 (Tunkin). This view was shared by a number of Governments, which opposed what was termed "judicial arbitration": see K.S. Carlston, 'Draft Convention on Arbitral Procedure of the International Law Commission', 48 AJIL (1954) 296 at 298.

[305] YBILC 1953, Vol. I, p. 43, para. 55 (Alfaro) and para. 56 (El-Khouri, saying that "[t]he jurisdiction of the International Court of Justice was not universally applicable and obligatory. But it should certainly be made so"); see also YBILC 1953, Vol. II, pp. 203–204, paras. 28–29. Lauterpacht took his passionate concern for the Court's jurisdiction to the Court itself: see I. Sinclair, 'International Law: The Court, Commission and Judges', in E. Jensen and T. Fisher (eds.), *The United Kingdom – The United Nations* (Macmillan 1990) 120 at 131–133. When the draft articles were reconsidered by the Commission in 1958 and turned into Model Rules on Arbitral Procedure,

Commission also took care to explain that its work on the topic was not meant to encourage a system of jurisdiction which might overlap or compete with that of the Court, and expressed its hope "that the activity and the jurisdiction of the International Court of Justice will substantially increase."[306] Draft articles providing for recourse to the Court were also included that same year in the Commission's draft conventions on 'Elimination of Future Statelessness' and 'Reduction of Future Statelessness'.[307]

Soon thereafter, however, in the course of the Commission's work on the law of the sea, some members argued that the question of the Court's jurisdiction was outside the competence of the Commission, whose task was of a purely legislative nature.[308] Yet others asserted that "the legislative rules proposed by the Commission on this subject were inevitably couched in such vague terms that any dispute regarding their application in specific cases would necessitate interpretation by a judicial body," and added that "[s]everal States would doubtless be unwilling to accept them without this guarantee."[309] In the debate, which was reminiscent of the controversy that arose within the Committee of Experts exactly thirty years earlier,[310] it was the latter view that finally prevailed: the draft articles on the topic, as adopted in 1956, provided that disputes that may arise between States concerning the interpretation or application of

the roles envisioned for the Court were retained and the commentary again clarified that criticisms of such provisions in the 1953 text "were made on the ground that this set up the International Court of Justice as a sort of super tribunal not subordinate to the agreement of the parties. Despite doubts expressed by certain of its members, the Commission did not consider these criticisms to be well-founded, particularly in the present context of the draft, according to which the articles in question will be binding upon the parties only in so far as they accept those articles and make them part of the arbitral agreement. On the other hand, the articles are necessary if the process of arbitration is not to be liable to possible frustration ... The practice of conferring functions upon the President of the International Court, or even upon the Court itself, is a fairly common one and has never given rise to any difficulty": YBILC 1958, Vol. II, pp. 86–87, para. 25.

306 YBILC 1953, Vol. II, p. 208, para. 56; see also YBILC 1953, Vol. 1, p. 316, para. 26 (Liang, Secretary to the Commission).

307 YBILC 1953, Vol. II, p. 227, paras. 156–157. The proposed dispute settlement provisions read, in pertinent part, as follows: "The Parties agree that any dispute between them concerning the interpretation or application of the Convention shall, if not referred to the tribunal provided for in paragraph 2, be submitted to the International Court of Justice."

308 See YBILC 1956, Vol. II, p. 4.

309 *Ibid.*

310 See Chapter 2, Section C.

the articles on the exploration and exploitation of the continental shelf "shall be submitted to the International Court of Justice at the request of any of the parties, unless they agree on another method of peaceful settlement."[311] At the same time, a proposal that all disputes concerning the breadth of the territorial sea would likewise be submitted to the compulsory jurisdiction of the Court was rejected by the Commission:[312] echoing again the debates of decades past, the majority of members "were unwilling to ask the Court to undertake the settlement of disputes on a subject regarding which the international community had not yet succeeded in formulating a rule of law."[313]

The general question whether the Commission should encourage recourse to the Court arose yet again some two years later, in 1958, when the Commission was finalizing its draft articles concerning diplomatic intercourse and immunities. Draft article 37 (later 45), as adopted in the previous year, provided that "[a]ny dispute between States concerning the interpretation or application of this Convention that cannot be settled through diplomatic channels, shall be referred to conciliation or arbitration or, failing that, shall be submitted to the International Court

[311] YBILC 1956, Vol. II, pp. 264, 300–301 (article 73). An earlier version had provided for settlement of such disputes by arbitration (making it clear that this "does not exclude any other procedure agreed upon by the parties as a means for the formal settlement of the dispute; in particular, they may agree, in matters of general importance, to refer the dispute to the International Court of Justice"): YBILC 1953, Vol. II, p. 217, para. 89. The Commission's eventual decision that arbitration should be replaced by recourse to the Court was made possible by the consideration that disputes concerning the exploration and exploitation of the continental shelf (unlike those concerning the conservation of the living resources of the sea) would not be of an extremely technical character, and would thus not be unsuited to adjudication by the Court. Even the commentary to article 57, however, on the settlement of disputes concerning the conservation of the living resources of the sea, made sure to clarify that "[t]he draft text leaves the parties entirely free as regards the method of settlement. They may submit their disputes to the International Court of Justice by agreement of or in accordance with mutual treaty obligations; they may set up courts of arbitration; they may, if they so desire, seek to compose their disagreements through a commission set up for the purpose, before resorting to these procedures. It is only where the parties fail to agree on the method of settling a dispute that the draft text provides for arbitration": *ibid*, at p. 291, paragraph (1) of the commentary.

[312] YBILC 1956, Vol. II, p. 266, para. 9 of the commentary to article 3.

[313] *Ibid* (adding that the majority of the Commission "did not wish to delegate an essentially legislative function to a judicial organ which, moreover, cannot render decisions binding on States other than the parties. For those reasons it considered that the question should be referred to the proposed conference").

of Justice."[314] When the article came up for reconsideration, Tunkin suggested its deletion, expressing his preference that the Commission's draft would not touch on the subject of the settlement of disputes: "the Commission's task was to codify existing international law and to promote the progressive development of international law," he explained, adding that "an article providing for the compulsory judicial settlement of disputes would not . . . further the Commission's purposes."[315] Quick to respond, García Amador observed that the proposed article did not expressly provide for compulsory jurisdiction; he then added that, in any event, "[i]t was particularly desirable that a body responsible for the codification and progressive development of international law should do its utmost to promote the ideal of compulsory judicial settlement."[316] In the ensuing discussion, several members concurred with the view that "[t]he task of the Commission was the codification of the law, not its implementation,"[317] but the majority shared the position that "[t]he aim of the Commission should be to promote and encourage recognition of the Court's jurisdiction."[318] In the end, the article – amended to enable recourse to the Court even "at the request of [only] one of the parties," as suggested by Ago in order to provide it with an

[314] YBILC 1957, Vol. II, p. 143.

[315] YBILC 1958, Vol. I, p. 184, paras. 60–61 (saying, moreover, that "an article on the settlement of disputes was not indispensable in the draft under discussion, for the settlement of disputes had practically nothing to do with diplomatic intercourse and immunities. A draft containing such an article would probably not be acceptable to many States").

[316] *Ibid*, at p. 185, paras. 62–63.

[317] *Ibid*, at para. 68 (François); see also YBILC 1958, Vol. I, p. 187, para. 2 (Sir Gerald Fitzmaurice saying that "it was questionable whether the Commission should insert a provision of that kind in a draft which did no more than codify the customary international law") and paras. 4, 5 (Amado saying that article 37 "was irrelevant to the Commission's task and altogether outside the scope of its work," and Žourek saying that "the problem of the pacific settlement of disputes was a separate problem which concerned the *application* of the international conventions and should not therefore be linked to the codification and progressive development of international law").

[318] YBILC 1958, Vol. I, p. 189, para. 15 (El-Khouri); see also p. 190, paras. 25 and 33 (Edmonds, García Amador), p. 186, paras. 74 and 76 (Yakota, Bartoš), and p. 189, paras. 17–18 (Alfaro). Some members, namely Hsu, Matine-Daftary, and Sir Gerald Fitzmaurice (and also the Secretary of the Commission, Liang), opined that a clause providing for dispute settlement should be included in the Commission's drafts only when it put forward proposed new law, as opposed to merely codified existing law. The option of including a dispute settlement provision in a separate protocol was also raised – and rejected.

element of compulsion – was adopted by 13 votes to 3, with 2 abstentions.[319] Before long, proposals were floated within the Commission for taking up a topic dedicated to 'The compulsory jurisdiction of the International Court of Justice'.[320]

The Commission's draft articles on the law of treaties of 1966, however, did not recommend that their application should be made subject to compulsory judicial settlement by the Court. Although some members of the Commission were strongly in favor of such a recommendation (and many proclaimed their allegiance to compulsory jurisdiction of the Court as an ideal), the view prevailed that "in the present state of international practice it would not be realistic for the Commission to put forward this [procedural] solution," as most States were unlikely to accept it.[321] No doubt having in mind the judgment by a very divided Court on the preliminary objections in the *South West Africa* cases (1962),[322] members of the Commission referred to "political realities" and to "the present climate of opinion,"[323] also pointing out that a compulsory jurisdiction clause had not been included in the Vienna conventions on diplomatic and consular relations (but only in a separate protocol).[324] It was again

[319] *Ibid*, at p. 191, para. 44.

[320] YBILC 1961, Vol. I, p. 207, para. 47 (Liang, Secretary of the Commission); several States speaking in the Sixth Committee that year viewed such an idea with favor. In the following year, a Secretariat working paper on possible future work for the Commission referred to the topic 'Obligatory jurisdiction of the International Court of Justice': YBILC 1962, Vol. II, p. 95, paras. 141–145. In the meantime, the idea that codification of the law was essential for strengthening the confidence of States in the Court's jurisdiction has not lost it hold on States: see A.E. Gotlieb, 'The International Law Commission', 4 CYIL (1966) 64 at 67–69.

[321] YBILC 1966, Vol. II, p. 262, para. 3 of the commentary to article 62 (on "Procedure to be followed in cases of invalidity, termination, withdrawal from or suspension of the operation of a treaty"). The lengthy debate on the question whether compulsory jurisdiction was acceptable or not may be found in YBILC 1963, Vol. I, pp. 170–182.

[322] *South West Africa Cases (Ethiopia* v. *South Africa; Liberia* v. *South Africa), Preliminary Objections, Judgment of 21 December 1962: I.C.J. Reports 1962*, p. 319.

[323] See, respectively, YBILC 1963, Vol. I, p. 177, para. 5 (El-Erian), and p. 181, para. 54 (Sir Humphrey Waldock). The view was also expressed that "the present composition of the Court was naturally not acceptable to a great many countries" (*ibid*, at p. 174, para. 59 (Tabibi)); see also p. 175, para. 69 (Yasseen referring to a "psychological problem" that "a more judicious allocation of seats on the Court might facilitate" the solution of). For Gros's sharp opposition to the view that the position in regard to acceptances of compulsory jurisdiction was due to the composition of the Court, see *ibid*, at p. 179, para. 40.

[324] *Ibid*, at p. 171, para. 6 (Tunkin, adding that "[a]dmittedly, articles on compulsory jurisdiction had been included in the Convention on Fishing and Conservation of the Living Resources of the High Seas in the teeth of strong opposition, but the ultimate fate

suggested that "[t]he settlement of disputes was a separate problem, which should not hold up the development of normative rules of international law,"[325] and some members went so far as to argue that proposing compulsory jurisdiction "would not be in line with the UN Charter, which only imposed an obligation to settle disputes by peaceful means."[326] The Commission eventually put forward, in connection with draft article 62 (on "Procedure to be followed in cases of invalidity, termination, withdrawal from or suspension of the operation of a treaty"), a very general provision according to which "the parties shall seek a solution through the means indicated in Article 33 of the Charter of the United Nations."[327]

The legitimacy crisis that befell the Court following its 1966 judgment in the *South West Africa* cases indeed did not go unnoticed by the Commission and has very likely contributed to the sense of realism that continued to prevent it from proposing recourse to the Court for fear that States would not accept it. The draft articles on special missions, adopted in 1967, contained no reference at all to dispute settlement, and in the following year the Commission similarly concluded that it was premature to take a decision on the question of the judicial settlement of disputes arising out of State succession.[328] In the draft articles on the

of that Convention was still unknown and the inclusion of those articles had certainly been instrumental in deterring many States from ratifying it").

325 *Ibid*, at p. 175, para. 66 (Yasseen); see also at p. 171, para. 7 (Tunkin suggesting that "[t]he settlement of disputes was an entirely separate branch of international law which certainly needed to be developed, and there were means of doing so, but it must be dealt with separately. The codification and progressive development of other branches of law should not be made dependent on the acceptance by States of compulsory jurisdiction"), and at p. 180, para. 46 (Tunkin reiterating that "[b]y endeavouring to make the acceptance of judicial settlement a condition for the acceptance of substantive rules of law, the advocates of compulsory jurisdiction, however good their intentions, were acting in a manner detrimental to the progress of international law ... Many States did not accept compulsory judicial settlement and had good reasons for that attitude").

326 *Ibid*, at p. 173, para. 35 (Rosenne) and para. 41 (Bartoš); the Chairman, Jiménez de Aréchaga, later took care to point out that "Article 36, paragraph 3, of the Charter provided that 'legal disputes should as a general rule be referred by the parties to the International Court of Justice in accordance with the provisions of the Statute of the Court'" (at p. 178, para. 28).

327 YBILC 1966, Vol. II, p. 185, para. 3. Kearney later said that he "particularly deplored the fact that no provision had been made in the draft articles on the law of treaties for interpretation by the Court to settle disputes, and hoped that that defect would be remedied at the second session of the Vienna Conference": YBILC 1968, Vol. I, p. 163, para. 28.

328 YBILC 1968, Vol. II, p. 220, para. 72.

representation of States in their relations with international organizations, as adopted on first reading in 1969, the Commission included a provision limited to the possible holding of consultations, having not "[found] it advisable" to include a provision referring disputes to the Court despite the Special Rapporteur's suggestion to that effect.[329] On second reading of the draft articles, in 1971, the Commission did leave some room for recourse to the Court, but only implicitly, in a safeguard provision accompanying a proposal focused on conciliation.[330] This was after members had heard from Judge Gros a year earlier that the issue of the limited acceptance of the Court's jurisdiction was a legal problem "of common interest to the judges of the Court and the members of the Commission": "the substance of the law and jurisdiction were two faces of the same coin," he told his former colleagues, adding that "the problem of the substance of the law and the problem of its application would never be solved separately."[331]

The draft articles on the prevention and punishment of crimes against diplomatic agents and other internationally protected persons, adopted in 1972, again did not refer to the Court, providing instead alternative formulations for a dispute settlement provision, one for the reference of a dispute to conciliation and the other to an optional form of arbitration.[332] In 1974, the Commission refrained from including any dispute settlement provision in its draft articles on succession of States in respect of treaties, leaving the matter for consideration by the General Assembly if it so wished.[333] The same approach was undertaken with regard to the draft articles on most-favoured-nation clauses (1978), the draft articles on succession of States in respect of State property, archives and debts

[329] See YBILC 1969, Vol. II, pp. 221, 222, para. 5 of the commentary to draft article 50; Fourth report on relations between States and international organizations by Mr. Abdullah El-Erian, Special Rapporteur, *ibid*, at p. 21, para. 5 of the commentary to the proposed draft article 49.

[330] YBILC 1971, Vol. II, Part One, p. 333 and p. 335, para. 13 of the commentary to draft article 82.

[331] YBILC 1970, Vol. I, p. 138, paras. 2, 4, 8.

[332] YBILC 1972, Vol. II, pp. 321–323, draft article 12. The Commission concluded that the conciliation or arbitration procedures "represent[ed] the largest measure of common ground that would appear to exist at present among Governments on the question of dispute settlement": *ibid*, at p. 322, para. 1 of the commentary. While the latter alternative included the possibility of referring the dispute to the Court if the parties failed to agree on the organization of the arbitration, it contained a provision expressly allowing the parties to make a reservation to that particular article (at para. 4).

[333] YBILC 1974, Vol. II, Part One, p. 173, paras. 79–81.

(1981), and the draft articles on jurisdictional immunities of States and their property (1991). The draft articles on the status of the diplomatic courier and the diplomatic bag not accompanied by diplomatic courier of 1989 did not contain any reference to judicial settlement of disputes: negotiation through diplomatic channels was envisaged instead.[334]

All along, however, the idea that judicial machinery may be essential to the implementation of international law had not been lost on members of the Commission, who understood that there may well be a difficulty in applying satisfactorily various draft articles proposed by the Commission unless they were accompanied by a system of adjudication.[335] Sir Humphrey Waldock thus referred to "the very real importance of the Court as the international organ concerned with completing the work of codification on which the Commission was engaged."[336] As he explained,

> [u]ndoubtedly one of the difficulties of codification was that it did not take place within a complete legal system with the full apparatus of the judicial process; there were many branches of the law in which an exact formula could not be found and the Commission had to be content with a statement of common ground. That meant that the judicial function

[334] See YBILC 1989, Vol. II, Part Two, p. 31, para. 9 of the commentary to article 18, and p. 36, draft article 22(5).

[335] See, for example, YBILC 1963, Vol. I, p. 19, para. 68 (Amado saying in the course of the debate on the law of treaties that "no set of rules [by the Commission] could cover all the cases that were liable to arise in practice. Exceptional cases might be settled peaceably by negotiation and arbitration, and it was there that the International Court of Justice would play its part"); YBILC 1966, Vol. II, p. 248, para. 5 of the commentary to draft article 50 of the Commission's draft articles on the law of treaties (acknowledging this difficulty in general terms), and p. 254, para. 5 of the commentary to draft article 57; YBILC 1966, Vol. I, Part I, p. 89, para. 52 (Briggs observing that "the rules of *jus cogens* set out in articles 37 and 45 were a threat to the stability of treaties, in the absence of compulsory international jurisdiction"); YBILC 1969, Vol. I, p. 72, para. 29 (Bartoš emphasizing "the importance of the compulsory jurisdiction of the Court – the only guarantee that the law would be applied"). Jennings recalled that a prominent member of the Commission has said that "the Commission has on more than one occasion found the absence of the possibility of compulsory judicial determination of situations a hindrance in the actual drafting of rules and principles": R.Y. Jennings, 'Recent Developments in the International Law Commission: Its Relation to the Sources of International Law', 13 ICLQ (1964) 385 at 394 (referring to Rosenne).

[336] YBILC 1969, Vol. I, p. 72, para. 27 (adding that "[h]e had noted in the past that, in dealing with the general principles of codification, the Commission had often found itself confronted with questions involving a mixture of facts and law and that it then became very difficult to push codification of general rules further without encountering sharp divergences of opinion. It was at that point that the work of the Court in interpretation and application became an essential complement to the work of the Commission").

> was extremely important for consolidation of the work of codification. And that work would be established on surer foundations if the Court were able to fill out the work of the Commission.[337]

For Ago, too, it was clear that:

> The conventions prepared on the basis of the Commission's drafts by diplomatic conferences must not remain abstract rules; they must be adapted to international life and applied to concrete cases. That was the task of the International Court of Justice, which could thus make a decisive contribution towards transforming the provisions of those conventions into living rules of law of the international community. The work of the International Court of Justice was valuable in that it completed, integrated and gave effect to the work which the International Law Commission was trying to accomplish.[338]

Members of the Commission have also kept in mind that their work in making the rules of international law more definite may of itself make judicial settlement by the Court more acceptable to States.[339] As Yasseen put it in 1969, "[t]he codification of international law could help to promote general acceptance of the compulsory jurisdiction of the International Court of Justice by making the rules of international law clearer, more precise and less controversial."[340] Indeed, even when the Commission shied away from proposing a compromissory clause in its draft articles, States have sometimes added one when adopting a treaty on their basis. An example of that was the eventual insertion by States,

[337] YBILC 1968, Vol. I, p. 162, para. 22.

[338] *Ibid*, at para. 18.

[339] See, for example, YBILC 1961, Vol. I, pp. 213–214, paras. 25–26 (Ago) and p. 215, paras. 40–41, 43 (Matine-Daftary); YBILC 1963, Vol. I, pp. 170–171, para. 5 (Tunkin), p. 175, para. 69 (Yasseen), and p. 180, para. 41 (Gros); YBILC 1967, Vol. I, p. 88, para. 8 (Waldock observing in the presence of judges Fitzmaurice and Lachs that "[t]he codification, elucidation and progressive development of the law was often said to be an essential prerequisite for extending the acceptance of the Court's jurisdiction and for its successful operation as a judicial instrument"). The President of the Court, Judge Jímenez de Arechaga, told members of the Commission in 1978 that the Court "was confident that [the Commission's] work would help to resolve the crisis that currently beset international justice": YBILC 1978, Vol. I, p. 41, para. 2.

[340] YBILC 1969, Vol. I, p. 71, para. 17 (adding that "[f]or instance, some countries which had not accepted the Court's compulsory jurisdiction had not hesitated, after the adoption of the Vienna Convention on Diplomatic Relations, to ratify the optional protocol on compulsory jurisdiction. What was more, the Commission's work had made it possible to widen the scope of compulsory jurisdiction, which, since the adoption of the Vienna Convention on the Law of Treaties, could henceforth extend to the question of incompatibility of treaties and rules of *jus cogens*").

into the Vienna Convention on the Law of Treaties, of a provision for interpretation by the Court to settle disputes concerning the provisions on *jus cogens*,[341] which led the Commission to try and reproduce this mechanism in its draft articles on the law of treaties between States and international organizations or between international organizations of 1982 despite the major procedural difficulty entailed by the impossibility of international organizations being parties to cases before the Court. It was only in view of "all the imperfections and uncertainties" of the solutions suggested that it decided eventually not to suggest recourse to the Court, but to conciliation and arbitration.[342]

The optimism of the post–Cold War period and the increasingly heavy case-load of the Court afforded the Commission greater comfort in encouraging the expansion of the Court's jurisdiction. It soon inserted into its draft articles on the law of the non-navigational uses of international watercourses (1994), with particular enthusiasm,[343] a reference to (non-compulsory) judicial settlement of disputes, making it clear in

[341] 1155 UNTS 331, article 66(a).

[342] YBILC 1982, Vol. II, Part Two, p. 65, para. 4 of the commentary to draft article 66. For the earlier proposal by Tammes, that the Commission take on the topic 'Status of international organizations before the International Court of Justice' in order to enable the United Nations and other international organizations to have the status of litigating parties before the Court, see YBILC 1970, Vol. II, p. 268, para. 138. Exploring such a possibility was again suggested by Sir Michael Wood in 2016, in his proposal for a topic entitled 'The settlement of international disputes to which international organizations are parties': YBILC 2016, Vol. II, Part Two, pp. 234–235, paras. 8–16.

[343] See, for example, YBILC 1994, Vol. I, p. 41, para. 33 (Yankov saying that "a reference to ICJ should be added at the end of paragraph 2(*c*) of the article. There was no valid reason for overlooking ICJ's role of adjudication"); p. 43, para. 2 and p. 52, para. 29 (Bowett saying that "[t]here would be no difficulty with that wording if the dispute was referred to ICJ . . . As far as the settlement of disputes was concerned, ICJ had recently established a special chamber for environmental disputes. In his view, to show some recognition for that initiative in its report, the Commission should include a reference to the Court in article 33"); p. 50, para. 15 (Vargas Carreño saying that "[t]he text proposed by the Special Rapporteur represented the bare-bones requirement. However, it would be more appropriate for article 33, paragraph 2*(c)*, to include a reference not only to binding arbitration by any permanent or ad hoc tribunal but also to judicial settlement, which would afford greater latitude and would explicitly provide for access to ICJ if the States parties to the dispute recognized its jurisdiction"); p. 51, para. 20 (Crawford saying that "[s]ome form of independent settlement, preferably by ICJ, was desirable"); p. 63, para. 11 (the Special Rapporteur, Rosenstock, summing up the debate in saying that "[t]here was plenty of room to strengthen the proposed article, with his wholehearted support, starting with the addition of a suitable reference to ICJ").

the commentary that the Court was what it had in mind.[344] Concurrently, an initiative of much grander scale was being considered. In 1993, the Special Rapporteur on the topic 'State responsibility', Arangio-Ruiz, proposed an ambitious three-tier regime corresponding in effect to binding dispute settlement for the whole of international law, at the apex of which he placed the Court.[345] This conformed to the view he had expressed in a debate on the matter already in 1986, according to which "the Commission should always make an effort to promote settlement of legal disputes by the Court… The members of the Commission, as independent lawyers acting in their personal capacity, should do all they could to enhance the role of the ICJ."[346]

Arangio-Ruiz's proposal was described within the Commission as "amounting to a radical revision of the system of adjudication at the international level, particularly that of ICJ, inasmuch as it made consensual jurisdiction compulsory in respect of a number of questions, some of which might not even qualify as legal matters."[347] It led to much discussion and mixed reactions, some of which once again raised the general question concerning the role of the Commission in the development of

[344] YBILC 1994, Vol. II, Part Two, pp. 134–135, draft article 33(c) and para. 11 of the commentary thereto.

[345] See YBILC 1993, Vol. II, Part Two, pp. 35–37, paras. 206–220. While focusing on disputes relating specifically to countermeasures, the Special Rapporteur (following in the footsteps of his predecessor) did make it clear that the conciliation, arbitration, or judicial settlement procedures envisaged for Part Three would deal not only with any such issues, but also with any other issue of fact or law concerning the interpretation or application of any of the articles of the future convention on State responsibility. See also YBILC 1993, Vol. I, p. 125, para. 28 (suggesting that "[a]ctually, ICJ was the only existing permanent body which possessed the competence and the technical means to determine the existence, attribution and consequences of an internationally wrongful act, including possibly a crime of State").

[346] YBILC 1986, Vol. I, pp. 60–61, paras. 27–28; for the debate more broadly, see pp. 56–85.

[347] YBILC 1993, Vol. II, Part Two, p. 45, para. 276. Pellet has written that such a mechanism would have "'judicialize[d]' international society": A. Pellet, 'Between Codification and Progressive Development of the Law: Some Reflections on the ILC', 6 *International Law FORUM du droit international* (2004) 15 at 18. The Commission's subsequent Special Rapporteur on the topic, Crawford, similarly observed that compulsory judicial settlement of disputes under the draft articles would mean that "any dispute between States as to the responsibility of one of them for a breach of an international obligation, whatever its origin, would involve the application if not the interpretation of the draft articles … A system of residual compulsory third-party dispute settlement would have the effect, for most purposes, of instituting third-party dispute settlement for the whole domain of international law, which is in so many ways concerned with the performance by a State of its international obligations": YBILC 2001, Vol. II, Part One, pp. 5–6, paras. 14, 18.

international law.[348] While several members observed that it was still premature to embark on compulsory dispute settlement procedures, and urged the Commission to distinguish between what was desirable and what was possible,[349] a large majority of members were generally "in favour of strengthening the role of the judge in the field of State responsibility."[350] Some suggested assigning an even greater role for the Court, by making room in the draft for advisory opinions and giving a more prominent role to the chambers procedure of the Court.[351]

Arangio-Ruiz's seventh report of 1995 put forward a revised, two-phased procedure, in which the UN General Assembly or the Security Council would make a preliminary political evaluation, and Court would make a decisive pronouncement on the existence of an international crime and then settle the disputes arising from its commission.[352] For the Special Rapporteur, "in the area of State responsibility for very serious breaches of international obligations, where the judicial application of the law was primary, the decision, prior to that of the *omnes* States themselves, had to rest ultimately with ICJ."[353] In the spirited discussion that followed, some members considered that the proposed scheme placed too much reliance on the Court, as it "failed to suggest any basis for believing that States which had so far shown reluctance to accept the jurisdiction of ICJ under Article 36, paragraph 2, of the Statute, would suddenly embrace such a role for the Court."[354] Concerns were also raised that the Court had no adequate techniques for independent fact-finding;[355] that it would not be able to act

348 YBILC 1993, Vol. II, Part Two, pp. 37–38, paras. 21–29.

349 *Ibid.* See also Rosenstock, *supra* note 93.

350 YBILC 1993, Vol. II, Part Two, p. 47, para. 282.

351 *Ibid*, at p. 46, para. 278 (recalling that the Court's President, Judge Jennings, had raised before the General Assembly in 1991 the suggestion that more advisory opinions should be sought). See also YBILC 1992, Vol. I, p. 73, para. 20 (Jacovides).

352 See YBILC 1995, Vol. II, Part One, p. 3; see also G. Cottereau, 'Resort to International Courts in Matters of Responsibility', in J. Crawford et al (eds.), *The Law of International Responsibility* (OUP 2010) 1113 at 1119–1121.

353 YBILC 1995, Vol. I, p. 87, para. 86.

354 *Ibid*, at p. 90, para. 23 (Rosenstock, having earlier said (at para. 19) that "[t]here were some who seemed committed, no matter what, to seeing the Court as the answer to all problems: they had been referred to as 'judicial romantics'"); see also p. 94, para. 50 (Bowett); p. 104, para. 23 (de Saram); p. 113, para. 26 (Rosenstock reiterating that "nothing in the Special Rapporteur's new proposals therefore cured the fatal problem of all his imaginative constructs, namely, that the compulsory jurisdiction of the Court would not be acceptable to States"); and Rosenstock, *supra* note 93.

355 YBILC 1995, Vol. I, p. 94, para. 52 (Bowett).

rapidly;[356] and that it would not be able to handle a very busy docket.[357] Other members welcomed the role assigned to the Court by the Special Rapporteur, asserting that the Commission "should not be overly concerned with realism lest it might become an accomplice of those States which refused to accept the jurisdiction of the competent international organs not only to evade the consequences of their acts, but also to retain complete freedom of action."[358] Ultimately, the Commission rejected the idea that States would accept such compulsory jurisdiction of the Court,[359] and the set of draft articles adopted on first reading in 1996 recommended compulsory recourse to arbitration (at the instance of any State subjected to countermeasures), with only a residual role for the Court in the event that the validity of the resulting arbitral award was disputed.[360]

When the second reading of the draft articles on State responsibility was completed in 2001, provisions concerning the pacific settlement of disputes were dropped altogether. This reflected the preference of the new Special Rapporteur for the topic, Crawford, who asserted (mistakenly) that "the Commission has so far refrained from proposing dispute settlement procedures in its final articles,"[361] and, more significantly, considered that there was no indication that States were ready to accept a system of residual compulsory third-party dispute settlement for essentially the whole domain of international law.[362] The Commission's

356 *Ibid*, at p. 95, para. 53 (Bowett); p. 97, para. 8 (Pellet); and p. 103, para. 9 (Bennouna). For the reply of the Special Rapporteur to this, see p. 100, para. 26; p. 101, para. 35; p. 126, para. 21; and p. 177, para. 28.

357 *Ibid*, at p. 93, para. 43 (Tomuschat); and p. 103, para. 15 (Bennouna). The Special Rapporteur said, with regard to the risk of a negative reaction by States to his proposals, that "the Commission, which was composed of independent experts, did not have to anticipate the possible objections of States, but must contribute to the progressive development of international law by striking a fair balance between the ideal and what was possible": YBILC 1995, Vol. II, Part Two, p. 58, para. 324.

358 YBILC 1995, Vol. II, Part Two, p. 54, para. 304.

359 See also YBILC 1996, Vol. I, p. 189, para. 5 (Arangio-Ruiz).

360 YBILC 1996, Vol. II, Part Two, pp. 64–65. Interestingly, Crawford then said that "[t]here was much to be said for the solution originally proposed by the former Special Rapporteur, namely, that disputes should be referred to ICJ": YBILC 1996, Vol. I, p. 191, para. 24.

361 YBILC 2001, Vol. II, Part One, p. 4, para. 5.

362 *Ibid*, at p. 6, paras. 17–18 (adding, at para. 19, that "[m]oreover, even if States were willing to undertake further commitments of a general character in relation to dispute settlement, there is no likelihood that they would do so in the framework of articles on State responsibility, aspects of which remain controversial. On the assumption that the articles were to be adopted by States in the form of a general convention, it cannot be expected that the convention would contain provisions for general and compulsory

decision not to provide for binding dispute settlement may have also been motivated by Crawford's suggestion that "provision for binding dispute settlement could only be included in a treaty,"[363] a form he and others did not consider appropriate for the draft articles.

The general interest among members of the Commission in seeing the Court's jurisdiction expanded was nevertheless carried into the new millennium. It received explicit encouragement from several presidents of the Court, one of whom told Commission members in 2010 that the decline of the optional clause on compulsory jurisdiction of the Court "was a situation which the United Nations and the international community as a whole must address."[364] On a number of occasions, members of the Commission have asked the Court's presidents expressly whether the Commission should contribute in some way to pursuing the objective of expanding the Court's compulsory jurisdiction, and received a positive reply.[365] When the broader issue of 'Peaceful settlement of

settlement of disputes by arbitration or adjudication"). Crawford's view was also that "[i]t [was] not necessary for the draft articles to provide yet another optional mechanism for the judicial settlement of disputes," as these were existing anyway, but he did suggest that adding a provision modelled on article 33 of the Charter could be considered (at paras. 13, 20). See also YBILC 2001, Vol. I, p. 4, paras. 20–25.

363 *Ibid*, at p. 4, para. 12.

364 YBILC 2010, Vol. I, p. 209, para. 34 (President Owada). See also, for example, YBILC 2014, Vol. I, p. 144, para. 24 (President Tomka telling Commission members that it was "unfortunate that only approximately one third of States Members of the United Nations had made the declaration under Article 36, paragraph 2, of the Statute of the Court").

365 In 2009, Melescanu asked President Owada whether the Commission "should contribute in some way to pursuing" the objective of expanding the Court's compulsory jurisdiction and received the reply that "it would be interesting for the Commission to take up that issue, but it was difficult to say whether that was a task best left to the Commission or to a political organ such as the Sixth Committee of the General Assembly": YBILC 2009, Vol. I, p. 126, paras. 55–56. Soon thereafter, Valencia-Ospina asked President Owada, "against the background of the relationship between the Commission and the Court," whether "the Commission should incorporate final clauses providing for the compulsory jurisdiction of the Court" in the final versions of draft articles that it recommended to the General Assembly for adoption; the President responded that "[w]ithout wishing to suggest that the Commission should take any such action, it would be useful for it to consider the matter": *Ibid*, at pp. 127–128, paras. 65–66. Valencia-Ospina again enquired in 2013 with President Tomka (who had emphasized before the Commission the need for the increased acceptance by States of the compulsory jurisdiction of the Court), "whether the Commission should consider including compromissory clauses concerning the jurisdiction of the Court in the final texts it adopted on its topics"; the President replied subtly that "further efforts should be made" to increase the number of multilateral conventions that contained compromissory clauses: YBILC 2013, Vol. I, p. 87, paras. 16, 20.

disputes' was considered by the Commission in 2011 (in connection with the future program of work),[366] a number of members pointed out that the Commission could thus contribute to enlarging the Court's jurisdiction.[367]

Still, the Commission's more recent practice in deciding whether or not to include a dispute settlement provision providing for recourse to the Court (or indeed a provision on dispute settlement at all) remains inconsistent, owing both to the mistaken perception that drafting such a clause has usually been left for States and to the prevalent impression that appetite among States for new multilateral treaties is in decline. The draft articles on diplomatic protection (2006) and the draft articles on the law of transboundary aquifers (2008) contained no dispute settlement provisions, and nor did the draft articles on the effects of armed conflicts on treaties (2011), the draft articles on expulsion of aliens (2012), and the draft articles on the protection of persons in the event of disasters (2016).

[366] The debate was held on the basis of a working paper prepared by Sir Michael Wood, which included a proposal concerning declarations under the optional clause: YBILC 2011, Vol. II, Part One, pp. 247–252.

[367] See, for example, YBILC 2011, Vol. I, p. 125, para. 23 (Vargas Carreño suggesting that "[i]f the Commission decided to formulate recommendations on dispute settlement, one of them ought to be that States should recognize as compulsory the jurisdiction of the ICJ"); p. 128, paras. 54, 56–57 (Dugard supporting the proposal that the Commission should examine the suggestion that the Statute of the Court be amended so to allow it to hear disputes between States and international organizations, further raising the idea that "[i]f the Commission did draft a model declaration [accepting the Court's compulsory jurisdiction], it might be easier for other bodies to press States to accept the optional clause," and adding that "[t]he Commission should not be afraid of considering the idea of investing the Secretary-General with the power to request advisory opinions from the ICJ"); p. 131, para. 6 (Hmoud being open to the idea that the Commission "could develop a model declaration that States could use to accept the optional clause recognizing the jurisdiction of the ICJ, indicate the required content of each declaration and specify the resulting legal obligations for States. That could assist States in accepting the Court's jurisdiction more readily, given that their reluctance was due in part to their lack of awareness of the consequences of such a step"); and p. 133, para. 26 (Jacobsson saying that "[t]he proposal contained in subparagraph (e) [of the Working Paper] concerning declarations under the optional clause, including the elaboration of model clauses for inclusion therein, was timely. The issue was less sensitive now and seemed to be undergoing a new and positive development, and the Commission could take advantage of the work done by other legal bodies"). At the same time, the view was also expressed, by Murase, that "[w]hile it might be desirable from the point of view of international organizations to amend the Statute of the International Court of Justice so that they could bring their claims as contentious proceedings, such a proposal must come from States and not from the International Law Commission": *ibid*, at p. 126, para. 35.

The draft guidelines on the protection of the atmosphere, adopted on second reading in 2021, suggest only generally that "[d]isputes between States relating to the protection of the atmosphere from atmospheric pollution and atmospheric degradation are to be settled by peaceful means," although the absence of reference to the Court may be explained by the stated recognition of the "fact-intensive and science-dependent character" of such disputes and the resulting need for particular technical expertise in resolving them.[368] On the other hand, in its draft articles on the responsibility of international organizations (2011), the Commission took care to note, against the background of the reluctance of most international organizations to accept methods for the compulsory settlement of disputes, that potential "mechanisms for the compulsory settlement of disputes are considered to include those involving the request for an advisory opinion of the International Court of Justice."[369] In its Guide to practice on reservations to treaties (also of 2011), the Commission contained the statement, in connection with the issue of permissibility of reservations, that "it cannot be argued that monitoring bodies – whether the International Court of Justice, an arbitral tribunal or a human rights treaty body – are prevented from assessing the permissibility of a reservation even if no objection has been raised to it."[370] More recently, while some in the Commission had hesitated whether it would be appropriate for the Commission to propose a provision on dispute settlement in the draft articles on prevention and punishment of crimes against humanity, adopted on second reading in 2019, the majority view was not only that such a provision should be included, but also that it should contain a novel formulation providing for immediate resort to the Court if the dispute is not settled by negotiation.[371] In the draft conclusions on

[368] A/76/10, *supra* note 202, at p. 50, draft guideline 12, paras. (1) and (2).

[369] YBILC 2011, Vol. II, Part Two, p. 95, fn. 345.

[370] YBILC 2011, Vol. II, Part Three, p. 245, para. 11 of the commentary to guideline 3.3.3.

[371] See the Statement of the Chairman of the Drafting Committee, Mr. Aniruddha Rajput (1 June 2017), available at <http://legal.un.org/docs/?path=../ilc/documentation/english/statements/2017_dc_chairman_statement_cah.pdf&lang=E>, pp. 16–17 ("Members of the Drafting Committee decided not to retain the original proposal made in the [Special Rapporteur's] third report, which was considered as giving precedence to arbitration over dispute resolution at the International Court of Justice, an approach viewed as inappropriate in the context of crimes against humanity. The adopted proposal is a new formulation not found in existing treaties, although inspired by article 22 of the International Convention on the Elimination of All Forms of Racial Discrimination").

peremptory norms of general international law (*jus cogens*), adopted that same year on first reading and not at all meant to assume the form of a convention,[372] the Commission, "in the spirit of avoiding unilateralism . . . found it appropriate, without obliging submission to the International Court of Justice, to encourage submission of the dispute to the International Court of Justice."[373] This position was maintained at the second reading stage in 2022,[374] illustrating yet again that codification of the law, as its early advocates had predicted, may well serve to bring more matters under the purview of the Court.[375]

C. Conclusion

The Court's jurisprudence has had a decisive and wide-ranging influence on the Commission's output, with its place in informing that work being second to none. As detailed above, this influence is not to be measured solely by the frequent and deferential references made by the Commission to the Court's case-law, but also by its choices concerning terminology and the topics to be added to its program of work. The Commission's deliberate efforts to protect and to extend the Court's authority more generally provide further indications of the Court's exceptional significance for it.

By systematically integrating the Court's pronouncements into its output as authoritative statements of general international law, and by according them greater weight than actual State practice, the

[372] The Commission did not consider it appropriate in the past to propose a fully-fledged dispute settlement mechanism in the context of instruments of a more flexible nature, such as the Guide to practice on reservations to treaties: see YBILC 2011, Vol. II, Part Two, p. 24, para. 67.

[373] A/74/10, *supra* note 31, at paragraph (8) of the commentary to draft conclusion 21 (on "Procedural requirements").

[374] See A/77/10, *supra* note 207, at p. 81, para. 3 of conclusion 21, and p. 84, para. 9 of the commentary thereto. One member of the Commission was pleased to tell the President of the Court that year that "two of the outcomes that the Commission was seeking to adopt at its current session, one on first reading and the other on second reading, were likely to include dispute settlement clauses that highlighted the role of the International Court of Justice as a forum in which States could resolve their disputes": UN Doc. A/CN.4/SR.3585: 'Provisional Summary Record of the Commission's 3585th Meeting' (1 June 2022), p. 8 (Murphy).

[375] See also H.P. Aust, 'The Normative Environment for Peace – On the Contribution of the ILC's Articles on State Responsibility', in G. Nolte (ed.), *Peace through International Law: The Role of the International Law Commission* (Springer 2009) 13–46.

Commission has treated the Court's decisions as directly applicable international law. In doing so it has afforded that case-law a role far more expansive than the subsidiary one that States have assigned it for the determination of the rules of international law, and has thus furthered the reach of a judicial institution whose jurisdiction and binding impact were rigidly circumscribed by its founders.

5

Interaction beyond the Printed Page

It is clear from what has gone before that the full extent of interplay between the Court and the Commission cannot be appreciated solely by reviewing the references frequently made by each organ to the output of the other: much of that interplay is more implicit and sometimes intangible. Yet the impact that the work of one body has on that of the other is itself only a part of the picture, as it draws upon and reinforces other links that unite the two. These links, including the movement of members from one institution to the other and the customary exchanges in Geneva between members of both, have indeed played a part in nourishing the "extremely subtle and not always evident intellectual ties"[1] that have bound the Court and the Commission since their early days. While these ties are not unknown, their history, scope, and effect remain mostly obscure. The following account seeks to illuminate this linkage in order to enable a broader and more accurate understanding of the inter-institutional relationship.

A. Personal Links

"Over and above the strong interest that the ICJ and ILC each take in the substantive work of the other," President Higgins once told the members of the Commission, "we also maintain significant personal links."[2] These links, formed primarily by the recurrent movement of Commission members to the Court as well as the frequent appearance of Commission members as counsel before the Court, have long played a critical role in shaping the institutional interaction. Being "the personal

[1] YBILC 1968, Vol. I, p. 163, para. 30 (Rosenne).

[2] Keynote Address by H.E. Judge Rosalyn Higgins, President of the International Court of Justice, at the Sixtieth Anniversary of the International Law Commission (19 May 2008), available at <http://legal.un.org/ilc/sessions/60/pdfs/english/president_higgins_speeche_ilc_60th.pdf>.

aspect of the relationship," as President Tomka referred to them,[3] such links have served – and still serve – to draw the Court and the Commission closer and to cultivate within them a joint spirit of interdependence and a common strategic purpose.

1. *A Membership "Often Interchangeable"*[4]

(i) Members of the Commission Become Members of the Court

Since the election to the Court in 1952 of Sir Benegal Rau, members of the Commission have regularly been elected to sit as judges of the Court, many of them during their term on the Commission or immediately after its expiration. Of the Court's 115 judges to date, as many as 43 (i.e. over one-third) had previously served as members of the Commission, and of these, 10 have become presidents of the Court (see Table 5.1). At times, a majority or nearly half of the Court's bench consisted of former members of the Commission.[5] In recent decades, "a frequent passage through the ILC" has indeed been identified as one component of the "increasingly more visible" profile of the Court's judges.[6] Before taking up their

[3] YBILC 2012, Vol. I, p. 146, para. 93 (addressing the Commission). See also, for example, YBILC 1968, Vol. I, p. 161, para. 8 (the Chairman, Ruda, saying that "[m]embers of the two bodies were also united by personal ties"); YBILC 2000, Vol. I, p. 358, para. 3 (President Guillaume telling Commission members that "[t]he two bodies were united by personal ties").

[4] YBILC 1997, Vol. I, p. 214, para. 65 (Judge Shi addressing the Commission).

[5] By way of example, in 1969 a third of the Court's fifteen judges were former members of the Commission (Fitzmaurice, Gros, Koretsky, Lachs, and Padilla Nervo); and in 1974, Judge Waldock said that "[i]n all, some fifteen members of the Commission had become judges of the Court, but the present number of seven could be called a high-water mark" (YBILC 1974, Vol. I, p. 69, para. 24). By 1980, nine of the judges were former members of the Commission (Ago, El-Erian, Elias, Gros, Lachs, Sette-Camara, Nagendra Singh, Ruda, and Waldock), but in 1997 the number again stood at five (Bedjaoui, Koroma, Schwebel, Shi, and Vereshchetin). In 2003, seven of the judges were former members of the Commission (Al-Khasawneh, Elaraby, Koroma, Shi, Simma, Vereshchetin, and Tomka), a number that was maintained in 2008 (Al-Khasawneh, Bennouna, Koroma, Sepulveda-Amor, Shi, Simma, and Tomka). The current bench (2024) has six former members (Aurescu, Gómez-Robledo, Nolte, Tladi, Tomka, and Xue).

[6] G. Abi-Saab, 'Ensuring the Best Bench: Ways of Selecting Judges', presentation recorded in C. Peck and R.S. Lee (eds.), *Increasing the Effectiveness of the International Court of Justice: Proceedings of the ICJ/UNITAR Colloquium to Celebrate the 50th Anniversary of the Court* (Martinus Nijhoff 1997) 165 at 168; see also C. Chinkin, 'Enhancing the International Law Commission's Relationship with Other Law-Making Bodies and Relevant Academic and

Table 5.1 *Members of the Court who previously served on the Commission*

Name	Member of the Commission	Member of the Court
Prince Bola Adesumbo Ajibola	1987–1991	1991–1994
Roberto Ago	1957–1978	1979–1995
Ricardo Joaquin Alfaro	1949–1953, 1958–1959	1959–1964
Awn Shawkat Al-Khasawneh	1987–1999	2000–2011
Mohammed Bedjaoui	1965–1981	1982–2001[a]
Mohamed Bennouna	1987–1998	2006–2024
James Richard Crawford	1992–2001	2015–2021
Roberto Córdova	1949–1954	1955–1964
Abdullah El-Erian	1957–1958, 1962–1978	1979–1981
Nabil Elaraby	1994–2001	2001–2006
Taslim Olawale Elias	1962–1975	1976–1991[a]
Jens Evensen	1979–1984	1985–1994
Sir Gerald Gray Fitzmaurice	1955–1960	1960–1973
Giorgio Gaja	1999–2011	2012–2021
Kirill Gevorgian	2012–2015	2015–2024
André Gros	1961–1963	1964–1982
Louis Ignacio-Pinto	1967–1969	1970–1979
Eduardo Jiménez de Aréchaga	1960–1969	1970–1979[a]
Feodor Ivanovitch Kozhevnikov	1952–1953	1953–1961
Vladimir M. Koretsky	1949–1951	1961–1970
Abdul G. Koroma	1982–1993	1994–2012
Manfred Lachs	1962–1966	1967–1993[a]
Sir Hersch Lauterpacht	1952–1954	1955–1960
Luis Padilla Nervo	1955–1963	1964–1973
Zhengyu Ni	1982–1984	1985–1994
Georg Nolte	2007–2021	2021–
Sir Benegal Rau	1949–1951	1952–1953
Patrick Lipton Robinson	1992–1996	2015–2024
José Maria Ruda	1964–1972	1973–1991[a]
Stephen M. Schwebel	1977–1980	1981–2000[a]
Bernardo Sepúlveda-Amor	1997–2005	2006–2015
José Sette-Câmara	1970–1978	1979–1988
Jiuyong Shi	1987–1993	1994–2010[a]
Bruno Simma	1997–2002	2003–2012
Nagendra Singh	1967–1972	1973–1988[a]
Jean Spiropoulos	1949–1957	1958–1967
Peter Tomka	1999–2002	2003–[a]
Vladlen Stepanovich Vereshchetin	1992–1994	1995–2006
Sir Humphrey Waldock	1961–1972	1973–1981[a]
Hanqin Xue	2002–2010	2010–
Bogdan Aurescu	2017–2024	2024–
Juan Manuel Gómez-Robledo	2012–2022	2024–
Dire D. Tladi	2012–2022	2024–

[a] Judges who also served as president of the Court.

position on the Court, serving members of the Commission have without exception resigned from the Commission.[7]

The departure of sitting members of the Commission from Geneva to The Hague following their election as judges has been viewed by some as detrimental to the Commission. One veteran member described the "systematic and continuing" movement of Commission members to the Court as "brain-drain," suggesting that "[w]hat was a gain for the Court was in some way a casualty for the Commission, especially when the jurists elected were active Special Rapporteurs in the middle of a project."[8] Another member explained that

Professional Institutions', in *Making Better International Law: The International Law Commission at 50* (United Nations 1998) 333 at 338. This has been seen by some as "proof of the great value which the representatives of sovereign States attached to the fact of membership in the Commission": YBILC 1982, Vol. I, p. 2, para. 8 (Suy, UN Legal Counsel); see also S. Sucharitkul, 'The Role of the International Law Commission in the Decade of International Law', 3 LJIL (1990) 15 at 25–26 (suggesting that "election results could be regarded as a form of appreciation for the work performed as members and as Special Rapporteurs of the Commission").

7 Article 16(1) of the Statute of the Court provides that "[n]o member of the Court may ... engage in any other occupation of a professional nature." Whether this covers participation in the Commission is unclear; it may be recalled that a virtually identical provision in the Statute of the Permanent Court of International Justice had not prevented members of that Court from being appointed as members of the Committee for the Progressive Codification of International Law (see Chapter 2, Section C). Some members of the Commission did continue to serve on it while holding other judicial positions: Sir Humphrey Waldock, for example, was concurrently a judge of the European Court of Human Rights; and Kateka's membership on the Commission overlapped for one year with his membership on the International Tribunal for the Law of the Sea (ITLOS). The Commission's own Statute is silent on the matter, probably given that members only serve part-time. The possible practical difficulties of holding both positions may be illustrated by the experience of Žourek, a member of the Commission and its Special Rapporteur on 'Consular intercourse and immunities' who was chosen in 1959 by the Government of Bulgaria to sit as judge ad hoc in the *Aerial Incident of 27 July 1955 (Israel* v. *Bulgaria)* case. This latter occupation caused him a significant delay in arriving for the Commission's eleventh session that year, and meant that work on the topic of consular intercourse and immunities could not be completed that year as originally planned: see YBILC 1959, Vol. I, p. 2, para. 28 as well as p. 52, para. 2 and pp. 74–75, paras. 1–13; YBILC 1959, Vol. II, p. 88, para. 7. The "rather slow progress" with the topic following Žourek's late arrival prompted the Commission's Chairman, on the Commission's authorization, to write to the President of the Court to request that the hearings which Žourek was to attend should be postponed by a week or two: see YBILC 1960, Vol. I, p. 66, para. 59. In his reply, "the President of the Court had stated that the case requiring Mr. Žourek's presence would not be proceeded with, and accordingly Mr. Žourek would not have to attend at The Hague": *ibid*, at pp. 110–111, para. 96.

8 Sucharitkul, *supra* note 6, at p. 25; see also J.S. Morton, *The International Law Commission of the United Nations* (University of South Carolina Press 2000) 16–17. For a different argument, according to which the perception of the Commission as a training ground for the

> [i]t is generally a setback to the Commission's work if the Special Rapporteur must be replaced in the midst of a project. In addition to the time lost in making the change, each special rapporteur introduces his own approach to the topic, which often cannot be reconciled with the work already done. Unfortunately, several times the Commission has had to appoint three or even four special rapporteurs for a single topic.[9]

This was the case, for example, in connection with the Commission's work on the topic 'Law of treaties', during which two special rapporteurs (Lauterpacht and Fitzmaurice) had to be replaced following their election to the Court and consequent resignation from the Commission. Similarly, the work on the topic 'Non-navigational uses of international watercourses' was "undoubtedly delayed"[10] by the fact that the (second) Special Rapporteur on the topic, Schwebel, was elected to the Court, only soon to be joined in The Hague by his own successor as Special Rapporteur, Evensen. In 1994, the Commission's working group on a draft statute for an international criminal court had to appoint, at a critical moment of completing a second draft, a successor to its Chairman, Koroma, who was elected to the Court in autumn of the preceding year. The Commission found itself in such a "delicate position"[11] in connection with other topics as well.[12]

Court's judges "might encourage caution against expressing radical opinions within the Commission and inhibit the sort of provocative debate that would be deemed unsuitable within the judiciary . . . to the detriment of innovation," see Chinkin, *supra* note 6.

9 B. Graefrath, 'The International Law Commission Tomorrow: Improving Its Organization and Methods of Work', 85 AJIL (1991) 595 at 605. Some special rapporteurs may also fail to get reelected to the Commission, or may not stand for reelection; sometimes, a new Special Rapporteur may well bring new impetus to a project.

10 S.C. McCaffrey, 'The International Law Commission Adopts Draft Articles on International Watercourses', 89 AJIL (1995) 395 at 396; see also S.C. McCaffrey, 'An Assessment of the Work of the International Law Commission', 36 *Natural Resources Journal* (1996) 297 at 299–300; and YBILC 1981, Vol. II, p. 164, para. 256(c).

11 YBILC 1979, Vol. I, p. 2, para. 17 (Chairman Šahović, saying that "[i]n consequence of the election of Mr. Ago, Mr. El-Erian and Mr. Sette Câmara to the International Court of Justice – and the Chairman wished them the fullest success in that new office – the Commission was in a delicate position. The vacancies that had arisen would have to be filled and new special rapporteurs would have to be appointed. He was sure, however, that, as on so many occasions in the past, the Commission would speedily meet the requirements of the situation").

12 In 1967, "one of the problems with which the Commission [had] to deal in the organization of its future work was the appointment of a new Special Rapporteur for the topic 'Succession of States and Governments,' to replace Mr. Lachs, the former Special Rapporteur, who had since been elected a Judge of the International Court of Justice": YBILC 1967, Vol. I, p. 127, para. 70 (the Chairman, Waldock). In 1973, the Commission

But any disadvantage suffered by the Commission as a result of the migration of its members to the Court appears outweighed by the benefits. Judges who are former members of the Commission are "consequently well aware of the Commission's valuable contribution to the codification of international law,"[13] and, in President Higgins's words, "ensure that the work of the ILC is always in the Court's sights."[14] Such judges indeed "[bring] an understanding and appreciation of the Commission's work to the Court;"[15] are familiar with the needs of the codification process;[16] and tend to view the Commission's output positively and favor its endorsement by the Court.[17] This general approach

appointed Sir Francis Vallat as the new Special Rapporteur for the topic of 'Succession of States in respect of treaties' following election to the Court of the former Special Rapporteur for this topic, Sir Humphrey Waldock. In 1978, Ago's election to the Court would have caused "troublesome interruption [to] the work in progress" on the topic 'State responsibility' if he were not permitted to return to the Commission to assist in completion of the first reading stage: YBILC 1979, Vol. I, p. 64, para. 7 (the Chairman, Šahović). Also in 1979, Díaz-González was appointed as Special Rapporteur for the second part of the topic 'Relations between States and international organizations' in place of El-Erian, who had shortly beforehand been elected as a member of the Court. The election of Simma to the Court in 2002 and his subsequent resignation from the Commission meant that he could not complete his assignment as Chairman of the Commission's Study Group on the Fragmentation of International Law, including a study that he committed to undertake on the topic 'The function and scope of the *lex specialis* rule and the question of "self-contained regimes"'.

[13] UN Doc. A/C.6/70/SR.21: 'Summary Record of the Sixth Committee's 21st Meeting' (6 November 2015), p. 6, para. 23 (President Abraham). See also A. Watts, *The International Law Commission 1949–1998* (OUP 1999) 13 ("many members of the International Court were themselves once members of the International Law Commission, and therefore have a natural regard for the quality of its work as well as direct personal knowledge of it").

[14] Higgins, *supra* note 2. See also R. Higgins et al, *Oppenheim's International Law: United Nations*, Vol. II (OUP 2017) 1182, para. 29.186. For the observation that "[i]ndividuals who move from one role to another are unlikely to remain uninfluenced by the ideas and considerations which impinge on them in their different capacities," see O. Schachter, 'The Invisible College of International Lawyers', 72 *Northwestern University Law Review* (1977) 217 at 218.

[15] S.M. Schwebel, 'The Inter-active Influence of the International Court of Justice and the International Law Commission', in C.A. Armas Barea et al (eds.), *Liber Amicorum 'In Memoriam' of Judge José María Ruda* (Kluwer Law International 2000) 479 at 480.

[16] See also YBILC 1979, Vol. I, p. 64, para. 6 (Chairman Šahović, saying that "the members of the Court [who] were former members of the Commission ... were thus well acquainted with all the details of the results of the codification process, and, having been personally involved in that process, were quite familiar with its methods and needs").

[17] This has indeed been the observation of several judges of the Court interviewed in April 2016 (interviews on file with the author). See also YBILC 1979, Vol. I, p. 65, para. 10 (President Waldock saying that "[t]hat interplay [between the Court and the

may be evident already at the stage of writing preliminary notes that express each judge's views on a case (and are distributed to the other judges) and then later in the deliberations of the Court;[18] it may well find expression in their judicial writing as well.[19]

By way of example, when the Court, in the *Kasikili/Sedudu Island* judgment (1999), recognized the principle of equitable utilization and treatment of shared water resources that was embodied in the 1997 Convention on the Non-Navigational Uses of International Watercourses (then not yet in force),[20] an inside observer pointed out that "[i]t is no coincidence that the chairman of the [Court's] Drafting Committee for this Judgment was President Schwebel, who submitted three reports as Special Rapporteur of the International Law Commission with regard to the topic 'Law of the Non-Navigational Uses of International Watercourses' between 1979 and 1982."[21] In the same vein, Judge Jiménez de Aréchaga suggested in the *Tunisia/Libya* case that the consistency between the interpretation adopted by the Court in 1969 for the term "natural prolongation" and the meaning earlier attributed to it by the Commission during its work on the law of the sea, was "confirmed by the fact that several Members of the Court in 1969 had taken an active part in the work of the International Law Commission."[22] And Judge Bedjaoui, who had been the Commission's Special Rapporteur on the topic 'Succession of States in respect of matters other than treaties', indicated in his Separate Opinion in the *Gabčíkovo-Nagymaros Project*

Commission], although inherent in the[ir] special functions ... was perhaps also due to the fact that nearly two thirds of the Court's present membership, including both its President and Vice-President, had formerly been members of the Commission"); YBILC 2012, Vol. I, p. 148, para. 109 (President Tomka addressing the Commission and saying that "[i]t was generally helpful to have former members of the Commission as members of the Court, since they tended to draw more on the work of the Commission"); Sucharitkul, *supra* note 6, at p. 37 ("even as draft articles on first reading, the work of the Commission has often been cited and discussed by the international judicial instance. This is not unnatural since many of the members of the International Court of Justice have come from the Commission").

18 Interview with member of the Court in April 2016 (on file with the author).

19 See also Chapter 3, Section C (with regard to judges of the Court that have referred in their individual opinions to their past work as members of the Commission).

20 *Kasikili/Sedudu Island (Botswana/Namibia), Judgment, I.C.J. Report 1999*, pp. 1107–1108, para. 103.

21 P.H.F. Bekker, *World Court Decisions at the Turn of the Millennium (1997–2001)* (Martinus Nijhoff 2002) 208.

22 *Continental Shelf (Tunisia/Libyan Arab Jamahiriya), Judgment, I.C.J. Reports 1982*, p. 113, para. 48 (Separate Opinion).

case (1997) that the Court should have given more attention to the question of Slovakia's succession to the treaty in question.[23]

Former members are also likely to follow more closely the Commission's work program and products.[24] Thus, while the percentage of former Commission members on the bench makes it clear that such prior membership has not been a precondition for the recurring judicial endorsement of the Commission's pronouncements (by larger and more diverse majorities), it has had a definite impact in terms of raising the Commission's profile within the Peace Palace. As Judge Ago put it, "a former member of the Commission never entirely ceased to belong to it."[25]

Yet past membership in the Commission does not mean automatic endorsement of its output. Previous attitudes are not always shed at the Court's doorstep, and thus a judge who as a member of the Commission developed a strong (albeit minority) position on a certain topic might carry that view into the Court, where he or she might then take a critical stance toward the Commission's pronouncements on the same subject, and oppose any move by the Court to endorse them. President Tomka referred to one such case when saying that

> [i]t was generally helpful to have former members of the Commission as members of the Court, since they tended to draw more on the work of the Commission, although that was not always the case. The one judge who had argued vehemently that article 48 of the articles on State responsibility did not reflect customary international law [and should not be endorsed as such by the Court] was a former member of the Commission.[26]

[23] *Gabčíkovo-Nagymaros Project (Hungary/Slovakia), Judgment, I.C.J. Reports 1997*, pp. 125–126, paras. 20–23; see also K. Wellens, 'The Court's Judgment in the Case concerning the Gabcikovo-Nagymaros Project (Hungary/Slovakia): Some Preliminary Reflections', in K. Wellens (ed.), *International Law: Theory and Practice – Essays in Honour of Eric Suy* (Martinus Nijhoff 1998) 765 at 769.

[24] Padilla Nervo, for instance, assured members of the Commission in 1964, after his resignation from the Commission following his election as a judge of the Court, that he "would follow their important work with the greatest interest": YBILC 1964, Vol. I, p. 40, para. 66.

[25] YBILC 1980, Vol. I, p. 268, para. 27 (addressing the Commission). Judge Waldock similarly said, when attending in 1974 the commemoration of the twenty-fifth anniversary of the opening of the Commission's first session, that "at the present meeting, where he was appearing on behalf of the International Court of Justice at the kind invitation of the Commission, he had the feeling, as a former member, of having come home": YBILC 1974, Vol. I, p. 69, para. 25.

[26] YBILC 2012, Vol. I, p. 148, para. 109 (addressing the Commission). President Tomka was referring to the Court's judgment in *Questions relating to the Obligation to Prosecute or Extradite (Belgium* v. *Senegal)* and most probably to Judge Xue (whose Dissenting

The election to the bench of former Commission members has also been beneficial for the Court, not least given the frequency in which products of the Commission feature in arguments put forward before the Court. President Bustamante y Rivero thus spoke of the "[l]eading international lawyers who had served on the Commission . . . [and] come with their knowledge and wisdom to strengthen the Court in the performance of its task of rendering justice and applying the law to specific cases."[27] Another benefit was highlighted by President Waldock, who said that "[i]n his view, it was a source of strength to the Court that such a large proportion of its members had had the experience of working together in the arduous forum of the Commission's deliberations."[28] Such advantages have also been provided by the significant number of sitting or former Commission members who have served on the Court as judges ad hoc.[29]

(ii) Members of the Court Become Members of the Commission

Traffic between the Commission and the Court has not been one way: even if only rarely, former judges have on occasion become members of the Commission after departing from The Hague. Manley O. Hudson was, of course, a judge on the PCIJ (1936–1946) before taking his place among the first members of the newly established Commission in 1949 (and serving until 1953). Sergei Borisovitch Krylov, who served on the Commission during the years 1954–1956, had previously been a member of the Court (1946–1952) – as was Luigi Ferrari Bravo, a member of the Commission during 1997–1998 and before that a judge of the Court in 1995–1997. One Commission member, Riphagen, was previously a judge

Opinion is instructive in this respect: see *Judgment, I.C.J. Reports 2012*, p. 571). See also UN Doc. A/CN.4/SR.3548: 'Provisional Summary Record of the Commission's 3548th Meeting' (22 July 2021), p. 10 (President Donoghue saying that "Members of the Court who had served on the Commission were often particularly attuned to its outputs but were not always well disposed towards every proposition that emerged from it").

27 YBILC 1969, Vol. I, p. 70, para. 8. For more recent praise see YBILC 2015, Vol. I, p. 233, para. 28 (President Abraham saying that "the presence of former members of the Commission among the judges of the Court made an invaluable contribution to the Court's work").

28 YBILC 1979, Vol. I, p. 65, para. 10 (adding that he, "for one, gladly acknowledged the debt he owed to the Commission for all he had learnt from participation in its work").

29 Some twelve sitting members of the Commission have served as judges ad hoc in cases before the Court: Ago, Brownlie, Castañeda, Dugard, Evensen, Gaja, Kateka, Mahiou, Nagendra Singh, Sepúlveda-Amor, Spiropoulos, and Žourek.

ad hoc on the Court. Also noteworthy is that Eduardo Jiménez de Aréchaga, a member of the Commission (1960–1969) and then a judge (1970–1979) and President (1976–1979) of the Court, attempted but failed to be reelected to the Commission after his judicial term of office had ended.[30]

On the Commission, the former judges have been flag-bearers for defending the Court's authority and standing. Prominent among them was Hudson, who by word and deed instilled in the Commission from its early days a pervasive ethos that the Court must command the respect of the Commission and intervened on several occasions to uphold this approach. As already noted,[31] during one such instance in 1950, when the Commission was debating whether it was desirable to establish a criminal chamber within the Court for the purpose of trying persons accused of genocide and certain other heinous crimes, Hudson turned anxiously to his fellow Commission members and said that "as the one who for thirty years had exerted every effort on behalf of the Court at the Hague, one of the essential organs of international life, [he] feared that it might mean the utter destruction of the Court's prestige if an international criminal jurisdiction were added to it."[32] He urged his colleagues that "[t]hey must avoid any step which might make that great institution a centre of grave controversy,"[33] and was ultimately able to steer the Commission to notify the General Assembly that it does not recommend such an option.[34]

Krylov, who said to members of the Commission at one point that "[d]uring his six years' service as a member of the International Court of Justice he had come to appreciate the value of that supreme tribunal,"[35] likewise made it known to his colleagues in Geneva that he "strongly

[30] This was in 1979, when Jiménez de Aréchaga sought to fill a casual vacancy caused by the election of three Commission members to the Court, but failed to win the vote of Commission members. According to one account, it was "too strange" for members of the Commission that Jiménez de Aréchaga would again sit among them; for him, that they elected instead Barboza (of Argentina) was "a humiliation": Interview with member of the Commission in May 2016 (on file with the author).

[31] See Chapter 4, Section B.1.

[32] YBILC 1950, Vol. I, p. 23, para. 60.

[33] *Ibid.* Hudson added, with much foresight, that "any international criminal jurisdiction was bound to become deeply embroiled in political controversies," and explained that "[t]his would mean less frequent recourse to the Hague Court in a sphere in which it had done admirable work, namely, in disputes between States; and even if States still submitted their disputes to the Court, its prestige would nevertheless be lowered": *ibid*, at p. 26, para. 34.

[34] YBILC 1950, Vol. II, pp. 378–379.

[35] YBILC 1956, Vol. I, p. 20, para. 27.

deprecated any effort to undermine the case-law created by the Court."[36] Mention has already been made of the instance in which several Commission members argued in 1955 that the criteria laid down in the *Fisheries Case* judgment for establishing a regime for straight base lines were too imprecise to merit inclusion in the Commission's draft articles on the regime of the territorial sea, and he sternly replied that he was "astonished by the unexpected attack made on the decision of the International Court of Justice."[37] In the following year, he rejected an updated proposal related to straight baselines because it "amounted to an attenuation of the finding of the Court in the Anglo-Norwegian Fisheries Case" and was "certainly against the spirit of the Court's decision."[38]

Safeguarding the Court's position did not come at the expense of seeking to ensure the success and integrity of Commission; the loyalty of former judges to the Court did not displace their allegiance to their current institution. Indeed, it was Hudson who insisted that the Commission must not be seen to give up its ability to study an issue merely for the reason that the Court took up a case involving that issue.[39] Krylov, in reply to a suggestion by another Commission member that claims relating to the breadth of a territorial sea beyond a 12-mile limit should be submitted to the Court for decisions that would be binding and generally applicable, asserted that "the Commission would be transgressing the terms of its statute if it sought to grant legislative power to the International Court of Justice."[40]

Commission members who were former judges of the Court also drew on their judicial experience in seeking to advance particular legal positions. Krylov referred expressly to his previous position as judge of the Court when telling his colleagues that he "had some experience of the bench and believed that in any specific instance a judge would be able to determine the meaning of the words 'to any appreciable extent'

[36] YBILC 1955, Vol. I, p. 202, para. 10; see also p. 278, para. 74 (Krylov saying with respect to a paragraph proposed to be included in the Commission's annual report that he "particularly disliked the second sentence in the second paragraph of the comment which seemed to criticize the judgement of the International Court in the Fisheries Case").

[37] YBILC 1955, Vol. I, p. 202, para. 9.

[38] YBILC 1956, Vol. I, p. 189, para. 20 (adding, at para. 22, that "in such a complex matter it would be preferable to do nothing that might disturb the decision of the Court"); see also p. 190, para. 35.

[39] See Chapter 6, Section B.2.

[40] YBILC 1955, Vol. I, p. 177, para. 67 (responding to Faris Bey el-Khouri's suggestion: see *ibid*, at p. 169, para. 40).

[suggested in a draft article on straight base lines] by a simple exercise in logic and would not return a verdict of *non liquet*."[41] He did not hesitate to refer the Commission to his own dissenting opinion in the *Corfu Channel* case when calling for the utmost prudence in formulating a principle on the passage of warships through territorial straits;[42] and he further drew on this experience when the Commission discussed ways and means of recording dissenting opinions of its members in its annual reports to the General Assembly.[43]

Ferrari Bravo, for his part, appeared to disclose inside information from the Court's deliberations in the preliminary objections stage of the ongoing case concerning *the Application of the Convention of the Prevention and Punishment of the Crime of Genocide (Bosnia and Herzegovina* v. *Yugoslavia)* during the Commission's discussion on whether a criminal responsibility of States may be said to exist. He stated that, although the Court had indicated that it was not in a position to declare that the government of Yugoslavia was criminal, "[o]ne nonetheless sensed that the Court was somewhat uncomfortable with that position and considered that a criminal entity was involved."[44] Riphagen, too, as Special Rapporteur on the topic 'State responsibility', said that his past experience as judge ad hoc in the *Barcelona Traction* case influenced his approach to the issue of "implementation" (*mise en oeuvre*) of international responsibility.[45]

(iii) Additional Significant Exchanges of Personnel

Also notable in this context of inter-institutional cooperation is the transition of key officials serving the Court or the Commission from one organ to the other. The Court's first Registrar, Edvard Hambro (who served between 1946 and 1953), was later a member of the Commission (1972–1976). In 1980, Torres-Bernárdez, the Deputy Secretary to the Commission, was appointed as Registrar of the Court, bringing to his new role much knowledge of the Commission's work at a time when the

[41] YBILC 1955, Vol. I, p. 202, para. 9 (adding that "[i]t was the special business of judges to be able to apply such provisos"). See also YBILC 1956, Vol. I, p. 203, para. 102.

[42] YBILC 1955, Vol. I, p. 150, para. 21; see also p. 254, para. 105.

[43] *Ibid*, at p. 242, para. 64 and p. 245, para. 37. In this connection see also YBILC 1950, Vol. I, p. 315, para. 7 (Hudson drawing on his experience at the Permanent Court of International Justice with respect to dissenting opinions, in a debate on how reservations by Commission members are to be handled).

[44] YBILC 1998, Vol. I, p. 140, para. 24. See also YBILC 1997, Vol. I, pp. 184–185, para. 58.

[45] YBILC 1983, Vol. I, p. 100, para. 5.

Court's Registry played a significant role in drafting the Court's decisions.[46] Upon his departure to The Hague, he assured members of the Commission that "for his part, he would do his utmost to strengthen the ties that already existed between the Commission and the International Court of Justice."[47] Judge Ago, who was present at the Commission's meeting in which tribute was paid to Torres-Bernárdez, said that the latter "would not feel exiled at The Hague ... especially because at the International Court of Justice he would find many friends who had known him in the Commission."[48] Ago then added that "[i]t was a good omen that an eminent official of the Commission was now to become the principal officer of the Court: at a time when the international community was not giving the law all the attention it merited, it was highly desirable that closer co-operation should be established between the two main legal organs of the United Nations."[49] Torres-Bernárdez later served as judge ad hoc in several cases before the Court. Another Deputy Secretary of the Commission, Valencia-Ospina, was appointed Deputy Registrar of the Court in 1984 and three years later was elected its Registrar, a role he fulfilled until 2000; in 2006, he was elected to be a member of the Commission, a position he held until 2022.

2. *Commission Members as Counsel before the Court*

Another significant factor contributing to the link between the work of the Court and that of the Commission is to be found in the fact that (past or present) members of the Commission often serve as counsel in proceedings before the Court. As President Shi has recognized, "[s]ome Commission members appeared regularly before the Court as counsel or agents of parties, bringing to bear not only their advocacy skills but also their valuable knowledge of the Commission's work, which in turn nourished the Court's deliberations."[50] Much like the Court's judges who were previously members of the Commission, such members serving as counsel indeed bear the indelible mark of their experience and

[46] For the role of the Court's Registry at that time, see H. Thirlway, 'The Drafting of ICJ Decisions: Some Personal Recollections and Observations', 5 CJIL (2006) 15–28.

[47] YBILC 1980, Vol. I, p. 270, para. 41.

[48] *Ibid*, at p. 268, para. 27; see also p. 267, para. 8 (Bedjaoui saying that Torres-Bernardez will be "rejoining many former members of the Commission, so that neither he nor they would feel exiled").

[49] *Ibid*, at p. 268, para. 27.

[50] YBILC 2003, Vol. I, p. 163, para. 3.

often promote the Commission's work within the Peace Palace. When incorporating the Commission's output into their pleadings, they effectively call upon the Court to consider and address it in its decisions. This was very much the case already in the *North Sea Continental Shelf* cases, when Sir Humphrey Waldock, while serving as a member of the Commission, acted both as counsel and advocate for Denmark and as counsel for The Netherlands; some years later, when speaking as a judge of the Court, he recalled that "[i]n the cases submitted to [the Court], counsel often found support of their arguments in the Commission's drafts and commentaries ... it was in the *North Sea Continental Shelf Cases* in 1969, that the Commission's work had for the first time been a central feature of the proceedings and had helped to guide the Court to its conclusions."[51] Similarly, Ago was a member of the Commission when he acted as counsel for Spain in the *Barcelona Traction* case; the approach ultimately taken by the Court "was a manifestation of Ago's view of the comprehensive scope of the law of State responsibility,"[52] a view that he would later advance in his role as the Commission's Special Rapporteur on the topic. Where counsel for both parties pled that the work product of the Commission is an authoritative statement of the law, the Court may find it particularly difficult to ignore that product. This situation occurred in the *Gabčíkovo-Nagymaros Project* case. In that instance, members (and former members) of the Commission represented litigants on both sides and argued that the existence of a state of necessity must be evaluated in the light of the criteria laid down in article 33 of the Commission's draft articles on State Responsibility (as adopted on first reading).[53]

[51] YBILC 1974, Vol. I, p. 70, para. 29.

[52] J. Crawford, 'The International Court of Justice and the Law of State Responsibility', in C.J. Tams and J. Sloan (eds.), *The Development of International Law by the International Court of Justice* (OUP 2013) 71 at 77. Other Commission members serving as counsel in that case were Jiménez de Aréchaga, Reuter, and Waldock.

[53] See *Gabčíkovo-Nagymaros Project (Hungary/Slovakia), Judgment, I.C.J. Reports 1997*, p. 39, para. 50. Crawford was among the counsel for Hungary; Mikulka, Bowett, McCaffrey, and Pellet were among the counsel for Slovakia. The Court's President, Judge Schwebel, said to the Commission in the following year that "[d]raft articles [produced by the Commission] were, of course, only drafts and therefore could not be accorded the same weight [as conventions elaborated on the basis of the Commission's drafts], but in cases where the parties to a dispute agreed that certain draft articles were an authoritative statement of the law on a particular point, the Court naturally gave relevant weight to them" (YBILC 1998, Vol. I, p. 145, para. 73); see also Schwebel, *supra* note 15, at p. 485 (adding that the Court's reliance on the reasoning of the Commission "seems to have been the result of the reliance of both parties on the Draft Articles on State

It is also notable that arguments put by counsel to the Court are later considered by the Commission, in its codification efforts, as State practice (and/or as evidence of acceptance as law).[54] The practice of Commission members who discharge the duties of counsel to the Court is useful to the Commission also by virtue of the lessons that such members may bring back to Geneva from The Hague with regard to the Court's procedure and jurisprudence. Rosenne, for example, advised in 1962 that the Commission's Drafting Committee working on draft articles on the law of treaties should consider carefully whether or not it wished to retain the word "deemed" in a proposed draft article on "participation in a treaty," given that "[t]hat word had the effect of creating a legal fiction, as he had learnt from painful personal experience when he had lost a case before the International Court that had turned on that word."[55] Gaja similarly shared with members of the Commission, during the debate on the topic 'Diplomatic protection', that "[h]is own claim to expertise in that field rested solely on the fact that he had assisted Roberto Ago in his pleadings on the question of diplomatic protection of shareholders in the *Barcelona Traction* case and had later been one of the counsel in the *ELSI* case."[56] Several such members of the Commission have not hesitated to use the opportunity afforded by the annual visit of the Court's President to the Commission (discussed below) to raise with the latter procedural issues that were of concern to them as counsel before the Court, such as the length of oral pleadings;[57] the value of such pleading as compared with written pleadings;[58] coverage of the Court's hearings by the media;[59] the

Responsibility"). At the same time, the extensive use that is often made of the Commission's text in pleadings before the Court is not always fully reflected in the Court's judgments in such cases: see also Chapter 3, Section B.2.

54 See also YBILC 1968, Vol. I, p. 163, para. 30 (Rosenne observing that "the Commission frequently studied the pleadings submitted to the Court and the position taken on behalf of the parties both by eminent counsel and by representatives of States").

55 YBILC 1962, Vol. I, pp. 208–209, para. 65.

56 YBILC 2003, p. 41, para. 51 (adding that "[o]n both occasions [of the *Barcelona Traction* and *ELSI* cases before the Court] he had been engaged on behalf of the respondent State, a fact that might affect his attitude to the present matter"). Other members have similarly drawn on their experience before the Court: see YBILC 1966, Vol. I, p. 45, para. 72 (Ago), and pp. 135–136, para. 19 (Sir Humphrey Waldock); YBILC 2005, Vol. I, p. 85, para. 29 (Pellet sharing, in connection with the topic of 'Responsibility of international organizations', his experience as counsel to Bosnia and Herzegovina).

57 See, for example, YBILC 2000, Vol. I, p. 361, para. 30 (Pellet); YBILC 2002, Vol. I, pp. 188, 189, paras. 12, 17 (Rao, Dugard).

58 See, for example, YBILC 2005, Vol. I, p. 141, para. 30 (Brownlie).

59 See, for example, YBILC 2000, Vol. I, p. 362, para. 36 (Simma).

collection and presentation of evidence;[60] and the appointment of judges ad hoc.[61]

But the concurrent service of Commission members as counsel before the Court may also have its inconveniences. Such members may feel constrained from expressing themselves freely during Commission debates that touch on matters related to the case they are currently involved in, not only because of the Commission's general preference to avoid taking a position on matters pending before the Court,[62] but also out of concern that their motives may be questioned (that is, they may be suspected of trying to promote within the Commission a particular position that would serve them in advancing a certain argument before the Court). For Simma, who served as Germany's co-agent and counsel in the *LaGrand* proceedings, referring to the (then ongoing) case during one of the Commission's debates on the topic of State responsibility was thus "unwelcome, as it placed members of the Commission who were involved in the case in a difficult situation."[63] Sir Michael Wood likewise refrained from saying much about the *Obiang* domestic court decisions discussed by the Commission in 2017 in the context on the topic 'Immunity of State officials from foreign criminal jurisdiction', by reason of his role as counsel for Equatorial Guinea before the Court in the case *Immunities and Criminal Proceedings*;[64] he also said that "since he was acting in a case in which the territorial exception was quite central, he had been careful not to take part in the [Commission's] debate on that issue, either in the Drafting Committee or in the ... plenary meeting."[65] Such instances harken back to and underscore the original

[60] See, for example, YBILC 2007, Vol. I, p. 128, para. 56 (Dugard).

[61] UN Doc. A/CN.4/SR.3380: 'Provisional Summary Record of the Commission's 3380th Meeting' (25 July 2017), p. 11 (Sir Michael Wood).

[62] See Chapter 6, Section B.2. For Tomka's general advice that "members of the Commission should refrain from siding with one or another of the parties and from taking positions on current or future proceedings," see YBILC 2000, Vol. I, pp. 247, para. 57.

[63] YBILC 2000, Vol. I, pp. 246–247, para. 47 (feeling obliged to correct the record with respect to Germany's actions in connection with the case). Simma earlier said that he has "a special interest in the issue of the implementation and enforcement of obligations *erga omnes*" (*ibid*, at para. 42).

[64] Sir Michael was one of two Commission members (the other being Kamto) representing Equatorial Guinea at a point in time when the Commission debated the issue of immunity of State officials from foreign criminal jurisdiction, which then stood at the heart of the *Immunities and Criminal Proceedings (Equatorial Guinea* v. *France)* case.

[65] UN Doc. A/CN.4/SR.3389: 'Provisional Summary Record of the Commission's 3389th Meeting' (4 August 2017), p. 22.

sense of unease felt by the drafters of the Commission's Statute about any interaction between the Court and the Commission concerning the latter's ongoing work.[66]

3. *Other Encounters*

Members of the Court and the Commission have various other opportunities to meet and interact. These frequently include academic conferences and workshops on international law (which are sometimes dedicated to discussing topics that are being dealt with by the Commission), as well as periodic meetings of international law societies. Judges of the Court traditionally take part in commemorative events of the Commission,[67] and Commission members are regular guests at the Court's anniversary celebrations. Members of the two bodies have sometimes sat together on arbitral tribunals, as was the case when Caflisch of the Commission served alongside judges Simma and Tomka (and former President Schwebel) on the tribunal of the *Indus Waters Kishenganga Arbitration*; and members of the Commission have often served as counsel in arbitral proceedings before judges of the Court sitting as arbitrators, as was the case when Sir Michael Wood appeared before Judge Greenwood in the *Chagos Maritime Protected Area Arbitration*.[68] The President of the Court and members of the Commission may also cross paths during 'International Law Week', held each October at the United Nations Headquarters in New York. On a few occasions, judges of the Court have commented on draft reports of the Commission's special rapporteurs before the latter have finalized and submitted them to the Commission for consideration.[69] Through many such instances, members of the two organs engage in a continuous process of communication and collaboration. The fact that this process is often informal, or that its full scale and effect is difficult to circumscribe, does not diminish

[66] See Chapter 2, Section D.2.

[67] This is so much so that in 1973, for example, "it had been decided [by the Commission] that it would be impractical to attempt to celebrate the Commission's twenty-fifth anniversary at the present session, since most of the Judges of the International Court who were former members of the Commission had intimated that they would be unable to attend such a ceremony. It had therefore been agreed that the Commission's anniversary should be celebrated at its next session in 1974": YBILC 1973, Vol. I, p. 103, para. 57.

[68] In October 2018, President Yusuf announced that the Court's judges would no longer be permitted to sit as arbitrators (other than in certain, limited circumstances).

[69] Interviews with two members of the Commission in May 2016 (on file with the author).

its intrinsic value in drawing the Court and the Commission closer and in fostering in them a sense of a shared mission.

B. Exchanges in Geneva

For several decades now, members of the Court have come to Geneva during the Commission's annual sessions to meet and confer with members of the Commission. Seeking to reinforce the inter-institutional relationship, such visits have supplied, in President Owada's words, "an opportunity for fruitful interaction between two key legal institutions of the United Nations."[70] While the nature and format of such exchanges have changed greatly over time, they have also come to symbolize the close relationship between the two organs and to serve as an ongoing link between them.

1. *1967–1996: Relaxed, Unbridled Discourse*

The tradition of courtesy visits to the Commission by the Court's judges dates back to 1967, when it began primarily as part of an exercise in public relations. In the harsh political aftermath of the 1966 *South West Africa* judgment, the Court was not only left without much work on its hands and vying for visibility, but was also conscious of the need for

[70] YBILC 2011, Vol. I, p. 158, para. 2 (addressing the Commission). The representatives of several other bodies frequently appear before the Commission as well, such as the Asian-African Legal Consultative Organization, the Inter-American Juridical Committee, the African Union Commission on International Law, the Committee of Legal Advisers on Public International Law of the Council of Europe, and the European Committee on Legal Cooperation. In 2008, the president of the International Tribunal for the Law of the Sea, Judge Rüdiger Wolfrum, and Philippe Gautier, the registrar of the Tribunal, paid a visit to the Commission with the intention to "share some information on the Tribunal's work but also to indicate to the Commission areas where the two institutions had common concerns and could cooperate easily": YBILC 2008, p. 247, para. 105 (as of 2023, no member of the Tribunal has visited in such capacity since). According to Tladi, "[w]hen, due to time pressures, the Commission decided to reduce the amount of time spent with each body to half a morning, it retained the full morning interaction with the President of the Court. Moreover when, due to the time pressures resulting from Covid-related changes in working methods in 2021, it decided not to have any interactions with external bodies, the President of the ICJ was still invited to interact with the Commission": D. Tladi, 'Representation, Inequality, Marginalization, and International Law-Making: The Case of the International Court of Justice and the International Law Commission', 7 *UC Irvine Journal of International, Transnational, and Comparative Law* (2022) 60 at 75, fn. 91. No visits are as festive an occasion as those made by a member of the Court.

closer cooperation with other organs of the United Nations.[71] Soon thereafter, as part of an orchestrated effort to get out of the courthouse more often, "the principle of contacts between the Court and the International Law Commission [was] unanimously accepted by the Court."[72] For the Commission, as Ago then described it, this "was the sign of a particularly important development: the International Court of Justice had grasped the great importance of the work of codification and had understood that the present age was that of the transformation of international law and that collaboration between the responsible legal organs of the United Nations was absolutely essential."[73] Thus began a "series [of visits] cementing the close relationship between the Commission and the Court."[74]

First to arrive in Geneva to address the Commission on behalf of the Court was Judge Fitzmaurice, himself a former member of the Commission, who was accompanied by another former member, Judge Lachs.[75] After a warm welcome by Chairman Waldock, Judge Fitzmaurice took the floor to say that the Court and the Commission "had a community of interest and a common legal foundation."[76] He explained that:

> The Court had to declare the law, not as an arbitrary process but in accordance with the provisions of Article 38, paragraph 1, of its Statute. The Commission's task was less circumscribed, for it was the main international codifying agency, but it still had to take into account the elements laid down in that article. The work of each influenced the other and they had a joint obligation to make every effort to promote the law.[77]

Judge Fitzmaurice saw fit to emphasize, moreover, that "[d]espite the obvious difference of functions, there were close links between the Court and the Commission and a number of members of the latter had become

[71] See also S. Engel, 'Annual Reports of the International Court of Justice to the General Assembly?', 44 BYIL (1970) 193 at 198.

[72] YBILC 1970, Vol. I, p. 138, para. 2 (Judge Gros addressing the Commission).

[73] YBILC 1968, Vol. I, p. 162, para. 16. Yasseen observed that "the International Court of Justice was quite right to maintain contact with the organs in which the international legal order was developed and norms of international law were framed; for international law was not static but dynamic, and its evolution must be followed in international life": *ibid*, at para. 11.

[74] YBILC 1980, Vol. I, p. 194, para. 1 (the Chairman, Pinto).

[75] YBILC 1967, Vol. I, p. 88, paras. 1–10 (it was originally the President of the Court, Judge Bustamante y Rivero, who was due to visit the Commission, but given schedule changes he deputed the task to Judge Fitzmaurice).

[76] *Ibid*, at para. 6.

[77] *Ibid*.

Judges of the Court."[78] Judge Lachs, for his part, added that "the mutual respect that existed between the Court and the Commission was a hopeful aspect in the development of international law."[79] In reply, Waldock sought to further highlight the interdependence of the two organs by pointing out that "[t]he codification, elucidation and progressive development of the law was often said to be an essential prerequisite for extending the acceptance of the Court's jurisdiction and for its successful operation as a judicial instrument";[80] he also mentioned "the feelings of personal friendship which existed between the Judges of the Court and members of the Commission."[81] Later on, in private, Waldock "availed himself of Mr. Lachs's . . . visit" to confer with him regarding the future direction of the Commission's work on the topic 'Succession of States and Governments'.[82]

In the following year, it was Vice-President Koretsky, another former member of the Commission, who was "asked by the President and the members of the Court to visit the International Law Commission in order to wish it every success in its work, which was so important for the consolidation and development of international law."[83] In so doing, Koretsky noted the "close and natural link" between the two institutions. No doubt aware of the attention paid that year in the *North Sea* case pleadings to the Commission's work on the legal regime pertaining to the continental shelf, he explained that the Commission

> played an increasingly active part in preparing what might be termed legislative drafts, in formulating the principles and norms of international law, and in the systematization, codification and progressive development of international law in the form of multilateral treaties. The Court, for its part, did not merely study the Commission's work; norms drafted by the Commission had crossed and continued to cross the threshold of the

78 *Ibid*, at para. 5.
79 *Ibid*, at para. 10.
80 *Ibid*, at para. 8 (adding that "the process was [also] certainly an indispensable condition for the peace and welfare of the international community").
81 *Ibid*, at para. 9.
82 See YBILC 1967, Vol. I, p. 127, para. 71 (Judge Lachs, who was Special Rapporteur for the topic until he resigned from the Commission following his election to the Court, "had expressed the view . . . that it would be practicable and probably helpful, as a first step, to treat as a separate topic the question of the succession of States and Governments with respect to treaties and, if desired, to appoint a separate special rapporteur for that question").
83 YBILC 1968, Vol. I, p. 161, para. 2.

> Peace Palace, where the Court sat, and were increasingly interpreted and applied by the Court in its examination of the cases referred to it.[84]

Koretsky further recognized that "there were personal relations between members of the two institutions," highlighting that "[t]hree of the Court's present judges had, as it were, assisted at the birth of the International Law Commission by helping to draft its Statute, and several other judges had been members of the Commission."[85] For members of the Commission, who paid ample tribute to Koretsky, his presence "was a symbol of the links between the Commission and the International Court of Justice."[86] Chairman Ruda explained that "the Commission was engaged in formulating rules for acceptance by States, which the Court would have to apply."[87]

In 1969, some four months after the *North Sea Continental Shelf* judgment was handed down, it was Judge Bustamante y Rivero who paid the Commission its first visit by a sitting President of the Court. For him, given that the Court and the Commission "were both working to promote and develop the law, and to perfect it as far as humanly possible," it was only "natural that the President and judges of the Court should from time to time have the pleasure of visiting the Commission and exchanging mutual good wishes for the success of their common endeavors."[88] In their "difficult task" of "adapting to the specific problems of a particular dispute the principles and rules formulated by the Commission," he added, "the members of the Court appreciated the help and encouragement of their friends in the Commission."[89] Members of the Commission, who devoted the whole meeting to the exchange with the President, acknowledged the complementary roles of the two institutions and called for the further strengthening of their ties.[90]

Judges of the Court continued to turn up at the Commission over the next two decades, their presence considered as "[bearing] witness to the close relations between the Court and the Commission."[91] As illustrated by Table 5.2, however, such visits did not follow a uniform pattern. Some

[84] *Ibid*, at para. 3.
[85] *Ibid*, at para. 4.
[86] *Ibid*, at p. 162, para. 20 (Sir Humphrey Waldock).
[87] *Ibid*, at para. 7.
[88] YBILC 1969, Vol. I, p. 69, para. 3.
[89] *Ibid*, at p. 70, paras. 7, 8.
[90] *Ibid*, at pp. 70–73, paras. 11–32.
[91] YBILC 1987, Vol. I, p. 140, para. 1 (the Chairman, McCaffrey).

Table 5.2 *Members of the Court who paid the Commission a visit (1967–2023)*

Year	Member(s) of the Court visiting the Commission
1967	Judges Fitzmaurice and Lachs
1968	Vice-President Koretsky
1969	President Bustamante y Rivero
1970	Judge Gros
1971	N/A
1972	Judges Jiménez de Aréchaga and Lachs
1973	N/A
1974	Judge Waldock
1975	President Lachs
1976	Judge Waldock
1977	N/A
1978	President Jiménez de Aréchaga; Vice-President Nagendra Singh; Judge Elias
1979	President Waldock; Vice-President Elias; and Judge Morozov; Judge Ago
1980	Judge El-Erian; Judge Sette-Câmara; Judge Ago
1981	Judge El-Erian; Judge Ago
1982	Judge Ago
1983	Judge Ago
1984	N/A
1985	Judge Ago; Judge Evensen
1986	Judge Ago
1987	Judge Ago; Judge Ruda; Judges Sette-Câmara and Evensen
1988	Judge Ago
1989	N/A
1990	Judges Ago and Guillaume
1991	N/A
1992	Judge Ajibola
1993	N/A
1994	N/A
1995	Judge Vereshchetin; Judge Oda; Judge Ajibola
1996	Judge Ferrari Bravo
1997	Judge Shi
1998	President Schwebel
1999	President Schwebel
2000	President Guillaume
2001	President Guillaume
2002	President Guillaume
2003	President Shi

Table 5.2 (*cont.*)

Year	Member(s) of the Court visiting the Commission
2004	President Shi
2005	President Shi
2006	President Higgins
2007	President Higgins
2008	President Higgins (and Judge Simma addressing the International Law Seminar)
2009	President Owada
2010	President Owada
2011	President Owada
2012	President Tomka
2013	President Tomka
2014	President Tomka
2015	President Abraham
2016	President Abraham
2017	President Abraham
2018	President Yusuf
2019	President Yusuf
2020	*[No ILC session because of the COVID-19 pandemic]*
2021	President Donoghue (via video link)
2022	President Donoghue (via video link)
2023	President Donoghue

years saw a single judge arriving in Geneva, while in others as many as four judges arrived (together or separately) or no judges seem to have visited at all. Some visits were held under the Commission's agenda item of "cooperation with other bodies," while others were not classified as such and sometimes not at all mentioned in the Commission's annual report covering the work of the relevant session. Not all judges were on an official visit on behalf of the Court, and some did not even address the Commission when attending one or more of its meetings. Following the visit of Judge Sette Câmara in 1980, for example, the Commission's Chairman "was not sure whether [or not] he had been present as an observer for the Court."[92] Similarly, no record seems to exist as to Judge

92 YBILC 1980, Vol. I, p. 300, para. 11. For Judge Sette Câmara's short remarks before the Commission, see *ibid*, at p. 240, para. 40.

Schwebel's return to Geneva in 1981, following his election to the Court and resignation from the Commission, to complete and then submit his third report on the topic 'Law of the non-navigational uses of international watercourses' (for which he had served as Special Rapporteur).[93] Private conversations between the judges and members of the Commission on matters of mutual interest no doubt took place in the corridors of the Palais des Nations during such visits.

Perhaps most intriguing in this context is the history of Judge Ago's visits to the Commission. Having served on the Commission in the years 1957–1978, including as Special Rapporteur for the topic 'State responsibility' from 1963 onward, Ago was elected judge of the Court in 1978. He subsequently resigned from the Commission, but given that he had previously submitted for consideration by the Commission his eighth report (relating to the final articles of Part One of the draft on State responsibility), a communication was addressed on behalf of the Commission to the President of the Court to inquire whether Ago would be able to introduce his report to the Commission and comment thereon despite his new office. By a letter dated March 12, 1979, President Waldock "had signified his consent, subject to certain conditions, in particular the condition that Mr. Ago would participate in the Commission's deliberations in his individual and personal capacity."[94] Judge Ago was back in Geneva with his former colleagues soon thereafter, and, for several weeks during the Commission's thirty-first session, took part in all plenary debates on his report, participated actively in the relevant Drafting Committee meetings, and oversaw the adoption of several draft articles together with their commentaries.[95]

93 Schwebel was elected to the Court in early 1981 and consequently resigned from the Commission, not taking part in its annual session later (May 4–July 24) that year; nevertheless, his third report carries the date of December 11, 1981 and still his title as Special Rapporteur. See also YBILC 1982, Vol. I, p. 2, para. 14 ("Despite the lack of a special rapporteur, the Commission had before it a third report on the topic submitted by the former Special Rapporteur (A/CN.4/348), who had begun the preparation of that report before he had resigned from the Commission"); the Commission did not take action on that third report.

94 YBILC 1979, Vol. I, p. 3, para. 1. See also Higgins et al, *supra* note 14, at 935 at fn. 47 (adding that "there was no question of his being appointed, designated, or given any official title such as 'expert consultant'; and priority would have to be given to his judicial duties"). For Šahović, the Court's authorization was "evidence of the Court's wish to continue to co-operate with the Commission in the codification and progressive development of international law": YBILC 1979, Vol. I, p. 4, para. 5.

95 According to the summary records of the Commission's session of that year, Ago attended plenary debates on May 16–18, 21–24, 28–29, and 31; June 1, 5; July 10, 16–20, and 30; and August 1–3: see YBILC 1979, Vol. I. On Ago's participation in

The following summer saw Judge Ago return to Geneva yet again, this time to introduce the addenda to his eighth report (more specifically, draft articles dealing with "State of necessity" and "Self-defence") and to take part in the completion of the first reading stage of Part One of the Commission's draft articles on State responsibility. Chairman Pinto welcomed him as a former Special Rapporteur who was now there as "a friend of the Commission,"[96] and for a total of some three weeks of the session that year,[97] Ago again navigated the Commission's work on the topic and played an active role in the adoption of additional draft articles and commentaries. In a tribute paid to him following the conclusion of the first reading stage, Riphagen, the new Special Rapporteur for the topic, said that members of the Commission "took their leave of Mr. Ago with a sense of awe, but knew that they could always count on him for assistance in their further work on the topic of State responsibility."[98] Ago, in reply, assured members of the Commission that indeed he would "remain at their disposal."[99] That he did: as detailed below, in the next decade he would visit the Commission no fewer than eight times, his visits – largely unreported by the Commission – almost always coinciding with the Commission's debates on State responsibility.

In 1981, in his capacity as a member of the Court, Judge Ago attended the Commission's first meeting on Riphagen's report on the content, forms, and degrees of international responsibility. "What had in the past seemed sometimes a formula of mutual courtesy," he said in reference to the question of cooperation between the Court and the Commission, "had come to have an extremely real significance" given, among other things, the increasing reference to the Commission's work, including that on State responsibility, in the Court's hearings and judgments.[100] Judge Ago sat in on some of the Commission's discussions on State

meeting of the drafting committee, see *ibid*, at p. 170, para. 2. Crawford has written that "[a] reflection of Ago's particular influence is that he managed to stay on as Special Rapporteur even after he was elected to the ICJ in 1979 and had ceased to be a member of the ILC. It is highly unlikely that such an arrangement would be permitted now; moreover, the current caseload of the Court would not allow it": Crawford, *supra* note 52, at p. 76.

[96] YBILC 1980, Vol. I, p. 153, para. 34.

[97] According to the summary records of the Commission's session of that year, Ago attended plenary debates on June 16–20, 23–27 and July 7–9, 17, 24–25 (see *ibid*); he also participated in meetings of the Drafting Committee.

[98] *Ibid*, at p. 308, para. 23.

[99] *Ibid*, at para. 25.

[100] YBILC 1981, Vol. I, p. 125, para. 5.

responsibility in 1982 and 1983 as well, in his capacity as a former member.[101] Arriving from The Hague yet again in 1985, he said that he believed that "frequent contacts between the Commission and the ICJ were useful and even necessary, since the Court's task of ruling on particular cases and settling disputes between States on points of law was the counterpart of the Commission's task of defining general rules, and the two tasks were essential for the international community."[102] This approach led him to attend the Commission's debates on State responsibility also in 1986,[103] 1987,[104] 1988,[105] and 1990.[106] There is little doubt that such visits afforded him an opportunity to coordinate or at least exchange views with the Commission on matters of substance.

2. *1997 Onward: A More Formal Engagement*

Social calls upon the Commission by members of the Court became a more formal affair in 1997, when the Commission, on the initiative of its Chairman that year, Pellet, unanimously decided to officially invite the President of the Court "to attend one of the meetings of the Commission and have an exchange of views with its members."[107] Pellet had felt that it was now the Commission that "was somewhat isolated within the United Nations" and that, although it did have close links with the Sixth Committee of the General Assembly, "it did not, for example, have any organizational link with the ICJ ... [with which] it would certainly be of interest to cultivate relations."[108] The idea was, he explained, "that the

[101] YBILC 1982, Vol. I, p. 230, para. 1; YBILC 1983, Vol. I, p. 234, para. 3 (the Chairman, Francis, acknowledging the presence of Judge Ago).

[102] YBILC 1985, p. 207, para. 3.

[103] YBILC 1986, Vol. I, p. 188, para. 1.

[104] YBILC 1987, Vol. I, p. 66, para. 1.

[105] YBILC 1988, Vol. I, pp. 31–32, para. 1 (attending the debate on international liability for injurious consequences arising out of acts not prohibited by international law).

[106] YBILC 1990, p. 298, para. 1 (attending debate on international liability for injurious consequences arising out of acts not prohibited by international law (as well as tribute to the memory of Paul Reuter)).

[107] YBILC 1997, Vol. I, p. 142, para. 1.

[108] *Ibid.* Interestingly, an idea that the Chairman of the General Assembly's Sixth Committee would annually address the Commission, "with a view to strengthening links between the two bodies and giving the Commission a clearer picture of the attitude of the Sixth Committee towards many of the projects the Commission was pursuing" (YBILC 1999, Vol. I, p. 57, para. 11 (Dugard)), has never been realized.

two institutions should create opportunities to meet and exchange views ... [in order to] engage in a fruitful dialogue."[109]

It did not take more than two weeks before Judge Shi, representing President Schwebel who was unable to travel for health reasons, arrived in Geneva, where, having previously served on the Commission himself, "he was glad to be thus reunited with his former colleagues and friends."[110] After providing an overview of the cases on the Court's docket, the decisions rendered by the Court in the previous year, and the Court's budgetary situation, he paid tribute to the Commission's achievements over the five decades of its existence. The "ICJ had always held the Commission's work in very high esteem," he stated, adding (perhaps in anticipation of the *Gabčíkovo-Nagymaros Project* judgment that was to be released some three months later) that the frequent reference to the Commission's products in decisions of the Court "bore witness to the excellent quality of the Commission's work and to the fact that the Court viewed the products of that work as evidence of the state of international law."[111] Members of the Commission did not hide their satisfaction, and in the short remaining time of the meeting posed various questions to Judge Shi, who replied patiently and openly.[112] The Commission soon made it known that it "found it useful to establish a dialogue with the Court and felt that this initiative [of visits] should continue."[113]

From then on, each year, without exception,[114] presidents of the Court have traveled to Geneva to address the Commission in plenary session. These visits, held under the Commission's agenda item of "cooperation with other bodies," have generally followed a uniform approach, with presidents first reading out a statement on the Court's docket (and possibly other institutional matters) and then, time permitting, engaging in an exchange of questions and answers with the members of the

[109] YBILC 1997, Vol. I, p. 212, paras. 49, 50 (revealing also that Pellet seems to have mistakenly thought that all previous visits by the Court's judges were "personal visits," that is, not in any capacity of representing the Court).

[110] *Ibid*, at para. 51.

[111] *Ibid*, at paras. 52–65.

[112] *Ibid*, at paras. 66–74.

[113] YBILC 1997, Vol. II, Part Two, p. 72, para. 242.

[114] The session scheduled for 2020 did not take place because of the sudden appearance of the COVID-19 pandemic; the pandemic also caused President Donoghue to address the Commission in 2021 and 2022 via video link.

Commission.[115] While it is difficult to think of a group of persons less in need of an update on the decisions rendered by the Court in any previous year,[116] the President's account does sometimes shed new light on the judgments of the Court or explicitly draws attention to aspects that have a special relevance to the Commission's work; occasionally it provides some information about the inner workings of the Court as well.[117]

The President's visits have also afforded them an opportunity to comment on the Commission's ongoing work, whether on their own initiative or in reply to a question by a member of the Commission. In 2002, for example, when the Commission had just taken up the topic of 'Fragmentation of international law', Xue asked President Guillaume "whether he could make any comments that might help the Commission in its consideration of the topic" and received an elaborate

[115] Pellet had originally envisaged that such "informal and mutually useful exchanges would be planned in the form, for example, of suggestions by the Court on the topics which the Commission intended to include in its agenda and symposia or workshops on subjects of common interest or concern": YBILC 1997, Vol. I, p. 212, para. 50.

[116] Addressing the Commission in 2015, President Abraham acknowledged that members probably need no updating on the Court's work which they surely follow closely, but thought a personal overview could stimulate the subsequent exchange: audio recording of the Commission's 3274th meeting (22 July 2015), available at <https://legal.un.org/ilc/sessions/67/bulletin.shtml> (minutes 2:59–3:313 in English). See also UN Doc. A/CN.4/SR.3478: 'Provisional Summary Record of the Commission's 3478th Meeting' (11 July 2019), p. 3 (President Yusuf). Nevertheless, not everyone is satisfied: Economides, for example, complained in 1999 that the relationship between the Court and the Commission "left a great deal to be desired," explaining that the Commission "had little or no knowledge of the Court's activities ... One 20-minute presentation delivered annually to the Commission by a member of the Court was not sufficient to provide the requisite information"; he added that "[i]n both bodies' interests, steps should be taken to ensure proper provision of full information, through regular exchanges of documents": YBILC 1999, Vol. I, p. 57, para. 9; see also at p. 58, para. 21 (Mr. He agreeing that the Commission should "strengthen its relations with ICJ").

[117] See, for example, YBILC 2003, Vol. I, p. 166, para. 25 (President Shi saying that members of the Court, who "were concerned about the fragmentation of international law ... had not discussed the matter formally, although they had exchanged views on the subject behind the scenes"); YBILC 2004, Vol. I, p. 157, para. 30 (President Shi providing details on the *Legal Consequences of the Construction of a Wall in the Occupied Palestinian Territory* Advisory Opinion that was to be made public only days later); YBILC 2012, Vol. I, p. 148, para. 109 (President Tomka revealing that "[t]he one judge who had argued vehemently [in the deliberations leading up to the judgment in *Questions relating to the Obligation to Prosecute or Extradite*] that article 48 of the articles on State responsibility did not reflect customary international law was a former member of the Commission"). See also YBILC 2001, Vol. I, p. 212, para. 28 (Melescanu welcoming the traditional visit by the President of the Court, "which provided the Commission with inside information about the activities of the Court").

reply.[118] In 2004, President Shi referred to the *Avena* judgment when suggesting to members of the Commission that the Court's findings with respect to the nature of Mexico's claim, and the question whether that claim was admissible despite the alleged lack of exhaustion of local remedies, were of relevance to the topic of diplomatic protection.[119] In 2007, it was President Higgins who suggested that, given the Court's rejection in the *Diallo* case of the Democratic Republic of Congo's argument that no real meaning should attach to the use of the term "refusal of entry" in place of "expulsion," the Commission "might wish to review" the position adopted in the second report of the Special Rapporteur on the topic 'Expulsion of aliens' (which suggested that no real terminological distinction could be drawn among the terms "expulsion," "escort to the border," and "*refoulement*").[120] She further remarked

[118] YBILC 2002, Vol. I, pp. 189–190, paras. 26, 30–31. A year earlier, when the Commission was wrapping up its work on the topic 'State responsibility', President Guillaume suggested, in reference to the *LaGrand* case and the Court's abstention from ordering the United States to pay indemnification for its failure to comply with its obligations, that "[t]he Court was thus suggesting, without making the point explicitly, that wrongful conduct did not always entail responsibility – something to which further consideration might be given": YBILC 2001, Vol. I, p. 211, para. 18.

[119] YBILC 2004, Vol. I. p. 155, para. 18; see also at p. 157, para. 27 (Sreenivasa Rao saying to President Shi that "the concepts of *jus cogens* and *erga omnes* obligations were a matter of particular interest to the Commission in the context of its consideration of the topic of fragmentation of international law," and then asking, "[g]iven that ICJ had, on several occasions, considered the scope, content and impact of the two concepts ... whether the President could give the Commission any further guidance").

[120] YBILC 2007, Vol. I, p. 126, para. 39. Given that the legal regime pertaining to refugees eventually fell outside the scope of the topic, no such review was deemed necessary. A year earlier, President Higgins said that "[t]he challenges raised by cases such as *Armed Activities on the Territory of the Congo (Democratic Republic of the Congo* v. *Uganda)* and *Application of the Convention on the Prevention and Punishment of the Crime of Genocide* were not only procedural, however. Those cases constituted exemplary material for the Commission's topic 'Fragmentation of international law: difficulties arising from the diversification and expansion of international law'"; referring to the *Pulp Mills on the River Uruguay (Argentina* v. *Uruguay)* case, she suggested that "[t]he Statute of the River Uruguay, whose provisions are at the centre of the dispute, should further be of particular interest to the ILC": YBILC 2006, Vol. I, pp. 214, 215, paras. 25, 35. President Higgins also said (according to the text of her speech), with regard to *Armed Activities on the Territory of the Congo (New Application: 2002)*, that "the Court had been prepared to accept that a statement made by the Minister of Justice to the Committee on Human Rights could bind a State (a matter perhaps of some interest for your work on unilateral acts)" and that "I imagine that the paragraphs of the Judgment on the reservation issues may be of some interest in the context of the work of the ILC on this topic": see Speech by H.E. Judge Rosalyn Higgins, President of the International Court of Justice, at the 58th Session of the International Law

that "[a]s the third report [of the Special Rapporteur] stated, the right to expulsion was not absolute and must be exercised in accordance with the fundamental rules of international law."[121] In 2009, President Owada drew the attention of the Commission, which was then working on the topic 'Reservations to treaties', to the Court's "interesting but also somewhat troubling [*Reservations*] Advisory Opinion of 28 May 1951," suggesting that the Commission "might wish to look into the matter" of whether a reservation to a compromissory clause setting aside an obligation arising from the Court's compulsory jurisdiction over substantive issues in the Convention itself, may be said to affect the object and purpose of a treaty.[122] Members themselves sometimes offered presidents of the Court their views on the Court's decisions, occasionally being critical.[123]

The exchanges have also afforded members of the Commission an opportunity to consult with presidents with regard to the Commission's work program, realizing to some degree an aspiration voiced back in 1973 by Ustor, who referred to article 17 of the Commission's Statute when suggesting that the Court, "as a principal organ of the United Nations, could well make interesting suggestions with regard to the Commission's future programme."[124] One such instance occurred in 2000, when Momtaz asked President Guillaume whether the Court, in

Commission (25 July 2006), available at <https://legal.un.org/ilc/sessions/58/pdfs/english/icj_president.pdf>.

121 YBILC 2007, Vol. I, p. 126, para. 38.

122 YBILC 2009, Vol. I, p. 128, para. 66.

123 See, for example, YBILC 2005, Vol. I, p. 141, para. 35 (Pambou-Tchivounda saying to President Shi that "[i]n the cases concerning Legality of Use of Force, the Court had taken great pains to determine whether a treaty was or was not in force vis-à-vis a State that was or was not a party to the Court's Statute; however, he himself did not feel that the issue had merited so much attention"); YBILC 2006, Vol. I, p. 218, para. 55 (Pellet telling President Higgins that the Court's Advisory Opinion on *Reservations to the Convention on Genocide* was a success, while the *North Sea Continental Shelf* judgment was a failure and the *Arrest Warrant* judgment "disastrous"); YBILC 2012, Vol. I, pp. 146–147, paras. 95–96 (Kittichaisaree), and p. 148, para. 106 (Forteau).

124 YBILC 1973, Vol. I, p. 163, para. 10. Article 17(1) of the Commission's Statute reads: "The Commission shall also consider proposals [for the progressive development of international law] and draft multilateral conventions submitted by Members of the United Nations, *the principal organs of the United Nations other than the General Assembly*, specialized agencies, or official bodies established by intergovernmental agreement to encourage the progressive development of international law and its codification, and transmitted to it for that purpose by the Secretary-General" (emphasis added).

referring in *Immunity from Legal Process of a Special Rapporteur* to the principle of the responsibility of international organizations despite the silence of treaty law on this issue, "was thus issuing to the international community, legal writers and more particularly the Commission, a kind of invitation to fill that gap by developing international law."[125] In another instance, already referred to,[126] Escarameia asked President Higgins whether there were any topics that "the Commission might take up that would be useful to the Court in its work."[127] Stressing that she could reply only in her personal capacity, President Higgins said that she "welcomed Ms. Escarameia's idea about the interplay between the work of the Court and that of the Commission" and added that "[o]ne topic on which she personally would warmly welcome a study by the Commission was the relationship between the global push for measures to combat impunity, on the one hand, and the international law in immunity, on the other."[128] The Commission did subsequently take up the topic 'Immunity of State officials from foreign criminal jurisdiction', and members of the Commission recalled President Higgins's expressed preference when highlighting the benefit of doing so.[129] In 2014, Forteau similarly asked President Tomka whether there was a need to clarify the rules of interpretation that applied to unilateral acts (to which the law of treaties did not apply), receiving the reply that this "might be a topic for possible consideration by the Commission, but it would not be an easy topic."[130] Forteau also asked President Abraham, in 2016,

125 YBILC 2000, Vol. I, p. 363, para. 48.

126 See Chapter 4, Section A.3.

127 YBILC 2006, Vol. I, p. 218, para. 50. In the following year, Escarameia asked President Higgins whether the Court would find it useful if the Commission, in its work on the topic of 'Fragmentation of international law', were to look into the issue of the relationship between courts (YBILC 2007, Vol. I, p. 127, para. 51); President Higgins seems to have avoided answering the question. In 2009, Escarameia similarly asked President Owada whether there was "any topic that the Commission could take up that might help the Court in its activities?": YBILC 2009, Vol. I, p. 125, para. 50.

128 YBILC 2006, Vol. I, p. 218, para. 52.

129 See YBILC 2008, Vol. I, p. 204, para. 2 (Jacobsson), p. 217, para. 18 (Vázquez-Bermúdez), and p. 226, para. 91 (Saboia). President Higgins saw it fit to tell Commission members that year (2008) that the *Certain Questions of Mutual Assistance in Criminal Matters* case "had raised a number of legal issues that the members of the Commission might find to be pertinent to their work," and that the Court "had found the area of immunity from criminal jurisdiction to be underdeveloped, and it therefore greatly welcomed that fact that it was receiving the Commission's serious attention": *ibid*, at p. 181, para. 102.

130 YBILC 2014, p. 144, para. 30.

"whether it might be useful" if the Commission were to undertake a study of the applicable law of compensation,[131] a question to which he received an affirmative answer.[132]

Yet presidents have not always been willing to express an opinion as to the Commission's work program. When President Owada was asked in 2009 whether there was "any topic that the Commission could take up that might help the Court in its activities," he replied that "it would be presumptuous of him to tell the Commission which [topic] it should study."[133] In a like manner, when Kittichaisaree inquired of President Tomka in 2012 whether he considered, "as a former member of the Commission," that the Commission should study the topic of the obligation to extradite or prosecute, the latter replied that "it was for the Commission to decide whether it could draw inspiration for its future work from the judgment in *Questions relating to the Obligation to Prosecute or Extradite*."[134] And President Abraham, in response to Šturma's question in 2015 of whether it might be useful, "in terms of judicial practice," for the Commission to study the matter of succession of States in respect of State responsibility, replied that "although he agreed that any issue of general international law was worthy of study, he would defer to the judgment of States and the Commission itself."[135] Such reluctance to reply seems however to stem more from considerations of courtesy than from the perception that the Court, for more substantive reasons, ought to stay clear of the Commission's ongoing work.

The formalization of visits from The Hague, while securing regular meetings between the Commission as a whole and a member of the Court, did come at a cost. Additional, more casual visits by judges of the Court have ceased altogether; and informal, behind the scenes, exchanges with those judges arriving in Geneva to represent the Court have virtually ended. Arrangements such as the one that afforded Judge

[131] YBILC 2016, Vol. I, p. 231, para. 17.

[132] *Ibid*, at p. 232, para. 19 (President Abraham replying that such a study "would certainly be very useful").

[133] YBILC 2009, Vol. I, p. 126, para. 53 (replying to Escarameia's question). President Owada's statement did, nevertheless, serve to inspire Sir Michael Wood's proposal that year to add the topic 'Dispute settlement clauses' to the Commission's work program: YBILC 2009, Vol. I, p. 208, para. 3 (mentioning other sources of inspiration as well).

[134] YBILC 2012, Vol. I, p. 146, para. 95 and p. 147, para. 100. It is not unlikely that President Tomka knew at the time that the question had been a controversial one within the Commission.

[135] YBILC 2015, Vol. I, p. 231, para. 20.

Ago's continued influence on the Commission's work on State responsibility, for example, would very likely no longer be permitted. But the visits have become more focused on substance rather than the exchange of courtesies, and do remain a unique opportunity for inter-institutional dialogue, one in which topics of common interest or concern may be raised, feedback may be given and received, and guidance and clarifications may be provided. The Commission continues to consider such visits to be a special honor and pleasure, a symbol of the "cordial and productive" relations between the two bodies.[136] Presidents of the Court have repeatedly stressed the importance that they (and the Court), too, attach to the visits,[137] which are indeed not to be taken for granted given the limited time and travel budget at their disposal.

C. Conclusion

In legal jargon common to the Court and the Commission it may well be said that their ties are not only *ratione materiae*, but also *ratione personae*.[138] These personal links, not always in the public eye or public record, have no doubt served to draw the two organs together, both reflecting and perpetuating their close institutional dialogue. They also enable a better appreciation of the members of the Court and the Commission for the community of practice in which they stand engaged, in the sense of a social entity bound together by the core dimensions of mutual engagement, collective definition of their joint enterprise, and a shared repertoire of concepts, words, and ways of doing things.[139] Within this community, the movement between functional roles (both sequential and simultaneous) has naturally made a significant difference to the work

[136] YBILC 1999, Vol. I, p. 122, para. 1 (the Chairman, Galicki, welcoming President Schwebel to the Commission).

[137] See, for example, YBILC 2003, Vol. I, p. 165, para. 18 (President Shi addressing the Commission in saying that "[t]he Court and the Commission, in performing their respective tasks, each had to be constantly aware of the work accomplished by the other"); YBILC 2006, Vol. I, p. 211, para. 3 (President Higgins saying that "the Court greatly appreciates such exchanges between the two bodies and the fact that they had become an annual event"); UN Doc. A/CN.4/SR.3380: 'Provisional Summary Record of the Commission's 3380th Meeting' (25 July 2017), p. 6 (President Abraham saying that his visits to the Commission as President "had been some of the most memorable moments of his time as President of the Court").

[138] See also YBILC 2001, Vol. I, p. 209, para. 1 (Kabatsi).

[139] See, more generally, E. Wenger, *Communities of Practice: Learning, Meaning Identity* (CUP 1998) 73–83; E. Adler, *Communitarian International Relations: The Epistemic Foundations of International Relations* (Routledge 2005) 13–15.

of the individuals concerned, as may be seen in the decisive role played by Manley O. Hudson, the former judge of the World Court-turned-first Chairman of the Commission, in laying the foundation for the exceptional regard with which the Court has been held within the Commission from the outset. The interaction between the two organs has also benefited from the long-established practice by which judges of the Court arrive in Geneva for an exchange with the Commission, thus further underlining the existence of a shared sense of purpose and the convergence of tasks. For the drafters of the Commission's Statute, who did not consider it appropriate that the Commission would ever consult with the Court, such visits and other forms of intercourse would likely have been deemed inconceivable. These too suggest that the inter-institutional relationship has turned out to be quite different than originally envisaged.

6

Just a Disagreement between Friends: When the Court and the Commission Diverge

The remarkable complementarity in the work of the Court and the Commission, and their mutual sense of respect and joint mission, do not mean that the two organs have always seen eye to eye. On a number of occasions during their long decades of parallel existence, they have adopted different or incompatible positions on the law. The extent of such disagreement, however, and the way it has been handled, very much attest to the strength and character of the inter-institutional relationship rather than undermine it.

A. Room for Disagreement

No formal obligation exists, either for the Court or for the Commission, to accept as authoritative the other's pronouncements on the law. Members of the Court, for one, certainly do not consider themselves obliged to follow the Commission's legal views, given the Court's position and mandate as the principal judicial organ of the United Nations. President Abraham thus had no compunction in telling members of the Commission in 2016 that "the Court remained free to establish its own position and was not bound by the [Commission's] recommendations or texts."[1] Even if the Commission's output were to be classified as "the teachings of the most highly qualified publicists of the various nations," and thus as a subsidiary means to be applied by the Court for the determination of rules of law according to article 38.1(*d*) of its Statute

[1] YBILC 2016, p. 232, para. 19. The early concern voiced by Stone, that if the Commission would formulate the general principles of law referred to in the Statute of the Court, the latter "would be deprived of creative discretions which it was certainly in the intention of the Powers [establishing it] to provide," thus seems exaggerated: J. Stone, 'On the Vocation of the International Law Commission', 57 *Columbia Law Review* (1957) 16 at 37.

(a view that not all of the judges necessarily accept[2]), this would not prevent the Court from going in an opposing direction.

The Commission has never considered itself strictly bound to follow the legal determinations of the Court either, a position that its members have exhibited – but also debated – on several occasions over the years. One such instance occurred in 2003, when the Special Rapporteur on the topic 'Diplomatic protection', Dugard, "appeared to be inciting the Commission to rebel against the Court"[3] by stating expressly in his fourth report that "[d]ecisions of the ICJ are not binding on the Commission."[4] Raising the question of whether the principle pronounced by the Court some thirty years earlier in the *Barcelona Traction* case should be adhered to by the Commission when formulating its draft articles on diplomatic protection, Dugard asserted that "[a]lthough there is an understandable reluctance on the part of the Commission to reject [decisions of the Court] … *Barcelona Traction* is not sacrosanct, untouchable. The Commission may, therefore, after careful consideration, decide not to follow it."[5] This statement provoked hardly any reaction in the ensuing plenary debate, perhaps not only because it was the subject of general agreement,[6] but also due to the fact that, after sharply criticizing the decision, the Special Rapporteur eventually recommended that the Commission follow it.[7] Only one member, Economides, said that he "personally disagreed" with the Special

[2] See Chapter 3, Section D.

[3] YBILC 2003, Vol. I, p. 44, para. 78 (Kateka, adding that he felt that "it was inappropriate for the Commission to openly challenge the Court").

[4] YBILC 2003, Vol. II, Part One, pp. 9–10, para. 24.

[5] *Ibid*; the Special Rapporteur described at length the criticism of the judgment both in the Separate Opinions appended to it and in academic writings (at pp. 7–9).

[6] Koskenniemi said that he "did not believe that the Commission was bound by the decisions of ICJ and, in particular, by the *Barcelona Traction* judgment. Those judgments had only the value that the Court's reasoning in them had"; and Chee said that "[a]s the Special Rapporteur pointed out … the decisions of ICJ were not binding on the Commission": YBILC 2003, Vo. I, p. 45, para. 3, and p. 54, para. 37, respectively. Brownlie, for his part, suggested that "[t]he Special Rapporteur asked in his report whether the decision of ICJ in the case bound the Commission, but no such problem should arise: the decision had been carefully argued by two important teams of international lawyers, was part of the literature and simply had to be taken very seriously"; he added later that "since the Commission was a deliberative body and not one that dealt with cases, the question of whether it should be bound by decisions of the ICJ should not arise": *ibid*, at p. 36, para. 3 and p. 239, para. 5.

[7] YBILC 2003, Vol. II, Part One, p. 15, para. 49 (saying that although "*Barcelona Traction* may be faulted on several grounds … it enjoys widespread acceptance on the part of States. In the light of this acceptance, and the objections to other tests for determining the

Rapporteur's statement that the Court's decisions were not binding on the Commission: "On the contrary," he added,

> the decisions of the Court, when it ruled on and applied international law, including customary law, bound the Commission as the body responsible for the codification of international law. The Commission could only depart from a particular customary solution in the interest of the progressive development of law; in so doing, it must explain why it was opting in favour of a new rule.[8]

Then, as on other occasions,[9] however, that view was a minority one.

Three reasons have been proffered in support of the position that the Commission is not bound by the Court's determinations of law, the first being that no rigid organizational hierarchy requires it: "the Court is not the Supreme Court of the world," as one Commission member has plainly put it.[10] A second reason has been that the Court's judgments are inherently case-specific and formally binding upon just the parties, and thus should not serve as a juridical foundation from which the Commission might seek to extract general rules of law. Such a contention was voiced as early as 1954 by Žourek, who criticized a draft article on the passage of warships that was based on the *Corfu Channel* judgment by saying that "it was wrong to base a general rule on a decision in a particular and very controversial case, and especially to apply the rule

nationality of corporations, the wisest course seems to be to formulate articles that give effect to the principles expounded in *Barcelona Traction*").

[8] YBILC 2003, Vol. I, p. 55, para. 44.

[9] See YBILC 1950, Vol. I, p. 257, para. 1a (Chairman Scelle arguing in vain with respect to the Court's advisory opinion on *Interpretation of Peace Treaties* that "[t]he Court had delivered its opinion by 11 votes to 2 . . . The Commission must bow to the Court's decision"); YBILC 1980, Vol. I, p. 40, para. 31 (Schwebel considering that "[m]ore generally . . . the Commission was not bound by the views of a United Nations organ on a point of law unless that organ was authorized to settle the law. Arguably, it might be bound by a decision of the International Court of Justice, though the Commission had not regarded itself as bound by the Court's opinion on reservations to treaties"); YBILC 1991, Vol. I, p. 194, para. 89 (Koroma saying that "[a]s international jurists, the members of the Commission were under an obligation to respect the jurisprudence of the ICJ"); YBILC 2016, Vol. I, p. 232, para. 25 (Kamto saying that the Commission "must, of course, strive to reflect the Court's rulings closely").

[10] Interview with member of the Commission in May 2016, on file with the author. Another member of the Commission, Pellet, has likewise commented that "[a]lthough the Commission had to pay careful attention to the case law of the International Court of Justice, it was not obliged to endorse all its tortuous reasoning, including its mistakes; first, because there was no hierarchical relationship between the two institutions . . .": YBILC 2011, Vol. I, p. 53, para. 57.

formulated by the Court to all straits, even those with a single coastal State."[11] In the following year, it was Scelle who openly "deplored the tendency of the Commission to turn into general principles rulings of the International Court of Justice which concerned specific instances" and stressed that "[i]t did not necessarily follow that because the International Court of Justice had given a ruling in a certain sense in a particular case, that ruling could be turned into an abstract point of law."[12] A similar view was later expressed, inter alia, in the context of the Commission's work on the topic 'State responsibility', where Ago as Special Rapporteur urged caution in endorsing the concept of obligations *erga omnes* by pointing out that it was mentioned by the Court in "comments [that] had been made *obiter* in a diplomatic protection case."[13] The opinion that it was "difficult to derive a uniform rule from the judgments of ICJ" because the Court ruled on questions *ex post facto* and taking into account specific facts was also voiced by Al-Khasawneh and Brownlie during the work on the topic 'Unilateral acts of States'.[14]

[11] YBILC 1954, Vol. 1, p. 161, para. 33; see also p. 190, para. 17.

[12] YBILC 1955, Vol. I, p. 260, para. 63; see also p. 204, para. 21 (referring to the criteria for a straight base line system enumerated in the *Fisheries case* judgment when saying that "[t]here could be no doubt whatsoever that the Court had not expounded any general principle or rule of international law. In any event, a single judicial decision was not enough to create case-law"). Scelle made the same point in the previous year, saying, with respect to the proposed article 6 on "Base Lines," that "the Special Rapporteur had described the Court's judgement in the *Fisheries* case as a statement of the law in force. Yet, a single court decision could not be said to lay down the law in force. The relevant rule of law would only be established in time, after a body of court decisions or precedents had been built up": YBILC 1954, Vol. I, p. 74, para. 20.

[13] YBILC 1976, Vol. I, p. 90, para. 31.

[14] YBILC 1999, Vol. I, p. 208, paras. 7–8 (Al-Khasawneh, adding that "[t]hat contextual approach was not available to legislators who, beforehand, wanted to provide an objective yardstick against which the intent of States to assume duties vis-à-vis other States could be ascertained"); YBILC 2002, Vol. I, p. 106, para. 62 (Brownlie arguing that that the case-law of the Court could not be invoked in support of the idea that there was a general concept of unilateral acts in international law as "[e]ach case was fact-related. The Court did not rely on a general theory of unilateral acts"). For similar arguments made in other contexts, see, for example, YBILC 1973, Vol. I, p. 64, paras. 52–33 (Sir Francis Vallat cautioning that it was "not at all easy" to base rather general arguments on the *Anglo-Iranian Oil Company case (jurisdiction)* decision where "[t]he fact was that, in that case, the International Court of Justice had had to deal essentially with a question of the interpretation of a particular treaty rather than with the character of the most-favoured-nation clause in general"); YBILC 1989, Vol. I, p. 212, para. 25 (Njenga saying that "it should be noted that the prevailing tendency to quote *obiter dicta* in support of a given point of view, while ignoring the essence of the decisions, had recently been criticized by Sir Robert Jennings at a meeting organized by the Netherlands Institute for the Law of the

It has also received a rather surprising support from Judge Xue, who cautioned (in her academic writing) that

> we must be careful in analyzing these decisions [by international courts] and their jurisprudence and applying them on a general basis. As I read the judgments by ICJ, for example, I felt that the Court is often predominantly concerned with finding a fair and reasonable solution to the pending dispute rather than focusing on the preservation of the nicety of treaties.[15]

A closely related third reason for the Commission not being bound by the Court's pronouncements is based on the different mandates of the two organs. According to this contention, the Court exists to resolve particular disputes and is not a law-making body; its pronouncements as a judicial organ that may resort to deduction may be insufficiently grounded in State practice; and the cases brought before it are in all events few and far between, accounting for only a very small share of any relevant international practice. Murase, for example, has thus "continued to be critical of the excessive reliance on the case law of the International Court of Justice to support commentaries" to the Commission's draft conclusions on the topic 'Identification of customary international law',

Sea. The criticism had been levelled at international law conferences and the ICJ, but it could very well have been directed at the Commission. It was not possible to recall offhand the number of times the *Corfu Channel* case, the *Lake Lanoux* arbitration, the *Trail Smelter* arbitration and the *North Sea Continental Shelf* cases had been cited in support of a particular point of view. Yet each of those cases dealt with a very specific issue"); YBILC 1998, Vol. I, p. 129, para. 51 (Addo referring to the *erga omnes* principle when saying that "the dictum on the principle handed down by ICJ in one case was not, in his view, meant to cover absolutely everything. For a proper understanding of it, the context in which it had been pronounced must be examined closely"); YBILC 2013, Vol. I, p. 26, para. 18 (Šturma saying that "the decisions of the International Court of Justice furnished answers to specific questions *in concreto*, not general rules. The Commission, on the other hand, had to prepare draft articles on assigned topics *in abstracto*, to draft restatements of general rules"); UN Doc. A/CN.4/SR.3399: 'Provisional Summary Record of the Commission's 3399th Meeting' (10 May 2018), p. 16 (Oral referring to suggested inclusion of the notion of specially affected States in the Commission's draft conclusions on 'Identification of customary international law' in saying that "one judgment and two separate opinions that referred to the concept did not provide a sufficient foundation for extrapolating a general rule"). Some members have argued that certain Court decisions may be motivated by political considerations particular to a given case: see, for example, YBILC 1992, Vol. I, p. 13, para. 37 (Shi, referring to one of the *Lockerbie* cases); YBILC 2000, Vol. I, p. 133, para. 36 (Simma, referring to the *Nuclear Tests* cases).

15 H. Xue, 'The Role of the ILC's Work in Promoting Peace and Security – Definition and Evaluation', in G. Nolte (ed.), *Peace through International Law: The Role of the International Law Commission* (Springer 2009) 183 at 186. See also B. Simma, 'Peace through Law: The Role of the ILC', in *Peace through International Law*, 189 at 190.

arguing that "[t]he primary function of the Court was to settle disputes between parties, and not to develop international law, while the Commission's function was to codify and progressively develop international law for the whole world."[16] Other members of the Commission, such as Pellet, have considered that the Commission is not bound to endorse the Court's pronouncements as the two institutions "did not perform the same functions. The Court had to base its decisions on positive law, *lex lata* ... whereas the Commission's first duty was the progressive development of international law."[17]

B. Managing Disagreement

Despite the existing potential for disagreement, both as regards institutional independence and the recurring opportunities of the Court and the Commission to review each other's output, instances where the two organs have diverged are rare. Equally remarkable is the way in which these differences of opinion have been handled. An examination of the techniques and justifications employed both by the Court and by the Commission in such instances illustrates a high level of mutual respect held by them as well as a conscious inclination to avoid openly challenging one another's authority.

[16] YBILC 2016, Vol. I, p. 96, para. 73 (adding that "[b]esides, as one writer had pointed out, the Court did not apply any coherent methodology with regard to its application of customary international law"); see also YBILC 2013, Vol. I, p. 83, para. 17 (Murase saying that "[t]he role of judges was not to identify general rules but to hand down rulings, based on the arguments presented by the parties, in the specific and subjective cases brought before them. Thus, debates before the International Court of Justice over the existence of a particular rule of customary international law did not have the same basis or objectives as the Commission's project"); YBILC 2014, Vol. I, p. 113, para. 39 (Park urging "caution in drawing generalizations from judgments of the International Court of Justice and similar bodies, as they dealt only with concrete cases brought by particular parties to a dispute").

[17] YBILC 2011, Vol. I, p. 53, para. 57. See also, for example, YBILC 1999, Vol. I, p. 58, para. 22 (Sreenivasa Rao saying that "while the relationship between the Commission ... and ICJ should be enhanced, that should not entail systematic integration of the work of one body with that of another. The place of each in the overall United Nations system had to be respected"); YBILC 2013, Vol. I, p. 20, para. 20 (Tladi saying that "the International Court of Justice, as the principal judicial organ of the United Nations, was endowed with unmatched authority. However, its primary mandate was the resolution of disputes between parties, and its rulings were binding only upon the parties. Even when the Court had ruled on an issue, therefore, the Commission had to conduct its own independent assessment of the relevant State practice").

1. *When the Court Disagrees with the Commission*

While it has certainly disagreed with the Commission on occasion, the Court has never made that disagreement explicit: instead, it has adopted two techniques for making indistinct any reservation it might have about a given pronouncement of the Commission. One technique has been simply to refrain from referring to the Commission's relevant product (as, admittedly, it has also done in some cases where it did agree with the Commission[18]). Such was the case when the Court, in its 2012 judgment on *Questions relating to the Obligation to Prosecute or Extradite*, omitted to mention the Commission's articles on State responsibility despite the fact that the Court was seized of the very issue of the right of a State, other than the injured State, to invoke responsibility.[19] As was later disclosed, this was because one judge had "argued vehemently [in the Court's deliberations] that article 48 of the articles on State responsibility did not reflect customary international law."[20]

A second means of avoiding explicit disagreement has been to refrain from deciding whether a certain rule promulgated by the Commission reflects the international law in force. One such instance may be found in the judgment rendered by the Court on the preliminary objections raised in the *Diallo* case. The Court was drafting its judgment when the Commission adopted, on second reading, its draft articles on diplomatic protection, a text that Guinea (represented by, *inter alios*, then Commission member Pellet) sought to rely on in its pleadings. In those draft articles the Commission recognized that, as "was strongly reaffirmed by the International Court of Justice in the *Barcelona Traction* case,"[21] the State of nationality of shareholders in a corporation is in principle not entitled to exercise diplomatic protection in respect of such shareholders in the case of an injury to the corporation. At the same time, the Commission suggested that customary international law provided for an exception to this rule in those cases in which the State of incorporation was itself responsible for inflicting injury on the

[18] See Chapter 3, Section B.2.

[19] *Questions relating to the Obligation to Prosecute or Extradite (Belgium* v. *Senegal), Judgment, I.C.J. Reports 2012*, p. 450, para. 69.

[20] YBILC 2012, Vol. I, p. 148, para. 109 (President Tomka addressing the Commission). It will be recalled, however, that the Court's overall approach in this instance was in fact consistent with that of the Commission, and may be seen as implicitly endorsing it: see also Chapter 3, Section B.2.

[21] YBILC 2006, Vol. I, Part Two, p. 39, para. (1) of the commentary to draft article 11.

corporation, stating that "it would be possible to sustain [this] general exception on the basis of [various instances of] judicial opinion."[22] Ultimately, however, the Commission proposed a more limited rule of such "protection by substitution": article 11(b) of its draft articles limits this exception to circumstances where the incorporation of a local corporation was required by the national State as a precondition for doing business there.

The Court clearly disagreed with the Commission when it held that "having carefully examined State practice and decisions of international courts and tribunals in respect of diplomatic protection of associés and shareholders, [it] is of the opinion that these do not reveal – at least at the present time – an exception in customary international law allowing for protection by substitution."[23] Given that the Commission had elected to propose a narrower exception, this divergence of views was neither blunt nor particularly damaging. But the Court did not seem to agree with the Commission that even the more limited exception was (or should be) a rule of positive international law either. In attempting to avoid saying so openly, it held – not entirely convincingly – that "this very special case does not seem to correspond to the one the Court is dealing with here."[24]

[22] *Ibid*, at p. 42, para. 12 of the commentary to draft article 11. The Commission appears to have been inaccurate in asserting, in paragraph (1) of the commentary to that article, that "[t]he Court in *Barcelona Traction* accepted that the State(s) of nationality of shareholders might exercise diplomatic protection on their behalf" in such a situation, as it was relying, in fact, on the separate opinions of Judges Fitzmaurice, Jessup, and Tanaka; the judgment itself had merely said in this context that "[w]hatever the validity of this theory may be, it is certainly not applicable to the present case." This is made clear in reading paragraphs 10 and 12 of the commentary.

[23] *Ahmadou Sadio Diallo (Republic of Guinea* v. *Democratic Republic of the Congo), Preliminary Objections, Judgment, I.C.J. Reports 2007*, p. 615, para. 89.

[24] *Ibid*, at pp. 615–616, paras. 92–93. See also Declaration of Judge ad hoc Mahiou, at p. 623, paras. 9–10 (arguing that in fact and in law, the *Diallo* case does lie within the reach of draft article 11(b)), and the Separate Opinion by Judge ad hoc Mampuya, p. 634 (suggesting that the Court's judgment confirms that "[i]nternational law as it now stands contains no customary rule enshrining the diplomatic protection by 'substitution' to which some writers … and the ILC's work have given the impression of subscribing"); A.M. Weisburd, 'The International Court of Justice and the Concept of State Practice', 31 *University of Pennsylvania Journal of International Law* (2009) 295 at 340; and A. Alvarez-Jiménez, 'Foreign Investors, Diplomatic Protection and the International Court of Justice's Decision on Preliminary Objections in the *Diallo* Case', 33 *North Carolina Journal of International Law and Commercial Regulation* (2008) 437 at 452. Pellet, then a member of the Commission, argued before the Court as Counsel for Guinea that the rule set out in article 11(b) of the Commission's draft articles was "hardly substantiated in positive law" (trying to rely instead on the more general exception that

A clear hint of this approach was provided by President Higgins herself in a speech before members of the Commission later that year, in which she revealed that "the question of whether article 11, paragraph (b), did or did not reflect customary international law had been, rather deliberately, left open."[25] This was an example, she suggested elsewhere, of the Court being "mindful of its two-way relationship with the ILC and [taking] every opportunity to foster mutual respect."[26]

The exceptional measure of respect with which the Court has treated the Commission may also be appreciated when contrasted with the way in which it has dealt with another institution that showed itself willing to reject the Court's pronouncements: the International Criminal Tribunal for the former Yugoslavia (ICTY). After the ICTY Appeals Chamber in *Tadić* applied its own test for State responsibility rather than the test formulated in the *Military and Paramilitary Activities in and against Nicaragua* case,[27] the Court did not let pass an opportunity to assert its position in determining the rules of general international law. Thus in the *Genocide* case, it explained at some length that "the argument in favour of that test [adopted by the ICTY] is unpersuasive" and "unsuitable," and made it clear that it does not "attach the utmost importance" to "positions adopted by the ICTY on issues of general international law" (meaning those "which do not lie within the specific purview of its jurisdiction and, moreover, the resolution of which is not always necessary for deciding the criminal cases before it").[28] Needless to add, the Court to date has never directed an admonition of this kind at the

he argued the Commission did recognize as customary international law in force): CR 2006/51 (28 November 2006), translation, p. 41, para. 20.

25 YBILC 2007, Vol. I, p. 127, para. 45. President Higgins added, when speaking about the difficulty of drawing upon draft articles of the Commission that may be considered by scholars as progressive development rather than codification, that "[a] case in point was article 11, subparagraph (b), of the draft articles on diplomatic protection, regarding which she believed there was general agreement that the provision did not represent customary international law. It would be for the Commission to decide whether it represented a useful development of that area of law": *ibid*, at p. 128, para. 55.

26 Keynote Address by H.E. Judge Rosalyn Higgins, President of the International Court of Justice, at the Sixtieth Anniversary of the International Law Commission (19 May 2008), available at <www.icj-cij.org/files/press-releases/8/14488.pdf>.

27 Technically, the Appeals Chamber was not applying a test of State responsibility but, rather, considering whether there existed an international armed conflict with respect to international humanitarian law.

28 *Application of the Convention on the Prevention and Punishment of the Crime of Genocide (Bosnia and Herzegovina* v. *Serbia and Montenegro), Judgment, I.C.J. Reports 2007*, p. 209, para. 403 and p. 210, paras. 404–406.

Commission in any case where the two bodies appeared to have divergent views.

2. *When the Commission Disagrees with the Court*

While the Court may simply ignore a pronouncement by the Commission (at least in the text of a judgment) or avoid a decision as to whether it reflects positive law, such options are not available to the Commission with respect to the Court's case-law. Not only does its own Statute require of it to consider judicial decisions, but the Court's position as the principal judicial organ of the United Nations, the wide resonance of its pronouncements, and the function it assumes in promulgating international legal rules of general application (a function that – as we have seen – the Commission itself endeavors to support), all mean that the Commission cannot overlook, or fail to engage with, a judgment that relates to its work on a particular topic. Commission members are mindful, however, that as opposed to the ease and legitimacy of endorsing a decision of the Court, diverging from it may undermine the stability of the law, harm the prestige of the Court, and expose the Commission to harsh criticism (including from the Court), which, in turn, may further weigh on legal certainty. From its very early days the Commission has thus been reluctant to challenge the Court openly or even to seem to be defying it, its members being well aware that there must be "very good reasons for doing so."[29]

One way for the Commission to try to avoid being at odds with the Court has been to postpone, where possible, debating or deciding a legal question that is pending before the Court. While such a choice may well be said to have an element of efficiency, it has undeniably been driven primarily by a desire to avoid friction among the two bodies.[30] This was

[29] YBILC 1954, Vol. I, p. 112, para. 62 (Lauterpacht recalling, in the context of debating the right of innocent passage through the territorial sea, that "the text submitted to the Commission took into account a very important decision adopted almost unanimously by the International Court of Justice [in the *Corfu Channel* case]. Unless it had very good reasons for doing so, the Commission should not disregard the authority of the Court's decision."). See also YBILC 2008, Vol. I, p. 74, para. 72 (Pellet suggesting that there would need to be a "valid reason" for "flying in the face of a view that has surely never been disputed since the ICJ has stated [it]").

[30] The Court, too, sees it as a matter of the Commission being respectful of the Court: see Higgins, *supra* note 26 (with regard to the Commission's decision to pause its consideration of the issue of promises of non-repetition until the Court had pronounced on the issue in a pending case).

the case when the Commission decided, in its very first session in 1949, to refrain from including in its draft Declaration on Rights and Duties of States an article relating to asylum by reason that the *Asylum* judgment was forthcoming. Although Yepes "did not think that the fact that the question was pending before the International Court of Justice stood in the way of the adoption of [the proposed] article 15 [on asylum],"[31] the Commission ultimately sided with Córdoba, who "considered the Commission unable at that stage to reach a decision upon article 15 ... [because] the decision of the International Court of Justice on the dispute submitted to it by Peru and Colombia should be awaited."[32] Such a position again won traction in the following year, after Hudson said that he "felt that the Commission could hardly deal with the question of the breadth of the territorial sea or methods of demarcating a line separating interior waters from territorial waters, because those questions were now before the International Court of Justice in the case between the United Kingdom and Norway concerning fisheries."[33] Again in 1951, Brierly, as Special Rapporteur on the law of treaties, pointed out with respect to the issue of reservations to treaties that the Commission "could take no decision until it knew the opinion of the International Court of Justice," which was then deliberating the matter of *Reservations to the Convention on the Prevention and Punishment of the Crime of Genocide*.[34] The Commission similarly decided in 2001 to wait for the Court's judgment in the *LaGrand* case before taking a final decision concerning the issue of assurances and guarantees of non-repetition that formed part of the topic of State responsibility.[35] And Galicki, as Special

31 YBILC 1949, pp. 148–149, para. 97.

32 *Ibid*, at p. 149, para. 102; see also p. 245, paras. 56, 61.

33 YBILC 1950, Vol. I, p. 204, para. 109.

34 YBILC 1951, Vol. I, p. 50, para. 76; see also p. 2, para. 23 (Spiropoulos saying that "it was advisable to await the opinion of the International Court of Justice on the question") and p. 32, para. 76 (François suggesting that "article 6 [of Brierly's report] should be left in abeyance until the International Court of Justice had given its advisory opinion"). Kerno, the UN Assistant Secretary-General, had earlier told the Commission that "[a]ccording to unofficial information from the International Court of Justice, the latter would be giving its opinion the following week with regard to reservations to multilateral conventions. The Commission would need to take that factor into consideration when discussing its agenda": *Ibid*, at p. 2, para. 15.

35 See YBILC 2001, Vol. I, p. 101, para. 103 ("taking into account that the provision was *sub judice*, the [Drafting] Committee had decided to place it in square brackets and reconsider it during the second part of the session"). Pellet did not approve of this: see *ibid*, at p. 106, para. 23 ("although the Commission should take account of the jurisprudence of the ICJ, it should not simply echo the views of the Court. It was therefore inappropriate

Rapporteur on the topic 'The obligation to extradite or prosecute (*aut dedere aut judicare*)', expressed in 2011 a preference to wait until the Court had rendered its final decision in *Questions relating to the Obligation to Prosecute or Extradite* before reaching a conclusion as to the customary basis for the obligation under discussion.[36] This view was maintained in the subsequent session by several members of the Commission, who "considered it prudent to await the judgment of the International Court of Justice ... before taking any definitive positions, since that judgment might clarify some of the issues."[37] It was further echoed by the Special Rapporteur on 'Immunity of State officials from foreign criminal jurisdiction,' Escobar Hernández, who suggested in 2020 that the Commission may proceed to consider issues pertaining to cooperation between national criminal tribunals and international criminal tribunals because "the [previously held] assumption that the International Court of Justice could pronounce on the matter does not seem feasible at this stage."[38]

for it to await a decision by the Court before taking a decision on article 30, subparagraph (*b*)"). For a mini-debate on the caution required in discussing cases that were ongoing before the Court, see also YBILC 2000, Vol. I, p. 247, paras. 54–58.

36 YBILC 2011, Vol. I, p. 245, para. 8. Vasciannie, however, thought that "[t]he Special Rapporteur should not await a decision of the International Court of Justice on the subject, but should reach his own conclusion, however difficult that might be": *ibid*, at p. 248, para. 38.

37 See the report of the Chairman of the Working Group on the topic, Kittichaisaree, in YBILC 2012, Vol. I, p. 175, para. 22. Kittichaisaree had earlier told the President of the Court, during the latter's visit to the Commission, that "the [Working] Group had been anxiously awaiting the judgment": *ibid*, at p. 146, para. 95. The Court eventually rendered its judgment "in the afternoon of Friday 20 July 2012, when the Working Group was supposed to have already concluded its substantive work during this session and report to the Plenary. The Working Group conducted a preliminary review of the judgment on 24 July 2012, at a meeting specially convened for that purpose. It was recognised that an in-depth analysis would be required to assess fully its implications for the topic. The Working Group requested its Chairman to prepare a working paper, to be considered at the sixty-fifth session of the Commission, reviewing the various perspectives in relation to the topic in light of the judgment of the International Court of Justice of 20 July 2012, any further developments, as well as comments made in the Working Group and the debate of the Sixth Committee": YBILC 2012, Vol. II, Part Two, p. 76, paras. 220–221.

38 A/CN.4/739: 'Eighth report on immunity of State officials from foreign criminal jurisdiction, by Concepción Escobar Hernández, Special Rapporteur' (2020), para. 22 (explaining that "the African Union, at its February 2020 summit, decided to urge African countries to withdraw the request for an advisory opinion that had been placed on the agenda of the General Assembly at their behest"). At least one member suggested that the

At the same time, the Commission has been careful not to imply that it is under any obligation to defer discussion of a topic simply because it was concurrently pending before the Court (in the way that the General Assembly is prohibited from making any recommendation with regard to a dispute or situation in respect of which the Security Council is exercising its mandate[39]). This, too, had been established early on, when in 1950 Yepes decided not to submit for the Commission's consideration a working paper on the right of asylum that he had completed, thinking (after some correspondence with the Secretariat) "it better not to submit it during the current session on the grounds that a case involving the question was pending before the International Court of Justice."[40] When he expressed his desire that the Commission's annual report would specify that his report was indeed ready on time but was not submitted merely for that reason, Hudson warned that the text of the report must not allow for the conclusion to be drawn "that the International Law Commission considered that it was no longer competent to study a problem once the Court took up a case involving that problem."[41] A drafting compromise had to be reached in order to ensure that no such precedent would appear to be set.[42]

Commission should keep waiting: see A/CN.4/SR.3521: Provisional summary record of the Commission's 3521st meeting (14 May 2021), pp. 8–9 (Rajput).

39 See Article 12(1) of the UN Charter.

40 YBILC 1950, Vol. I, p. 273, paras. 2, 4. Spiropoulos recalled in 1957 that "[i]t was true that the Commission had asked Mr. Yepes to prepare a working paper on the subject [of the right of asylum], but it had done so before it knew that a case which bore on it was being submitted to the International Court of Justice. As soon as it had learnt of that case, it had thought it preferable to postpone its own study": YBILC 1957, Vol. I, p. 55, para. 52.

41 For Hudson, "[s]urely the reason why the topic had been deferred was that the paper had not been submitted; there was no point in going into detail": YBILC 1950, Vol. I, p. 273, para. 3. Hudson had similarly objected, in the previous year, to specifying in the Commission's report to the General Assembly that a proposed article on Asylum was put aside in the context of the work on the draft Declaration on Rights and Duties of States by reason that the *Asylum* case was pending before the International Court of Justice: YBILC 1949, p. 252, paras. 56–57.

42 In the face of Yepes's insistence, the text eventually adopted at the suggestion of the Chairman read: "At its first session, the Commission invited Mr. M. Yepes to prepare, for its consideration, a working paper on the topic of the right of asylum. At the beginning of the second session, Mr. Yepes stated that, in view of the fact that a case involving the right of asylum was pending before the International Court of Justice, he would for the time being, postpone the submission of this working paper which had already been prepared. The Commission accordingly decided not to include the topic of the right of asylum in the agenda of its second session" (YBILC 1950, Vol. II, p. 366, para. 12). This was understood to remedy Mr. Hudson's concern and "to avoid creating any precedent, since

As decades of summary records exhibit, it is only rarely that Commission members criticize the Court in their debates and for the most part they do so with great courtesy.[43] One member has spoken about "the first unofficial rule of membership: we must not harm the Court."[44] In those rare instances where a judgment had already been rendered and the Commission nevertheless sought to adopt a rule different to the one previously pronounced by the Court, care has been taken to avoid any perception of open defiance of the Court's authority. As discussed below, a number of justifications have been employed by the Commission in such circumstances, namely, that it was engaging in progressive development of the law rather than in codification; that the relevant judgment had been devoted to a problem specific to the parties or facts of the case; that much time had passed since the decision was handed down and the law or practice have since then evolved; or that the Court itself was sharply divided on the relevant point and its decision had indeed proven to be highly criticized. An additional method for making a divergence indistinct has been to present an interpretation of the Court's judgment that effectively concealed a difference of opinion which, in fact, did exist.

The Commission's first (and perhaps best-known) departure from a rule pronounced by the Court may be traced to its third session in 1951. A year earlier, the General Assembly adopted a resolution inviting both the Court and the Commission, in an indication of the related yet distinct roles designated for each, to pronounce themselves on the question of reservations to multilateral conventions.[45] In the absence of a settled rule of international law on the matter, such reservations (and objections to

it would involve only Mr. Yepes'[s] preference, and not a decision on the part of the Commission": YBILC 1950, Vol. I, p. 273, para. 5.

43 In addition to the several instances mentioned in this chapter, see YBILC 1985, Vol. I, p. 110, para. 12 (Francis referring to the *South West Africa Cases (Preliminary Objections)* judgment as one "that had been severely criticized and was, in his humble submission, wrong"); YBILC 1999, Vol. I, p. 286, para. 93 (Pellet saying that "[p]artial control or direction still engaged State responsibility for the internationally wrongful act. In the case concerning *Military and Paramilitary Activities in and against Nicaragua*, for example, ICJ had probably reasoned wrongly in considering that"); YBILC 2008, Vol. I, p. 48, para. 4 (Hmoud opining that "[i]n the *Lockerbie* cases . . . the ICJ had stated – unfortunately – that decisions under Chapter VII of the Charter of the United Nations took precedence over other obligations of a State").

44 Interview with member of the Commission in May 2016, on file with the author.

45 UNGA resolution of 478(V) of 16 November 1950. See also 'Legal Matters', 5 *International Organization* (1951) 165 at 167.

them) had given rise to difficulties for the UN Secretary-General in performing his depositary functions, and thus he drew the General Assembly's attention to the issue and sought its guidance. While the Court was requested to give an advisory opinion on the question only in so far as it concerned the Convention on the Prevention and Punishment of the Crime of Genocide, the Commission was invited to study the question more generally, "both from the point of view of codification and from that of the progressive development of international law," in the course of its then-ongoing work on the law of treaties.

In deliberating this question, the Court had before it, among other materials, the first report on the law of treaties compiled for the Commission a year earlier by its Special Rapporteur, Brierly; the summary of the meeting of the Commission in which that report was discussed; and the annual report of the Commission on the proceedings of its second session.[46] These all clearly suggested that the Commission, following the lead of the Special Rapporteur, had favored the so-called unanimity rule according to which a State formulating a reservation could become a party to the treaty only if and when all other parties had accepted the reservation. But in its Advisory Opinion of May 28, 1951, rendered soon after the Commission convened in Geneva for its third session, the Court held by a majority of 7 votes to 5 (and without making any reference to the Commission's preliminary work in progress) that under international law no such unanimous consent by all parties to a treaty was required. Instead, it asserted as a criterion that unless otherwise agreed upon in the treaty itself, a reservation must be compatible with the object and purpose of the convention in question.[47]

In the report he submitted a month earlier for dissemination during the Commission's third session,[48] the Special Rapporteur (Brierly) laid out some of the relevant issues but at the outset, as noted above, expressed himself that:

> Before proceeding to the consideration of the subject of reservations it is desirable to point out that this Report is necessarily of a tentative character, for until the International Court has rendered its opinion

[46] These documents were submitted to the Court by the UN Secretary-General: *Reservations to the Convention on Genocide, Advisory Opinion: I.C.J. Reports 1951*, p. 68.

[47] *Ibid*, at pp. 23–26, 29. Interestingly, in their Joint Dissenting Opinion, Judges Guerrero, McNair, Read, and Hsu Mo referred to the work of the League of Nations Committee for the Progressive Codification of International Law (*ibid*, at pp. 34–35).

[48] YBILC 1951, Vol. II, p. 1.

> on the questions referred to it by the Assembly's resolution of 16 November 1950, any study of the subject by the Commission, whether from the standpoint of codification or the progressive development of international law, can hardly be definitive.[49]

The Special Rapporteur further opined that "until the Court has rendered its opinion, the Commission may most usefully occupy itself with examining the possibility of drafting model clauses which would be suitable for insertion in conventions, and which would settle, in so far as those conventions are concerned, the various problems which may arise regarding reservations."[50] But the Court's pronouncement did not make Brierly change his original position, and after studying the *Reservations* advisory opinion, he presented the Commission with a brief report suggesting that the Court's approach was "not suitable for wholesale application to multilateral conventions."[51] Memoranda submitted by Amado and Scelle expressed continued support for the unanimity rule as well, the latter offering scathing criticism of the Court's decision.[52] In the ensuing debate, other members of the Commission, drawing some encouragement from the Joint Dissent by four of the Court's judges, likewise rejected the principles pronounced in the advisory opinion. Among them was Yepes, who seemed to voice the collective view when he said that "[h]owever worthy of respect the opinion expressed by the

[49] *Ibid*, at para. 3; in concluding his report he once again stated that "[i]n view … of the questions now pending before the International Court of Justice it is considered that it would be inappropriate to make recommendations on this point until the Court has rendered its opinion" (*ibid*, at p. 4, para. 16).

[50] *Ibid*, at p. 3, para. 11.

[51] See YBILC 1951, Vol. I, p. 169, para. 9.

[52] See YBILC 1951, Vol. II, pp. 23–26, at paras. 22–24 (Scelle saying that "[n]ous ne saurions bien entendu nous rallier à l'avis consultatif de la CIJ du 28 mai 1951. L'opinion dissidente collective des quatre juges, L. Exc. J. G. Guerrero, Arnold D. MacNair, John E. Read, Hsu Mo, nous paraît l'avoir réfuté victorieusement. La compatibilité des réserves avec « l'objet et le but de la convention » ne constitue pas un critère utilisable, attendu qu'il dépend de l'opinion subjective de chaque État intéressé, comme le montre bien le paragraphe a de la réponse à la question 2. En outre, l'avis détruit toute l'unité ou l'intégrité de l'instrument conventionnel, ce qui est cependant essentiel à la valeur sociale de tout instrument de nature législative. C'est un point sur lequel nous n'avons pas insisté parce qu'il nous paraît aller de soi que tout instrument d'ordre législatif au sein d'un ordre juridique quelconque doit être un (exception faite des cas particuliers qu'il peut viser), sous peine de n'être plus général et d'engendrer l'anarchie. L'avis de la Cour aboutirait, en principe, à reproduire tous les inconvénients de la méthode exceptionnelle et très dangereuse adoptée par l'Union panaméricaine. Enfin, nous nous séparons de l'avis de la Cour parce que nous mettons sur la même ligne les Parties (États ayant ratifié ou adhéré sans réserves) et les Parties éventuelles (signataires originaires)").

International Court of Justice . . ., the Court's conclusions were not well-founded."[53] Being "well aware of the seriousness of such a decision," he nevertheless asserted that "the Commission could not adopt the Court's opinion."[54]

In restating the traditional rule of unanimous consent in the annual report it prepared for the General Assembly that year, the Commission gave protracted consideration to the draft of the report presented by Brierly, so as not to "run counter to the Court's Opinion so obviously."[55] Hudson primarily, but also other members, suggested several amendments to the text with the intention to "make it easier for the Commission to justify the divergent conclusions it proposed to adopt as regards the question in general."[56] When considering the paragraph that aimed to explain why the criterion adopted by Court was rejected, in particular, members of the Commission were asked to review the sentences carefully one by one (as opposed to approving the paragraph as a whole, as was usual practice).[57] It was then that El Khouri said that for the Commission to give its reasons for not following the opinion of the Court would be "a dangerous proceeding"[58] and suggested deleting the paragraph "entirely, since it implied criticism of the Court's opinion."[59] Spiropoulos soon joined him, saying that the Commission "should avoid criticizing the Court's opinion . . . [as it] had every reason to try to enhance the prestige of that body."[60] When this objection was put to a

[53] YBILC 1951, Vol. I, p. 160, para. 3.

[54] *Ibid*; Yepes further said that "it was [necessary for the Commission] . . . to weigh the responsibility it would assume in adopting a decision contrary to the opinion of the International Court of Justice" (*ibid*, at p. 162, para. 30).

[55] *Ibid*, at p. 370, para. 5 (Scelle); see also p. 170, paras. 28, 43 (Hudson, Spiropoulos).

[56] *Ibid*, at p. 163, paras. 43, 44; see also p. 368, para. 110. Hudson believed "the existing law was inadequate" and this may explain his agreement to [go against the Court on this question]: *ibid*, at p. 176, para. 160.

[57] *Ibid*, at p. 169, para. 12 (Brierly); see also p. 171, para. 59 (Hudson). Scelle thought that the paragraph "must not be scrutinized too minutely. The Commission might remember that when Byzantium was taken by the Turks in 1453 the local theologians in the Basilica of S. Sophia were arguing about the sex of the angels! The Commission must beware of following their example"; but François said that, to the contrary, "the Commission should put everything under the microscope. It was not accepting the opinion of the Court; consequently every statement it made would be gone through with a fine-tooth comb, and it would be adversely criticized if it produced a text which was not juridically flawless": *ibid*, at p. 171, para. 52 and pp. 171–172, para. 65, respectively.

[58] *Ibid*, at p. 166, paras. 100–101; see also p. 167, para. 104 (Spiropoulos).

[59] *Ibid*, at p. 169, para. 15.

[60] *Ibid*, at p. 171, para. 55.

vote, however, it was rejected by 10 votes to 2,[61] as Brierly and the other members "did not see how it was possible to avoid criticizing the Court."[62] In the text eventually adopted, the Commission made sure to note, before stating its belief that the criterion applied by the Court to the Genocide Convention was not suitable for application to multilateral conventions more generally (by reason of its subjective character), that it felt at liberty to do so only because,

> first, that the Court's opinion had been strictly limited to the particular case of the Genocide Convention and, secondly, that while the Court had given its opinion on the basis of existing law, the Commission had been expressly asked to study the question "both from the point of view of codification and from that of the progressive development of international law."[63]

The Commission made clear that it suggested "the practice which it considers the most convenient for States to adopt for the future,"[64] and did not fail to mention that the advisory opinion was given by 7 votes to 5 and "was accompanied by two dissenting opinions of four judges and one judge respectively. The International Law Commission has studied these opinions with care."[65]

During that same 1951 session, the Commission also rejected the reasoning adopted by the Court's predecessor, the PCIJ, in the *Lotus* case. The question of jurisdiction with regard to crimes committed outside national territory had been inscribed on the Commission's list of topics for codification some two years earlier, after Hudson (himself a former Judge of that Court, but not in that case) said that "it was generally agreed that The Hague Court had shown excessive discretion in the case of the *Lotus*. A further study of the problem could therefore usefully be made, the more so as there were among States more points of agreement in the matter of criminal jurisdiction than was usually

61 *Ibid*, at para. 57.

62 *Ibid*, at p. 169, para. 16 (Brierly); Spiropoulos added that "if the Commission made no mention of the Court's opinion, its very silence would be tantamount to criticism" (*ibid*, at para. 17).

63 YBILC 1951, Vol. II, p. 128, para. 24 and p. 126, para. 17. On the Commission's willingness to pronounce *de lege ferenda* where the Court had pronounced *de lege lata*, see also YBILC 1950, Vol. I, pp. 256–257 (in connection with the Court's advisory opinion on *Interpretation of Peace Treaties* and the Commission's work on the topic 'Arbitral procedure').

64 YBILC 1951, Vol. II, p. 126, para. 17.

65 *Ibid*, at pp. 125–126, para. 16.

supposed."[66] Following a debate on the topic of 'Regime of the high seas' in 1950, the Commission (again at the suggestion of Hudson) "considered it important ... to determine which court was competent in criminal cases arising out of collision [of two vessels on the high seas] and that, after the case of the *Lotus* and its repercussions throughout the world, it could not remain silent on the subject."[67] When the Special Rapporteur, François, elaborated in the subsequent session on the criticism with which the *Lotus* judgment had been met and suggested that the Commission take a different position,[68] he added that:

> If the Commission adopted the proposal he submitted ... it would be departing from the view taken by the Permanent Court of International Justice. Admittedly it had done that before, but in different circumstances. In the case in point, a decision opposed to the judgment of the Court was justified by the very small majority by which that judgment had been reached, by the time which had since elapsed, and, finally, by the criticisms which that judgment had aroused. The Commission should nevertheless consider whether it wished to go against a judgment of the Court.[69]

The discussion that ensued revealed how hesitant members of the Commission were to stand in opposition to the Court, in particular after Kerno, the UN Assistant Secretary-General present in the room, intervened to say that he

> appreciated the gravity of the situation. He was sure that all the organs of the United Nations and all jurists would always do everything in their power to enhance the prestige of The Hague Court and it was certain that the Commission would not lightheartedly arrive at any solution other than that of the Court in the *Lotus* case.[70]

66 YBILC 1949, p. 42, paras. 53, 54.

67 YBILC 1950, Vol. II, p. 383, para. 187. The Special Rapporteur on the topic was thus requested to make a study of the subject and to propose a solution to the Commission at its next session. Hudson had earlier said that he "would be sorry if the Commission did not deal with the question of collision. After the *Lotus* case and its repercussions throughout the world, he did not feel it possible for the Commission to keep silent and would request the Rapporteur to examine the question": YBILC 1950, Vol. I, p. 196, para. 12a. Hudson then added, however, that "[h]e still felt that in the *Lotus* case the Court had come to a just decision. The Rapporteur could present a detailed report on the point the following year" (*ibid*).

68 YBILC 1951, Vol. II, pp. 79–80.

69 YBILC 1951, Vol. I, p. 334, para. 128. See also YBILC 1952, Vol. I, p. 143, para. 6.

70 YBILC 1951, Vol. I, p. 334, para. 129.

Amado, speaking first, said that "he was convinced that the Court would not give the same judgment at the present day,"[71] prompting Hudson to respond that

> the Court's decision in the *Lotus* case had been reached as a result of the President's casting vote but one of the judges, Judge J.B. Moore, who had expressed a dissenting opinion, had agreed with the Court's judgment on the main point at issue. Out of twelve judges, therefore, seven had voted in favour of the judgment and five against.[72]

Well aware, however, that the judgment was received by some States with consternation, Hudson added that "[i]f the Commission adopted a provision such as that proposed by the rapporteur, it should add a comment noting the criticism of the judgment in the countries of northern Europe, and indicating, at the same time, that the provision was adopted for the future."[73] He then stressed that he

> would not like it to be said that the majority of the Court had been mistaken. It was not for the Commission to say so and it would be bad for the prestige of the Court if it did. The comment should indicate that the Commission was not in a position to criticize what the Court had decided in 1927. It would thus lay down a principle for the future.[74]

Brierly concurred that the Commission's suggestion should be couched in terms of progressive development of the law: "It was feasible to tackle the subject without declaring that the Permanent Court of International Justice had been in the wrong. The Commission might state that, whatever the law in force at present it considered that the law in the future should be as formulated by it."[75]

Yet several members, among them Hudson, were still perturbed,[76] despite the Special Rapporteur's insistence that the Commission's "terms of reference were not merely codification, but also the progressive

[71] *Ibid*, at para. 130.
[72] *Ibid*, at pp. 334–335, para. 131.
[73] *Ibid*, at p. 335, para. 139.
[74] *Ibid*.
[75] *Ibid*, at p. 337, para. 4. Brierly earlier said that "it was quite clear that if the Commission adopted the rule proposed by Mr. François it would not necessarily be saying that the Court was wrong. It would be suggesting that, in future, it would be preferable to adopt such a rule. It was a question of the progressive development of law. Numerous criticisms had been made of the judgment in the *Lotus* case and particular importance should be attached to the opinion of the seafaring community": *ibid*, at p. 336, para. 147.
[76] See *ibid*, at p. 336, paras. 145 and 1–2 (Sandström, Hudson).

development of the law,"[77] and Liang (the Secretary to the Commission) opining that any fears that the Commission would be seen as criticizing the judgment were "somewhat exaggerated."[78] Yepes then attempted to bring the matter to a close:

> All the pros and cons had already been advanced. The views of those who were against Mr. François's proposal appeared to have been influenced by the judgment of the Permanent Court of International Justice, which should not be accepted unreservedly. In the first place it had been given only by the President's casting vote, and anyway, the authority of the Court was no argument for adopting a course contrary to that proposed by Mr. François. All the leading authorities on international law had come out against the Court's award. The French Government representative, Mr. Basdevant, who was now President of the International Court of Justice, had contested the majority argument and almost won the day with purely scientific reasoning. Another judge of the International Court of Justice, Mr. de Visscher, had expressed an opinion which differed considerably from that of the Permanent Court of International Justice.[79]

But this forceful plea did not remove all doubts: when the proposed article was put to a vote, there were 6 votes for and 6 against, with the result that the principle laid down by François's was not adopted.[80] Hudson soon seemed remorseful and suggested that if the Commission would indeed propose the article as a new rule of international law, he would support a new vote (with him abstaining, "so as not to stand in the way of a vote by six members of the Commission in favour of continuing the examination of the problem").[81] In an unusual move, the article was put to vote yet again, this time to be adopted by 6 votes to 4, with 2 abstentions.[82] The commentary eventually adopted together with what became article 35 (on "Penal jurisdiction in matters of collision") of the Commission's articles concerning the law of the sea recorded that the "[*Lotus*] judgment, which was carried by the President's casting vote after an equal vote of six to six, was very strongly criticized and caused serious disquiet in international maritime circles"; it further noted the disagreement with which the judgment was received by the diplomatic

[77] *Ibid*, at p. 337, para. 12.

[78] *Ibid*, at p. 335, para. 142 (explaining that "[t]he judgment in question had [already] been criticized both in maritime circles and by lawyers").

[79] *Ibid*, at p. 338, para. 25.

[80] *Ibid*, at p. 339, para. 39.

[81] *Ibid*, at pp. 339–340, 342, paras. 40, 42, 44, 69.

[82] *Ibid*, at p. 342, para. 71.

conference held at Brussels in 1952 and the international treaty that followed it.[83]

Decades were to pass before the Commission would again consider challenging the Court's jurisprudence. To a large extent, this may be due simply to the nature of the topics that came before it (and whether these had previously been dealt with by the Court) as well as to an appreciation of a developing inter-institutional relationship that needed to be nurtured. But it may also be due to the fact that, after its initial show of independence, by 1962 the Commission had eventually aligned itself with the Court's position on reservations to treaties, a move that left an institutional scar serving as a reminder of the need carefully to consider whether departing from a rule pronounced by the Court was indeed wise or constructive. While the first two special rapporteurs on the law of treaties who succeeded Brierly, Sir Hersch Lauterpacht and Sir Gerald Fitzmaurice, generally clung to the unanimity rule,[84] the fourth Special

[83] YBILC 1956, Vol. II, p. 281.

[84] The former of the two found the divergence of opinion between the Court and the Commission to be "somewhat strange," observing that "[i]t is a matter for reflection that while the International Court of Justice, whose function it is to *apply* existing law, in its advisory opinion on the question of Reservations to the Convention on Genocide, devoted itself mainly to the *development* of the law in this sphere by laying down the novel principle of compatibility of reservations with the purpose of the treaty, the International Law Commission whose task is both to codify and develop international law, limited itself substantially to a statement of existing law": YBILC 1954, Vol. II, p. 131, para. 3 (original emphasis). See also A. Pellet, 'The ILC Guide to Practice on Reservations to Treaties: A General Presentation by the Special Rapporteur', 24 EJIL (2013) 1061 at 1064–1065. It bears mention that Judge Alvarez, in his dissenting opinion appended to the Court's advisory opinion on *Reservations to the Convention on the Prevention and Punishment of the Crime of Genocide*, said that "[a]ccording to current opinion, this Court has to apply the principles of international law deemed to be in existence at the moment when it delivers its judgment or opinion, without considering whether they have undergone any more or less sudden changes, or whether they are in accord with the new conditions of international life; it appertains – we are told – to the International Law Commission created by the United Nations to determine what modifications should be made in international law. That is a view which it is impossible to accept. As a result of the great changes in international life that have taken place since the last social cataclysm, it is necessary that the Court should determine the present state of law in each case which is brought before it and, when needed, act constructively in this respect, all the more so because in virtue of Resolution 171 of the General Assembly of the United Nations of 1947, it is at liberty to develop international law, and indeed to create law, if that is necessary, for it is impossible to define exactly where the development of this law ends and its creation begins. To proceed otherwise would be to fail to understand the nature of international law, which must always reflect the international life of which it is born, if it is not to be discredited": *Reservations to the Convention on Genocide, Advisory Opinion: I.C.J. Reports 1951*, p. 50.

Rapporteur on the topic, Sir Humphrey Waldock, suggested in his first report that "[t]he situation of the Commission today with regard to this question [of reservations] differs in several important respects from its situation when it drew up its report in 1951," among them "the opposition of many States to the unanimity principle, and ... the Court's refusal to consider that principle as having been 'transformed into a rule of law'."[85] Expressing his belief that criticisms of the Court's criterion were well founded, he opined that the latter "[n]evertheless ... does express a valuable concept,"[86] and thus incorporated that criterion into the alternative, more flexible legal regime of reservations that he proposed.[87] The Commission agreed,[88] and that same year, in its commentary to the relevant draft article, reversed its earlier position entirely so as to say that "the Court's principle of 'compatibility with the object and purpose of the treaty' is one suitable for adoption as a general criterion of the legitimacy of reservations to multilateral treaties and of objections to them."[89] Many years later, the original disagreement with the Court would still be remembered among Commission members as "a mistake."[90]

85 YBILC 1962, Vol. II, pp. 63–64, para. 4. See also YBILC 1968, Vol. I, p. 162, para. 21 (Sir Humphrey saying that the Court's Advisory Opinion "had marked a turning point in the development of the law on reservations").

86 YBILC 1962, Vol. II, p. 66, para. 10.

87 *Ibid* (referring to the Court's criterion as "a general principle to be taken into account").

88 Amado, for example, said that he "had since [1951] modified his views, having re-examined the question in the light of the advisory opinion of the International Court of Justice," and later added that since 1951 "the deep and mature wisdom of the Court in delivering an advisory opinion which promoted the universality of treaties had become more widely recognized": YBILC 1962, Vol. I, pp. 139–140, para. 10 and p. 290, para. 64, respectively. Bartoš similarly said that "if his thinking on reservations had evolved, it had done so between 1950 and 1962, and in any case not in the matter of doctrine... He had revised his practical position in order to take account of the development of international law and because he had observed that his opinion was no longer compatible with the new positive rules of international law which had emerged from the jurisprudence of the Court and from the General Assembly resolution [that took it into account]": YBILC 1965, Vol. I, p. 147, para. 51. Yet not everyone was converted: Ruda said in 1965 that "[t]he requirement that a reservation must be 'compatible with the object and purpose of the treaty' had no legal foundation. It was taken from a passage in the 1951 Advisory Opinion of the International Court of Justice on reservations to the Genocide Convention, but the Court itself had expressly stated that its opinion was limited strictly to the particular Convention": *ibid*, at para. 55.

89 YBILC 1962, Vol. II, p. 178, para. 10.

90 YBILC 1998, Vol. I, p. 128, paras. 42 (Addo, adding that "[i]t had taken the Commission 11 years to see the obvious" and adopt the Court's criterion).

Be that as it may, in 2001 the Commission was again ready to reject a reasoning adopted by the Court, this time when adopting article 48 of its draft articles on State responsibility. The commentary to the article, which recognizes the right of a State other than the injured State to invoke responsibility, could not be more explicit: "Cf., however, the much-criticized decision of ICJ in *South West Africa, Second Phase, Judgment, I.C.J. Reports 1966*, p. 6, from which article 48 is a deliberate departure."[91] This criticism, however, was perhaps not so difficult to voice: the notorious judgment (again decided by the President's casting vote, the votes of the judges being equally divided), had already been repudiated by the Court itself in a well-known *obiter dictum* in the *Barcelona Traction* judgment. Dugard nevertheless recalled several years later that

> [during] the work on the draft articles on State responsibility, an entire session had been devoted to deciding whether to criticize the 1966 judgment of the ICJ in the *South West Africa* cases. Some members of the Commission had taken the view that one could never disagree with a decision of the ICJ, which was nonsense, of course, but showed how seriously judicial decisions [of the Court] . . . were taken.[92]

In the draft articles on State responsibility, the Commission also included a provision concerning non-repetition of internationally wrongful acts that did not fit squarely with the conception of such remedial consequences that the Court had just recently adopted in *LaGrand*. There the Court did not consider assurances and guarantees of non-repetition to be an autonomous and automatic consequence binding on the State

[91] YBILC 2001, Vol. II, Part Two, p. 127, fn. 725. Kamto had earlier said during the work on the topic (with regard to the different issue of countermeasures) that "[a] side issue that also arose was the question of the Commission's normative policy: should the practice of ICJ, whose decisions did not necessarily become accepted rules suitable for codification, be automatically endorsed?": YBILC 1999, Vol. I, p. 163, para. 9.

[92] YBILC 2009, Vol. I, p. 19, para. 32. Dugard referred also to decisions of the European Court of Human Rights, but when Xue intervened to say that "it was . . . important to draw a distinction between the decisions of the European Court of Human Rights and those of the ICJ," he soon "agreed that decisions of the ICJ were perhaps more persuasive than those of the European Court of Human Rights": *ibid*, at p. 20, paras. 39, 42. See also YBILC 2006, Vol. I, p. 283, para. 54 (Dugard recalling that "the Commission had debated for two days whether it should repudiate the *South West Africa* decision in its draft articles" and adding that "it was now accepted that it had done so"); and YBILC 2006, Vol. II, Part Two, p. 51, para. 2 of the commentary to article 16 of the Draft articles on diplomatic protection.

responsible for an internationally wrongful act,[93] but the Commission soon proposed precisely such a general rule in draft article 30.[94] For the Special Rapporteur, Crawford, the difference in approach illustrated the different roles of the Court and the Commission: while the former is a discrete settlement mechanism that is not an enforcer of its own judgments, the Commission seeks to cover a broader range of situations in diplomatic relations.[95] To blur or soften that difference, however, the Commission qualified the provision with the words "if circumstances so require."[96]

In the following year, the Commission "severely limited the scope"[97] of the *Nottebohm* judgment when defining the State of nationality for the purpose of diplomatic protection. Article 4 on 'State of nationality of a natural person', as its commentary explains, "does not require a State to prove an effective or genuine link between itself and its national, along the lines suggested in the *Nottebohm* case, as an additional factor for the exercise of diplomatic protection, even where the national possesses only one nationality."[98] But the commentary also explained that "[d]espite divergent views as to the interpretation of the case, the Commission took the view that there were certain factors that limited *Nottebohm* to the facts of the case in question . . .," and that "the Court did not intend to expound a general rule applicable to all States."[99] The Commission

93 See also P. Couvreur, 'The ICJ and the Implementation of the Law on State Responsibility', in *The International Court of Justice and the Effectiveness of International Law* (Brill 2016) 205 at 230–236.

94 YBILC 2001, Vol. II, Part Two, p. 88.

95 See YBILC 2001, Vol. I, p. 213, para. 37 (also expressing gratitude to the Court for not adopting a stance clearly contradictory to that favored by Commission on this matter); J. Crawford, 'The International Court of Justice and the Law of State Responsibility', in C.J. Tams and J. Sloan, *The Development of International Law by the International Court of Justice* (OUP 2013) 71 at 82.

96 YBILC 2001, Vol. II, Part Two, p. 91, para. 13 of the commentary to draft article 30 (explaining the formulation of the obligation in such flexible terms, however, in the need "to prevent the kinds of abusive or excessive claims which characterized some demands for assurances and guarantees by States in the past"). The actual intention may be gleaned from the account of the Drafting Committee debate: YBILC 2001, Vol. I, p. 239, para. 65.

97 YBILC 2003, Vol. II, Part One, p. 9, para. 24 (Fourth report on diplomatic protection by Mr. John R. Dugard, Special Rapporteur). See also YBILC 2002, Vol. I, p. 130, para. 16 (Yamada, Chairman of the Drafting Committee, drawing the Commission's attention to the "important point" that "the article did not adopt the effective link requirement enunciated by the ICJ in the *Nottebohm* case").

98 YBILC 2002, Vol. II, Part Two, pp. 69–70, para. 6.

99 *Ibid.*

further justified its choice by referring to the time that had passed since the Court's decision, saying that it

> was mindful of the fact that if the genuine link requirement proposed by *Nottebohm* was strictly applied it would exclude millions of persons from the benefit of diplomatic protection, as in today's world of economic globalization and migration there are millions of persons who have drifted away from their State of nationality and made their lives in States whose nationality they never acquire, or who have acquired nationality by birth or descent from States with which they have a tenuous connection.[100]

Yet another example in which the Commission has sought to avoid any appearance of disagreement with the Court may be found in the explanation it provided to guideline 3.1.5.3 of its Guide to practice on reservations to treaties of 2011, according to which "[t]he fact that a treaty provision reflects a rule of customary international law does not in itself constitute an obstacle to the formulation of a reservation to that provision."[101] In formulating this guideline, the Commission had to bear in mind that in a much-criticized passage in the *North Sea Continental Shelf* judgment, the Court had suggested quite the opposite by holding that "some faculty of making unilateral reservations may, within certain limits, be admitted" in the case of "purely conventional rules and obligations," but that "this cannot be so in the case of general or customary law rules."[102] To avoid being seen to be at odds with the Court, the Commission simply offered an interpretation of the judgment according to which an inability to formulate reservations to treaty provisions that codify customary rules cannot be deduced from it. It suggested (rather unconvincingly) that even if "the wording adopted by the Court is certainly not the most felicitous," once the passage in question "is put back into its context," then "it is not true that the Court affirmed the inadmissibility of reservations in respect of customary law."[103]

A more recent instance of divergence between the Commission and the Court concerns the scope of the class of beneficiaries of immunity *ratione personae* among holders of high-ranking office in a State. In the *Arrest Warrant* judgment of 2002 (and again in *Certain Questions of Mutual Assistance in Criminal Matters* some six years later), the Court

[100] *Ibid.*

[101] YBILC 2011, Vol. II, Part Three, p. 220.

[102] *North Sea Continental Shelf, Judgment, I.C.J. Reports 1969*, p. 38, para. 63.

[103] YBILC 2011, Vol. II, Part Three, p. 221, paras. (3)–(6) of the commentary to guideline 3.1.5.3.

held that "in international law it is firmly established that … certain holders of high-ranking office in a State, such as the Head of State, Head of Government and Minister for Foreign Affairs, enjoy immunities from jurisdiction in other States, both civil and criminal."[104] The words "such as" have been widely understood to mean that the Court did not draw up an exhaustive list of beneficiaries of immunity *ratione personae*, but rather implied a broader ambit than the three high-ranking State officials that it enumerated (also known as 'the troika'). In its work on the topic 'Immunity of State officials from foreign criminal proceedings', however, the Commission has elected to restrict immunity *ratione personae* to the troika. Although the first Special Rapporteur on the topic, Kolodkin, supported by several members of the Commission, considered in 2008 that the Court clearly recognized that (full) immunity *ratione personae* extends beyond the troika,[105] some members voiced harsh criticism of the *Arrest Warrant* judgment and the debate soon returned to the question of whether the Commission may, or should, distance itself from a decision of the Court. Pellet, to begin with, expressed himself "unable to share the Special Rapporteur's reverential respect for the stance of the ICJ in the *Arrest Warrant* case," and clarified that

> [w]hile it was appropriate for the Commission to pay close attention to the positions adopted by the ICJ, it was not necessarily bound by them, and the Court's far too conservative position in its 2002 judgment … which ran counter to the general trend at the time towards the communal development of international law, should not unduly intimidate the Commission.[106]

Dugard "wholeheartedly" agreed, adding that the Commission "was under no obligation to follow the Court's decisions blindly" and stressing that "the Court had not had any basis at the time for finding in its judgment that there was a customary rule establishing immunity for

[104] *Arrest Warrant of 11 April 2000 (Democratic Republic of the Congo* v. *Belgium), Judgment, I.C.J. Reports 2002*, pp. 20–21, para. 51; *Certain Questions of Mutual Assistance in Criminal Matters (Djibouti* v. *France), Judgment, I.C.J. Reports 2008*, pp. 236–237, para. 170.

[105] See YBILC 2008, Vol. II, Part One, p. 188, para. 117 (Preliminary report on immunity of State officials from foreign criminal jurisdiction, by Roman Anatolevich Kolodkin, Special Rapporteur); see also YBILC 2008, Vol. I, pp. 198–199, para. 54.

[106] YBILC 2008, Vol. I, p. 185, paras. 7, 11–12 (also referring to the judgment as "disastrous").

Ministers for Foreign Affairs."[107] Jacobsson, too, observed that "the Commission should not hesitate to distant itself from the Court's decision in the case and should examine the dissenting opinions" appended to the judgment,[108] explaining that the Commission "had not only the procedural right but also the duty systematically to address the implications of important decisions such as the one in the *Arrest Warrant* case and to keep an open mind when doing so."[109] Vasciannie, on the other hand, cautioned that "while he would not support uncritical acceptance of decisions, even those of the ICJ, considerable weight should be attached to a pronouncement by the Court that a rule of international law was 'firmly established'."[110] In a similar vein, Nolte suggested that a solution might be found in seeking to interpret the judgment,[111] and Hmoud agreed that "the Commission need not necessarily go against the Court on the issue of immunity" as "some exceptions may be found within the confines of general international law."[112] By the end of the debate that year it appeared that "[a]lthough views had diverged on the *Arrest Warrant* case, there seemed to be general consensus that the judgment was not beyond criticism and might be in need of

[107] *Ibid*, at p. 187, para. 17. Brownlie, in reply, said that the Court "had the rather splendid prerogative of making judicial general international law," and that in the *Arrest Warrant* case, "the Court had had to fill a gap and, being the International Court of Justice, it had had the prerogative – and indeed the duty – not only to apply the law, but also to make the law"; he then noted by contrast that "[t]he Commission could not generate international law, but it could make some informed choices based on informed discussions of policy": *ibid*, at p. 198, para. 53.

[108] *Ibid*, at p. 204, para. 7.

[109] *Ibid*, at p. 224, para. 73.

[110] *Ibid*, at p. 220, para. 44 (adding that "[s]econdly, the decision in that case was fairly recent, and it was hard to argue with force, as some had tried to do, that subsequent developments in the law were of sufficient significance to warrant a shift from the majority perspective of the Court" (at para. 45)).

[111] *Ibid*, at p. 221, para. 59 and p. 223, para. 66.

[112] *Ibid*, at p. 224, para. 71; see also p. 225, para. 80. The Special Rapporteur, Kolodkin, said, in summarizing the debate, that "he was convinced, contrary to some members of the Commission, that the judgment of the ICJ in the *Arrest Warrant* case was correct and important and that it provided a clear picture of the current state of international law in the area under consideration. The judgment had been adopted by 13 votes to 3, an overwhelming majority … He would continue to base his analysis of the foregoing issues on the sources used to prepare the preliminary report, namely: State practice, including legislation and judicial decisions; decisions of international courts and tribunals (particularly the ICJ); and academic writings": *ibid*, at p. 233, paras. 39–40.

reappraisal."[113] Similar positions were voiced when discussion of the topic resumed in 2011.[114]

In 2013, the new Special Rapporteur on the topic, Escobar Hernández, suggested that the extension of immunity *ratione personae* to ministers for foreign affairs "was not in doubt in light of the judgment of the International Court of Justice in the *Arrest Warrant* case."[115] Seeking to limit the scope of immunity to the troika alone without openly challenging the Court, however, she argued that "despite [the] literal meaning [of the words 'such as' in the judgment], when read in context it was difficult to conclude that the Court was referring to the existence of an open-ended list of persons who enjoy immunity *ratione personae*."[116] She further highlighted, on a number of occasions, that the Commission was in any event approaching the topic "from the dual perspective of *lex lata* and *lege ferenda*."[117] Some members, arguing for an even narrower scope of immunity, thought that the Special Rapporteur had paid too much respect to the Court. Murase, for example, recounted the argument that "[t]he judgments of the International Court of Justice on which the Special Rapporteur based her arguments were binding only on the parties and were limited to the particular cases."[118] Tladi, acknowledging that "the International Court of Justice, as the principal judicial organ of the United Nations, was endowed with unmatched authority," similarly said that "its primary mandate was the resolution of disputes between parties, and its rulings were binding only upon the parties. Even when the Court had ruled on an issue, therefore, the Commission had to conduct its own independent assessment of the relevant State practice."[119] But other

[113] *Ibid*, at p. 227, para. 99 (Dugard); see also para. 100 (Brownlie).

[114] See YBILC 2011, Vol. I, p. 42, para. 34 (Dugard stressing again that he "was not convinced that the decision of the International Court of Justice in that [*Arrest Warrant*] case had been correct," and thinking it "necessary to mention that the International Court of Justice did not include many international criminal law specialists, which meant that there was all the more reason to listen to those who were"), and p. 53, para. 57 (Pellet reiterating his position that "[a]lthough the Commission had to pay careful attention to the case law of the International Court of Justice, it was not obliged to endorse all its tortuous reasoning, including its mistakes"). Vasciannie again cautioned that "the majority view in the *Arrest Warrant* case should not be lightly dismissed": *ibid*, at p. 56, para. 85.

[115] YBILC 2013, Vol. II, Part One, p. 45, para. 58.

[116] *Ibid*, at p. 46, para. 62.

[117] YBILC 2013, Vol. I, p. 40, para. 4.

[118] *Ibid*, at p. 20, para. 17.

[119] *Ibid*, at para. 20. Tladi expressed the same position as Special Rapporteur on the topic 'Peremptory norms of general international law (*jus cogens*)': see A/CN.4/747: 'Fifth

members insisted that the scope of immunity should be defined in light of the Court's case-law. Among them was Sir Michael Wood, who protested that the Special Rapporteur "seemed to depart, without any real explanation, from the opinion of the International Court of Justice in the *Arrest Warrant* case," and added that "[i]t was hardly an answer to say that that was a 'literal reading' of that judgment."[120] Several members likewise expressed the view that the Special Rapporteur should have undertaken a closer analysis of recent State practice in order to support her suggestion, in particular given the Court's pronouncement on the matter.[121]

The debate raged on (albeit unrecorded) in the Commission's Drafting Committee, which eventually adopted, under protest by several members,[122] a draft article limiting the scope of immunity *ratione personae* to the troika alone.[123] Remarkably, the draft commentary to the article does not at all mention the consideration of the so-called "fight against impunity" that motivated many of the members who favored a more limited scope of immunity. Nor does it record any of the criticisms voiced in this context with respect to the *Arrest Warrant* judgment. Instead, in attempting to disguise any hint of disagreement with the Court, it portrays the limiting of immunity to the troika as a possible interpretation of the Court's case-law.[124]

Report on Peremptory Norms of General International Law (*jus cogens*) by Dire Tladi, Special Rapporteur' (2022), para. 180.

120 YBILC 2013, Vol. I, p. 31, para. 22.

121 See, for example, *ibid*, at p. 23, para. 12 (Huang), p. 25, para. 8 (Murphy), p. 32, para. 1 (Nolte), and p. 35, para. 44 (Gevorgian).

122 The Report of the Chairman of the Drafting Committee records, in quite unusual fashion, that "[a] reservation was nevertheless expressed regarding draft article 3 as a whole. It was contended that the Drafting Committee, as well as the Commission in Plenary, had not given adequate consideration to whether the list of persons in draft article 3 precisely reflected the state of international law on this subject. Such a point of view was opposed by some members": Statement of the Chairman of the Drafting Committee, Mr. Dire Tladi (7 June 2013), available at <http://legal.un.org/docs/?path=../ilc/sessions/65/pdfs/immunity_of_state_officials_dc_statement_2013.pdf&lang=E>, pp. 11–13.

123 YBILC 2013, Vol. II, Part Two, p. 43 (draft article 3).

124 *Ibid*, at pp. 45–46, paras. 8–9. Surprisingly, the commentary does mention some of the criticisms voiced with respect to the Court's particular recognition of ministers for foreign affairs as entitled to immunity *ratione personae* (*ibid*, at p. 45, para. 5); but this is done against the background of a draft article that does adopt the Court's position on this point.

That same approach – of offering an interpretation of a decision of the Court as being in conformity with a view that the Commission seeks to advance, despite the fact that that is probably not the case, so as not to be seen as defying the Court – may also be seen in the Commission's decision in 2019 to list "the right of self-determination" among the norms having the status of *jus cogens*.[125] In the face of some resistance within the Commission to do so, on the grounds that the Court had refused to recognize self-determination in this way in the *Chagos* advisory opinion,[126] the Special Rapporteur made a passionate plea according to which the Court "had not said that self-determination was not a peremptory norm of international law."[127] On this basis he advocated, and the Commission as a whole seemed to accept, that the Commission "could only conclude that the Court had, without using the words, accepted self-determination as a peremptory norm of general international law."[128]

C. Is All Disagreement Necessarily Bad?

The fact that disagreement between the Court and the Commission has been both rare and mostly camouflaged has owed, at least to some extent, to a concern that such contention may prove detrimental to the authority of both organs[129] and of international law more broadly. Such was indeed the case in the 1950s when the divergence of views on the issue of reservations to treaties gave rise to a fairly confused period during which the law remained unsettled.[130] Disagreement in evaluating State practice,

125 A/74/10: 'Report of the International Law Commission on the Work of Its Seventy-First Session' (29 April–7 June and 8 July–9 August 9 2019), p. 147 ("Annex"). The position was maintained in the final text adopted in 2022.

126 See, for example, UN Doc. A/CN.4/SR.3460: 'Provisional Summary Record of the Commission's 3460th Meeting' (9 May 2019), p. 9 (Murphy).

127 UN Doc. A/CN.4/SR.3465: 'Provisional Summary Record of the Commission's 3465th Meeting' (16 May 2019), p. 7 (Tladi).

128 *Ibid.* Later in that same session, President Yusuf told members expressly that in fact "the Court had deemed it unnecessary to address the matter of whether the right to self-determination was a peremptory norm of international law in its advisory opinion on the *Legal Consequences of the Separation of the Chagos Archipelago from Mauritius in 1965*, because that had not been the point at issue" (UN Doc. A/CN.4/SR.3478: 'Provisional Summary Record of the 3478th Meeting' (11 July 2019), p. 10).

129 More so that of the Commission, some judges are keen to stress: Interviews with three members of the Court in April 2016, on file with the author.

130 The response of the General Assembly to the conflicting replies received from the Court and the Commission came in the form of resolution 598 (VI) of January 12, 1952, where

in particular, might serve to imply that the very process of law ascertainment is overly subjective.[131]

Yet disagreement between the Court and the Commission should not be considered as inherently pernicious. As one member of the Commission suggested, if the Commission has erred, it would be useful for the international legal system if the Court were to point that out.[132] A judge of the Court has similarly submitted that any disagreement should preferably be made explicit, as it could promote a genuine development of the law and the subsequent consolidation of a coherent view.[133] By the same token, President Donoghue suggested to members of the Commission that a critical reading of each other's texts may actually serve to strengthen both organs by compelling each to be more rigorous in its work:

> The two institutions should ... be cautious about placing too much weight on cross-citation, by which she meant the Court's citation of the Commission's outputs as authoritative and the Commission's frequent citation of the Court as an authority. Cross-citation as a means of supporting a particular proposition was convenient and efficient, and could also be considered to reflect the respect that each institution had for the other, but the two institutions should not be overly reliant on that method of reasoning. They had a duty to the States Members of the United Nations and other readers to set out convincing substantive reasons for their conclusions that went beyond simply observing that the other institution had stated a concordant view. If the two institutions offered only meagre reasons for their conclusions on the existence and

the Assembly requested the UN Secretary-General to conform to the Court's Advisory Opinion with respect to the Genocide Convention, and, with respect of other conventions, to accept the deposit of instruments containing or relating to reservations without passing upon their legal effect. Being sharply divided on the merits of the Commission's proposal, the Assembly thus left unanswered the questions of which States should have the right to lodge objections to reservations and what should the legal effect of such objections be. See also the 'Historical summary of the question of reservations to multilateral conventions', in YBILC 1962, Vol. II, p. 77, paras. 6–7 (explaining, inter alia, that some States considered that a more general application could be given to the Court's criterion); and YBILC 1997, Vol. I, p. 88, para. 3 (Pellet).

131 See also S. Talmon, 'Determining Customary International Law: The ICJ's Methodology between Induction, Deduction and Assertion', 26 EJIL (2015) 417 at 433 (referring to the disagreement between the Court and the Commission in 1951 on the legal regime of reservations to treaties when arguing that "[t]he fact that such wide disagreement is possible on the question of state practice underlines the subjectivity involved in evaluating the evidence before the ICJ").

132 Interview with member of the Commission in May 2016, on file with the author.

133 Interview with member of the Court in April 2016, on file with the author.

> content of customary international law and relied excessively on cross-citation, they ran the risk of being criticized for establishing what Judge James Crawford had once described as "customary international law by stealth." The substance of the institutions' specific conclusions and the overall authority of their pronouncements could be diminished as a result.[134]

Still more deeply, the different roles of the Court and the Commission suggest that disagreement among the two may sometimes not only be useful, but also legitimate and possibly desirable. This may well be true if codification by the Commission injects an unwelcome rigidity, and the Court feels compelled in a certain case to take into account new or special circumstances. Divergence of views may be even more advantageous with respect to the Commission adopting a view different to one that the Court has taken, bearing in mind its dual mandate of codifying and progressively developing international law.

Judicial decisions reached in particular cases may indeed require review and adaptation when a rule of a more general application is sought to be established. This may also be the case if the Court has erred,[135] or has left the legal situation unclear: as Lauterpacht observed, "experience has shown that on occasions decisions of international tribunals themselves, far from supplying the missing element of completeness [in the uncertain rules of international law], may infuse an element of doubt and uncertainty where hitherto there existed relative clarity and agreement."[136] Departing from a rule stated by the Court will

134 UN Doc. A/CN.4/SR.3548: 'Provisional Summary Record of the Commission's 3548th Meeting' (22 July 2021), p. 7.

135 Akande has focused on quality control when similarly suggesting that "to the extent that the ILC has the function of setting out what the law is or a law-making function, it should be part of its function to consider whether judicial bodies have correctly applied the law. Controversial as it may be, part of the codification (and also law-making) function is to reverse judicial bodies if they get it wrong": D. Akande, 'Should the International Law Commission Overrule the ICJ in Its Articles on Immunity of State Officials from Foreign Criminal Jurisdiction?', *EJIL: Talk!* (5 August 2013), available at <www.ejiltalk.org/should-the-international-law-commission-overrule-the-icj-in-its-articles-on-immunity-of-state-officials-from-foreign-criminal-jurisdiction/>.

136 H. Lauterpacht, 'Codification and Development of International Law', 49 AJIL (1955) 16 at 21 (adding that "on occasions judicial activity, far from supplying the missing link of certainty and clarity, may achieve the opposite effect," and explaining that this may be done "in two directions: it may disturb or do away with the conviction, hitherto operative, of the existence of an agreed rule of law; after having done that, it may accentuate the anomaly by laying down a principle which is incomplete and which requires further elaboration if it is to be of practical value").

also be appropriate when codification is undertaken a long time after the judicial decision in question has been rendered and the law had since been developing, especially as the Court itself – which can only deal with those matters that come before it – has no program of its own and may not necessarily have an opportunity to revisit a given issue.[137] One such adjustment may be found in the definition of diplomatic protection adopted by the Commission in its 2006 draft articles on the subject: here the Commission decided eventually to abandon the fiction, proclaimed by the PCIJ in the *Mavrommatis Palestine Concessions* case some eighty years earlier, that the sending State was vindicating its own rights,[138] and the Court soon after accepted this new definition as reflective of customary international law.[139]

The cause of progressive development of the law, in particular, may justify a departure from judicial pronouncements, resonating with Mahatma Gandhi's well-known remark that "honest disagreement is often a good sign of progress." In the international legal system, where the question of the peaceful change of the law has attracted particular concern, this may prove to be of exceptional significance, also bringing to mind that one of the main objections put forward in the early twentieth century to any compulsory jurisdiction of the PCIJ (and later to that of its successor, the Court) was that no international legislature exists as a safety valve to correct decisions of the Court and bring the law into

[137] For the suggestion that a judgment dating back "nearly half a century" is possibly no longer reliable as a statement of the law, see also YBILC 1995, Vol. I, p. 78, para. 9 (Mikulka, Special Rapporteur on the topic 'State succession and its impact on the nationality of natural and legal persons', referring to the *Nottebohm* decision). See also A.A. D'Amato, 'The Concept of Special Custom in International Law', 63 AJIL (1969) 211 at 215 ("In international law in particular, the lack of compulsory jurisdiction and centralized enforcement procedures make it very difficult for an international tribunal to reverse itself or to depart from its own precedents in future cases, for most of the court's authority depends upon the soundness and consistency of its reasoning").

[138] See also A. Pellet, 'The Second Death of Euripide Mavrommatis? Notes on the International Law Commission's Draft Articles on Diplomatic Protection', 7 LAPE (2008) 33–58; J. Crawford, 'The International Law Commission's Articles on Diplomatic Protection Revisited', in T. Maluwa et al (eds.), *The Pursuit of a Brave New World in International Law: Essays in Honour of John Dugard* (Brill Nijhoff 2007) 135 at 137–140. The Commission had done so 'diplomatically', by defining diplomatic protection "[f]or the purposes of these draft articles" and thus not challenging the PCIJ's previous determinations on the matter.

[139] *Ahmadou Sadio Diallo (Republic of Guinea* v. *Democratic Republic of the Congo), Preliminary Objections, Judgment, I.C.J. Reports 2007*, p. 599, para. 39.

harmony with justice and progress when circumstances so required.[140] Viewed in this light, the general approach within the Commission, that it must first try to codify the rules of international law based on the Court's decisions and only then fill in lacunae as necessary while being very cautious with any proposal for progressive development,[141] is even more remarkable. At the same time, by turning more openly to progressive development, the Commission would doubtless make it increasingly difficult for the Court to have any recourse to its work in performing its judicial function. Surely, that has not been lost on its members.

D. Conclusion

Given their institutional independence, distinct mandates, and recurring opportunities to review each other's work, one would be justified in expecting more than only a handful of cases where the Court and the Commission, in their long decades of coexistence, would show themselves to be opposed. Yet both organs have generally been averse to disagree; even more so, they have been committed to handling differing views that do arise in a careful and collegial manner, so as not to inflict any harm on the image or authority of the other. Thus these rare instances of disagreement do not stand as any measure of rivalry or disharmony, but rather are further evidence of a unique interaction characterized by great respect and a sense of partnership.

[140] See Chapter 2, Section C. For more on this argument (and the response to it), see H. Lauterpacht, 'The Absence of an International Legislature and the Compulsory Jurisdiction of International Tribunals', 11 BYIL (1930) 134–157; H. Kelsen, 'Compulsory Adjudication of International Disputes', 37 AJIL (1943) 397 at 400–401. Brierly had earlier contrasted international law with municipal law for lacking the safeguard possessed by the latter, namely that decisions of courts "may be corrected and the law brought into harmony with public opinion by the legislature": J.L. Brierly, *The Law of Nations* (OUP 1928) 189.

[141] See, for example, YBILC 1955, Vol. I, p. 203, para. 20 (Addo saying that "to go beyond the judgment of the Court into the realm of the progressive development of the law . . . would give rise to even greater objections than those levelled against any objectionable decision of the Court. It might also invite retaliation by the Court, which could result in instability of the law"); YBILC 2000, Vol. I, p. 45, para. 70 (Tomka saying, in reference to the topic 'Diplomatic protection', that "[t]here had been a number of decisions by PCIJ and ICJ on diplomatic protection, and it was important to build on them . . . The Commission must be cautious with the proposal for progressive development. It must first try to codify the rules of customary international law and only then fill in lacunae as necessary").

The desire on the part of the Court and the Commission to maintain and promote a common position on the law may, however, come at a cost. In particular, in blurring and avoiding incompatible positions the two organs might hinder the operation of effective checks and balances that can be crucial to well-grounded relations between legislative and adjudicative bodies, such as advancement of codification in order to cancel out a ruling for the future or to reestablish what had previously been regarded as the status quo. More significantly, the prevalent attachment of one organ to the statements of the law by the other very much limits the potential for development of the law, the adaptation of which may sometimes be more necessary and advantageous than its stability. This is particularly consequential when considering that the Commission is expressly mandated with promoting the progressive development of international law and remains an agency for such development where the risks of demanding it from the Court itself may be too great.

7

The Court and the Commission: A 'Special Relationship'

The preceding chapters have established that the relationship forged between the Court and the Commission during their seven-odd decades of mutual coexistence is exceptional in both quality and consequence. It is clear from what has gone before that the work of each organ has had a profound influence on that of the other; that this influence has not been limited to the mere reciprocal borrowing of each other's work, but extends to a more fertile realm of intellectual synergy that is not always fully in sight; that "respect for one another," as one member of the Court has put it, "is part of the furniture of both organs";[1] and that each of them has consciously taken care to cultivate the inter-institutional connection.

All of this would justify labeling the connection as a 'special relationship', to borrow the term popularized by British Prime Minister Winston Churchill and later employed as shorthand for the extensive network of links between the United Kingdom and the United States.[2] Anglo-American relations have been depicted in terms of "an intimate, harmonious bond between the two nations celebrated on State occasions with suitably hyperbolic prose,"[3] and have been said to be based, inter alia, upon an identity of interests, feelings of affinity and trust, mutual consideration, and willingness to assist each other when necessary.[4] These relations have also been considered as uniquely important not only for

[1] Interview with a member of the Court in April 2016, on file with the author.

[2] See, for example, J. Dumbrell, 'The US–UK "Special Relationship" in a World Twice Transformed', 17 *Cambridge Review of International Affairs* (2004) 437–450; J. Rasmussen and J.M. McCormick, 'British Mass Perceptions of the Anglo-American Special Relationship', 108 *Political Science Quarterly* (1993) 515–541. The concept is not uniquely Anglo-American, however, in that it has been applied occasionally to ties between the United States and others of its allies; nor does it connote pure harmony.

[3] D. Reynolds, 'A "Special Relationship"? America, Britain and the International Order since the Second World War', 62 *International Affairs* (1986) 1.

[4] See, for example, B.M. Russett, *Community and Contention: Britain and American in the Twentieth Century* (MIT Press 1963).

the two countries, but also for the international order as a whole. The analogy is, of course, quite distant, but, as this concluding chapter seeks to illustrate, a similar appreciation of the relationship between the Court and the Commission is nevertheless appropriate.

A. The Foundations of the 'Special Relationship'

The expectation that the Court and the Commission would have a natural link between them was grounded from the outset in a functional conception according to which their tasks were both complementary and distinctly different. The Court, as a judicial organ, applies the rules of international law in force, while the Commission, having a vocation of a legislative nature, is engaged in drafting them.[5] This notion also implied, in the *trias politica* tradition, that some distance between the two organs can – and should – be maintained.

Yet the past also has shown that sharp lines could not be drawn so easily in dividing the labor between the Court and the Commission; that codification of the law and its progressive development in fact were within the remit of both of them.[6] After all, in determining the content of customary international law on any particular point, the Court too performs an act of codification: precisely such articulation of the existing rules of international law had fallen primarily to international tribunals before the Commission was set up.[7] By the same token, pushing the

[5] See Chapter 2, Section D.2.

[6] See Chapter 2. See also, for example, A. Pellet, 'Shaping the Future of International Law: The Role of the World Court in Law-Making', in M.H. Arsanjani et al (eds.), *Looking to the Future: Essays in International Law in Honor of W. Michael Reisman* (Martinus Nijhoff 2011) 1065 at 1076 (suggesting that "only the 'product' differs"); N. Singh, 'Codification and Progressive Development: The Role of the International Court of Justice', 18 IJIL (1978) 1–16.

[7] That both organs are tasked with saying what the law is may further be seen in the proposals occasionally voiced that the Commission, like the Court, could provide UN organs with advisory opinions on legal issues of importance to the international community: see, for example, YBILC 1951, Vol. I, p. 7, para. 33 and p. 8, paras. 52a–53 (Spiropoulos); YBILC 1990, Vol. II, Part Two, p. 107, fn. 366 (recording a recommendation by a Working Group established by the Commission to consider its long-term program of work that "the Commission could indicate to the General Assembly its readiness to receive from the Assembly requests for legal opinions on some pressing legal issues of the international community"); S. McCaffrey, 'Is Codification in Decline?', 20 HICLR (1996) 639 at 658 (suggesting that the General Assembly "should feel free to call upon the Commission to answer questions on points of law that are not, for whatever reason, suitable for referral to the International Court of Justice"); *Making Better*

envelope of positive law is not the sole preserve of the Commission either. Although the duty to insist on the distinction between *lex lata* and *lex ferenda* is an essential part of the judicial function,[8] codification of customary international law was early on understood to involve "as an incident in the process an element of what is really legislation,"[9] and it was anyway considered – rather ambiguously – that "one of the Court's important tasks [was] to contribute, through its jurisprudence, to the development of international law."[10] Further, though the point should not be pressed too far, the Court, "in perhaps the majority of cases . . . will have to state as settled law what is in fact not entirely settled."[11] It has

International Law: The International Law Commission at 50 (United Nations 1998) 89, 98, and 180, para. (*d*) (Orrego Vicuña). One may also recall that in 1950 the General Assembly invited both the Court and the Commission to pronounce themselves on the question of reservations to multilateral conventions: see Chapter 6, Section B.2. Similarly, in 1970, the President of the Security Council addressed a letter both to the Court and to the Commission as the "appropriate organs of the United Nations" for whom the matter of infringements of the inviolability of diplomatic agents may be of concern: YBILC 1970, Vol. II, pp. 273–274.

[8] See, for example, *South West Africa, Second Phase, Judgment, I.C.J. Reports 1966*, p. 34, para. 49; *Fisheries Jurisdiction (United Kingdom* v. *Iceland), Merits, Judgment, I.C.J. Reports 1974*, pp. 23–24, para. 53; *Legality of the Threat or Use of Nuclear Weapons, Advisory Opinion, I.C.J. Reports 1996*, p. 237, para. 18. See also H. Thirlway, 'Reflections on *Lex Ferenda*', 32 NYIL (2001) 3 at 8.

[9] J.L. Brierly, 'The Future of Codification', 12 BYIL (1931) 1 at 3.

[10] Report and Draft Scheme Presented to the [League of Nations'] Assembly by the Third Committee, in *Documents concerning the Action Taken by the Council of the League of Nations under Article 14 of the Covenant and the adoption by the Assembly of the Statute of the Permanent Court* (League of Nations 1921) 206, 211.

[11] H. Thirlway, 'The Contribution of the International Court of Justice to the Development of International Law', in L. Zeng and Y. Xiao (eds.), *Wuhan University Lectures on International Law*, Vol. II (Wuhan University Press 2006) 32 at 43. See also H. Thirlway, 'Unacknowledged Legislators: Some Preliminary Reflections on the Limits of Judicial Lawmaking', in R. Wolfrum and I. Gätzschmann (eds.), *International Dispute Settlement: Room for Innovations?* (Springer 2013) 311 ("It is a cardinal and well-known principle that tribunals do not make law: they only apply it. It is also an open secret that in practice this is simply not true"); YBILC 2008, Vol. I, p. 198, para. 53 (Brownlie suggesting that "the ICJ had the rather splendid prerogative of making judicial general international law"); A. Pellet and D. Müller, 'Article 38', in A. Zimmerman et al (eds.), *The Statute of the International Court of Justice: A Commentary*, 3rd ed. (OUP 2019) 819 at 958, MN 333 ("It can be accepted that 'the Court is moving in the direction of the mandate that the UN gave to the ILC' in that the ICJ is participating [in] the 'progressive development' of international law, which confirms the difficulty met by the ILC in making a clear-cut distinction between the two parts of its mandate" (citations omitted)).

itself conceded that "in stating and applying the law, [it may] necessarily [have] to specify its scope and sometimes note its general trend."[12]

The fact that the tasks performed by the Court and the Commission in the international legal system are not sealed compartments has not escaped the attention of their members.[13] President Bustamante y Rivero, for example, spoke before the Commission of "the common task of developing the law,"[14] and Judge Ago has observed that the Court and the Commission "each . . . had for its purpose the subject of international law, its definition, development and application."[15] In a similar vein, President Higgins has noted that "[t]he ICJ and the ILC are both fully engaged in the interpretation and development of international law, while each performing rather different functions."[16] Such an appreciation of the significant commonality between the tasks of the two organs no doubt has contributed to the sense of a shared mission instilled in them. Indeed, members of the Court have considered that "[t]he Commission and the Court served the same grand design: the furtherance of the rule of law in the international community,"[17] while members of the

[12] *Legality of the Threat or Use of Nuclear Weapons, Advisory Opinion, I.C.J. Reports 1996*, p. 237, para. 18; see also the statement of the Chamber of the Court in the *Gulf of Maine* case, according to which the judgment in the *North Sea Continental Shelf* cases, "while well known to have attributed more marked importance to the link between the legal institution of the continental shelf and the physical fact of the natural prolongation than has subsequently been given to it, is nonetheless the judicial decision which has made the greatest contribution to the formation of customary law in this field. From this point of view, its achievements remain unchallenged": *Delimitation of the Maritime Boundary in the Gulf of Maine Area, Judgment, I.C.J. Reports 1984*, p. 293, para. 91.

[13] Although there are exceptions: see, for example, YBILC 1955, Vol. I, p. 243, para. 9 (Garcia Amador); YBILC 1998, Vol. I, p. 81, para. 36 (Economides).

[14] YBILC 1969, Vol. I, p. 70, paras. 3, 9.

[15] YBILC 1981, Vol. I, p. 125, para. 5.

[16] Keynote Address by H.E. Judge Rosalyn Higgins, President of the International Court of Justice, at the Sixtieth Anniversary of the International Law Commission (19 May 2008), available at <www.icj-cij.org/files/press-releases/8/14488.pdf>. President Guillaume has similarly said that the two organs "were united by a common aim – the development of international law, by methods that were admittedly different," and President Shi referred to the "respective and complementary roles played by both institutions in promoting and developing international law": see, respectively, YBILC 2000, Vol. I, p. 358, para. 3, and YBILC 2004, Vol. I, p. 153, para. 2. See also UN Doc. GA/L/3240, available at <www.un.org/press/en/2003/gal3240.doc.htm> (President Shi affirming in October 2003 "the close link between the International Law Commission and the Court in that both were responsible and intricately linked in the development of international law").

[17] YBILC 1974, Vol. I, p. 70, para. 26 (Judge Sir Humphrey Waldock addressing the Commission). See also, for example, YBILC 1967, Vol. I, p. 88, para. 6 (Judge Fitzmaurice referring to a "joint obligation to make every effort to promote the law");

Commission have similarly regarded the work of the two bodies as being "part and parcel of the same aspiration: to promote harmonious and friendly relations between the members of the international community on the basis of international law and justice."[18] The judges at The Hague thus referred to members of the Commission as "their brothers in the law within the family of the United Nations,"[19] and Commission members, in their turn, have spoken in Geneva of an "international legal fraternity."[20] Notwithstanding the Commission's formal role as a subsidiary organ of the General Assembly, they have shared the view that the Court and the Commission are "the principal judicial and legal organs of the United Nations, respectively."[21] All this reflects not just sentiment, but also a professional solidarity that should not be underestimated.

YBILC 1981, Vol. I, p. 125, paras. 6, 8 (Judge Ago saying that "[i]t was essential that the Court and the Commission should co-operate in actually defending the law in the field of international relations … He was thus convinced that the Court and the Commission were called upon to co-operate even more closely, not limiting themselves to mere reciprocal borrowing of each other's work, to safeguard international law and the essential function it fulfilled in the life of the international community"); YBILC 2003, Vol. I, p. 163, para. 3 (President Shi saying that "[t]he link between the two spoke for itself. Both contributed to the strengthening of international law").

18 YBILC 1981, Vol. I, p. 125, para. 2 (Chairman Thiam); see also, for example, YBILC 1968, Vol. I, p. 163, para. 30 (Rosenne saying that "[t]he Commission and the Court shared, from different viewpoints, a general responsibility for the improvement and modernization of the whole body of international law so urgently needed in the contemporary world"); YBILC 1969, Vol. I, p. 69, para. 1 (Chairman Ushakov observing that "[t]he Court and the Commission pursued a common aim proclaimed in the preamble to the Charter of the United Nations: 'to establish conditions under which justice and respect for the obligations arising from treaties and other sources of international law can be maintained'"), and p. 71, para. 18 (Tabibi saying that "both served the same ultimate objective under the United Nations Charter, the one as quasi-legislative and the other as a judicial organ"); YBILC 1979, Vol. I, p. 64, para. 5 (Šahović saying that "the Court and the Commission both pursued the same purpose, which was to promote peace and security, and international co-operation based on the rule of law. It was there, above all, that the true *raison d'etre* of the bond uniting the Court and the Commission, and of the relations that had been established between then, was to be found"); YBILC 1997, Vol. I, p. 214, para. 67 (Sreenivasa Rao saying that "[t]he mutual respect felt by the two institutions could be attributed to common interests, the consensual element in the work of both, the persuasion that they used to secure the recognition and application of international law and the culture of promotion of the rule of law and justice that they shared").

19 YBILC 1974, Vol. I, p. 70, para. 32 (Judge Waldock addressing the Commission); see also YBILC 1969, Vol. I, p. 70, para. 9 (President Bustamante y Rivero speaking of members of both organs as belonging "to the same unique family").

20 YBILC 1981, Vol. I, p. 125, para. 2 (Chairman Thiam).

21 YBILC 2012, Vol. I, p. 146, para. 92 (President Tomka addressing the Commission); see also, for example, YBILC 1974, Vol. II, Part One, p. 310, para. 208 (the Commission

Members of the two institutions, by definition, do have much in common, not least because the prescriptions contained in the Commission's Statute with regard to its composition were drafted by those who very much had in mind the corresponding provisions of the Statute of the Court.[22] According to these two founding documents – and subject to a mandatory geographic spread similarly enshrined in them so as to ensure representation of the world's main civilizations and principal legal systems – "[i]n both cases members were elected by governments, not as representatives of countries but in their personal capacity as jurists, and they had a scientific task to perform in accordance with their consciences."[23] As international legal experts, they tend to share a style and structure of thought and argument. Moreover, serving the only international tribunal with a general subject-matter jurisdiction, or the only official international body with wide competence to promote the codification of international law as a whole, they typically hold a

opining that "[i]f a comparison must be made between the Commission and another United Nations body, it is with the International Court of Justice that such a comparison should be made. The Court is entrusted with the task of applying international law to controversies between States, while the Commission performs the task of formulating draft rules of international law. The work done by the Court, at the judicial level, and that done by the Commission, at the legislative level, are complementary and make those bodies, respectively, the principal judicial and legal organs of the United Nations system"); YBILC 1980, Vol. I, p. 268, para. 27 (Judge Ago referring to the Court and the Commission as "the two main legal organs of the United Nations"). On the distinction between principal and subsidiary United Nations organs, see H. Kelsen, *The Law of the United Nations: A Critical Analysis of Its Foundational Problems* (second reprinting, The Lawbook Exchange 2001) 136–145.

22 See Chapter 2, Section D.2. In the early years, which saw a Court and a Commission both composed of fifteen members, the comparison was even more easily drawn, with members of the Commission seeing it as "the equal of the International Court of Justice": YBILC 1949, p. 19, para. 45 (Scelle). See also, for example, YBILC 1951, Vol. I, p. 7, paras. 38–39 (Spiropoulos suggesting that members of the Commission should be accorded equal status with the judges of the Court, and calling for the Commission to have an independent structure, like that of the Court (while working in cooperation with the General Assembly)); H.W. Briggs, *The International Law Commission* (Cornell University Press 1965) 103 (detailing Hudson's suggestion to the General Assembly's Fifth (budget) Committee in 1949 that Commission members be treated, for purposes of the *per diem* fee, not as just another UN sub-commission, but on the same basis of ad hoc judges of the Court).

23 YBILC 1967, Vol. I, p. 88, para. 5 (Judge Fitzmaurice addressing the Commission); see also Y.-L. Liang, 'The First Session of the International Law Commission: Review of Its Work by the General Assembly', 44 AJIL (1950) 527 at 542. The statutes of both organs refer to a membership comprising persons of "recognized competence in international law": Statute of the International Court of Justice, article 2; Statute of the International Law Commission, article 2(1).

generalist perspective of international law (as opposed to a 'specialist' perspective grounded in a particular field of the discipline),[24] which commits them to a common conception of international law as a unified system and to supporting its universalist aspiration.[25] This shared profile, too, has incited the gravitational pull among the members of both institutions toward one another. As preceding chapters have demonstrated, they may well be said to form a visible college of international lawyers dedicated to a joint intellectual enterprise and continuously engaging in a process of communication and collaboration.[26]

Personal links have certainly been an important factor bolstering the close inter-institutional connection: some have observed that "relations between the International Law Commission and the International Court of Justice had evolved from a personal to an organic basis."[27] Here it is not only the cordial relationships among members of the two organs that have contributed to this result, but even more so the overlap of individuals who wore the hats of both codifier and judge. As we have seen, the number of persons who served on both the Court and the Commission is remarkable, and has not been without significance.[28] When recalling that engagement with codification as well as international adjudication by the very same international lawyers may be traced back to the earlier era of the PCIJ and the League of Nations Committee for the Progressive Codification of International Law,[29] the importance of this human factor in the advancement of both causes comes even further to the fore.

[24] See J. Crawford, 'Chance, Order, Change: The Course of International Law', 365 RdC (2013) 252 (suggesting that both the Court and the Commission, among the key institutions that shape international law, "continue to nudge international law in the direction of universality"); M. Andenas and E. Bjorge, 'Introduction', in M. Andenas and E. Bjorge (eds.), *A Farewell to Fragmentation: Reassertion and Convergence in International Law* (CUP 2015) 1 at 29 (referring to members of the two organs as "two totems of the 'specialist of the general'").

[25] Both organs do accept more localized tendencies in international law, but only to the extent that they "can be accommodated within the ordinary framework of international law": Crawford, *supra* note 24, at p. 249 (referring to the Court). For example, rules of particular customary international law (that apply only among a limited number of States) have been recognized in this way in both the Court's case-law and the Commission's conclusions on 'Identification of customary international law'.

[26] To borrow from O. Schachter, 'The Invisible College of International Lawyers', 72 *Northwestern University Law Review* (1977) 217–226.

[27] YBILC 1968, Vol. I, p. 162, para. 16 (Ago).

[28] Chapter 5, Section A.1.

[29] See Chapter 2, Section C.

Beyond the shared mission and personal links it is, of course, self-interest that binds the Court and the Commission together, as each side derives significant benefit from the work of the other and from maintaining a close inter-institutional cooperation. As already indicated, for both the Court and the Commission, deference to the findings of the other is generally easier than conducting an independent inquiry into the state of international law on any given question.[30] It also reduces the 'persuasion cost' and reinforces the legitimacy of a determination on the matter by making it appear as an objective outcome not dependent on the identity of the decision-maker.[31] Disregarding the stated position of the other might cause instability, by casting doubt on the status of the law on a certain question if not the methods of international law more broadly.[32]

There is, however, much more to it. For the Commission, the judicial application of the rules drafted by it clearly gives effect to the task that it is trying to accomplish: Sir Humphrey Waldock thus spoke in the late 1960s of "the very real importance of the Court as the international organ concerned with completing the work of codification on which the Commission was engaged."[33] This claim has taken on a whole new meaning with the Court's increasing recourse not only to conventional provisions based on the Commission's work, but also to propositions contained in the Commission's own output. In repeatedly turning to such propositions as authoritative statements of international law even without a seal of approval set upon them by States, the Court has contributed to a prevalent perception that the Commission's output is generally declaratory of existing law, unless there is compelling evidence that a

[30] See Chapter 3, Section D and Chapter 4, Section A.

[31] See also, more generally, F. Zarbiyev, 'Saying Credibly What the Law Is: On Marks of Authority in International Law', 9 JIDS (2018) 291 at 303.

[32] See Chapter 6, Section C.

[33] YBILC 1969, Vol. I, p. 72, para. 27 (adding that "in dealing with general principles of codification, the Commission had often found itself confronted with questions involving a mixture of fact and law and ... it then became very difficult to push codification of general rules further without encountering sharp divergences of opinion. It was at that point that the work of the Court in interpretation and application became an essential complement to the work of the Commission"); see also YBILC 1968, Vol. I, p. 162, para. 18 (Ago) and para. 22 (Sir Humphrey Waldock, saying that "[codification] would be established on surer foundations if the Court were able to fill out the work of the Commission").

particular proposition was introduced as *lex ferenda*.[34] By this, the Court has greatly advanced the Commission's persuasive authority and law-making potential.

More significantly still, the Court has given the Commission a momentous boost by making explicit in several of its decisions that the consolidation of emerging customary international law may well take place through the Commission's work, and by treating the reaction of Governments to that work as giving rise to, or evincing, the customary rules in force. In the *North Sea Continental Shelf* judgment, delivered as it was in the very same year that saw the conclusion of the last major law-making treaty based on the Commission's work, the Court expressly pointed out that determining the status of a certain rule under customary international law may depend "mainly on the processes that led the Commission to propose it."[35] In taking such a line and consistently maintaining it,[36] the Court has not only nudged States to give particular consideration to the Commission's work, it also has further encouraged the Commission's role in the development of customary international law alongside its role in generating treaties.

For the Court, too, the inter-institutional relationship affords considerable advantages. It will already be clear from previous chapters that the Commission's work has been invaluable to the Court in avoiding any declaration of *non liquet* and has appreciably promoted the acceptance of

[34] On the "lazy assumption, whether amongst writers, governments or even courts, that, merely because something is included in a proposal by the ILC, it is therefore international law – unless it has been specifically disapproved," see F. Berman, 'The ILC within the UN's Legal Framework: Its Relationship with the Sixth Committee', 49 GYIL (2006) 107 at 127, fn. 74. See also J. Crawford, 'The International Court of Justice and the Law of State Responsibility', in C.J. Tams and J. Sloan (eds.), *The Development of International Law by the International Court of Justice* (OUP 2013) 71 at 86 (referring in these terms to the Commission's articles on State responsibility, and adding that such a status took the Vienna Convention on the Law of Treaties thirty years to reach). For a broader perspective on "non-legislative codifications" as texts that the legal profession accepts as authoritative despite the fact that they have not been enacted by official law-making entities designated for that purpose by the relevant political community, see N. Jansen, *The Making of Legal Authority: Non-Legislative Codifications in Historical and Comparative Perspectives* (OUP 2010) 7–8.

[35] *North Sea Continental Shelf, Judgment, I.C.J. Reports 1969*, p. 3, at p. 38, para. 62.

[36] See, for example, *Continental Shelf (Tunisia/Libyan Arab Jamahiriya), Judgment, I.C.J. Reports 1982*, pp. 45–46, paras. 41–42; *Jurisdictional Immunities of the State (Germany* v. *Italy: Greece intervening), Judgment, I.C.J. Reports 2012*, p. 123, para. 55 and p. 135, para. 77; *Maritime Dispute (Peru* v. *Chile), Judgment, I.C.J. Reports 2014*, p. 47, para. 117.

its jurisdiction.[37] The Commission also proved useful to the Court in times of need, namely, in the harsh political aftermath of the 1966 *South West Africa* judgment and when the risks of fragmentation of international law loomed large.[38] More than that, however, the privileged position reserved for the Court's case-law in the Commission's output greatly enhances – if not effectively institutionalizes – the Court's role in the codification and progressive development of international law. Put differently, the systematic incorporation of the Court's pronouncements in the Commission's work product has served to expand their reach far beyond the contours of any given case. Rulings that concerned concrete situations, even novel or eccentric views of customary international law, have been taken up by the Commission for general application. Doing so ensures that the Court's judgments do not remain isolated but become integrated into (or cornerstones of) comprehensive legal regimes, thereby assisting the Court to deliver an impact far greater than the transactional settlement of discrete disputes.

The mutual benefit that accrues to both organs from cooperation has become ever more vital in an era where State interest in expanding the Court's compulsory jurisdiction, or in being bound by new multilateral conventions based on Commission drafts, appears mostly to be in decline.[39] The Court's recourse to the Commission's work products even without (or prior to) their transformation into binding treaties, in particular, has thrown the Commission a lifesaver, in that it sustains the Commission's relevance at a time when the utility of its efforts has openly been called into question.[40] Other tendencies threatening to undermine

[37] See Chapter 4, Section B.3.

[38] See, respectively, Chapter 5, Section B.1, and Chapter 4, Section A.3.

[39] An investigation into why that is so would go beyond the bounds of the present study; as the bibliography attached to it makes clear, however, literature on the topic is abundant.

[40] See also Pellet and Müller, *supra* note 11, at p. 962, MN 341 ("there might be some paradox in the World Court paying increasing attention to the ILC's work at a time when the Commission itself gives the impression of suffering an identity crisis and thus losing part of its prestige"). For other critical writings, see, for example, M. El Baradei, T.M. Franck and R. Trachtenberg, *The International Law Commission: The Need for a New Direction* (UNITAR 1981); K. Zemanek, 'Codification of International Law: Salvation or Dead End?', 1 *Le Droit International à l'Heure de sa Codification* (1987) 581–601; J. Dugard, 'How Effective Is the International Law Commission in the Development of International Law? A Critique of the International Law Commission on the Occasion of Its Fiftieth Anniversary', 23 SAYIL (1998) 34–44; C. Tomuschat, 'The International Law Commission – An Outdated Institution?', 49 GYIL (2006) 77–105. But see O. Sender and M. Wood, 'The Work of the International Law Commission between 1997 and 2022: A Positive Assessment', 25 MPYUNL (2022) 645–681.

general international law's reach and potential – not least the proliferation of specialized tribunals and ad hoc law-making efforts that appropriate particular fields of the discipline – have been a fertile ground for deeper inter-institutional cooperation as well.[41]

In these circumstances, it is hardly surprising that the Court and the Commission have made allies of one another, and that nurturing their special relationship is a principle guiding both institutions. By visibly promoting the work of one another or otherwise amplifying its effect, they have not only consecrated the standing and authority of the other, but also of their own.[42] The links uniting the Court and the Commission are thus strong not merely "because of the ways in which the work of the two bodies on particular issues have influenced each other,"[43] but ultimately because allowing for such influence helps maintain them both at the center of the international legal system.

B. The Special Relationship's Special Importance: Law Made by Judge and Company

The discussion above leads naturally into consideration of the broader impact produced by the special relationship between the Court and the Commission, especially in view of the model originally adopted for their operation.

As detailed in Chapter 2, the sovereign will of States was to play a fundamental role in international law-making for the legal system carefully put in place by States since the Peace of Westphalia, including when creating an international court under the League of Nations and the United Nations. This finds clear expression in article 38.1 of the Court's Statute, which – by referring to conventions "establishing rules

41 See also Chapter 4, Section A.3 with regard to the Commission's work on the topic 'Fragmentation of international law: Difficulties arising from the diversification and expansion of international law'.

42 See also Y. Chen, 'Structural Limitations and Possible Future of the Work of the International Law Commission', 9 CJIL (2010) 473, at 483, fn. 33 ("The cross-references to each other's work by the ILC and ICJ can be explained as a strategy of self-empowerment through mutual empowerment").

43 S.M. Schwebel, 'The Inter-active Influence of the International Court of Justice and the International Law Commission', in C.A. Armas Barea et al (eds.), *Liber Amicorum "In Memoriam" of Judge José María Ruda* (Kluwer Law International 2000) 479 at 480. In this sense it is equally misleading to suggest that the links between the Court and the Commission are strong "[d]espite their different functions" (*ibid* at 479; see also Crawford, *supra* note 34, at p. 74).

expressly recognized by the contesting states," international custom "as evidence of a general practice accepted as law," and "the general principles of law recognized by civilized nations" – establishes State consent as delineating "the outer limits" of the law's validity.[44] Article 38.1 further provides, in the same vein, that "judicial decisions and the teachings of the most highly qualified publicists of the various nations" are to serve merely as "subsidiary means for the determination of rules of law"; the underlying understanding was that "[d]octrine and jurisprudence no doubt do not create law."[45] The significance of State consent was further embodied in article 59 of the Court's Statute, according to which the Court's own decisions are to bind only the States parties to the contentious proceedings in question, and in respect of that particular case alone. The same sentiment was enshrined in the Commission's Statute, both by distinguishing between codification of existing law and its progressive development, and by placing in the hands of States in the General Assembly the ultimate decision as to whether any binding force may attach to the Commission's work.

The special relationship forged between the Court and the Commission since 1949 has put this basic tenet of the international legal system under considerable strain.

For a start, when accepting the pronouncements of the other as authoritative restatements of international law without verifying their foundation in actual State practice, the Court and the Commission circumvent the prescriptions of their constituent instruments. As we have seen, the work of both organs has been accorded a degree of authority that transcends the roles designated for such work in their respective statutes as only "subsidiary means." This departure may well explain both organs' discomfort in describing the work product of the other (as well as their own) in such terms.[46]

[44] S. Yee, 'Article 38 of the ICJ Statute and Applicable Law: Selected Issues in Recent Cases', 7 JIDS (2016) 472 at 474. For a deeper inquiry into the role of consent in the law referred to in article 38.1, see G. Fitzmaurice, 'Some Problems regarding the Formal Sources of International Law', in *Symbolae Verzijl: Présentées au professeur J.H.W. Verzijl à l'occasion de son LXX-ième anniversaire* (Martinus Nijhoff 1958) 153–176.

[45] See Chapter 2, Section B (quoting Baron Descamps); see also M.O. Hudson, *The Permanent Court of Justice 1920–1942* (Macmillan 1943) 612 ("Judicial decisions and the teachings of publicists are not rules to be applied, but sources to be resorted to for finding applicable rules").

[46] See Chapter 3, Section D and Chapter 4, Section B.1. It is indeed paradoxical that while both organs seek to promote (and operate within) the approach to law-finding enshrined in article 38.1 (including by treating one another as the *ne plus ultra* of the two categories

The Court and the Commission may of course assume that the output of the other is the result of careful consideration of material evidences of the law, as is often the case. But any uncritical deference to the propositions of the other remains questionable when bearing in mind that such propositions may not necessarily reflect the existing law. This is certainly the case as regards the Commission, which has long ago abandoned the distinction established in its Statute between codification and progressive development, and only rarely specifies whether a certain provision proposed by it falls into one or the other category.[47] Having by now plucked most of the low-hanging fruit of subjects that were ripe for codification, much of what it does, "in a real sense . . . is progressive development, although not necessarily seen or characterized as such."[48] Nor does the Court, when partaking of development of the law, always state the *lex lata* when asserting a non-treaty rule: as Hersch Lauterpacht wrote, "[m]any an act of judicial legislation may in fact be accomplished under the guise of the ascertainment of customary international law."[49] In these circumstances, for the Court or the Commission to adopt the position of the other without sufficient probing into its normative status may well amount to unduly according that position the force of law. This is strikingly illustrated by the several instances where decisions of the Court have drawn on the views of the Commission, which earlier had

referred to as "subsidiary means"), they essentially turn it on its head it when thwarting the notion of State consent that underlies it.

47 See also YBILC 1956, Vol. II, pp. 255–256, paras. 25–26.

48 D. McRae, 'The Work of the International Law Commission, 2007–2011: Progress and Prospects', 106 AJIL (2012) 322 at 324. See also D.M. McRae, 'The International Law Commission: Codification and Progressive Development after Forty Years', 25 CYIL (1987) 355 at 362.

49 H. Lauterpacht, *The Development of International Law by The International Court* (Stevens & Sons 1958) 368. See also Pellet and Müller, *supra* note 11, at p. 917, MN 236 ("it must be admitted at the same time that in some cases those assertions [by the Court] were made in regard to 'rules' [of customary international law] which are far from self-evident"). With the exception of relying on a treaty, the Court often simply asserts a rule without specifying the source of such law or by using the ambiguous term "general international law": M. Mendelson, 'The International Court of Justice and the Sources of International Law', in V. Lowe and M. Fitzmaurice (eds.), *Fifty Years of the International Court of Justice: Essays in Honour of Sir Robert Jennings* (CUP 1996) 63 at 64. See also R. Higgins, *Problems and Process: International Law and How We Use It* (Clarendon Press 1994) 37 (observing that the Court itself "often seems to approach the question of sources with a certain looseness").

supported those views by reference to the Court's decisions; one observer referred to such occurrences as "a normative Ponzi scheme."[50]

Concerns over undue reliance of this sort have been aggravated at a time when the Commission's formulations are increasingly designed to be contained not in treaties (that States may choose whether or not to become parties to) but in non-binding instruments. Recent decades have seen the Commission – whose success or failure was once measured by whether a general law-making treaty based on its work had been achieved – repeatedly favoring the pursuit either of expository codes (using such terms as "guidelines," "conclusions," "principles," and the like), or of draft articles that it does not recommend to the General Assembly for formulation as a new convention.[51] One well-known example is the draft articles on State responsibility – dealing as they do with "that most traditional and yet most elusive, unsettled and intractable problem which lies at the very core of any notion of an international law"[52] – which the Commission in 2001 sent to the General Assembly with the recommendation that it simply take note of them and consider only at a later stage the possibility of concluding a convention on their basis.[53] Other examples include the draft articles on the effects of armed

[50] S. Villalpando, 'On the International Court of Justice and the Determination of Rules of Law', 26 LJIL (2013) 243 at 248 (also referring to an "autocatalytic process" by which the consolidation of legal regimes is achieved through informal channels in the absence of formal negotiation by Governments). See also N. Krisch, 'The Dynamics of International Law Redux', 74 *Current Legal Problems* (2021) 269 at 294 (referring to the Commission's frequent reference to the Court's decisions and the Court's reliance, in turn, on the Commission's work, as "a citation cartel"); C.J. Tams, 'The ICJ as a "Law-Formative Agency": Summary and Synthesis', in C.J. Tams and J. Sloan, *The Development of International Law by the International Court of Justice* (OUP 2013) 377 at 386 (referring to the Commission as the Court's "partner in legal development"); F.R. Tesón, 'Fake Custom', in B. Lepard (ed.), *Reexamining Customary International Law* (CUP 2017) 86 at 96 (suggesting that citing a false proposition of customary international law may be referred to as a "corrupt pedigree fallacy").

[51] For more detailed accounts of this paradigm shift, see, for example, J. Katz Cogen, 'The Changing Form of the International Law Commission's Work', 108 *AJIL Unbound* (2014) 4–7; F.L. Bordin, 'Reflections of Customary International Law: The Authority of Codification Conventions and ILC Draft Articles in International Law', 63 ICLQ (2014) 535–567; and N.Y. Morris-Sharma, 'The ILC's Draft Articles before the 69th Session of the UNGA: A Reawakening?', 7 *Asian Journal of International Law* (2017) 1–12.

[52] R.Y. Jennings, 'Recent Developments in the International Law Commission: Its Relation to the Sources of International Law', 13 ICLQ (1964) 385 at 396.

[53] For a close examination of the endgame of the Commission's forty-plus year work on the topic, see D.D. Caron, 'The ILC Articles on State Responsibility: The Paradoxical Relationship between Form and Authority', 96 AJIL (2002) 857 at 861–866. See also

conflict on treaties; the draft articles on the responsibility of international organizations; the draft articles on expulsion of aliens; the guiding principles applicable to unilateral declarations of States capable of creating legal obligations; and the draft conclusions on subsequent agreements and subsequent practice in relation to interpretation of treaties.

The turn by the Commission to such "codification light," as it has been called,[54] came no doubt in response to the declining interest among States in taking upon themselves new treaty obligations, and the failure of even widely ratified conventions to achieve universal adherence.[55] But it may also be attributed to the awareness within the Commission that because of the Court's recurring recourse to its output, there was little merit in the view according to which its efforts would be "wasted if, after some five or ten years of work, a broad majority of states in the General Assembly cannot be persuaded to support the draft or to convene an international diplomatic conference to conclude a convention on the subject."[56] Such awareness has been evolving since the days of the *North Sea Continental Shelf* cases,[57] but it was after the Court's

J. Crawford and S. Olleson, 'The Continuing Debate on a UN Convention on State Responsibility', 54 ICLQ (2005) 959–971.

54 S. Villalpando, 'Codification Light: A New Trend in the Codification of International Law at the United Nations', 8 *Anuario brasileiro de direito internacional* (2013) 117–155.

55 See also, for example, R. Higgins, 'The United Nations at 70 Years: The Impact upon International Law', 65 ICLQ (2016) 1 at 2. Suggestions that the Commission should turn to codification by instruments other than treaties, given the delays in ratification of (or accession to) the conventions proposed by it, were voiced beginning in the early 1970s, but clearly left it to States to then determine the fate of the instrument chosen: see, for example, YBILC 1974, Vol. I, pp. 68–69, paras. 18–19 (Suy, the United Nations Legal Counsel); M. El Baradei, T.M. Franck, and R. Trachtenberg, 'The International Law Commission: The Need for a New Direction', 1 *Policy and Efficacy Studies* (1981) 11 at 26–27; McRae, 'The International Law Commission', *supra* note 48, at pp. 361–366. Jessup suggested in 1970 (when serving as a member of the Court) that the Court might apply the rules enshrined in a treaty based on the Commission's work even where its conclusion or entry into force may be delayed, but only if the parties concerned had so agreed: P.C. Jessup, 'To form a more perfect United Nations', 129 RdC (1970) 22.

56 B. Graefrath, 'The International Law Commission Tomorrow: Improving Its Organization and Methods of Work', 85 AJIL (1991) 595 at 600.

57 See, for example, YBILC 1968, Vol. I, p. 197, para. 75 (Yasseen); YBILC 1972, Vol. I, pp. 29–30, paras. 38–40 (Sir Humphrey Waldock suggesting that the difficulty of ratification taking a long time was "inherent in the method of using as an instrument of codification a multilateral treaty of the ordinary kind," but that this "did not seriously diminish the value of the work of codification," also because the Court may treat provisions of such instruments as an expression of rules of international law already in force); M. Šahović, 'The Present Stage in the Activities of the UN International Law Commission', 1 *Jugoslovenska Revija za Međunarodno Pravo* (1980) 85 at 87; and, more

remarkable reliance on the Commission's work in the *Gabčíkovo-Nagymaros Project* judgment[58] that Lukashuk told his colleagues in Geneva that "[w]e were witnessing a new trend in the progressive development of international law: the Commission stated the rule which it believed existed or should exist and the ICJ recognized the rule as a norm of positive international law."[59] President Schwebel soon confirmed this observation, saying that the Court's recurring practice of recognizing as positive international law various rules adopted by the Commission in the belief that they were – or should be – part of international law, "accelerated the incorporation of the work product of the Commission into the body of customary international law."[60] This echoes the suggestion voiced almost a century ago by the U.S. member of the Committee for the Progressive Codification of International Law, who observed that restatements of the law seeking to assist the World Court "might be a less difficult method [for codification] than one which

recently, the observation by Valencia-Ospina, as Special Rapporteur on the topic 'Protection of persons in the event of disasters', that "[t]he draft articles are not, in themselves, binding. Their binding effect would result from their being embodied in an international convention or judicially proclaimed to be rules of customary international law": UN Doc. A/CN.4/697: 'Eighth Report on the Protection of Persons in the Event of Disasters by Eduardo Valencia-Ospina, Special Rapporteur' (2016), para. 410.

58 See Chapter 3, Section A.2.

59 YBILC 1999, Vol. I, p. 27, para. 47. The Commission indeed made it known already in 1974 that its success was not to be measured simply by those international instruments which had resulted from the its final drafts or reports during its first twenty-five years, as its work "had exercised a definite influence on the formation of legal opinion throughout the international community," including in the Court: YBILC 1974, Vol. II, Part One, p. 162, para. 17. In 1979, the President of the Court, Sir Humphrey Waldock, told Commission members that "[t]he success of the Commission's work was not to be measured solely in terms of the conventions it produced: at a time when not only the rules of international law, but the very structure of the international community, were undergoing an unprecedented evolution, the importance of the Commission's reports in consolidating legal opinion and furthering the general consensus in many branches of international law was a factor of the greatest consequence for the future security of international law": YBILC 1979, Vol. I, pp. 64–65, para. 9. Two years later, Judge El-Erian made it explicit that the Commission's work "was indeed useful to the Court even before it became an international convention," for being illustrative of customary international law: YBILC 1981, Vol. I, p. 208, para. 5.

60 YBILC 1999, Vol. I, p. 124, para. 19. Judge Xue, writing in a personal capacity, has cautioned that "if a convention is prematurely adopted and few States would be willing to be bound by it, consequently, treaty provisions are likely to turn into dead letters. This is something that the ILC should try to avoid with its final products": H. Xue, 'The Role of the ILC's Work in Promoting Peace and Security – Definition and Evaluation', in G. Nolte (ed.), *Peace through International Law: The Role of the International Law Commission* (Springer 2009) 183 at 186.

sought the assent of Governments to formal agreements of International Law to be embodied in treaties."[61]

To be sure, the Commission's Statute does envisage the production of output other than draft conventions; one reason for providing therein for the method of scientific restatement was precisely the meager results that codification by international treaties had achieved up to that point.[62] Yet this scientific restatement was reserved for the "formulation and systematization of rules of international law in fields where there already has been extensive State practice, precedent and doctrine" – that is, for projects primarily concerned with codification of the law already in force.[63] Progressive development, on the other hand, was to be pursued by draft conventions,[64] so as to afford States the possibility of negotiating the rules contained therein before deciding whether they wish to be bound by them. When the Commission early on avoided the distinction between codification and progressive development as unworkable, it thus saw fit to put forward an outcome formally designated to be pursued as a treaty.[65] To employ the expository code where the Commission blends codification with progressive development of the law, however, "in a situation where no further State action is envisaged, and with the expectation that the draft articles will simply be seen as 'the law', potentially casts the Commission in the role of legislator."[66] It also erodes the crucial distinction between treaty and custom, and affords the Court a

[61] See Chapter 2, Section C (quoting Wickersham).

[62] See Chapter 2, Section D.2.

[63] See Statute of the International Law Commission (1947), articles 15, 20. When completing such a project by preparing a final draft and explanatory report, the Commission may recommend to the General Assembly that it either (a) take no action; (b) take note of or adopt the report by resolution; (c) recommend the draft to members with a view to the conclusion of a convention; or (d) convoke a conference to conclude a convention (*ibid*, at article 23(1)).

[64] *Ibid*, at article 15.

[65] See, for example, YBILC 1956, Vol. II, pp. 255–256, paras. 25–27 (recognizing that in the circumstances of doing away with the distinction between codification and progressive development in its work on the law of the sea, "in order to give effect to the project as a whole, it will be necessary to have recourse to conventional means"). The Commission also considered that giving States an opportunity to participate directly in the formulation of the law would be more effective for its consolidation: YBILC 1962, Vol. II, p. 160, para. 17 (justifying its decision to favor a convention on the law of treaties rather than an expository code); see also F. Vallat, 'The Work of the International Law Commission on the Law of Treaties', 22 NILR (1975) 327 at 336.

[66] S.D. Murphy, 'Codification, Progressive Development, or Scholarly Analysis? The Art of Packaging the ILC's Work Product', in M. Ragazzi (ed.), *Responsibility of International Organizations: Essays in Memory of Sir Ian Brownlie* (Brill 2013) 29 at 35. See also Katz

controlling function originally reserved for States in terms of determining that the purported codification correctly expresses the existing international law.[67]

The original systemic design adopted by States has been upended in yet another significant way. If the drafters of the Commission's Statute considered it elementary that the Court would abstain from giving any opinion on the Commission's working drafts, and that the Commission itself would never approach the Court for such a purpose,[68] that underlying understanding has been lost in time. As we have seen, the two bodies maintain a constant dialogue concerning the process of codification and progressive development of the law, including by the Court's occasional recourse (and attribution of significant weight) to the Commission's unfinished work as evidence of the current state of the law. This is yet another avenue by which the Court has effectively taken part in a feedback loop reserved for States, albeit in a "less direct and more subtle" way.[69]

States, for their part, seem largely unmoved by the current situation, for which a large share of the responsibility may be laid squarely at their own feet – if only for their appearing to acquiesce in it.[70] The failure of a

Cogen, *supra* note 51, at p. 7; K. Daugirdas, 'The International Law Commission Reinvents Itself?', 108 *AJIL Unbound* (2014) 79 at 80; Caron, *supra* note 53, at p. 866.

67 See also A. Pellet, 'Conclusions générales', in *Colloque d'aix-en-Provence: La codification du droit international* (Pedone 1999) 329 at 339 (agreeing with a statement attributed to Judge Guillaume, according to which the Court "était un « vérificateur » de la solidité de la codification" by the Commission); A. Watts, M. Wood, and O. Sender, 'Codification and Progressive Development of International Law', in MPEPIL (2021), para. 21 ("Reluctant itself to make clear distinctions between those parts of its draft articles which involve codification and those parts which involve progressive development, the ILC has been content to allow others – particularly judicial tribunals, and notably the ICJ – to determine, if necessary and on a case-by-case basis, into which category particular provisions fall"); Villalpando, *supra* note 54, at pp. 153–154. As Murphy explains, in sending forward its draft articles without any recommendation that they be transformed into a convention, the Commission preempts a situation in which a decision by States not to pursue a convention despite a recommendation of the Commission to that effect would imply that the Commission's work was not acceptable to them because it failed to capture properly the law concerning that topic: Murphy, *supra* note 66, at p. 34.

68 See Chapter 2, Section D.2.

69 J. Crawford, 'The ILC's Articles on Responsibility of States for Internationally Wrongful Acts: A Retrospect', 96 AJIL (2002) 874 at 875.

70 Judge Gaja, for example, considered that the General Assembly "seemingly encouraged these references [by the Court to the Commission's draft articles on State responsibility before their final adoption] by annexing the articles to its resolution 56/83 and 'recommending them to the attention of Governments, without prejudice to the question of

meaningful oversight role exercised by the General Assembly's Sixth (Legal) Committee, in particular,[71] has no doubt facilitated the strengthening of relations between the Commission and the Court. Moreover, States have kept some of the Commission's draft articles lodged in the General Assembly by repeatedly deferring a decision as to their final form;[72] and have typically "commended" the Commission's output to the attention of States after removing the word 'draft', which had hitherto "denoted the subsidiary status of the Commission's text and the role of the Commission itself."[73]

their future adoption or other appropriate action"': G. Gaja, 'Interpreting Articles Adopted by the International Law Commission', 85 BYIL (2015) 10 at 11. On the limited capacity of States to react to the work of the Court and the Commission, see, for example, D. Bethlehem, 'The Secret Life of International Law', 1 CJICL (2012) 23 at 32–33; D. Tladi, 'The Fate of the Draft Articles on State Responsibility: Act Soon or Face the Further Erosion of the Role of States in the International Law-Making Process', APDI 2013 (2015) 87 at 91. See also S. Sivakumaran, 'Beyond States and Non-State Actors: The Role of State-Empowered Entities in the Making and Shaping of International Law', 55 *Columbia Journal of Transnational Law* (2017) 343 at 393. On some possible signs of "reawakening" among States, see Morris-Sharma, *supra* note 51.

71 For the observation that "States do not show a serious interest in the work of the Commission," see A. Pellet, 'Between Codification and Progressive Development of the Law: Some Reflections from the ILC', 6 *International Law Forum du droit international* (2004) 15 at 19; McRae, 'The International Law Commission', *supra* note 48, at pp. 365–366. One may recall Lauterpacht's words of admonition, according to which "[a] government which proclaims its devotion to an object of international endeavor and co-operation and which at the same time fails in its duty to make the best contribution, in so far as it lies with it, to the membership of the organ concerned, lays itself open to a charge of contradictory conduct inimical to international interest. It is probable that this aspect of governmental action or omission constitutes, as a matter of moral duty and international trust, one of the crucial problems of international organization in general": H. Lauterpacht, 'Codification and Development of International Law', 49 AJIL (1955) 16 at 40.

72 See also M. Wood, 'The General Assembly and the International Law Commission: What Happens to the Commission's Work and Why?', in I. Buffard et al (eds.), *International Law between Universalism and Fragmentation: Festschrift in Honour of Gerhard Hafner* (Brill 2008) 373, at 382–386 (explaining the various considerations that may be applicable to choice of form); Tomuschat, *supra* note 40, at p. 91 (observing that "[o]n the whole, States seem to have become rather tired of the tight network of international obligations which progressively restrict their sovereign freedom of action. Therefore, they do not hasten to bring new treaties into force, rather being inclined to watch for a considerable number of years what advantages they may expect of formal acceptance of the instrument concerned which they, in any event, often resort to as guideline for their conduct").

73 J. Katz Cogen, 'The Decline of "Drafts"', 11 IOLR (2014) 1 at 3–4 (adding that "the deletion of that term suggests that the Assembly no longer considers the Commission's work provisional in nature . . . Dropping the word 'draft' eliminated the insinuation that the texts were necessarily preliminary to a future treaty-drafting exercise (where they

The result, to use Jeremy Bentham's catchphrase, is law made by "Judge and Company."[74] The inherent malleability of custom as unwritten law, coupled with the chronic difficulty of upholding in practice the conceptual distinction between codification and progressive development, leave the Court and the Commission with significant discretion in saying what the law is. It allows both organs to relegate to "customary international law" rules that they consider to be important, even where no general practice accepted as law has been identified. When one of them endorses as authoritative such a proposition of the other, the effect may then be that the rule contained in such a proposition passes into the stream of international law without meeting the requisite of State consent. What were meant to be "pre-normative instruments"[75] (in the case of the Commission's output) or case-specific pronouncements binding only on the parties thereto (in the case of the Court's decisions) thus infiltrate the general process of international law-making and soon

would undergo revisions), and hence that they should not be considered on their own terms... The decline of 'drafts' is a constitutive change. It has turned the International Law Commission into the finalizer of international legal texts (not just their originator), replacing the collective law-making by states that once occurred in diplomatic conferences").

74 J. Bentham, in J. Bowring (ed.), *The Works of Jeremy Bentham*, Vol. V (William Tait 1843) 369 (referring, in a wholly different context and in a critical manner not at all intended by the present author, to joint endeavors by the bench and the bar). One may here recall the view put forward by Judge Alvarez back in 1950: "... In future, it is to the General Assembly of the United Nations, to the International Court of Justice and to the jurists that we shall look, more than to anyone, for the creation of the new international law. Consequently, whether in regard to old questions which assume new aspects, or in regard to entirely new questions, the Court has to give decisions, not in accordance with traditional international law – that would be an anomaly – but in accordance with the international law which is now emerging and which the court itself is able to create. It might be said that this law is merely *lex ferenda* and not an existing law at the present time; but both these types of law coincide. In many cases, so far as the Court is concerned, the task of determining, establishing and applying the law go hand in hand": *Competence of Assembly regarding Admission to the United Nations, Advisory Opinion: I.C. J. Reports 1950*, p. 13 (Dissenting Opinion).

75 G. Hafner, 'The International Law Commission and the Future Codification of International Law', 2 *ILSA Journal of International & Comparative Law* (1996) 671 at 676. See also M. Reisman, 'Metamorphoses: Judge Shingeru Oda and the International Court of Justice', 33 CYIL (1995) 185 at 203 (saying the Commission has "no competence to bind States by its *ipse dixit* because the Assembly simply does not have that power to delegate").

exercise direct influence as law.[76] With the subsidiary character of the output of the Court and the Commission being lost, legal opinion essentially claims the rank of binding legal authority, challenging the exclusive power of States in the creation of international law.

Granted, both the Court and the Commission enjoy an aura of authority by themselves, and their statements of law carry great weight on their own.[77] It is the endorsements of their output by one another, however, that effectively removes the shackles purposely placed upon that output by their respective mandates, as the normative labeling of customary international law makes the rule in question opposable to all States irrespective of article 59 of the Court's Statute or the procedures laid down in that of the Commission. Such interaction between the Court and the Commission may allow them to give less careful consideration to the balance between making substantial progress and achieving wide acceptance among States. It also legitimates their legal propositions and law-making more generally, especially as authority in international law "is not coextensive with formal juridical competence; it is a socially sanctioned deference entitlement."[78]

[76] There are numerous examples of the great extent to which the propositions of the Court and the Commission are later cited in legal practice, including by domestic and international courts and tribunals, as authoritative statements of the law. In the context of State responsibility, for example, see UN Docs. A/62/62 and Corr.1 and Add.1, A/65/76, A/68/72, and A/71/80. One rather astonishing statement in this regard is attributed to the UN Legal Counsel, Corell, who said, following the adoption of the draft articles on State responsibility, that "[t]he published articles now formed part of international law and a basis for decision-making by ICJ and other bodies throughout the world": YBILC 2002, Vol. I, p. 84, para. 2.

[77] This is particularly true of the Court. Judge Jessup has observed that "the influence of the Court's decisions is wider than their binding force": *Barcelona Traction, Light and Power Company, Limited, Judgment, I.C.J. Reports 1970*, p. 163, para. 9 (Separate Opinion).

[78] Zarbiyev, *supra* note 31, at p. 313 (adding that, as such, authority "may exist in the absence of a formal juridical competence or on top of it"). The bureaucratization (in the Weberian sense) of international society, which increases the authority of specialists as well as their use of that authority in order to shape the world around them, provides an appropriate setting for such an impact: see P. Allott, 'State Responsibility and the Unmaking of International Law', 29 HILJ (1988) 1 at 9–11 (referring to codification by the Commission as symbolizing such bureaucratization); M. Barnett and M. and Finnemore, *Rules for the World: International Organizations in Global Politics* (Cornell University Press 2004) (discussing international organizations more broadly, and referring also to the phenomenon of mission creep in bureaucracies); M. Finnemore and S.J. Toope, 'Alternatives to "Legalization": Richer Views of Law and Politics', 55 *International Organization* (2001) 743 at 750–751. For Schachter's observation that "the expression of an international consensus by the professional community may well have a persuasive effect in many cases," see Schachter, *supra* note 26, at p. 221.

Several members of the Commission, writing in their private capacity, have pointed to this reality as well, if only in terms of the expansion of the Commission's impact. Sir Michael Wood, for example, has called the Commission a "potentially dangerous place," explaining that "[i]t is not dangerous in itself; it is the attitude of others, including courts and tribunals, that make it so, in the sense that undue homage is sometimes paid to its work, whether that work is good, bad or indifferent, and whatever stage it has reached."[79] In the same vein, Professor Dire Tladi has observed that "[t]he problem is that the reverence with which the [Commission's] product is held has had the effect of excluding the State, the principal international law-maker, from the law-making process."[80] These reflections bring to mind the debates of the past yet again, in particular the concern voiced in 1947 within the Committee of Seventeen that without sufficient input from Governments, codification may become "a monopoly of the fifteen scientists of the ILC [while] it was a basic principle of the Charter of the United Nations that this organization was not a super-State."[81]

The exercise of public authority without a correlating mandate is but one legality concern arising from the Court and the Commission acquiring de facto the role of legislators.[82] Another is the blurring of judicial and legislative endeavors, which was indeed originally sought to be avoided. Equally unsettling is the erosion of the essential distinction between actual and desirable law, a distinction without which "any present law cannot be held as a constraining factor in social decision."[83]

[79] M. Wood, '"Weighing" the Articles on Responsibility of International Organizations', in M. Ragazzi (ed.), *Responsibility of International Organizations: Essays in Memory of Sir Ian Brownlie* (Brill 2013) 55 at 65 (adding that "[i]t is entirely understandable that the Commission should heed the International Court of Justice; it is perhaps less understandable that the International Court should heed the Commission. The Court's decisions are authoritative. The Commission's output is normally less so").

[80] Tladi, *supra* note 70, at p. 91.

[81] UN Doc. A/AC.10/SR.27: 'Summary Record of the Twenty-Seventh Meeting of the Committee on the Progressive Development and Its Codification' (13 June 1947), p. 7 (Bartoš).

[82] See also Bordin, *supra* note 51, at pp. 562–563 (referring to the Commission and pointing to the paradox of jeopardizing basic elements of the rule of law in an effort to enhance the rule of law in international affairs).

[83] M. Koskenniemi, *From Apology to Utopia: The Structure of International Legal Argument* (CUP 1989) 209.

Additional concerns arise as well. First, legislative policy is generally held to be a matter far too political to be decided just by the lawyers.[84] Even if the Court and the Commission do generally wish to enlist the support of Governments for their work, any juridical thinking that is divorced from actual State interests might again "challenge the traditional checks and balances in international law-making, which was mainly achieved through international conventions negotiated by governments and customary international law, with its two constitutive elements of State practice and (State) *opinio juris.*"[85] (Suggestions that members of the Court and the Commission are politically unaccountable, however, are not wholly accurate, as the electoral processes for their election and reelection are profoundly political.) To this it may be added that the pattern according to which members of the Commission go on to become judges of the Court has been said to have "certainly served to concentrate influence over the development of international law within too few hands."[86]

Second, there is the danger that the close alignment between the Court and the Commission might impinge upon their institutional independence. Beyond the repeated reciprocal endorsement of the each other's output, mention has already been made of the Commission's reluctance to make changes to draft provisions that had been held by the Court to reflect existing law,[87] as well as the conscious effort by the two organs to

[84] See also Pellet, *supra* note 71, at pp. 16–17 ("It would be absolutely disastrous and extremely arrogant that [members of the Commission] assume the role of a legislator; 'codification makers' they are; law-makers (even quasi-legislators) they are not… legal development is, globally, something much too serious to be entrusted to lawyers"); Schachter, *supra* note 26, at p. 226 (raising such problems more generally in connection with the role played by international lawyers as a professional community in the process of creating new law and in extending existing law to meet emerging needs). On the sharp differences expressed before the Commission began its work, on the question whether codification of international law should be a scientific or political task, see O. Schachter, *International Law in Theory and Practice* (Martinus Nijhoff 1991) 66–68.

[85] S. Villalpando, 'The "Invisible College of International Lawyers" Forty Years Later', *European Society of International Law Conference Paper Series*, Paper No. 5/2013 (2013), available at <https://papers.ssrn.com/sol3/papers.cfm?abstract_id=2363640##>, p. 14. The Commission, for its part, not infrequently chooses not to accept suggestions made by States: see also Tladi, *supra* note 70, at p. 92 (referring, as an example, to the draft articles on 'Expulsion of aliens').

[86] C. Chinkin, 'Enhancing the International Law Commission's Relationship with Other Law-Making Bodies and Relevant Academic and Professional Institutions', in *Making Better International Law: The International Law Commission at 50* (United Nations 1998) 333 at 338.

[87] See Chapter 3, Section A.2.

avoid or downplay any divergence of views between them.[88] Such 'bootstrapping', by which the Court or the Commission defer to the position of the other without challenge, might prove adverse to the fulfillment of their distinct functions and, in particular, jeopardize any genuine efforts at progressive development of the law.[89]

All this leads to the question whether the impact jointly assumed by the Court and the Commission beyond the parameters initially drawn for them may nevertheless be seen as legitimate, even desirable. The answer – and here we come full circle to the principle still formally underlying all international law-making – lies with the consent of States. As long as an international legislature in a full-blown sense remains unacceptable to the members of the international society, the Court and the Commission can serve as an effective machinery for the development of international law where the prospects of multilateral action are dim: this is, indeed, precisely the void that they have sought to fill. If States are fully aware of the way in which these two organs interact – as hopefully this study may better enable them to be – they could then exercise greater caution and control, thus retaining their sovereign right to shape the law that guides their international dealings.

C. Conclusion

Having come to the end of our examination of the relationship between the Court and the Commission as it has been shaped through decades of coexistence, we may now endeavor briefly to set out the main conclusions that emerge from it.

The Court and the Commission are both the products of a two-century effort to advance the rule of law in international affairs, and the roots of their relationship are thus found deep in the historical experience of international law. Indeed, the long-standing movements for a world court and for a world code were not unrelated: both endorsed the notion that the judicial settlement of international disputes and the codification (and development) of international law would ideally go hand in hand. Any evaluation today of the relationship between the Court and the Commission must take account of this rich historical context. It should

[88] See Chapter 6, Section B.
[89] See Chapter 6, Section C.

also recognize that both organs were configured so as to make States their partners in making international law more definite, and that at the dawn of the United Nations it was clearly understood that a certain distance would no doubt be maintained between the jurists in Geneva working to reduce the law of nations to writing, and those at The Hague who would administer it.

Inquiry into the work of the Court and the Commission reveals, however, that the original vision for their interaction was either forgotten or quietly set aside. The recurring reciprocal action, by which the Commission builds on the rules pronounced by the Court, and the Court, in turn, endorses in its decisions the Commission's formulations, is only the tip of the iceberg, and goes beyond the protection of the prerogatives of a collateral UN organ. In fact, the Court and the Commission have maintained a deeper and more subtle dialogue that has profoundly influenced their output. Both on and beyond the printed page of their work product, they have jointly been able to establish a highly developed body of international law, brushing aside not only the distinction between codification and progressive development, but also the rank formally accorded by States to their respective pronouncements as mere evidence of customary international law.

The special relationship forged between the Court and the Commission has thus been a partnership for a purpose.[90] In an international society that differs greatly from the one into which they were born, where States have less recourse to them than initially envisaged, the two bodies have turned to one another in order to advance their causes and to deliver a greater impact. By often treating the pronouncements of the other as immutable statements of the law, they have together affected a significant expansion of their authority, constructed much of the vocabulary for international relations, and in effect created a short-circuited method of law-making.

Even if the activities of the Court and the Commission remain intrinsically linked with the trust that States place in them, the original design of both institutions, which sought to guarantee that no agency could impose its will on States, has been modified over time. States may well

[90] To borrow once again a description of the US–UK relationship, here by British Prime Minister Gordon Brown, quoted in W. Wallace and C. Phillips, 'Reassessing the Special Relationship', 85 *International Affairs* (2009) 263.

decide to exercise greater control in the future, and reclaim their role in shaping the law that binds them. Yet they should also bear in mind that in the persistent absence of any central organ of formal legislative authority in the international legal system, the special relationship between the Court and the Commission has emerged as a rather constructive means for modifying and supplementing a body of law that must surely continue to evolve in order to remain effective.

* * * * * * * * * *

Annex 1

Statute of the International Court of Justice (*excerpts*)

Article 1

The International Court of Justice established by the Charter of the United Nations as the principal judicial organ of the United Nations shall be constituted and shall function in accordance with the provisions of the present Statute.

Chapter I
Organization of the Court

Article 2

The Court shall be composed of a body of independent judges, elected regardless of their nationality from among persons of high moral character, who possess the qualifications required in their respective countries for appointment to the highest judicial offices, or are jurisconsults of recognized competence in international law.

Article 16

1. No member of the Court may exercise any political or administrative function, or engage in any other occupation of a professional nature.
2. Any doubt on this point shall be settled by the decision of the Court.

Chapter II
Competence of the Court

Article 38

1. The Court, whose function is to decide in accordance with international law such disputes as are submitted to it, shall apply:

   a. international conventions, whether general or particular, establishing rules expressly recognized by the contesting states;

b. international custom, as evidence of a general practice accepted as law;
c. the general principles of law recognized by civilized nations;
d. subject to the provisions of Article 59, judicial decisions and the teachings of the most highly qualified publicists of the various nations, as subsidiary means for the determination of rules of law.

2. This provision shall not prejudice the power of the Court to decide a case *ex aequo et bono*, if the parties agree thereto.

Chapter III
Procedure

Article 59

The decision of the Court has no binding force except between the parties and in respect of that particular case.

Annex 2

Statute of the International Law Commission *(excerpts)*

Article 1

1. The International Law Commission shall have for its object the promotion of the progressive development of international law and its codification.
2. The Commission shall concern itself primarily with public international law, but is not precluded from entering the field of private international law.

Chapter I
Organization of the International Law Commission

Article 2

1. The Commission shall consist of thirty-four members who shall be persons of recognized competence in international law.
2. No two members of the Commission shall be nationals of the same State.
3. In case of dual nationality a candidate shall be deemed to be a national of the State in which he ordinarily exercises civil and political rights.

Chapter II
Functions of the International Law Commission

Article 15

In the following articles the expression "progressive development of international law" is used for convenience as meaning the preparation of draft conventions on subjects which have not yet been regulated by international law or in regard to which the law has not yet been sufficiently developed in the practice of States. Similarly, the expression "codification of international law" is used for convenience as meaning the more precise formulation and systematization of rules of international law in fields where there already has been extensive State practice, precedent and doctrine.

A. *Progressive Development of International Law*

Article 16

When the General Assembly refers to the Commission a proposal for the progressive development of international law, the Commission shall follow in general a procedure on the following lines:

(a) It shall appoint one of its members to be Rapporteur;
(b) It shall formulate a plan of work;
(c) It shall circulate a questionnaire to the Governments, and shall invite them to supply, within a fixed period of time, data and information relevant to items included in the plan of work;
(d) It may appoint some of its members to work with the Rapporteur on the preparation of drafts pending receipt of replies to this questionnaire;
(e) It may consult with scientific institutions and individual experts; these experts need not necessarily be nationals of Members of the United Nations. The Secretary-General will provide, when necessary and within the limits of the budget, for the expenses of these consultations of experts;
(f) It shall consider the drafts proposed by the Rapporteur;
(g) When the Commission considers a draft to be satisfactory, it shall request the Secretary-General to issue it as a Commission document. The Secretariat shall give all necessary publicity to this document which shall be accompanied by such explanations and supporting material as the Commission considers appropriate. The publication shall include any information supplied to the Commission in reply to the questionnaire referred to in subparagraph (c) above;
(h) The Commission shall invite the Governments to submit their comments on this document within a reasonable time;
(i) The Rapporteur and the members appointed for that purpose shall reconsider the draft, taking into consideration these comments, and shall prepare a final draft and explanatory report which they shall submit for consideration and adoption by the Commission;
(j) The Commission shall submit the draft so adopted with its recommendations through the Secretary-General to the General Assembly.

Article 17

1. The Commission shall also consider proposals and draft multilateral conventions submitted by Members of the United Nations, the principal organs of the United Nations other than the General Assembly, specialized agencies, or official bodies established by intergovernmental agreement to

encourage the progressive development of international law and its codification, and transmitted to it for that purpose by the Secretary-General.

2. If in such cases the Commission deems it appropriate to proceed with the study of such proposals or drafts, it shall follow in general a procedure on the following lines:

   (a) The Commission shall formulate a plan of work, and study such proposals or drafts, and compare them with any other proposals and drafts on the same subjects;
   (b) The Commission shall circulate a questionnaire to all Members of the United Nations and to the organs, specialized agencies and official bodies mentioned above which are concerned with the question, and shall invite them to transmit their comments within a reasonable time;
   (c) The Commission shall submit a report and its recommendations to the General Assembly. Before doing so, it may also, if it deems it desirable, make an interim report to the organ or agency which has submitted the proposal or draft;
   (d) If the General Assembly should invite the Commission to proceed with its work in accordance with a suggested plan, the procedure outlined in article 16 above shall apply. The questionnaire referred to in paragraph (c) of that article may not, however, be necessary.

B. *Codification of International Law*

Article 18

1. The Commission shall survey the whole field of international law with a view to selecting topics for codification, having in mind existing drafts, whether governmental or not.
2. When the Commission considers that the codification of a particular topic is necessary and desirable, it shall submit its recommendations to the General Assembly.
3. The Commission shall give priority to requests of the General Assembly to deal with any question.

Article 19

1. The Commission shall adopt a plan of work appropriate to each case.
2. The Commission shall, through the Secretary-General, address to Governments a detailed request to furnish the texts of laws, decrees, judicial decisions, treaties, diplomatic correspondence and other documents relevant to the topic being studied and which the Commission deems necessary.

Article 20

The Commission shall prepare its drafts in the form of articles and shall submit them to the General Assembly together with a commentary containing:

(a) Adequate presentation of precedents and other relevant data, including treaties, judicial decisions and doctrine;
(b) Conclusions defining: (i) The extent of agreement on each point in the practice of States and in doctrine; (ii) Divergencies and disagreements which exist, as well as arguments invoked in favour of one or another solution.

Article 21

1. When the Commission considers a draft to be satisfactory, it shall request the Secretary-General to issue it as a Commission document. The Secretariat shall give all necessary publicity to the document, including such explanations and supporting material as the Commission may consider appropriate. The publication shall include any information supplied to the Commission by Governments in accordance with article 19. The Commission shall decide whether the opinions of any scientific institution or individual experts consulted by the Commission shall be included in the publication.
2. The Commission shall request Governments to submit comments on this document within a reasonable time.

Article 22

Taking such comments into consideration, the Commission shall prepare a final draft and explanatory report, which it shall submit with its recommendations through the Secretary-General to the General Assembly.

Article 23

1. The Commission may recommend to the General Assembly:

   (a) To take no action, the report having already been published;
   (b) To take note of or adopt the report by resolution;
   (c) To recommend the draft to Members with a view to the conclusion of a convention;
   (d) To convoke a conference to conclude a convention.
2. Whenever it deems it desirable, the General Assembly may refer drafts back to the Commission for reconsideration or redrafting.

Article 24

The Commission shall consider ways and means for making the evidence of customary international law more readily available, such as the collection and publication of documents concerning State practice and of the decisions of national and international courts on questions of international law, and shall make a report to the General Assembly on this matter.

Chapter III
Cooperation with Other Bodies

Article 25

1. The Commission may consult, if it considers it necessary, with any of the organs of the United Nations on any subject which is within the competence of that organ.
2. All documents of the Commission which are circulated to Governments by the Secretary-General shall also be circulated to such organs of the United Nations as are concerned. Such organs may furnish any information or make any suggestions to the Commission.

Article 26

1. The Commission may consult with any international or national organizations, official or non-official, on any subject entrusted to it if it believes that such a procedure might aid it in the performance of its functions.
2. For the purpose of distribution of documents of the Commission, the Secretary-General, after consultation with the Commission, shall draw up a list of national and international organizations concerned with questions of international law. The Secretary-General shall endeavour to include on this list at least one national organization of each Member of the United Nations.
3. In the application of the provisions of this article, the Commission and the Secretary-General shall comply with the resolutions of the General Assembly and the other principal organs of the United Nations concerning relations with Franco Spain and shall exclude both from consultations and from the list, organizations which have collaborated with the nazis and fascists.
4. The advisability of consultation by the Commission with intergovernmental organizations whose task is the codification of international law, such as those of the Pan American Union, is recognized.

Annex 3

Members of the Court and the Commission Interviewed *(in alphabetical order)*

1. Mr. Ronny Abraham
2. Mr. Mohamed Bennouna
3. Mr. James Crawford
4. Ms. Joan Donoghue
5. Mr. Mathias Forteau
6. Mr. Giorgio Gaja
7. Mr. Mahmoud Hmoud
8. Ms. Marie Jacobsson
9. Mr. Maurice Kamto
10. Mr. Roman Kolodkin
11. Mr. Shinya Murase
12. Mr. Georg Nolte
13. Mr. Ki Gab Park
14. Mr. Stephen Schwebel
15. Mr. Bruno Simma
16. Mr. Dire Tladi
17. Mr. Peter Tomka
18. Mr. Eduardo Valencia-Ospina
19. Sir Michael Wood
20. Ms. Xue Hanqin

BIBLIOGRAPHY

Abi-Saab, G. 'Ensuring the Best Bench: Ways of Selecting Judges', presentation recorded in C. Peck and R.S. Lee (eds.), *Increasing the Effectiveness of the International Court of Justice: Proceedings of the ICJ/UNITAR Colloquium to Celebrate the 50th Anniversary of the Court* (Martinus Nijhoff 1997) 165.

Abraham, R. 'Presentation of the International Court of Justice over the Last Ten Years', 7 JIDS (2016) 297.

Adler, E. and Pouliot, V. 'International Practices', 3 *International Theory* (2011) 1.

Akande, D. 'Should the International Law Commission Overrule the ICJ in Its Articles on Immunity of State Officials from Foreign Criminal Jurisdiction?', *EJIL: Talk!* (5 August 2013), available at <www.ejiltalk.org/should-the-international-law-commission-overrule-the-icj-in-its-articles-on-immunity-of-state-officials-from-foreign-criminal-jurisdiction/>.

Allott, P. 'State Responsibility and the Unmaking of International Law', 29 HILJ (1988) 1.

Alschner, W. and Charlotin, D. 'The Growing Complexity of the International Court of Justice's Self-Citation Network', 29 EJIL (2018) 83.

Alvarez, A. 'Impressions Left by the First Hague Conference for the Codification of International Law', 16 *Transactions of the Grotius Society* (1931) 119.

'The Reconstruction and Codification of International Law', 1 *International Law Quarterly* (1947) 469.

Alvarez-Jiménez, A. 'Foreign Investors, Diplomatic Protection and the International Court of Justice's Decision on Preliminary Objections in the *Diallo* Case', 33 *North Carolina Journal of International Law and Commercial Regulation* (2008) 437.

Anand, R.P. 'Enhancing the Acceptability of Compulsory Procedures of International Dispute Settlement', 5 MPYUNL (2001) 1.

Andenas, M. 'Reassertion and Transformation: From Fragmentation to Convergence in International Law', 46 GJIL (2015) 685.

Andenas, M. and Bjorge, E. (eds.) *A Farewell to Fragmentation: Reassertion and Convergence in International Law* (CUP 2015).

Andenas, M. and Leiss, J.R. 'The Systemic Relevance of "Judicial Decisions" in Article 38 of the ICJ Statute', 77 *Zeitschrift für ausländisches öffentliches Recht und Völkerrecht* (2017) 907.

Anderson, M.R. et al (eds.) *The International Law Commission and the Future of International Law* (BIICL 1998).

Arsanjani, M.H. 'The United Nations and International Law-Making', 362 RdC (2013) 9.

Aust, H.P. 'The Normative Environment for Peace: On the Contribution of the ILC's Articles on State Responsibility', in G. Nolte (ed.), *Peace through International Law: The Role of the International Law Commission* (Springer 2009) 13.

Barnett, M. and Finnemore, M. 'The Politics, Power, and Pathologies of International Organizations', 53 *International Organization* (1999) 699.

Rules for the World: International Organizations in Global Politics (Cornell University Press 2004).

Baylis, E. 'The International Law Commission's Soft Law Influence', 13 *FIU Law Review* (2019) 1007.

Bederman, D.J. 'Counterintuiting Countermeasures', 96 AJIL (2002) 817.

Bekker, P.H.F. *World Court Decisions at the Turn of the Millennium (1997–2001)* (Martinus Nijhoff 2002).

Berman, F. 'The ILC within the UN's Legal Framework: Its Relationship with the Sixth Committee', 49 GYIL (2006) 107.

'The International Court of Justice as an "Agent" of Legal Development?', in C.J. Tams and J. Sloan (eds.), *The Development of International Law by the International Court of Justice* (OUP 2013) 7.

'Authority in International Law', KFG Working Paper Series, No. 22, Berlin Potsdam Research Group (2018), available at <https://publishup.uni-potsdam.de/opus4-ubp/frontdoor/deliver/index/docId/42284/file/kfg_wps22.pdf>.

Bethlehem, D. 'The Secret Life of International Law', 1 CJICL (2012) 23.

Bishop, W.W. 'General Course of Public International Law', 115 RdC (1965) 147.

Bodeau-Livinec, P. 'Circumstances Precluding Wrongfulness', in S. Forlati, M.M. Mbengue and B. McGarry (eds.), *The Gabčíkovo-Nagymaros Judgment and Its Contribution to the Development of International Law* (Brill 2020) 131.

Bordin, F.L. 'Reflections of Customary International Law: The Authority of Codification Conventions and ILC Draft Articles in International Law', 63 ICLQ (2014) 535.

Boyle, A. and Chinkin, C. *The Making of International Law* (OUP 2007).

Bradley, C.A. and Kelley, J.G. 'The Concept of International Delegation', 71 *Law and Contemporary Problems* (2008) 1.

Brierly, J.L. *The Law of Nations* (OUP 1928).

'The Future of Codification', 12 BYIL (1931) 1.

Briggs, H.W. 'Official Interest in the Work of the International Law Commission: Replies of Governments to Requests for Information or Comment', 48 AJIL (1954) 603.

The International Law Commission (Cornell University Press 1965).

Buergenthal, T. 'Lawmaking by the ICJ and Other International Courts', 103 PASIL (2009) 403.

Caminos, H. 'The Growth of Specialized International Tribunals and the Fears of Fragmentation of International Law', in N. Boschiero et al (eds.), *International Courts and the Development of International Law* (T.M.C. Asser Press 2013) 55.

Candioti, E. 'Comment: International Law of Shared Natural Resources and Peace', in G. Nolte (ed.), *Peace through International Law: The Role of the International Law Commission* (Springer 2009) 151.

Cannizzaro, E. et al (eds.) *Decisions of the ICJ as Sources of International Law?*, Gaetano Morelli Lecture Series, Vol. 2 (International and European Papers Publishing 2018).

Carlston, K.S. 'Draft Convention on Arbitral Procedure of the International Law Commission', 48 AJIL (1954) 296.

Caron, D.D. 'The ILC Articles on State Responsibility: The Paradoxical Relationship between Form and Authority', 96 AJIL (2002) 857.

Cassese, A. 'The *Nicaragua* and *Tadić* Tests Revisited in Light of the ICJ Judgment on Genocide in Bosnia', 18 EJIL (2007) 649.

Cassese, A. and Weiler, J.H.H. (eds.) *Change and Stability in International Law-Making* (Walter de Gruyter 1988).

Chen, Y. 'Structural Limitations and Possible Future of the Work of the International Law Commission', 9 CJIL (2010) 473.

Chigara, B.A. 'The Administration of International Law in National Courts and the Legitimacy of International Law', 17 *International Criminal Law Review* (2017) 909.

Chinkin, C. 'Enhancing the International Law Commission's Relationship with Other Law-Making Bodies and Relevant Academic and Professional Institutions', in *Making Better International Law: The International Law Commission at 50* (United Nations 1998) 333.

Condorelli, L. 'Protection diplomatique réussie et réparation due: une glose', in D. Alland et al (eds.), *Unity and Diversity of International Law: Essays in Honour of Professor Pierre-Marie Dupuy* (Brill 2014) 477.

Cottereau, G. 'Resort to International Courts in Matters of Responsibility', in J. Crawford et al (eds.), *The Law of International Responsibility* (OUP 2010) 1113.

Couvreur, P. *The International Court of Justice and the Effectiveness of International Law* (Brill Nijhoff 2016).

Corten, O. and Klein, P. 'La Commission du droit international comme agent de formalisation du droit de la responsabilité: Modalités et significations de l'utilisation d'arbitages partiellement détaches du droit positif', in D. Alland et al (eds.), *Unity and Diversity of International Law: Essays in Honour of Professor Pierre-Marie Dupuy* (Martinus Nijhoff 2014) 399.

Crawford, J. 'Universalism and Regionalism from the Perspective of the Work of the International Law Commission', in *International Law on the Eve of the Twenty-First Century: Views from the International Law Commission* (United Nations 1997) 99.

'The ILC's Articles on Responsibility of States for Internationally Wrongful Acts: A Retrospect', 96 AJIL (2002) 874.

'The International Law Commission's Articles on Diplomatic Protection Revisited', in T. Maluwa et al (eds.), *The Pursuit of a Brave New World in International Law: Essays in Honour of John Dugard* (Brill Nijhoff 2007) 135.

'The International Court of Justice and the Law of State Responsibility', in C.J. Tams and J. Sloan, *The Development of International Law by the International Court of Justice* (OUP 2013) 71.

'The Progressive Development of International Law: History, Theory and Practice', in D. Alland et al (eds.), *Unity and Diversity of International Law: Essays in Honour of Professor Pierre-Marie Dupuy* (Martinus Nijhoff 2014) 3.

Crawford, J. and Olleson, S. 'The Continuing Debate on a UN Convention on State Responsibility', 54 ICLQ (2005) 959.

Crema, L. 'The ILC's New Way of Codifying International Law, the Motives Behind It, and the Interpretive Approach Best Suited to It', in P. Merkouris, J. Kammerhofer and N. Arajarvi (eds.), *The Theory, Practice, and Interpretation of Customary International Law* (CUP 2022) 161.

Cullen, M. 'Separation of Powers in the United Nations System? Institutional Structure and the Rule of Law', 17 IOLR (2020) 1.

D'Amato, A.A. 'The Concept of Special Custom in International Law', 63 AJIL (1969) 211.

d'Aspremont, J. 'Canonical Cross-Referencing in the Making of the Law of International Responsibility', in S. Forlati, M.M. Mbengue and B. McGarry (eds.), *The Gabčíkovo-Nagymaros Judgment and Its Contribution to the Development of International Law* (Brill 2020) 22.

'Bypassing the Authority of International Law: The Virtue of Modern Self-Referentiality', *forthcoming* in G. Hernandez and G. Jokubauskaite (eds.), *Constructing Authority in International Law*, available on SSRN at <https://papers.ssrn.com/sol3/papers.cfm?abstract_id=3040975>.

Daugirdas, K. 'The International Law Commission Reinvents Itself?', 108 *AJIL Unbound* (2014) 79.

de Serpa Soares, M. '75 Years of International Law-Making at the United Nations', 23 MPYUNL (2020) 1.

de Visscher, C. 'La codification du droit international', 6 RdC (1925) 325.

'Stages in the Codification of International Law: The Hague 1930 – Geneva 1958 – Vienna 1969', in W. Friedmann et al (eds.), *Transnational Law in a Changing Society: Essays in Honour of Philip C. Jessup* (Columbia University Press 1972) 17.

Dhokalia, R.P. *The Codification of Public International Law* (MUP 1970).

'Reflections on International Law-Making and Its Progressive Development in the Contemporary Era of Transition', in R.S. Pathak and R.P. Dhokalia (eds.), *International Law in Transition: Essays in Memory of Judge Nagendra Singh* (Martinus Nijhoff 1992) 203.

Donoghue, J. 'The Effectiveness of the International Court of Justice', 108 *Proceedings of the Annual Meeting (American Society of International Law)* (2014) 114.

Đorđeska, M. 'The Process of International Law-Making: The Relationship between the International Court of Justice and the International Law Commission', 15 *International and Comparative Law Review* (2015) 7.

Dugard, J. 'How Effective Is the International Law Commission in the Development of International Law? A Critique of the International Law Commission on the Occasion of Its Fiftieth Anniversary', 23 SAYIL (1998) 34.

Dupuy, P.-M., 'Droit des traités, codification et responsabilité internationale', 43 *Annuaire Français de Droit International* (1997) 7.

Eagleton, C. 'Preparation for the International Law Commission', 43 AJIL (1949) 325.

'First Session of the International Law Commission', 43 AJIL (1949) 758.

El Baradei, M., Franck, T.M. and Trachtenberg, R. 'The International Law Commission: The Need for a New Direction', 1 *Policy and Efficacy Studies* (1981) 11.

Engel, S. 'Annual Reports of the International Court of Justice to the General Assembly?', 44 BYIL (1970) 193.

Eyffinger, A. *The 1899 Hague Peace Conference: The Parliament of Man, the Federation of the World* (Martinus Nijhoff 1999).

Finnemore, M. *National Interests in International Society* (Cornell University Press 1996).

Finnemore, M. and Sikkink, K. 'International Norm Dynamics and Political Change', 52 *International Organization* (1998) 887.

Finnemore, M. and Toope, S.J. 'Alternatives to "Legalization": Richer Views of Law and Politics', 55 *International Organization* (2001) 743.

Fitzmaurice, G. 'Some Problems regarding the Formal Sources of International Law', in *Symbolae Verzijl: Présentées au professeur J.H.W. Verzijl à l'occasion de son LXX-ième anniversaire* (Martinus Nijhoff 1958) 153.

Fitzmaurice, M. 'The History of Article 38 of the Statute of the International Court of Justice: The Journey from the Past to the Present', in S. Besson and J.

d'Aspremont (eds.), *The Oxford Handbook of the Sources of International Law* (OUP 2017) 179.

Fleck, D. 'London Naval Conference (1908–1909)', in MPEPIL (2015).

Fleischhauer, C.-A. and Simma, B. 'Article 13', in B. Simma et al (eds), *The Charter of the United Nations: A Commentary*, Vol. I, 3rd ed. (OUP 2012) 525.

Follesdal, A. and Ulfstein, G. (eds.) *The Judicialization of International Law: A Mixed Blessing?* (OUP 2018).

Forteau, M. 'The Diversity of Applicable Law before International Courts and Tribunals as a Source of Forum Shopping and Fragmentation of International Law: An Assessment', in R. Wolfrum and I. Gätzschmann (eds.), *International Dispute Settlement: Room for Innovations?* (Springer 2013) 417.

Franck, T.M. and El Baradei, M. 'The Codification and Progressive Development of International Law: A UNITAR Study of the Role and Use of the International Law Commission', 76 AJIL (1982) 630.

Gaja, G. 'The Protection of General Interests of in the International Community', 364 RdC (2012).

'Interpreting Articles Adopted by the International Law Commission', 85 BYIL (2015) 10.

Gattini, A. 'Breach of the Obligation to Prevent and Reparation Thereof in the ICJ's Genocide Judgment', 18 EJIL (2007) 695.

Goswami, S. *Politics in Law-Making: A Study of the International Law Commission of the UN* (Ashish Publishing House 1986).

Gotlieb, A.E. 'The International Law Commission', 4 CYIL (1966) 64.

Gradoni, L. 'La Commissione del diritto internazionale riflette sulla rilevazione dela consuetudine', 97 *Rivista di diritto internazionale* (2014) 667.

Graefrath, B. 'The International Law Commission Tomorrow: Improving Its Organization and Methods of Work', 85 AJIL (1991) 595.

Grant T.G. and Nicholson, R. 'The Early *United Nations* Advisory Opinions (1948–62)', in E. Bjorge and C. Miles (eds.), *Landmark Cases in Public International Law* (Hart 2017) 222.

Gray, J.C. *The Nature and Sources of Law* (Macmillan 1931).

Gregory, C.N. 'The Proposed International Prize Court and Some of Its Difficulties', 3 AJIL (1908) 458.

Gross, L. 'The United Nations and the Role of Law', 19 *International Organization* (1965) 537.

Guerrero, J.G. 'The International Court of Justice', 1 *United Nations World* (February 1947) 54.

Guillaume, G. 'The Future of International Judicial Institutions', 44 ICLQ (1995) 848.

'Le juge international et la codification', in *La codification du droit international* (Pedone 1999) 301.

'The Use of Precedent by International Judges and Arbitrators', 2 JIDS (2011) 5.

Hackworth, G.H. 'The International Court of Justice and the Codification of International Law', 31 *American Bar Association Journal* (1946) 81.

Hafner, G. 'The International Law Commission and the Future Codification of International Law', 2 *ILSA Journal of International & Comparative Law* (1996) 671.

Hernández, G. *The International Court of Justice and the Judicial Function* (OUP 2014).

Hernández, G.I. 'Sources and the Systematicity of International Law: A Co-Constitutive Relationship?', in S. Besson and J. d'Aspremont (eds.), *The Oxford Handbook of the Sources of International Law* (OUP 2017) 604.

Hershey, A.S. 'An International Prize Court', *Articles by Maurer Faculty*, Paper 1960 (1907) 652.

Higgins, R. *Problems and Process: International Law and How We Use It* (Clarendon Press 1994).

'A Babel of Judicial Voices? Ruminations from the Bench', 55 ICLQ (2006) 791.

Themes & Theories: Selected Essays, Speeches, and Writings in International Law (OUP 2009).

'The United Nations at 70 Years: The Impact upon International Law', 65 ICLQ (2016) 1.

Higgins R. et al. *Oppenheim's International Law: United Nations*, Vol. II (OUP 2017).

Hudson, M.O. 'The Permanent Court of International Justice', 35 HLR (1922) 245.

'The First Conference for the Codification of International Law', 24 AJIL (1930) 447.

The Permanent Court of Justice: A Treatise (Macmillan 1934).

The Permanent Court of Justice, 1920–1942 (Macmillan 1943).

International Tribunals: Past and Future (Carnegie Endowment for International Peace and Brookings Institution 1944).

'The New World Court', *Foreign Affairs* (October 1945) 75.

'The Twenty-Third Year of the Permanent Court of International Justice and Its Future', 39 AJIL (1945) 1.

Hurst, C. 'A Plea for the Codification of International Law on New Lines', 32 *Transactions of the Grotius Society* (1946) 135.

Jacob, M. 'Precedents: Lawmaking through International Adjudication', in A. von Bogdandy and I. Venzke (eds.), *International Judicial Lawmaking* (Springer 2012) 35.

Jansen, N. *The Making of Legal Authority: Non-Legislative Codifications in Historical and Comparative Perspectives* (OUP 2010).

Jenks, C.W. 'The Need for an International Legislative Drafting Bureau', 39 AJIL (1945) 163.

Jennings, R.Y. 'The Progressive Development of International Law and Its Codification', 24 BYIL (1947) 301.

'Recent Developments in the International Law Commission: Its Relation to the Sources of International Law', 13 ICLQ (1964) 385.

'Treaties as "Legislation"', in G.M. Wilner et al (eds.), *Jus et Societas: Essays in Tribute to Wolfgang Friedmann* (Martinus Nijhoff 1979) 159.

'The Identification of International Law', in B. Cheng (ed.), *International Law: Teaching and Practice* (Stevens & Sons 1982) 3.

'Customary Law and General Principles of Law as Sources of Space Law', in K.-H. Böckstiegel (ed.), *Environmental Aspects of Activities in Outer Space: State of the Law and Measures of Protection* (Carl Heymanns Verlag KG 1990) 149.

'International Lawyers and the Progressive Development of International Law', in J. Makarczyk (ed.), *Theory of International Law at the Threshold of the Twenty-first Century* (Kluwer Law International 1996) 413.

'Reflections on the Subsidiary Means for the Determination of Rules of Law', in *Studi di diritto internazionale in onore di Gaetano Arangio-Ruiz* (Editoriale Scientifica 2004) 319.

Jessup, P.C. 'To Form a More Perfect United Nations', 129 RdC (1970) 1.

Jiménez de Aréchaga, E. 'The Work and the Jurisprudence of the International Court of Justice 1947–1986', 58 BYIL (1987) 1.

Johnson, D.H.N. 'The Preparation of the 1958 Geneva Conference on the Law of the Sea', 8 ICLQ (1959) 122.

Katz Cogen, J. 'The Changing Form of the International Law Commission's Work', 108 *AJIL Unbound* (2014) 4.

'The Decline of "Drafts"', 11 IOLR (2014) 1.

Kawano, M. 'Kokuren Kokusaiho-Iinkai to Kokusai-Shiho-Saibansho' ['UN International Law Commission and International Court of Justice'], in S. Murase and K. Tsuruoka (eds.), *Henkakuki no Kokusai Ho Iinkai: Yamada Chusei Taishi Sanju Kinen* [*The International Law Commission at Time of Reform: In Celebration of the 80th Birthday of Ambassador Chusei Yamada*] (Shinzansha 2011) 51–78 (in Japanese).

Kearney, R.D. 'Comments on the Future Work of the International Law Commission', 25 *South Carolina Law Review* (1973–1974) 555.

Keith, K. 'The International Law Commission's Work and the Shaping of International Law', in *Making Better International Law: The International Law Commission at 50* (United Nations 1998) 285.

'The Processes of Law-Making: The Law relating to International Organizations as an Example', in M. Ragazzi (ed.), *Responsibility of International Organizations: Essays in Memory of Sir Ian Brownlie* (Brill 2013) 15.

Kelsen, H. 'Compulsory Adjudication of International Disputes', 37 AJIL (1943) 397.

The Law of the United Nations: A Critical Analysis of Its Fundamental Problems (second reprinting, The Lawbook Exchange 2000).

Kerno, I. 'The International Law Commission', 35 *American Bar Association Journal* (1949) 487.

Kolb, R. *The International Court of Justice* (Hart 2014).

Koskenniemi, M. *From Apology to Utopia: The Structure of International Legal Argument* (CUP 1989).

'The Politics of International Law', 1 EJIL (1990) 4.

'International Legislation Today: Limits and Possibilities', 23 *Wisconsin International Law Journal* (2005) 61.

Koskenniemi, M. and Leino, P. 'Fragmentation of International Law? Postmodern Anxieties', 15 LJIL (2002) 553.

Kulick, A. 'From Problem to Opportunity?: An Analytical Framework for Vagueness and Ambiguity in International Law' 59 GYIL (2016) 257.

Kunz, J.L. 'Continental Shelf and International Law: Confusion and Abuse', 50 AJIL (1956) 828.

Lachs, M. 'Some Reflections on the Contribution of the International Court of Justice to the Development of International Law', 10 *Syracuse Journal of International Law and Commerce* (1983) 239.

Lang, A. 'The Role of the International Court of Justice in a Context of Fragmentation', 62 ICLQ (2013) 777.

Lanovoy, V. 'Customary International Law in the Reasoning of International Courts and Tribunals', in P. Merkouris, J. Kammerhofer and N. Arajärvi (eds.), *The Theory, Practice, and Interpretation of Customary International Law* (CUP 2022) 231–255.

Lauterpacht, H. 'The Absence of an International Legislature and the Compulsory Jurisdiction of International Tribunals', 11 BYIL (1930) 134.

'The Legal Aspect', in C.A.W. Manning (ed.), *Peaceful Change: An International Problem* (Macmillan 1937) 135.

'The Grotian Tradition in International Law', 23 BYIL (1946) 1.

'Codification and Development of International Law', 49 AJIL (1955) 16.

The Development of International Law by the International Court (Stevens & Sons 1958, reprinted by Grotius Publications 1982).

The Function of Law in the International Community (1933, reprinted by OUP 2011).

Leathley, C. 'An Institutional Hierarchy to Combat the Fragmentation of International Law: Has the ILC Missed an Opportunity?', 40 *New York University Journal of International Law & Politics* (2007) 259.

Lee, L.T. 'The International Law Commission Re-examined', 59 AJIL (1965) 545.

Lekkas, S.-I. 'The Uses of the Outputs of the International Law Commission in International Adjudication: Subsidiary Means or Artefacts of Rules?', 69 NIRL (2022) 327–359.

Liang, Y.-L. 'The Progressive Development of International Law and Its Codification under the United Nations', 41 PASIL (1947) 24.

'The General Assembly and the Progressive Development and Codification of International Law', 42 AJIL (1948) 66.

'Le développement et la codification du droit international', 73 RdC (1948) 407.

'The First Session of the International Law Commission: Review of Its Work by the General Assembly', 44 AJIL (1950) 527.

Loder, C.J. 'The Permanent Court of International Justice and Compulsory Jurisdiction', 2 BYIL (1920–1921) 6.

MacWhinney, E. 'The International Court of Justice and International Law-Making: The Judicial Activism/Self-Restraint Antimony', 5 CJIL (2006) 3.

Matheson, M.J. 'The Fifty-Eighth Session of the International Law Commission', 101 AJIL (2007) 407.

McCaffrey, S.C. 'International Environmental Law and the Work of the International Law Commission', 77 PASIL (1983) 414.

'The International Law Commission Adopts Draft Articles on International Watercourses', 89 AJIL (1995) 395.

'An Assessment of the Work of the International Law Commission', 36 *Natural Resources Journal* (1996) 297.

'Is Codification in Decline?', 20 HICLR (1996) 639.

McRae, D.M. 'The International Law Commission: Codification and Progressive Development after Forty Years', 25 CYIL (1987) 355.

'The Work of the International Law Commission 2007–2011: Progress and Prospects', 106 AJIL (2012) 322.

Mejia-Lemos, D.G. 'On Self-Reflectivity, Performativity, and Conditions for Existence of Sources of Law in International Law', 57 GYIL (2014) 289.

Mendelson, M. 'The International Court of Justice and the Sources of International Law', in V. Lowe and M. Fitzmaurice (eds.), *Fifty Years of the International Court of Justice: Essays in Honour of Sir Robert Jennings* (CUP 1996) 63.

Messenger, G. 'The Practice of Litigation at the ICJ: The Role of Counsel in the Development of International Law', in M. Hirsch and A. Lang (eds.), *Research Handbook on the Sociology of International Law* (Edward Elgar, forthcoming).

Meyer, H.N. *The World Court in Action: Judging among the Nations* (Rowman & Littlefield 2002).

Milanović, M. 'State Responsibility for Genocide: A Follow-Up', 18 EJIL (2007) 669.

Miles, C. 'Thoughts on Domestic Adjudication and the Identification of Customary International Law', 27 *Italian Yearbook of International Law* (2017) 133.

Miller, H. 'The Hague Codification Conference', 24 AJIL (1930) 674.

Morris-Sharma, N.Y. 'The ILC's Draft Articles before the 69th Session of the UNGA: A Reawakening?', 7 *Asian Journal of International Law* (2017) 1.

Morton, J.S. *The International Law Commission of the United Nations* (University of South Carolina Press 2000).

Murphy, S.D. 'Codification, Progressive Development, or Scholarly Analysis? The Art of Packaging the ILC's Work Product', in M. Ragazzi (ed.), *Responsibility of International Organizations: Essays in Memory of Sir Ian Brownlie* (Brill 2013) 29.

'Deconstructing Fragmentation: Koskenniemi's 2006 ILC Project', 27 *Temple International & Comparative Law Journal* (2013) 293.

'The Relevance of Subsequent Agreement and Subsequent Practice for the Interpretation of Treaties', in G. Nolte (ed.), *Treaties and Subsequent Practice* (OUP 2013) 82.

'What a Difference a Year Makes: The International Court of Justice's 2012 Jurisprudence', 4 JIDS (2013) 539.

'Immunity *Ratione Personae* of Foreign Government Officials and Other Topics: The Sixty-Fifth Session of the International Law Commission', 108 AJIL (2014) 41.

'Identification of Customary International Law and Other Topics: The Sixty-Seventh Session of the International Law Commission', 109 AJIL (2015) 822.

'Protection of Persons in the Event of Disasters and Other Topics: The Sixty-Eighth Session of the International Law Commission', 110 AJIL (2016) 718.

'Anniversary Commemoration and Work of The International Law Commission's Seventieth Session', 113 AJIL (2019) 90.

Nelson, L.D.M. 'The North Sea Continental Shelf Cases and Law-Making Conventions', 35 *Modern Law Review* (1972) 52.

Nicholson, R. 'The International Court of Justice as a "Shortcut" to Identifying Custom', 20 LAPE (2021) 490.

O'Connell, M.E. and VanderZee, L. 'The History of International Adjudication', in C.P.R. Romano, K.J. Alter and Y. Shany (eds.), *The Oxford Handbook of International Adjudication* (OUP 2014) 40.

O'Keefe, R. 'Jurisdictional Immunities', in C.J. Tams and J. Sloan (eds.), *The Development of International Law by the International Court of Justice* (OUP 2013) 147.

Oda, S. 'The International Court of Justice Viewed from the Bench (1976–1993)', 244 RdC (1993).

Olivier, M.E. 'The International Court of Justice and the Development of International Law over the Past Ten Years', 29 SAYIL (2004) 23.

Oppenheim, L. 'The Science of International Law: Its Task and Method', 2 AJIL (1908) 313.

Pacht, L.T. 'The Case for a Convention on State Responsibility', 83 *Nordic Journal of International Law* (2014) 439.

Palchetti, P. 'Is It Time to Take a Decision on the Final Form of ARIO?', 20 IOLR (2023) 103.

Park, L. 'The International Court and Rule-Making: Finding Effectiveness', 39 *University of Pennsylvania Journal of International Law* (2018) 1065.

Parlett, K. 'Diplomatic Protection and the International Court of Justice', in C.J. Tams and J. Sloan (eds.), *The Development of International Law by the International Court of Justice* (OUP 2013) 87.

Patel, B.N. 'Recommendations on the Enhancement of the Role and Effectiveness of the International Court of Justice and State Practice: The Gap Between Recommendation and Practice (1971–2006)', 11 *Singapore Yearbook of International Law* (2007) 99.

Peil, M. 'Scholarly Writings as a Source of Law: A Survey of the Use of Doctrine by the International Court of Justice', 1 CJICL (2012) 136.

Pellet, A. 'Conclusions générales', in *Colloque d'aix-en-Provence: La codification du droit international* (Pedone 1999) 329.

'Responding to New Needs through Codification and Progressive Development', in V. Gowlland-Debbas (ed.), *Multilateral Treaty-Making: The Current Status of Challenges to and Reforms Needed in the International Legislative Process* (Martinus Nijhoff 2000) 13.

'La CIJ et les réserves aux traités: Remarques cursives sur une révolution jurisprudentielle', in N. Ando et al (eds.), *Liber Amicorum Judge Shigeru Oda*, Vol. I (Kluwer Law International 2002) 481.

'Between Codification and Progressive Development of the Law: Some Reflections from the ILC', 6 *International Law Forum du droit international* (2004) 15.

'L'adaptation du droit international aux besoins changeants de la société internationale', 329 RdC (2007) 9.

'The Second Death of Euripide Mavrommatis? Notes on the International Law Commission's Draft Articles on Diplomatic Protection', 7 LAPE (2008) 33.

'The ILC Adrift? Some Reflexions from Inside', in *M. Pogačnik (ed.), Challenges of Contemporary International Law and International Relations: Liber Amicorum in Honour of Ernest Petrič* (Evropska Pravna Fakulteta 2011) 299.

'Shaping the Future of International Law: The Role of the World Court in Law-Making', in M.H. Arsanjani et al (eds.), *Looking to the Future: Essays in International Law in Honor of W. Michael Reisman* (Martinus Nijhoff 2011) 1065.

'Some Remarks on the Recent Case Law of The International Court of Justice on Responsibility Issues', in P. Kovács (ed.), *International Law – A Quiet Strength* (Pázmány Press 2011) 111.

'The ILC Guide to Practice on Reservations to Treaties: A General Presentation by the Special Rapporteur', 24 EJIL (2013) 1061.

Pellet, A. and Müller, D. 'Article 38', in A. Zimmerman et al (eds.), *The Statute of the International Court of Justice: A Commentary*, 3rd ed. (OUP 2019) 819.

Pronto, A.N. 'Some Thoughts on the Making of International Law', 19 EJIL (2008) 601.

Quentin-Baxter, R.Q. 'The International Law Commission', 17 *Victoria University Wellington Law Review* (1987) 1.

Ramcharan, B.G. *The International Law Commission: Its Approach to the Codification and Progressive Development of International Law* (Brill Nijhoff 1977).

Ranganathan, S. 'Between Philosophy and Anxiety? The Early International Law Commission, Treaty Conflict and the Project of International Law', 83 BYIL (2013) 82.

Reisman, W.M. 'Metamorphoses: Judge Shingeru Oda and the International Court of Justice', 33 CYIL (1995) 185.

'The Democratization of Contemporary International Law-Making Processes and the Differentiation of Their Application', in R. Wolfrum and V. Röben (eds.), *Developments of International Law in Treaty Making* (Springer 2005) 15.

Reynolds, D. 'A "Special Relationship"? America, Britain and the International Order since the Second World War', 62 *International Affairs* (1986) 1.

Riphagen, W. 'State Responsibility: New Theories of Obligation in Inter-State Relations', in R.St.J. MacDonald and D.M. Johnston (eds.), *The Structure and Process of International Law: Essays in Legal Philosophy, Doctrine and Theory* (Martinus Nijhoff 1983) 581.

Root, E. 'The Outlook for International Law', 10 AJIL (1916) 1.

'Address by the Secretary of State of the United States before the American Society of International Law, at Washington, D.C., April 27, 1923', 9 *International Conciliation* (1923) 319.

'The Codification of International Law', 19 AJIL (1925) 675.

Rosenne, S. *The International Court of Justice: An Essay in Political and Legal Theory* (Sijthoff 1957).

'The Rôle of the International Law Commission', 64 AJIL (1970) 24.

(ed.) *League of Nations Committee of Experts for the Progressive Codification of International Law (1925–1928)* (Oceana Publications 1972).

'Codification Revisited after 50 Years', 2 MPYUNL (1998) 1.

Rosenstock, R. 'The Forty-Fourth Session of the International Law Commission', 87 AJIL (1993) 138.

'The Forty-Sixth Session of the International Law Commission', 89 AJIL (1995) 390.

Rosenstock, R. and Kaplan, M. 'The Fifty-Third Session of the International Law Commission', 96 AJIL (2002) 412.

Ross, A. *A Textbook of International Law* (Longmans, Green & Co. 1947).

Ruda, J.M. 'Some of the Contributions of the International Court of Justice to the Development of International Law', 24 *New York University Journal of International Law and Politics* (1991) 35.

Russett, B.M. *Community and Contention: Britain and American in the Twentieth Century* (MIT Press 1963).

Šahović, M. 'The Present Stage in the Activities of the UN International Law Commission', 1 *Jugoslovenska Revija za Međunarodno Pravo* (1980) 85.

Schachter, O. 'The Invisible College of International Lawyers', 72 *Northwestern University Law Review* (1977) 217.

International Law in Theory and Practice (Martinus Nijhoff 1991).

'The UN Legal Order: An Overview', in C.C. Joyner (ed.), *The United Nations and International Law* (CUP 1997) 3.

Schauer, F. 'Authority and Authorities', 94 *Virginia Law Review* (2008) 1931.

Schwebel, S.M. 'The Influence of the International Court of Justice on the Work of the International Law Commission and the Influence of the Commission on the Court', in *Making Better International Law: The International Law Commission at 50* (United Nations 1998) 161.

'Speech by Judge Stephen M. Schwebel on the Report of the International Court of Justice', 92 AJIL (1998) 612.

'The Inter-active Influence of the International Court of Justice and the International Law Commission', in C.A. Armas Barea et al (eds.), *Liber Amicorum 'In Memoriam' of Judge José María Ruda* (Kluwer Law International 2000) 479.

Justice in International Law (CUP 2011).

Scott, J.B. 'The Proposed Court of Arbitral Justice', 2 AJIL (1908) 772.

The Project of a Permanent Court of International Justice and Resolutions of the Advisory Committee of Jurists (Carnegie 1920).

'Advancement of International Law Essential to an International Court of Justice', 15 PASIL (1921) 21.

Scott, S. 'Codification of State Responsibility in International Law: A Review and Assessment', 9 *ASILS International Law Journal* (1985) 1.

Sender, O. 'The Importance of Being Earnest: Purpose and Method in Scholarship on International Law', 54 *Case Western Reserve Journal of International Law* (2022) 53.

Sender, O. and Wood, M. 'The International Court of Justice and Customary International Law: A Reply to Stefan Talmon', *EJIL:Talk!* (30 November 2015), available at <www.ejiltalk.org/the-international-court-of-justice-and-customary-international-law-a-reply-to-stefan-talmon/>.

'The Work of the International Law Commission between 1997 and 2022: A Positive Assessment', 25 MPYUNL (2022) 645.

Sepúlveda, C. 'Methods and Procedures for the Creation of Legal Norms in the International System of States: An Inquiry into the Progressive Development of International Law in the Present Era', 33 GYIL (1990) 432.

Sette-Camara, J. 'The International Law Commission: Discourse and Method', in *International Law at the Time of Its Codification: Essays in Honour of Roberto Ago* (Dott. A. Giuffrè Editore 1987) 467.

Shaw, M.N. 'The International Court of Justice: A Practical Perspective', 46 ICLQ (1997) 831.

Simma, B. 'Peace through Law: The Role of the ILC', in G. Nolte (ed.), *Peace through International Law: The Role of the International Law Commission* (Springer 2009) 189.

Sinclair, I. *The International Law Commission* (Grotius Publications 1987).

'International Law: The Court, Commission and Judges', in E. Jensen and T. Fisher (eds.), *The United Kingdom – The United Nations* (Macmillan 1990) 120.

'The International Lawyer and the Codification of International Law', in C. Wickremasinghe (ed.), *The International Lawyer as Practitioner* (BIICL 2000) 41.

Singh, N. 'Codification and Progressive Development: The Role of the International Court of Justice', 18 IJIL (1978) 1.

Sirpaul, S. 'Developments in the Legal Machinery of the United Nations', 11 ICLQ (1962) 573.

Sivakumaran, S. 'The Influence of Teachings of Publicists on the Development of International Law', 66 ICLQ (2017) 1.

'Beyond States and Non-State Actors: The Role of State-Empowered Entities in the Making and Shaping of International Law', 55 *Columbia Journal of Transnational Law* (2017) 343.

Sloan, F.B. 'Advisory Jurisdiction of the International Court of Justice', 38 *California Law Review* (1950) 830.

Smith, H.A. 'Codification of International Law', 12 *Journal of Comparative Legislation and International Law* (1930) 131.

Sotirios-Ioannis, L. 'The Uses of the Outputs of the International Law Commission in International Adjudication: Subsidiary Means or Artefacts of Rules?', 69 NILR (2022) 327.

Spiermann, O. '"Who Attempts Too Much Does Nothing Well": The 1920 Advisory Committee of Jurists and the Statute of the Permanent Court of International Justice', 73 BYIL (2002) 187.

'A Permanent Court of International Justice', 72 *Nordic Journal of International Law* (2003) 399.

International Legal Argument in the Permanent Court of International Justice: The Rise of the International Judiciary (CUP 2010).

'The History of Article 38 of the Statute of the International Court of Justice: "A Purely Platonic Discussion"?', in S. Besson and J. d'Aspremont (eds.), *The Oxford Handbook of the Sources of International Law* (OUP 2017) 165.

Sreenivasa Rao, P. 'International Law Commission (ILC)', in R. Wolfrum (ed.), MPEPIL (2017).

Stockton, C.H. 'The International Naval Conference of London, 1908–1909', 3 AJIL (1909) 596.

Stone, J. 'On the Vocation of the International Law Commission', 57 *Columbia Law Review* (1957) 16.

Sucharitkul, S. 'The Role of the International Law Commission in the Decade of International Law', 3 LJIL (1990) 15.

'Legal Multiculturalism and the International Law Commission', in S. Yee and J.-Y. Morin (eds.), *Multiculturalism and International Law* (Brill 2009) 310.

Talmon, S. 'Determining Customary International Law: The ICJ's Methodology between Induction, Deduction and Assertion', 26 EJIL (2015) 417.

Tammes, A.J.P. 'Codification of International Law in the International Law Commission', 22 NILR (1975) 319.

Tams, C.J. 'The ICJ as a "Law-Formative Agency": Summary and Synthesis', in C.J. Tams and J. Sloan (eds.), *The Development of International Law by the International Court of Justice* (OUP 2013) 377.

'Law-Making in Complex Processes: The World Court and the Modern Law of State Responsibility', in C. Chinkin and F. Baetens (eds.), *Sovereignty, Statehood and State Responsibility: Essays in Honour of James Crawford* (CUP 2015) 287.

'Die Identifikation des Völkergewohnheistrechts', in N. Dethloff et al (eds.), *Freiheit und Regulierung in der Cyberwelt: Rechtsidentifikation zwischen Quelle und Gericht* (C.F. Miller 2016) 323.

Tanaka, Y. 'Rethinking *Lex Ferenda* in International Adjudication', 51 GYIL (2008) 467.

Tesón, F.R. 'Fake Custom', in B. Lepard (ed.), *Reexamining Customary International Law* (CUP 2017) 86.

Thirlway, H.W.A. *International Customary Law and Codification* (A.W. Sijthoff 1972).

'Reflections on *Lex Ferenda*', 32 NYIL (2001) 3.

'The Contribution of the International Court of Justice to the Development of International Law', in L. Zeng and Y. Xiao (eds.), *Wuhan University Lectures on International Law*, Vol. II (Wuhan University Press 2006) 32.

'The Drafting of ICJ Decisions: Some Personal Recollections and Observations', 5 CJIL (2006) 15.

The Law and Procedure of the International Court of Justice: Fifty Years of Jurisprudence, vols. I and II (OUP 2013).

'Unacknowledged Legislators: Some Preliminary Reflections on the Limits of Judicial Lawmaking', in R. Wolfrum and I. Gätzschmann (eds.), *International Dispute Settlement: Room for Innovations?* (Springer 2013) 311.

The Sources of International Law, 2nd ed. (OUP 2019).

Tladi, D. 'The Fate of the Draft Articles on State Responsibility: Act Soon or Face the Further Erosion of the Role of States in the International Law-Making Process', APDI 2013 (2015) 87.

'Representation, Inequality, Marginalization, and International Law-Making: The Case of the International Court of Justice and the International Law Commission', 7 *UC Irvine Journal of International, Transnational, and Comparative Law* (2022) 60.

Tomka, P. 'Remarks', 106 PASIL (2012) 195.

'The Contribution of the International Court of Justice to the Law of the Sea', in D.J. Attard, M. Fitzmaurice and N.A. Martínez (eds.), *The IMLI Manual on International Maritime Law – Volume I: The Law of the Sea* (OUP 2014) 618.

'Customary International Law in the Jurisprudence of the World Court: The Increasing Relevance of Codification', in L. Lijnzaad and Council of Europe (eds.), *The Judge and International Custom* (Brill Nijhoff 2016) 1.

Tomuschat, C. 'International Law', in C. Tomuschat (ed.), *The United Nations at Age Fifty: A Legal Perspective* (Kluwer Law International 1995) 281.

'The International Law Commission – An Outdated Institution?', 49 GYIL (2006) 77.

Treves, T. 'The Expansion of International Law', 398 RdC (2015).

Tryon, J.L. 'The International Prize Court and Code', 20 YLJ (1911) 604.

United Nations (ed.). *The International Law Commission Fifty Years After: An Evaluation – Proceedings of the Seminar Held to Commemorate the Fiftieth Anniversary of the International Law Commission, 21–22 April 1998* (United Nations 2000).

Seventy Years of the International Law Commission: Drawing a Balance for the Future (Brill Nijhoff 2021).

Venzke, I. 'Judicial Authority and Styles of Reasoning: Self-Presentation between Legalism and Deliberation', in J. Jemielniak, L. Nielsen and H. Palmer Olsen (eds.), *Establishing Judicial Authority in International Economic Law* (CUP 2016) 240.

Verma, D.P. 'Rethinking about New International Law-Making Process', 29 IJIL (1989) 38.

Vermeer-Künzli, A. '*Diallo* and the Draft Articles: The Application of the Draft Articles on Diplomatic Protection in the *Ahmadou Sadio Diallo* case', 20 LJIL (2007) 941.

Villagrán Kramer, F. 'The First Fifty Years of the U.N. International Law Commission', 16 *Chinese Taiwan Yearbook of International Law and Affairs* (1997) 1.

Villalpando, S. 'Le codificateur et le juge face à la responsabilité internationale de l'État: interaction entre la CDI et la CIJ dans la détermination des règles secondaires', 55 AFDI (2009) 39.

'Codification Light: A New Trend in the Codification of International Law at the United Nations', 8 *Anuario brasileiro de direito internacional* (2013) 117.

'On the International Court of Justice and the Determination of Rules of Law', 26 LJIL (2013) 243.

'The "Invisible College of International Lawyers" Forty Years Later', *European Society of International Law Conference Paper Series*, Paper No. 5/2013 (2013), available at <https://papers.ssrn.com/sol3/papers.cfm?abstract_id=2363640##>.

Wallace, W. and Phillips, C. 'Reassessing the Special Relationship', 85 *International Affairs* (2009) 263.

Watts, A. *The International Law Commission 1949–1998*, Vol. I (OUP 1999).

'The International Court and the Continuing Customary International Law of Treaties', in N. Ando et al (eds.), *Liber Amicorum Judge Shigeru Oda*, Vol. I (Kluwer Law International 2002) 251.

Watts, A., Wood, M. and Sender, O. 'Codification and Progressive Development of International Law', in MPEPIL (2021).

Weeramantry, C.G. 'The Function of the International Court of Justice in the Development of International Law', 10 LJIL (1997) 309.

Weil, P. '"The Court Cannot Conclude Definitively . . .": *Non Liquet* Revisited', 36 *Columbia Journal of Transnational Law* (1998) 109.

Weisburd, A.M. 'The International Court of Justice and the Concept of State Practice', 31 *University of Pennsylvania Journal of International Law* (2009) 295.

Wellens, K. 'The Court's Judgment in the Case concerning the Gabcikovo-Nagymaros Project (Hungary/Slovakia): Some Preliminary Reflections', in K. Wellens (ed.), *International Law: Theory and Practice – Essays in Honour of Eric Suy* (Martinus Nijhoff 1998) 765.

'The International Court of Justice, Back to the Future: Keeping the Dream Alive', 64 NILR (2017) 193.

Westlake, J. 'The Hague Conferences', in L. Oppenheim (ed.), *The Collected Papers of John Westlake on Public International Law* (CUP 1914) 531.

Wickersham, G.W. 'The Codification of International Law', 4 *Foreign Affairs* (1926) 237.

Wilcox, F.O. 'The United States Accepts Compulsory Jurisdiction', 40 AJIL (1946) 699.

Wolfke, K. 'Materials Used in the UN Practice of International Law-Making', 7 *Polish Yearbook of International Law* (1975) 256.

'Can the Codification of International Law Be Harmful?', in J. Makarczyc (ed.), *Essays in International Law in Honour of Judge Manfred Lachs* (Brill 1984) 313.

Wood, M. 'The General Assembly and the International Law Commission: What Happens to the Commission's Work and Why?', in I. Buffard et al (eds.), *International Law between Universalism and Fragmentation: Festschrift in Honour of Gerhard Hafner* (Brill 2008) 373.

'"Weighing" the Articles on Responsibility of International Organizations', in M. Ragazzi (ed.), *Responsibility of International Organizations: Essays in Memory of Sir Ian Brownlie* (Brill 2013) 55.

'Teachings of the Most Highly Qualified Publicists (Art. 38(1) ICJ Statute)', in MPEPIL (2017).

'The UN International Law Commission and Customary International Law', in E. Cannizzaro et al (eds.), *Discourses on Methods in International Law: An Anthology*, Gaetano Morelli Lectures Series, Vol. 3 (International and European Papers Publishing 2020) 65.

Worster, W.T. 'The Transformation of Quantity into Quality: Critical Mass in the Formation of Customary International Law', 31 *Boston University International Law Journal* (2013) 1.

Xue, H. 'The Role of the ILC's Work in Promoting Peace and Security – Definition and Evaluation', in G. Nolte (ed.), *Peace through International Law: The Role of the International Law Commission* (Springer 2009) 183.

Yee, S. 'Article 38 of the ICJ Statute and Applicable Law: Selected Issues in Recent Cases', 7 JIDS (2016) 472.

Zarbiyev, F. 'Saying Credibly What the Law Is: On Marks of Authority in International Law', 9 JIDS (2018) 291.

Zemanek, K. '*Codification of International Law: Salvation or Dead End?*', in *International Law at the Time of Its Codification: Essays in Honour of Roberto Ago* (Dott. A. Giuffrè Editore 1987) 581.

* * * * * * * * * *

INDEX

CAMBRIDGE STUDIES IN INTERNATIONAL AND COMPARATIVE LAW

Books in the Series

187 *International Law-Making by the International Court of Justice and International Law Commission: Partnership for Purpose in a Decentralized Legal Order*
Omri Sender

186 *The Rebirth of Territory*
Gail Lythgoe

185 *Reimagining Sustainable Development in International Law: Perspectives from African Legal Cosmologies*
Godwin Eli Kwadzo Dzah

184 *Collective Self-Defence in International Law*
James A. Green

183 *Weaponising Evidence: A History of Tobacco Control in International Law*
Margherita Melillo

182 *The Justice Factory: Management Practices at the International Criminal Court*
Richard Clements

181 *A Communitarian Theory of WTO Law*
Chi Carmody

180 *Drones and International Law: A Techno-Legal Machinery*
Mignot-Mahdavi

179 *The Necessity of Nature: God, Science and Money in 17th Century English Law of Nature*
Mónica García-Salmones

178 *Making the World Safe for Investment: The Protection of Foreign Property 1922–1959*
Andrea Leiter

177 *National Governance and Investment Treaties*
Josef Ostřanský and Facundo Pérez Aznar

176 *Who Owns Outer Space? International Law, Astrophysics, and the Sustainable Development of Space*
Michael Byers and Aaron Boley

175 *Intervening in International Justice: Third States before Courts and Tribunals*
Brian McGarry

174 *Reciprocity in Public International Law*
Arianna Whelan

173 *When Environmental Protection and Human Rights Collide*
Marie-Catherine Petersmann

172 *The International Law of Sovereign Debt Dispute Settlement*
Kei Nakajima

171 *The Everyday Makers of International Law: From Great Halls to Back Rooms*
Tommaso Soave

170 *Virtue in Global Governance: Judgment and Discretion*
Jan Klabbers

169 *The Effects of Armed Conflict on Investment Treaties*
Tobias Ackermann

168 *Investment Law's Alibis: Colonialism, Imperialism, Debt and Development*
David Schneiderman

167 *Negative Comparative Law: A Strong Programme for Weak Thought*
Pierre Legrand

166 *Detention by Non-State Armed Groups under International Law*
Ezequiel Heffes

165 *Rebellions and Civil Wars: State Responsibility for the Conduct of Insurgents*
Patrick Dumberry

164 *The International Law of Energy*
Jorge Viñuales

163 *The Three Ages of International Commercial Arbitration*
Mikaël Schinazi

162 *Repetition and International Law*
Wouter Werner

161 *State Responsibility and Rebels: The History and Legacy of Protecting Investment Against Revolution*
Kathryn Greenman

160 *Rewriting Histories of the Use of Force: The Narrative of 'Indifference'*
Agatha Verdebout

159 *The League of Nations and the Protection of the Environment*
Omer Aloni

158 *International Investment Law and Legal Theory: Expropriation and the Fragmentation of Sources*
Jörg Kammerhofer

157 *Legal Barbarians: Identity, Modern Comparative Law and the Global South*
Daniel Bonilla Maldonado

156 *International Human Rights Law Beyond State Territorial Control*
Antal Berkes

155 *The Crime of Aggression under the Rome Statute of the International Criminal Court*
Carrie McDougall

154 *Minorities and the Making of Postcolonial States in International Law*
Mohammad Shahabuddin

153 *Preclassical Conflict of Laws*
Nikitas E. Hatzimihail

152 *International Law and History: Modern Interfaces*
Ignacio de la Rasilla

151 *Marketing Global Justice: The Political Economy of International Criminal Law*
Christine Schwöbel-Patel

150 *International Status in the Shadow of Empire*
Cait Storr

149 *Treaties in Motion: The Evolution of Treaties from Formation to Termination*
Edited by Malgosia Fitzmaurice and Panos Merkouris

148 *Humanitarian Disarmament: An Historical Enquiry*
Treasa Dunworth

147 *Complementarity, Catalysts, Compliance: The International Criminal Court in Uganda, Kenya, and the Democratic Republic of Congo*
Christian M. De Vos

146 *Cyber Operations and International Law*
François Delerue

145 *Comparative Reasoning in International Courts and Tribunals*
Daniel Peat

144 *Maritime Delimitation as a Judicial Process*
Massimo Lando

143 *Prosecuting Sexual and Gender-Based Crimes at the International Criminal Court: Practice, Progress and Potential*
Rosemary Grey

142 *Capitalism As Civilisation: A History of International Law*
Ntina Tzouvala

141 *Sovereignty in China: A Genealogy of a Concept Since 1840*
Adele Carrai

140 *Narratives of Hunger in International Law: Feeding the World in Times of Climate Change*
Anne Saab

139 *Victim Reparation under the Ius Post Bellum: An Historical and Normative Perspective*
Shavana Musa

138 *The Analogy between States and International Organizations*
Fernando Lusa Bordin

137 *The Process of International Legal Reproduction: Inequality, Historiography, Resistance*
Rose Parfitt

136 *State Responsibility for Breaches of Investment Contracts*
Jean Ho

135 *Coalitions of the Willing and International Law: The Interplay between Formality and Informality*
Alejandro Rodiles

134 *Self-Determination in Disputed Colonial Territories*
Jamie Trinidad

133 *International Law as a Belief System*
Jean d'Aspremont

132 *Legal Consequences of Peremptory Norms in International Law*
Daniel Costelloe

131 *Third-Party Countermeasures in International Law*
Martin Dawidowicz

130 *Justification and Excuse in International Law: Concept and Theory of General Defences*
Federica Paddeu

129 *Exclusion from Public Space: A Comparative Constitutional Analysis*
Daniel Moeckli

128 *Provisional Measures before International Courts and Tribunals*
Cameron A. Miles

127 *Humanity at Sea: Maritime Migration and the Foundations of International Law*
Itamar Mann

126 *Beyond Human Rights: The Legal Status of the Individual in International Law*
Anne Peters

125 *The Doctrine of Odious Debt in International Law: A Restatement*
Jeff King

124 *Static and Evolutive Treaty Interpretation: A Functional Reconstruction*
Christian Djeffal

123 *Civil Liability in Europe for Terrorism-Related Risk*
Lucas Bergkamp, Michael Faure, Monika Hinteregger and Niels Philipsen

122 *Proportionality and Deference in Investor-State Arbitration: Balancing Investment Protection and Regulatory Autonomy*
Caroline Henckels

121 *International Law and Governance of Natural Resources in Conflict and Post-Conflict Situations*
Daniëlla Dam-de Jong

120 *Proof of Causation in Tort Law*
Sandy Steel

119 *The Formation and Identification of Rules of Customary International Law in International Investment Law*
Patrick Dumberry

118 *Religious Hatred and International Law: The Prohibition of Incitement to Violence or Discrimination*
Jeroen Temperman

117 *Taking Economic, Social and Cultural Rights Seriously in International Criminal Law*
Evelyne Schmid

116 *Climate Change Litigation: Regulatory Pathways to Cleaner Energy*
Jacqueline Peel and Hari M. Osofsky

115 *Mestizo International Law: A Global Intellectual History 1842–1933*
Arnulf Becker Lorca

114 *Sugar and the Making of International Trade Law*
Michael Fakhri

113 *Strategically Created Treaty Conflicts and the Politics of International Law*
Surabhi Ranganathan

112 *Investment Treaty Arbitration As Public International Law: Procedural Aspects and Implications*
Eric De Brabandere

111 *The New Entrants Problem in International Fisheries Law*
Andrew Serdy

110 *Substantive Protection under Investment Treaties: A Legal and Economic Analysis*
Jonathan Bonnitcha

109 *Popular Governance of Post-Conflict Reconstruction: The Role of International Law*
Matthew Saul

108 *Evolution of International Environmental Regimes: The Case of Climate Change*
Simone Schiele

107 *Judges, Law and War: The Judicial Development of International Humanitarian Law*
Shane Darcy

106 *Religious Offence and Human Rights: The Implications of Defamation of Religions*
Lorenz Langer

105 *Forum Shopping in International Adjudication: The Role of Preliminary Objections*
Luiz Eduardo Salles

104 *Domestic Politics and International Human Rights Tribunals: The Problem of Compliance*
Courtney Hillebrecht

103 *International Law and the Arctic*
Michael Byers

102 *Cooperation in the Law of Transboundary Water Resources*
Christina Leb

101 *Underwater Cultural Heritage and International Law*
Sarah Dromgoole

100 *State Responsibility: The General Part*
James Crawford

99 *The Origins of International Investment Law: Empire, Environment and the Safeguarding of Capital*
Kate Miles

98 *The Crime of Aggression under the Rome Statute of the International Criminal Court*
Carrie McDougall

97 *'Crimes against Peace' and International Law*
Kirsten Sellars

96 *Non-Legality in International Law: Unruly Law*
Fleur Johns

95 *Armed Conflict and Displacement: The Protection of Refugees and Displaced Persons under International Humanitarian Law*
Mélanie Jacques

94 *Foreign Investment and the Environment in International Law*
Jorge E. Viñuales

93 *The Human Rights Treaty Obligations of Peacekeepers*
Kjetil Mujezinović Larsen

92 *Cyber Warfare and the Laws of War*
Heather Harrison Dinniss

91 *The Right to Reparation in International Law for Victims of Armed Conflict*
Christine Evans

90 *Global Public Interest in International Investment Law*
Andreas Kulick

89 *State Immunity in International Law*
Xiaodong Yang

88 *Reparations and Victim Support in the International Criminal Court*
Conor McCarthy

87 *Reducing Genocide to Law: Definition, Meaning, and the Ultimate Crime*
Payam Akhavan

86 *Decolonising International Law: Development, Economic Growth and the Politics of Universality*
Sundhya Pahuja

85 *Complicity and the Law of State Responsibility*
Helmut Philipp Aust

84 *State Control over Private Military and Security Companies in Armed Conflict*
Hannah Tonkin

83 *'Fair and Equitable Treatment' in International Investment Law*
Roland Kläger

82 *The UN and Human Rights: Who Guards the Guardians?*
Guglielmo Verdirame

81 *Sovereign Defaults before International Courts and Tribunals*
Michael Waibel

80 *Making the Law of the Sea: A Study in the Development of International Law*
James Harrison

79 *Science and the Precautionary Principle in International Courts and Tribunals: Expert Evidence, Burden of Proof and Finality*
Caroline E. Foster

78 *Transition from Illegal Regimes under International Law*
Yaël Ronen

77 *Access to Asylum: International Refugee Law and the Globalisation of Migration Control*
Thomas Gammeltoft-Hansen

76 *Trading Fish, Saving Fish: The Interaction between Regimes in International Law*
Margaret A. Young

75 *The Individual in the International Legal System: Continuity and Change in International Law*
Kate Parlett

74 *'Armed Attack' and Article 51 of the UN Charter: Evolutions in Customary Law and Practice*
Tom Ruys

73 *Theatre of the Rule of Law: Transnational Legal Intervention in Theory and Practice*
Stephen Humphreys

72 *Science and Risk Regulation in International Law*
Jacqueline Peel

71 *The Participation of States in International Organisations: The Role of Human Rights and Democracy*
Alison Duxbury

70 *Legal Personality in International Law*
Roland Portmann

69 *Vicarious Liability in Tort: A Comparative Perspective*
Paula Giliker

68 *The Public International Law Theory of Hans Kelsen: Believing in Universal Law*
Jochen von Bernstorff

67 *Legitimacy and Legality in International Law: An Interactional Account*
Jutta Brunnée and Stephen J. Toope

66 *The Concept of Non-International Armed Conflict in International Humanitarian Law*
Anthony Cullen

65 *The Principle of Legality in International and Comparative Criminal Law*
Kenneth S. Gallant

64 *The Challenge of Child Labour in International Law*
Franziska Humbert

63 *Shipping Interdiction and the Law of the Sea*
Douglas Guilfoyle

62 *International Courts and Environmental Protection*
Tim Stephens

61 *Legal Principles in WTO Disputes*
Andrew D. Mitchell

60 *War Crimes in Internal Armed Conflicts*
Eve La Haye

59 *Humanitarian Occupation*
Gregory H. Fox

58 *The International Law of Environmental Impact Assessment: Process, Substance and Integration*
Neil Craik

57 *The Law and Practice of International Territorial Administration: Versailles to Iraq and Beyond*
Carsten Stahn

56 *United Nations Sanctions and the Rule of Law*
Jeremy Matam Farrall

55 *National Law in WTO Law: Effectiveness and Good Governance in the World Trading System*
Sharif Bhuiyan

54 *Cultural Products and the World Trade Organization*
Tania Voon

53 *The Threat of Force in International Law*
Nikolas Stürchler

52 *Indigenous Rights and United Nations Standards: Self-Determination, Culture and Land*
Alexandra Xanthaki

51 *International Refugee Law and Socio-Economic Rights: Refuge from Deprivation*
Michelle Foster

50 *The Protection of Cultural Property in Armed Conflict*
Roger O'Keefe

49 *Interpretation and Revision of International Boundary Decisions*
Kaiyan Homi Kaikobad

48 *Multinationals and Corporate Social Responsibility: Limitations and Opportunities in International Law*
Jennifer A. Zerk

47 *Judiciaries within Europe: A Comparative Review*
John Bell

46 *Law in Times of Crisis: Emergency Powers in Theory and Practice*
Oren Gross and Fionnuala Ní Aoláin

45 *Vessel-Source Marine Pollution: The Law and Politics of International Regulation*
Alan Khee-Jin Tan

44 *Enforcing Obligations Erga Omnes in International Law*
Christian J. Tams

43 *Non-Governmental Organisations in International Law*
Anna-Karin Lindblom

42 *Democracy, Minorities and International Law*
Steven Wheatley

41 *Prosecuting International Crimes: Selectivity and the International Criminal Law Regime*
Robert Cryer

40 *Compensation for Personal Injury in English, German and Italian Law: A Comparative Outline*
Basil Markesinis, Michael Coester, Guido Alpa and Augustus Ullstein

39 *Dispute Settlement in the UN Convention on the Law of the Sea*
Natalie Klein

38 *The International Protection of Internally Displaced Persons*
Catherine Phuong

37 *Imperialism, Sovereignty and the Making of International Law*
Antony Anghie

36 *Principles of the Institutional Law of International Organizations*
C. F. Amerasinghe

35 *Necessity, Proportionality and the Use of Force by States*
Judith Gardam

34 *International Legal Argument in the Permanent Court of International Justice: The Rise of the International Judiciary*
Ole Spiermann

33 -

32 *Great Powers and Outlaw States: Unequal Sovereigns in the International Legal Order*
Gerry Simpson

31 *Local Remedies in International Law (second edition)*
Chittharanjan Felix Amerasinghe

30 *Reading Humanitarian Intervention: Human Rights and the Use of Force in International Law*
Anne Orford

29 *Conflict of Norms in Public International Law: How WTO Law Relates to Other Rules of International Law*
Joost Pauwelyn

28 -

27 *Transboundary Damage in International Law*
Hanqin Xue

26 -

25 *European Criminal Procedures*
Edited by Mireille Delmas-Marty, and J. R. Spencer

24 *Accountability of Armed Opposition Groups in International Law*
Liesbeth Zegveld

23 *Sharing Transboundary Resources: International Law and Optimal Resource Use*
Eyal Benvenisti

22 *International Human Rights and Humanitarian Law*
René Provost

21 *Remedies against International Organisations*
Karel Wellens

20 *Diversity and Self-Determination in International Law*
Karen Knop

19 *The Law of Internal Armed Conflict*
Lindsay Moir

18 *International Commercial Arbitration and African States: Practice, Participation and Institutional Development*
Amazu A. Asouzu

17 *The Enforceability of Promises in European Contract Law*
James Gordley

16 *International Law in Antiquity*
David J. Bederman

15 *Money Laundering: A New International Law Enforcement Model*
Guy Stessens

14 *Good Faith in European Contract Law*
Reinhard Zimmermann and Simon Whittaker

13 *On Civil Procedure*
J. A. Jolowicz

12 *Trusts: A Comparative Study*
Maurizio Lupoi and Simon Dix

11 *The Right to Property in Commonwealth Constitutions*
Tom Allen

10 *International Organizations before National Courts*
August Reinisch

9 *The Changing International Law of High Seas Fisheries*
Francisco Orrego Vicuña

8 *Trade and the Environment: A Comparative Study of EC and US Law*
Damien Geradin

7 *Unjust Enrichment: A Study of Private Law and Public Values*
Hanoch Dagan

6 *Religious Liberty and International Law in Europe*
Malcolm D. Evans

5 *Ethics and Authority in International Law*
Alfred P. Rubin

4 *Sovereignty over Natural Resources: Balancing Rights and Duties*
Nico Schrijver

3 *The Polar Regions and the Development of International Law*
Donald R. Rothwell

2 *Fragmentation and the International Relations of Micro-States: Self-Determination and Statehood*
Jorri C. Duursma

1 *Principles of the Institutional Law of International Organizations*
C. F. Amerasinghe

For EU product safety concerns, contact us at Calle de José Abascal, 56–1°,
28003 Madrid, Spain or eugpsr@cambridge.org.

www.ingramcontent.com/pod-product-compliance
Lightning Source LLC
LaVergne TN
LVHW011807200926
848484LV00005B/1094